The United States and Torture

D0948100

The United States and Torture
Interrogation, Incarceration, and Abuse

EDITED BY

Marjorie Cohn

NEW YORK UNIVERSITY PRESS

New York and London

NEW YORK UNIVERSITY PRESS
New York and London
www.nyupress.org

© 2011 by New York University
All rights reserved

Library of Congress Cataloging-in-Publication Data
The United States and torture : interrogation, incarceration, and abuse /
edited by Marjorie Cohn.
p. cm.   Includes bibliographical references and index.
ISBN 978–0–8147–1732–5 (cl : alk. paper)
1. Terrorism—Prevention—Law and legislation—United States.
2. War on Terrorism, 2001–2009. 3. Torture—United States.
4. Unlawful combatants—United States. I. Cohn, Marjorie, 1948–
KF9430.U55   2010
364.6'70973—dc22   2010027843

New York University Press books are printed on acid-free paper,
and their binding materials are chosen for strength and durability.
We strive to use environmentally responsible suppliers and materials
to the greatest extent possible in publishing our books.

Manufactured in the United States of America
10 9 8 7 6 5 4 3 2 1

To the victims

Contents

Acknowledgments

My heartfelt thanks to Sister Dianna Ortiz and all of our contributors for their fine work. I am also grateful to my gifted editor, Debbie Gershenowitz, for her invaluable assistance and commitment to this project, as well as her assistant, Gabrielle Begue, and my assistant, James McAllister. This extraordinary team worked together almost seamlessly as the book took shape. I am also appreciative of my husband and editor, Jerry Wallingford; my parents, Leonard and Florence Cohn; and my sons, Victor and Nicolas Cohn-López, for their love and encouragement. Thanks to my dean, Rudy Hasl, for his support, as well as Nuri Albala, Dennis Bernstein, John Conyers, Claire Didion, Vaughdean Forbes, Jeanne Friedman, Despina Papazoglou Gimbel, Ann Fagan Ginger, Karen Hershman, David Swanson, Carlos Villarreal, and Doris Brin Walker. I salute all who have courageously challenged those responsible for the torture and abuse of prisoners in U.S. custody. It is your efforts that will achieve justice and accountability.

Preface

SISTER DIANNA ORTIZ

Experience, we are told, is a great teacher. If this is so, then my class-room was a clandestine prison and my teachers, experts in the commission of crimes against humanity. There were others on this cruel faculty as well, drawn from two governments, the Guatemalan and my own.

It was in the fall of 1987 that my dream was realized. I had come to my new home in the highlands of Guatemala to live and work alongside the Mayan people as a Catholic missionary. My ministry was teaching children how to read and write in their native language, and with them, to celebrate their culture—a culture devalued by that country's oligarchy. There I hoped to live the rest of my life.

That dream was short-lived, as had been the dream of democracy for the Guatemalan people. In 1954, the United States had overthrown the democratically elected government of Guatemala, whose land reform program had incurred the wrath of the United Fruit Company. During the ensuing decades, Guatemala was the scene of torture, disappearance, massacres, and death. Some 200,000 Guatemalans suffered this fate. As a long, cruel civil war raged, the government, the military, and the oligarchy committed genocide against the Mayan people. All of this occurred with the support of the U.S. government.

It was in this setting that on November 2, 1989, I was abducted by members of the Guatemalan security forces, put into a police car, blindfolded, and taken to a clandestine prison, where I encountered a world I never could have imagined. In that place, I came face to face with evil. There, my life changed forever.

So often it is assumed that torture is conducted for the purpose of gaining information. It is much more often intended to threaten populations into silence and submission. What I was to endure was a message, a warning to others—not to oppose, to remain silent, and to yield to power without question. In Guatemala, the Catholic Church sought to walk in company with the suffering poor. I was to be a message board upon which those in power would write a warning to the Church to cease its opposition or be prepared to face the full force of the state.

First came the "interrogation." They played what they called a "game." If I answered a question in a way they liked, I would be allowed to smoke. If I answered in a way they didn't like, I would be burned with a cigarette. For every answer I gave, they burned me. Days after my escape, a doctor would find more than 111 second-degree burns on my back alone.

After they tired of this game, they gambled to see who would rape me first. "Heads, I go first," said the policeman. After he raped me, the proud winner whispered into my ear, "Your God is dead." (I didn't argue.) And then the others took their turns.

I regained consciousness and found myself in a courtyard of some type. They then lowered me into an open pit filled with human bodies—bodies of children, women, and men—some decapitated, some caked with blood, some dead, some alive. I remember them, those barely alive—crying out. Our cries joined together to become one terrible declaration of hopelessness—as the rats danced about, feasting on the already dead.

The next step in my descent into hell, I was placed in a dark room. Gradually, I became aware of someone else there, terribly tortured herself, on a table, covered with a foul smelling, blood-stained sheet. We spoke briefly. Then the torturers came in, one with a video camera. They placed a knife in my hand and I felt grateful for I thought that, somehow, it was to be used to kill me. Instead, as the filming began, hands were placed over mine and the knife was thrust into the woman. Her screams met mine as my torturers gloated. When it was finished they told me, "Now, you are just like us."

Left alone in the dark cell, I prayed to a deaf God to be rescued from this nightmare. Then I sensed someone—or something—approaching. For a moment, I thought I might actually be rescued, but as it neared me, I saw the dog's two dark eyes and snarling teeth. It was then that all hope died.

There is more that happened during my captivity, but I will add only this. My torturers had referred to "Alejandro" as their "boss"; that's what they called him. As they prepared to rape me again, one called out, "Hey, Alejandro, come and have some fun." Their boss had arrived but instead of joining in, he cursed in English and then spoke to the torturers in U.S.-

accented Spanish. Apparently, my disappearance had been the subject of much publicity.

"Alejandro" told me he would take me to a friend of his at the U.S. embassy who would help me leave the country. I asked if he was a North American (i.e., from the United States) and he asked why I wanted to know. Then he added, referring to death threats I had received, "We tried to warn you." *We*, not they—*we*. When we became ensnarled in traffic, I jumped out of the vehicle and ran.

Immediately after my escape, I reached a religious house in Guatemala City. A friend was warned by a U.S. official that I was not to speak of "Alejandro." However, I did, and the cost has been high. The first lie circulated by U.S. and Guatemalan officials was that I had not been tortured at all, that it was a publicity stunt to help defeat a bill in Congress dealing with military aid to Guatemala. But there were all those second-degree burns and so now the story changed. I still had not been tortured; rather, I had been involved in "kinky lesbian sex" that "got out of hand." I already had little faith in the Guatemalan government. Now I would learn to have no faith in my own.

Upon returning to the United States, I asked my government for information about "Alejandro" and what had been done to me. I did so not only for myself but because I believed the Guatemalan people had a right to know why an American was the head of a Guatemalan torture squad, and thus, presumably, involved in the torture of that nation's people.

I had been tortured and lied about during the administration of George H.W. Bush. Now my direct appeals to President Clinton produced nothing. One hundred and three members of Congress appealed to Mr. Clinton to release relevant documents—to no avail. A five-week silent vigil and a bread and water fast across from the White House finally produced documents, none relevant to my case. While there was nothing of value for me, one very important document came to light: the Report of the President's Intelligence Oversight Board, dated June 1996. In it, finally, the U.S. government acknowledged the torture texts used at the School of the Americas at Fort Benning, Georgia.

It is no surprise that the documents I have sought have never been released. The U.S. government, regardless of administration, protects those who order torture. Our government has been involved in this crime against humanity stretching back many years. The difference with the George W. Bush administration was that its actions were so blatant, so clear for all to see. That the major figures of that administration continue to walk free is consistent with the way we do these things. As of this writing, the change-oriented Obama administration has followed the same path by carefully avoiding investigating violations of U.S. law attributable to its high-level predecessors. Where, I ask, is the outrage?

At the darkest moment I prayed for death. When I learned that my prayer would not be answered, that I was doomed to return to life, it was more painful than anything done to me in that clandestine prison. Even today, 20 years later, I remain shackled to the memories of that time. But even the pain carries a molecule of hope. In a world where torture is so prevalent, in a nation that mixes self-proclaimed leadership in human rights with its own practice of torture, it may be difficult to hope. I have been to a place where there seemed none at all and I will not go there again. As hard as it may be to justify, I still hope. I still do hope for a world that one day will be torture-free.

Introduction

An American Policy of Torture

MARJORIE COHN

Emboldened by the terrorist attacks of September 11, 2001, the Bush administration lost no time establishing a policy that authorized the use of "enhanced interrogation techniques," that is, torture and abuse. Cofer Black, head of the CIA Counterterrorist Center, testified at a joint hearing of the House and Senate intelligence committees in September 2002: "This is a very highly classified area, but I have to say that all you need to know: There was a before 9/11, and there was an after 9/11. After 9/11 the gloves come off."[1] Indeed, in his January 2003 State of the Union Address, President Bush admitted: "All told, more than 3,000 suspected terrorists have been arrested in many countries. Many others have met a different fate. Let's put it this way—they are no longer a problem to the United States and our friends and allies."[2] Bush was tacitly admitting to the illegal practice of summary execution.[3]

The first indication that Bush officials would employ torture in their "War on Terror" occurred in December 2001, after U.S. citizen John Walker Lindh was captured in Afghanistan. Lindh's American interrogators stripped and gagged him, strapped him to a board, and displayed him to the press. He was writhing in pain from a bullet which U.S. officials would leave in his body for weeks in order to "preserve the chain of custody of the evidence" against him.[4] A Navy admiral told the intelligence officer who interrogated Lindh, "The secretary of defense's counsel has authorized him to 'take the gloves off' and ask whatever he wanted."[5] Although Lindh was initially charged with terrorism crimes that exposed him to three life terms plus 90 years, then-Attorney General John Ashcroft permitted him to plead guilty to lesser offenses that garnered him 20 years. The condition: that Lindh declare he suffered "no deliberate mistreatment" while in custody.[6] The cover-up was under way.

In December 2002, to the consternation of the U.S. State Department, the documentary titled *Afghan Massacre*[7] was broadcast on German television. It shows interviews with eyewitnesses to the torture and slaughter of 3,000 Taliban POWs, who surrendered to U.S. and allied Afghan forces. The film demonstrates the complicity of the U.S. Army command in the killing of these 3,000 men. Some of the prisoners died from suffocation while being transported in closed containers that lacked any ventilation. An Afghan soldier who traveled with the convoy reported that he was ordered by an American commander to fire shots into the containers to provide air, knowing he would hit the men inside. One of the drivers recounted the fate of survivors of the transport—dumped in the desert, shot and left to be eaten by dogs, as 30 to 40 American soldiers looked on. These allegations suggest evidence of war crimes and crimes against humanity under the statute of the International Criminal Court (ICC). It is precisely liability for actions such as these that Bush sought to avoid when he removed the United States' signature from the ICC treaty in May 2002.

A week after the documentary aired in Germany, the *Washington Post* reported that "stress and duress" tactics were being used on captured al-Qaeda operatives and Taliban commanders being interrogated in the CIA's secret detention center at the U.S.–occupied Bagram air base in Afghanistan.[8] Those who remained uncooperative could be kept standing or kneeling for hours, wearing black hoods and spray-painted goggles. Some were held in awkward, painful positions and deprived of sleep with a bombardment of lights for 24 hours. The article quotes "Americans with direct knowledge and others who have witnessed the treatment." They reported that military police and U.S. Army Special Forces troops beat captives and confined them in tiny rooms. Many were blindfolded, thrown into walls, tethered in painful positions, subjected to loud noises, and deprived of sleep. Witnesses also described prisoners bound to stretchers with duct tape for transport, much like the treatment Lindh suffered. At least two prisoners are known to have died at Bagram, one of a pulmonary embolism, the other of a heart attack.

The Bush administration experienced a public relations disaster with the 2004 publication of grotesque photographs from Abu Ghraib depicting naked Iraqis piled on top of each other, forced to masturbate, and led around on leashes like dogs. Shock waves reverberated around the world.

The United States, which routinely criticizes other countries for human rights violations, was exposed as a major rights violator itself. People of Arab and Muslim descent were outraged at the treatment of people of color in the Iraqi prison. Former Navy General Counsel Alberto Mora told Congress, "There are serving U.S. flag-rank officers who maintain that the first and second identifiable causes of U.S. combat deaths in Iraq—as judged by their effectiveness in recruiting insurgent fighters into combat—are, respectively the symbols of Abu Ghraib and Guantánamo."[9]

After the Abu Ghraib photos became public, Bush declared, "I shared a deep disgust that those prisoners were treated the way they were treated."[10] Yet less than a year later, his Justice Department issued secret opinions endorsing the harshest interrogation techniques the CIA had ever used.[11] The memos justify banging heads into walls 30 times in a row, prolonged nudity, repeated facial and abdominal slapping, dietary manipulation, and dousing with water as cold as 41 degrees. They countenance shackling in a standing position for 180 hours, sleep deprivation for 11 days, confinement of people in small dark boxes with insects for hours, and waterboarding to create the perception of suffocation and drowning. Moreover, the memos permit many of these techniques to be used in combination for a 30-day period.[12] Yet, Bush insisted, "This government does not torture people."[13]

Evidence of cruel treatment has continued to emerge. One form of torture CIA interrogators plied was "stress positions," suspending the prisoner from the ceiling or wall by his wrists, handcuffed behind his back. Iraqi Manadel Jamadi was subjected to this technique before he died in CIA custody at Abu Ghraib in November 2003. Tony Diaz, an MP who witnessed Jamadi's torture, said that blood gushed from his mouth like "a faucet had turned on" after Jamadi was lowered to the ground.[14]

As more stories of torture and cruelty surfaced from U.S. prisons in Afghanistan, Iraq, Guantánamo Bay, and the secret CIA black sites, it became clear there was an interrogation policy set at the top levels of our government that authorized the mistreatment. The "torture memos," written by former lawyers in the Justice Department's Office of Legal Counsel, contained twisted legal reasoning that purported to define torture more narrowly than U.S. law allows. Torture constitutes a war crime under the U.S. War Crimes Act.[15] The memos advised high Bush officials how to avoid criminal liability under the act.[16]

The Convention against Torture and Other Cruel, Inhuman or Degrading Treatment or Punishment, a treaty the United States has ratified, making it U.S. law under the Supremacy Clause of the Constitution,[17] contains an absolute ban on torture: "No exceptional circumstances whatsoever, whether a state of war or a threat of war, internal political instability or any other public emergency, may be invoked as a justification of torture."[18] The prohibition against torture is so fundamental it is considered *jus cogens,* a peremptory norm of international law binding on all countries, even if they have not ratified the Torture Convention.

Despite our laws prohibiting torture, the U.S. government has also employed it in American prisons. Torture in this country goes back at least to the nineteenth century. Slaves were often whipped and tortured in other ways, and the United States has frequently aided and abetted repressive regimes that have tortured and abused their people. The CIA developed torture manuals and the U.S. Army trained future torturers at the School of the Americas. Following this tradition, the Bush administration, under the guise of the "War on Terror," set policies that led to the torture and abuse of prisoners.

This collection details the complicity of the U.S. government in the torture and cruel treatment of prisoners both at home and abroad. In her compelling preface, Sister Dianna Ortiz describes the unimaginable treatment she endured in 1987, when she was in Guatemala doing missionary work while the United States was supporting the dictatorship there. She survived and founded the Torture Abolition and Survivors Support Coalition International, and her work has made her a national symbol of the struggle to abolish torture.

In Part I, The History and Character of Torture, chapters written by an historian, a lawyer, and a political scientist trace the history of CIA torture and U.S. complicity in torture throughout Latin America. A philosopher and a lawyer then analyze the character of torture—the ticking time bomb scenario, and parallels between torture and "one-sided warfare."

Part II, Torture and Cruel Treatment of Prisoners in U.S. Custody, brings the study into the current context of the War on Terror. A journalist examines the Bush administration's "extraordinary rendition" program, in which a person is abducted without any legal proceedings and transferred to a foreign country for detention and interrogation, often tortured. Two lawyers look at the treatment of detainees at Guantánamo. The role played by psychologists in the Bush torture program is set forth by one of the leaders of the movement to end that involvement. And a journalist brings the debate home with his description of the torture of prisoners in U.S. supermax prisons.

Finally, in Part III, Accountability for Torture, three lawyers explain strategies for bringing to justice the officials and lawyers who participated in establishing the Bush administration's policy that led to torture and abuse. Finally, a sociologist finds links between torture, war, and presidential power.

The Bush administration revived Cold War–era torture in its terror war, historian Alfred McCoy explains in our first chapter. McCoy details how the CIA has refined the "art" of torture by developing techniques to manipulate human consciousness. Since drug research had been unsuccessful, the CIA explored sensory deprivation and stress positions, to be used offensively by CIA interrogators and defensively to train U.S. troops to resist enemy interrogators. In 1963, the CIA created the Counter-Intelligence Interrogation Manual (KUBARK), which codified secret research on mind control. McCoy observes how they dialectically used heat and cold, light and dark, noise and silence, feast and famine, and sensory overload and deprivation, to pursue their sordid ends.

During the 1970s and 1980s, dictators and military leaders in Chile, Bolivia, Colombia, Guatemala, El Salvador, Honduras, and Paraguay utilized skills they learned at the U.S. Army's School of the Americas (SOA) to torture and execute dissidents. Attorney Bill Quigley's chapter documents how SOA graduates assassinated bishops, priests, labor leaders, women, children, and community workers, and massacred entire communities. Although in 2001 the school was cosmetically renamed the Western Hemisphere Institute for Security Cooperation (WHINSEC) at Fort Benning, Georgia, the U.S. government continues to resist accountability for those complicit in the egregious human rights violations perpetrated by the school's students. There is a growing protest movement against the SOA/WHINSEC. Since the assassination of Archbishop Oscar Romero in El Salvador in 1980, protesters have increasingly engaged in lobbying and civil disobedience, including regular teach-ins, demonstrations, and prayer vigils. Up to 20,000 demonstrators descend on Fort Benning each year. They want the U.S. government to admit what it has done at the school, allow an independent investigation, and accept responsibility for the consequences. They are demanding that the torture school be closed.

Political scientist Terry Karl, in the next chapter, reports that thousands were tortured and murdered by the government and death squads of El Salvador while the United States was training, financing, and advising its army and intelligence establishment. She describes how the United States uses "deniability" to cover up state terror by its allies, refashioning them into "freedom fighters" in order to maintain the support of the American people.

Latin America is not the only place where the United States has historically sponsored torturers. In 1953, the CIA engineered a coup in Iran that ousted Prime Minister Mohamed Mossedeq, whose government had refused to capitulate to Western property claims when it nationalized the Anglo-Iranian Oil Company two years before. After the coup, the United States helped install Mohammed Reza Shah Pahlavi, who ruled Iran with a fist of terror for the next 25 years until the 1979 Iranian revolution.

One year before the revolution, when I visited that country on a mission of the International Association of Democratic Lawyers, hundreds of U.S. corporations were doing business in Iran, the largest customer of U.S. arms at the time.

As many as 100,000 political prisoners had been incarcerated in the Shah's dungeons. Several former prisoners who risked their lives to speak with me described the brutal torture they had suffered. Their torturers utilized a helmet which magnified tenfold the prisoner's screams inside his head. The sounds of the screams, they said, were worse than the original treatment that caused them to scream in the first place. They showed me the web of scars on their bodies, a lasting memorial of their torture. In 1976, Amnesty International reported allegations of whipping and beating, electric shocks, the extraction of nails and teeth, boiling water pumped into the rectum, heavy weights hung on testicles, tying the prisoner to a table heated to white heat, inserting a broken bottle into the anus, and rape in Iran's prisons. Allegations of death under torture were not uncommon.[19] During this time, the United States continued to support the Shah's torturous regime.

Although there is general consensus that torture does not work—the subject will say anything to get the torture to stop—what if it did work? Would that justify torturing people into providing information? Philosopher John Lango's chapter asks whether an extreme emergency can ever trump the absolute prohibition of torture. Lango rejects the nuclear weapon and ticking bomb scenarios as "fantasy" and declares, "Terrorism can never warrant terroristic torment." He suggests a protocol to the Convention against Torture to fortify the moral prohibition of torture and cruel treatment.

The moral equivalence of torture and "one-sided warfare" is explored in Professor Richard Falk's provocative chapter. He critiques the liberal moral outrage at torture but uncritical acceptance of one-sided warfare. Nations, particularly the United States, inflict horrific pain on primarily non-white people in other countries, but suffer no consequences. Falk draws an analogy between the torture victim and the subjects of one-sided warfare—both are under the total control of the perpetrator. He recommends adherence to international humanitarian law and repudiation of "wars of choice."

Bush's "Operation Iraqi Freedom" is a war of choice. Weapons inspectors insisted that Saddam Hussein had no weapons of mass destruction; his military capacity had been neutered by the first Gulf War, a decade of punishing sanctions, and the nearly daily bombings in the "no-fly zones." So Bush endeavored to create a connection between Hussein and al-Qaeda to justify the 2003 invasion of Iraq. Top Bush officials put heavy pressure on Pentagon interrogators to get Khalid Sheikh Mohammed and Abu Zubaydah to reveal a link between Hussein and the 9/11 hijackers, according to a report of the Senate Armed Services Committee.[20]

The CIA waterboarded Khalid Sheikh Mohammed 183 times and Abu Zubaydah 83 times.[21] Waterboarding has long been considered torture.[22] One of Deputy Assistant Attorney General Stephen Bradbury's 2005 memos asserted that "enhanced techniques" on Zubaydah yielded the identification of Mohammed and an alleged radioactive bomb plot by Jose Padilla.[23] But FBI supervisory special agent Ali Soufan, who interrogated Zubaydah from March to June 2002, wrote in the *New York Times* that Zubaydah produced that information under traditional interrogation methods, before the harsh techniques were ever used.[24]

Journalist Jane Mayer's chapter recounts the case of Ibn al-Sheikh al-Libi, who was tortured into providing information the CIA knew to be false. Yet Colin Powell cited al-Libi's falsehoods to the Security Council to bolster the case for Bush's war with Iraq.[25] Mayer chronicles the sordid record of Bush's "extraordinary rendition" program.

Another victim of the Bush torture program is Adnan Farhan Abdul Latif, a Yemeni prisoner who has been held at the U.S. prison camp at Guantánamo for several years. Latif is one of hundreds of men and boys who have appeared before the Combatant Status Review Tribunals (CSRTs)—kangaroo courts the Bush administration established to determine whether a detainee is an "enemy combatant." Detainees were denied the right to counsel, with access only to a "personal representative" who owed no duty of confidentiality to his client and often did not even advocate on behalf of the detainee; one even argued the government's case. The detainee did not have the right to see much of the evidence against him and was very limited in the evidence he could present. The CSRTs were criticized by military participants in the process. Lt. Col. Stephen

Abraham, a veteran of U.S. intelligence, said they often relied on "generic" evidence and were set up to rubber-stamp the "enemy combatant" designation. When he sat as a judge in one of the tribunals, Abraham and the other two judges—a colonel and a major in the Air Force—"found the information presented to lack substance," and noted that statements presented as factual "lacked even the most fundamental earmarks of objectively credible evidence." After they determined there was "no factual basis" to conclude the detainee was an enemy combatant, the government pressured them to change their conclusion, but they refused. Abraham was never assigned to another CSRT panel.[26]

Latif's personal representative, attorney Marc Falkoff, collected information from his litigation notebooks, military documents, and his client's letters and poems. The resulting chapter is a powerful narrative in Latif's own words. "This place is like a hideous ghost," he writes. Falkoff could see the scars on the wrists of Latif, one of the hunger strikers at Guantánamo.

More than a third of the prisoners at Guantánamo have refused food to protest being held incommunicado for years with no hope of release. They have concluded that death could not be worse than the living hell they are forced to endure. Attorney Julia Tarver recounts how two of her clients described being force-fed by the guards:

> Yousef was the second detainee to have an NG [nasal gastric] tube inserted into his nose and pushed all the way down his throat and into his stomach, a procedure which caused him great pain. Yousef was given no anesthesia or sedative for the procedure; instead, two soldiers restrained him—one holding his chin while the other held him back by his hair, and a medical staff member forcefully inserted the tube in his nose and down his throat. Much blood came out of his nose. Yousef said he could not speak for two days after the procedure; he said he felt like a piece of metal was inside of him. He said he could not sleep because of the severe pain.[27]

When Yousef and others "vomited up blood, the soldiers mocked and cursed at them, and taunted them with statements like 'look what your religion has brought you.'"

In 2006, the United Nations Human Rights Commission determined that the violent force-feeding of detainees by the U.S. military at Guantánamo amounts to torture.[28] The commission confirmed that "doctors and other health professionals are participating in force-feeding detainees." It cited the Declarations of Tokyo and Malta, the World Medical Association, and the American Medical Association, which prohibit doctors from taking part in the force-feeding of detainees, provided the detainee is capable of understanding the consequences of refusing food. International Committee of the Red Cross guidelines state: "Doctors should never be party to actual coercive feeding. . . . Such actions can be considered a form of torture and under no circumstances should doctors participate in them on the pretext of saving the hunger striker's life."[29]

Psychologists were also an essential component of the Bush torture regime, psychologist Stephen Soldz writes in the next chapter. They helped develop, supervise, implement, and disseminate abusive interrogation techniques, modeled on the U.S. military's Survival, Evasion, Resistance and Escape (SERE) program. Bush administration officials "reverse engineered" SERE techniques to design counter-resistance methods in order to break detainees.

Soldz explains how the American Psychological Association (APA), the nation's largest professional mental health organization, "provided essential cover" for the psychologists' assistance to the torture regime. Notably, a group of activist psychologists opposed the APA's complicity. The movement achieved several major successes, which forced a change in APA policies. Soldz's chapter documents that movement.

Center for Constitutional Rights (CCR) president and attorney Michael Ratner's chapter traces the abusive treatment and struggles endured by clients of CCR, which initiated the Guantánamo litigation. Ratner describes CCR's victories in the U.S. Supreme Court as well as its efforts to convince Germany to prosecute U.S. leaders for torture under the well-established doctrine of "universal jurisdiction." If the United States fails to investigate and prosecute those who committed war crimes, other countries can do so under universal jurisdiction. This is a theory that countries, including the United States, have used for many years to bring to justice foreign nationals for crimes that shock the conscience of the global community. It provides a critical legal tool to hold accountable people who commit crimes against the law of nations, including war crimes and crimes against humanity. Without universal jurisdiction, many of the most notorious criminals would go free.

Israel used universal jurisdiction to prosecute, convict, and execute Adolph Eichmann, often called "the architect of the Holocaust," for crimes unconnected to Israel. Eichmann orchestrated the deportations but was not necessarily present at the gas chambers when millions were murdered. A U.S. federal court in Miami also used universal jurisdiction to convict Chuckie Taylor, son of the former Liberian president, of torture that occurred in Liberia, and sentence him to 97 years in prison in January 2009.[30]

Universal jurisdiction complements, but does not supersede, national prosecutions. So if the United States was investigating the Bush officials and lawyers, other countries would refrain from doing so. Spain launched an investigation of six Bush-era lawyers for their complicity in the U.S. torture policy. As this book went to press, the Spanish legislature had weakened its universal jurisdiction statute but the investigation of John Yoo, Jay Bybee, Alberto Gonzales, David Addington, William Haynes, and Douglas Feith in Spain was ongoing.

In other judicial developments, two courts issued significant decisions in extraordinary rendition cases—one in the United States and the other in Italy. On November 2, 2009, a sharply divided U.S. federal court of appeals dismissed Canadian citizen Maher Arar's case against U.S. officials for sending him to Syria to be tortured.[31] CCR had filed a lawsuit in which Arar alleged he was held in a "grave cell," beaten with an electrical cable, and threatened with electric shocks until he falsely confessed to being in Afghanistan. The Canadian government exonerated Arar and awarded him a multi-million-dollar judgment for its role in the travesty. But the U.S. court deferred to the executive on foreign policy matters and relied on the state secrets privilege to shield the officials from liability. Two days later, an Italian judge convicted 22 CIA operatives and a U.S. Air Force colonel of arranging the kidnapping of a Muslim cleric in Milan in 2003, then flying him to Egypt where he was tortured. Hassan Mustafa Osama Nasr told Human Rights Watch in 2007 that he was "hung up like a slaughtered sheep and given electrical shocks" in Egypt. "I was brutally tortured and I could hear the screams of others who were tortured too," he added.[32] The convicted Americans face arrest if they travel outside the United States.

The torture of prisoners in U.S. custody did not begin in Iraq, Afghanistan, and Guantánamo. "I do not view the sexual abuse, torture and humiliation of Iraqi prisoners by American soldiers as an isolated event," says Terry Kupers, a psychiatrist who testifies about human rights abuses in U.S. prisons.

The plight of prisoners in the United States is strikingly similar to that of the Iraqis who were abused by American GIs. Prisoners are maced, raped, beaten, starved, left naked in freezing cold cells, and otherwise abused in too many American prisons, as substantiated by findings in many courts that prisoners' constitutional rights to remain free of cruel and unusual punishment are being violated.[33]

Journalist Lance Tapley's chapter describes the torture of prisoners, especially those who suffer from mental illness, in the supermax prisons of the United States. "Cell extraction" is one of the most common forms of abuse. The guard slams the inmate's head against the wall and drops him on the floor while handcuffed. In another variation of this technique, the "point man" smashes his large body shield into the prisoner, knocks him down, jumps on him, maces him in the face, pushes him onto the bed, twists his arms behind his back, and handcuffs him. The guard carries the prisoner naked through the cell block, continuing to mace him, then binds him to a restraint chair and leaves him there for hours, naked, cold, and screaming. Tapley notes that one inmate's arm was broken during the cell extraction. Solitary confinement, which can result in hallucination, depression, and catatonia, is a form of torture.

Torture techniques the United States has used in other countries are all too familiar in U.S. prisons as well. Hooded, robed figures with electrical wiring attached to them have been observed at the city jail in Sacramento, California. Male prisoners in Maricopa County jails in Phoenix, Arizona were forced to wear women's underwear. And guards in the Utah prison system piled naked bodies in grotesque and uncomfortable positions.[34]

The connection between mistreatment of prisoners here and abroad is even more striking. For example, John Armstrong ran Connecticut's Department of Corrections from 1995 to 2003, before being sent to Iraq as a prison adviser in September 2003. On his Connecticut watch, two mentally ill prisoners died while being restrained by guards. Two more inmates died in custody after guards mistreated them. Armstrong once made a remark that equated the death penalty with euthanasia.[35]

More than 100 African American men alleged that they were tortured by officers in the Chicago Police Department from 1973 to 1991. Allegations include the use of cattle prods that delivered electric shocks and mock executions. The city of Chicago approved a $20 million settlement with four former death row inmates who had been tortured by officers in the Chicago Police Department. Former Chicago Police Lt. Jon Burge was convicted of perjury and obstruction of justice for lying about the torture of African American suspects. The statute of limitations on torture crimes had run because of a cover-up by Chicago prosecutors, according to attorney Flint Taylor.[36] And in Michigan, the state agreed to pay $100 million to more than 500 female prisoners who alleged sexual assault by guards.[37]

In the wake of the September 11 attacks, more than 1,200 Muslim, South Asian, and Arab non-citizens were rounded up by the Immigration and Naturalization Service and the FBI in one of the most extensive incidents of racial profiling in the United States since people of Japanese descent were interned during World War II. None were ever charged with any connection to terrorism. A December 2003 report by the Department of Justice's Office of Inspector General investigated allegations of physical and verbal abuse of non-citizen prisoners by the Federal Bureau of Prisons' Metropolitan Detention Center (MDC) in Brooklyn, New York.[38] The report concluded that several MDC staff members slammed and bounced detainees into the walls, twisted or bent their arms, hands, wrists, or fingers, pulled their thumbs back, tripped them, and dragged them on the floor. CCR filed a class action lawsuit in 2002, on behalf of people detained by the United States in the racial profiling dragnet after 9/11.[39] In November 2009, five of the seven plaintiffs settled their claims for $1.26 million from the United States.

The U.S. Supreme Court has applied the Eighth Amendment's ban on cruel and unusual punishment to conditions of confinement incompatible with the evolving standards of decency that mark the progress of a maturing society.[40] The United Nations' Economic and Social Council promulgated the Standard Minimum Rules for the Treatment of Prisoners.[41] They provide that corporal punishment, punishment by placing in a dark cell, and all cruel, inhuman, or degrading punishments shall be completely prohibited as punishments for disciplinary actions. The Supreme Court in *Estelle v. Gamble* specified that these rules should be included in the measurement of "evolving standards of decency."[42] Indeed, Fyodor Dostoevsky once said, "The degree of civilization in a society can be judged by entering its prisons."[43]

Torture is absolutely forbidden in all circumstances. It is considered a *jus cogens* norm. Attorney Jeanne Mirer's chapter points out that no country can ever pass a law that authorizes torture any more than it can legitimize slavery, genocide, or wars of aggression. There is no statute of limitations, no immunity from prosecution, and no defense of obedience of superior orders for violation of a *jus cogens* norm. Mirer notes that every U.S. circuit court that has reviewed the issue had concluded that torture violates well-established customary international law.

In spite of the absolute legal ban on torture, John Yoo, one of the most notorious torture memo authors, told contributing author Jane Mayer that Congress "can't prevent the president from ordering torture." When asked whether any law could stop the president from "crushing the testicles of the person's child," Yoo answered, "No treaty." Asked if another law could forbid it, Yoo qualified his answer, saying, "I think it depends on why the president thinks he needs to do that."[44]

Yoo and Jay Bybee wrote a memorandum the same month Bush invaded Iraq, in which they announced that the Department of Justice would construe U.S. criminal laws as not applicable to the president's detention and interrogation of enemy combatants. According to Bybee and Yoo, the federal statutes against torture, assault, maiming, and stalking do not apply to the military in the conduct of the war.[45] The behavior prohibited by these statutes is appalling. For example, the federal maiming statute makes it a crime for someone "with the intent to torture, maim, or disfigure," to "cut, bite, or slit the nose, ear or lip, or cut out or disable the tongue, or put out or destroy an eye, or cut off or disable a limb or any member of another person." It further prohibits individuals from "throw[ing] or pour[ing] upon another person any scalding water, corrosive acid, or caustic substance," with like intent.[46]

Bybee-Yoo also redefined torture to require that the victim experience intense pain or suffering equivalent to that associated with physical injury so severe that death, organ failure, or permanent damage resulting in loss of significant body functions will likely result. This definition contravenes the definition in the Convention Against Torture.[47]

Yoo and Bybee said self-defense or necessity could be used as a defense to war crimes prosecutions for torture, notwithstanding the Torture Convention's categorical prohibition against torture in all circumstances, even in wartime. Their memos provided the basis for the administration's torture of prisoners.

When asked in a *New York Times Magazine* interview, "Do you regret writing the so-called torture memos, which claimed that President Bush was legally entitled to ignore laws prohibiting torture?" Yoo responded, "No, I had to write them. It was my job. As a lawyer, I had a client [President Bush and 'the U.S. government as a whole.'] The client needed a legal question answered."[48] In his chapter, British barrister and international law expert Philippe Sands grapples with the question of whether an international lawyer should fully advise a client or merely provide "legal cover" for the client's lawbreaking. Citing Bush lawyers who wrote memos to circumvent international law, Sands demonstrates how they provided an after-the-fact basis to "green-light" the harsh interrogation procedures.

Law professor Jordan Paust's chapter analyzes the torture memos and explains why they did not provide a "Golden Shield" for those who planned, ordered, authorized, abetted, or perpetrated torture and cruel, inhumane, and degrading treatment. He describes the "common, unifying" plan to violate international law in the treatment and interrogation of detainees that emerged in the Bush administration.

On February 7, 2002, Bush signed a memo erroneously stating that the Geneva Conventions,[49] which require humane treatment, did not apply to al-Qaeda and the Taliban. But the Supreme Court made clear that Geneva protects all prisoners.[50] Bush admitted that he approved of high-level meetings of the Principals Committee in which harsh interrogation techniques, including waterboarding, were authorized by Dick Cheney, Condoleezza Rice, John Ashcroft, Colin Powell, Donald Rumsfeld, and George Tenet.[51]

Cheney and Bush have also publicly confessed to ordering war crimes. Asked about waterboarding in an *ABC News* interview, Cheney replied, "I was aware of the program, certainly, and involved in helping get the process cleared." He also said he still believes waterboarding was an appropriate method to use on terrorism suspects.[52] Cheney said the enhanced interrogation techniques yielded the "desired results."[53] Bush also acknowledged to the Economic Club of Grand Rapids, Michigan that he had waterboarded Khalid Sheik Mohammed and said he would "do it again to save lives."[54]

The bipartisan December 11, 2008 report of the Senate Armed Services Committee concluded that, "senior officials in the United States government solicited information on how to use aggressive techniques, redefined the law to create the appearance of their legality, and authorized their use against detainees."[55]

As a result of the Watergate scandal, President Jimmy Carter asked Congress to pass a law authorizing the appointment of a special prosecutor to investigate and prosecute unlawful acts by high government officials. The Ethics in Government Act empowered the attorney general to conduct a preliminary 90-day investigation when serious allegations arose involving a high government official.

Under the act, the attorney general could drop the investigation if he or she determined it was unsupported by the evidence. But if he found some merit to the charges, he was required to apply to a three-judge panel of federal court judges who would appoint a special prosecutor to investigate, prosecute, and issue a report. This procedure was used to select Kenneth Starr, whose witch hunt led to President Bill Clinton's impeachment. As a result, Congress allowed the independent counsel statute to expire by its own terms in 1999. It is time for the American people to demand that Congress re-enact an independent counsel statute.

The Constitution requires President Obama to faithfully execute the laws.[56] "My view is . . . that nobody's above the law, and if there are clear instances of wrongdoing, that people should be prosecuted just like any ordinary citizen," Obama stated. "But," he added, "that generally speaking, I'm more interested in looking forward than I am in looking backwards."[57] Obama's attorney general must prosecute lawbreakers—not just the bank robber, but also the CIA agent who tortured or abused a prisoner, and the officials and lawyers who set the policy. When the United States ratified the Geneva Conventions and the Convention against Torture, thereby making them part of U.S. law, we agreed to punish those who violate their prohibitions. Our law forbids torture and cruel, inhuman, or degrading treatment, and requires that those who subject people to such treatment be punished.[58] The Convention against Torture compels us to refer all torture cases for prosecution or to extradite the suspect to a country that will undertake a criminal investigation. The Geneva Conventions proclaim an "obligation" to bring people who have committed torture and cruel treatment before our "own courts." Two federal statutes—the Torture Statute[59] and the War Crimes Act—provide for life imprisonment and even the death penalty if the victim dies as a result of torture. Unfortunately, the Torture Statute only punishes torture committed abroad. Congress should amend this law to cover torture committed inside the United States as well.[60]

Lt. Gen. Antonio Taguba, who investigated the Abu Ghraib scandal, said, "There is no longer any doubt as to whether the current [Bush] administration has committed war crimes. The only question that remains to be answered is whether those who ordered the use of torture will be held to account."[61]

Lawyers who wrote the memos that purported to immunize government officials from war crimes liability include John Yoo, Jay Bybee, William Haynes, David Addington, Stephen Bradbury, Robert J. Delahunty, and Alberto Gonzales. There is precedent in our law for holding lawyers criminally liable for participating in a common plan to violate the law. In *United States v. Altstoetter*, Nazi lawyers were convicted of war crimes and crimes against humanity for advice they provided on how to disappear political suspects to special detention camps.[62]

Altstoetter and the case of the Bush lawyers share common aspects. Both dealt with people detained during wartime who were not prisoners of war; in both, it was reasonably foreseeable that the advice they provided would result in great physical or mental harm or death to many detainees; and in both, the advice was legally erroneous. More than 100 people have died in U.S. detention since 9/11, many from torture.[63] And the Department of Justice's Office of Legal Counsel later withdrew one of the most egregious Yoo-Bybee memos,[64] an admission that the advice in it was defective.

The legislative branch of our government was also complicit in the Bush torture policy, as sociologist Thomas Reifer contends in our final chapter. He writes that torture worked to extract false confessions that were used to gain congressional approval for Bush's illegal war of aggression in Iraq. Citing the "liberal culture of torture," Reifer criticizes Obama for shielding the executive branch under a cloak of secrecy in order to prevent further revelations about torture.

Indeed, Obama's Department of Justice supported the dismissal of lawsuits filed by victims of CIA extraordinary renditions. Justice Department lawyers also asked the Ninth Circuit Court of Appeals to dismiss a civil case brought against John Yoo by Jose Padilla, the U.S. citizen held incommunicado and tortured after his arrest at Chicago's O'Hare Airport. And when four Britons sued Donald Rumsfeld and other Bush officials to obtain relief for the torture they suffered, Obama's Justice Department argued that their lawsuit should be dismissed.[65]

Obama insists that his administration does not engage in torture. But if the officials, lawyers, and operatives from the Bush administration who ordered, committed, aided, and abetted torture are not held legally accountable, what will prevent the next administration from authorizing cruel treatment? And if we countenance impunity for those who participated in the torture and abuse, we will give the terrorists a third recruiting tool—along with Abu Ghraib and Guantánamo. The "War on Terror" has been uncritically accepted by most in this country. But terrorism is a tactic, not an enemy. One cannot declare war on a tactic. The way to combat terrorism is by identifying and targeting its root causes, including poverty, lack of education, and foreign occupation. As long as the United States continues to wage wars of choice and support unsavory regimes that treat their people inhumanely, there will be blowback. Starting illegal and unnecessary wars will make us more vulnerable to terrorism, not less. A complete reexamination of U.S. foreign policy is in order.

NOTES

1. Cofer Black, *9/11 Congressional Inquiry*, Washington, DC, Sept. 26, 2002.

2. George W. Bush, *State of the Union Address*, Washington, DC, Jan. 28, 2003.

3. See Marjorie Cohn, *Cowboy Republic: Six Ways the Bush Gang Has Defied the Law* (Sausalito: PoliPointPress, 2007), pp. 49–50.

4. See Jane Mayer, *The Dark Side* (New York: Doubleday, 2008), 92.

5. See Richard Serrano, "Prison Interrogators' Gloves Came Off Before Abu Ghraib," *Los Angeles Times*, June, 9, 2004.

6. Author's conversation with John Walker Lindh's attorney, George Harris; Mayer, *Dark Side*, p. 97.

7. See Jamie Doran and Najibullah Quraishi, *Afghan Massacre: The Convoy of Death*, 2002, http://www.acftv.com/archive/article.asp?archive_id=1 (last visited Nov. 10, 2009); Anderson Cooper, "Obama Orders Review of Alleged Slayings of Taliban in Bush Era," *CNN*, July 13, 2009, http://edition.cnn.com/2009/POLI-TICS/07/12/obama. afghan.killings/ (last visited Nov. 10, 2009).

8. See Dana Priest and Barton Gellman, "U.S. Decries Abuse But Defends Interrogations," *Washington Post*, Dec. 26, 2002, http://www.washingtonpost.com/wp-dyn/content/article/2006/06/09/AR2006060901356.html (last visited Nov. 16, 2009).

9. U.S. Senate Armed Services Committee, *Statement of Alberto J. Mora*, June 17, 2008, p. 5, http://armed-services.senate.gov/statemnt/2008/June/Mora%20 06-17-08.pdf (last visited Nov. 10, 2009).

10. George W. Bush, remarks at press availability, Rose Garden, White House, Washington, DC, Apr. 30, 2004, http://georgewbush-whitehouse.archives.gov/news/releases/2004/04/20040430-2.html (last visited Nov. 10, 2009).

11. See Scott Shane, David Johnston, and James Risen, "Secret Endorsement of Severe Interrogations," *New York Times*, Oct. 4, 2007, http://www.nytimes.com/2007/10/04/washington/04interrogate.html (last visited Nov. 10, 2009).

12. See Jay S. Bybee, *Memorandum for John Rizzo, Acting General Counsel of the Central Intelligence Agency, Interrogation of al Qaeda Operative*, Aug. 1, 2002, http://luxmedia.vo.llnwd.net/o10/clients/aclu/olc_08012002_bybee.pdf (last visited Nov. 10, 2009).

13. See Sheryl Gay Stolberg, "Bush Says Interrogation Methods Aren't Torture," *New York Times*, Oct. 6, 2007, http://www.nytimes.com/2007/10/06/us/nationalspecial3/06interrogate.html (last visited Nov. 10, 2009).

14. See Mayer, *Dark Side*, 255.

15. 18 U.S.C. 2441.

16. See, for example, John C. Yoo, memorandum to William Haynes regarding "Application of Treaties and Laws to al Qaeda and Taliban Detainees," Jan. 9, 2002, http://www.gwu. edu/~nsarchiv/NSAEBB/NSAEBB127/02.01.09. pdf (last visited Nov. 10, 2009); Alberto Gonzales, memorandum to President Bush regarding "Application of the Geneva Convention on Prisoners of War to the Conflict with al Qaeda and the Taliban," Jan. 25, 2002, http://www.gwu. edu/~nsarchiv/NSAEBB/NSAEBB127/02.01.25.pdf (last visited Nov. 10, 2009).

17. U.S. Constitution, art. VI, para. 2.

18. *The Convention against Torture and Other Cruel, Inhuman or Degrading Treatment or Punishment*, G.A. res. 39/46, annex, 39 U.N. GAOR Supp. (No. 51) at 197, U.N. Doc. A/39/51 (1984), art. 2.

19. Amnesty International, *Amnesty International Briefing: Iran* (London: Amnesty International, 1976), pp. 8–9.

20. See U.S. Senate Armed Services Committee, *Inquiry into the Treatment of Detainees in U.S. Custody*, Nov. 20, 2008, pp. 16–18, http://armed-services. senate.gov/Publications/Detainee%20Report%20Final_April%2022%202009.pdf (last visited Nov. 16, 2009).

21. See Stephen G. Bradbury, memorandum to John Rizzo regarding "Application of United States Obligations Under Article 16 of the Convention Against Torture to Certain Techniques that May Be Used in the Interrogation of High Value al Qaeda Detainees," May 30, 2005, p. 37, http://luxmedia.vo.llnwd.net/ 010/clients/aclu/olc_05302005_bradbury.pdf (last visited Nov. 10, 2009).

22. See, for example, *U.S. v. Lee*, 744 F.2d 1124 (5th Cir. 1984).

23. See Bradbury, memo regarding Art. 16 of CAT, p. 10.

24. Ali Soufan, "My Tortured Decision," *New York Times*, Apr. 22, 2009, http:// www.nytimes.com/2009/04/23/opinion/23soufan.html (last visited Nov. 10, 2009).

25. See Marjorie Cohn, *Cowboy Republic: Six Ways the Bush Gang Has Defied the Law* (Sausalito: PoliPointPress, 2007), pp. 13–14.

26. U.S. Senate Armed Services Committee, *Statement of Stephen E. Abraham*, July 26, 2007, pp. 5, 10, http://armedservices.house.gov/pdfs/FC072607/ Abraham_Testimony072607.pdf (last visited Nov. 10, 2009).

27. Julia Tarver, *Supplemental Declaration of Julia Tarver*, Oct. 13, 2005, para. 30, http://humanrights.ucdavis.edu/projects/the-guantanamo-testimonials-project/testimonies/prisoner-testimonies/supplemental-declaration-of-julia-tarver-october-13-2005 (last visited Nov. 10, 2009).

28. See U.N. Commission on Human Rights, *Situation of Detainees at Guantánamo Bay*, 62nd sess., Feb. 15, 2006, http://www.nytimes.com/packages/pdf/ international/20060216gitmo_report.pdf (last visited Nov. 10, 2009).

29. International Committee of the Red Cross, "Maltreatment and Torture," *Research in Legal Medicine*, vol. 19, 1998.

30. Editorial, "Taylors' Son Jailed for 97 Years," *BBC News*, Jan. 9, 2009, http://news.bbc.co.uk/2/hi/americas/7820069.stm (last visited Nov. 11, 2009).

31. *Arar v. Ashcroft, et al.*, U.S. 2nd Court of Appeals, 06-4216-cv (Nov. 2, 2009). The Supreme Court refused to review the case.

32. See Human Rights Watch, "Italy/US: Ruling Expected in Historic CIA Rendition Case," Nov. 3, 2009, http://www.hrw. org/en/news/2009/11/03/italyus-ruling-expected-historic-cia-rendition-case (last visited Nov. 11, 2009); Rachel Donadio, "Italy Convicts 23 Americans for CIA Renditions," *New York Times*, Nov. 4, 2009, http://www.nytimes.com/2009/11/05/world/europe/05italy.html (last visited Jan. 5, 2010).

33. See Norman Solomon, "From Attica to Abu Ghraib—and a Prison Near You," *Common Dreams*, Aug. 6, 2004, http://www.commondreams.org/views04/0806-02.htm (last visited Nov. 11, 2009).

34. See Anne-Marie Cusac, "Abu Ghraib, USA," *The Progressive*, Aug. 7, 2008, http://www.progressive.org/mag_amcabu (last visited Nov. 11, 2009).

35. See Antonio Ponver III, "Iraqi Prisoner Abuse: Why Are We Surprised?" *CounterPunch*, June 12, 2004, http://www.counterpunch.org/ponver06132004.html (last visited Nov. 16, 2009).

36. See Monica Davey and Emma Graves Fitzsimmons, "Officer Accused of Torture Is Guilty of Perjury," *New York Times*, June 28, 2010, http://www.nytimes.com/2010/06/29/us/29burge.html; "Trial Begins for Ex-Chicago Police Lt. Accused of Torturing More Than 100 African American Men," *Democracy Now!* May 24, 2010, http://democracynow.org/2010/5/24/trial_begins_for_ex_chicago_police; Gary Washburn, "City Council Settles Burge Police Torture Cases," *Chicago Tribune*, Jan. 9, 2008, http://newsblogs.chicagotribune.com/clout_st/2008/01/city-council-se.html.

37. See Jeff Seidel and Dawson Bell, "$100 million ends prisoner sex-abuse suit: Women started their legal fight in 1996," *Freep.com*, July 16, 2009, http://www.freep.com/article/20090716/NEWS06/101250006/0/MULTI/100-million-ends-prisoner-sex-abuse-suit (last visited Jan. 28, 2010); David Eggert, "10 Get $15.5 Million for Mich. Prison Sex Abuse," *USA Today*, Feb. 1, 2008, http://www.usatoday.com/news/nation/2008-02-01-3553096094_x.htm (last visited Nov. 13, 2009); *Neal v. Michigan Dept. of Corrections*, 230 Mich. App. 202 (1998).

38. U.S. Dept. of Justice, Office of the Inspector General, *Supplemental Report on September 11 Detainees' Allegations of Abuse at the Metropolitan Detention Center in Brooklyn, New York*, Dec. 2003, http://www.fas.org/irp/agency/doj/oig/detainees1203.pdf (last visited Nov. 11, 2009).

39. Class Action Complaint and Demand for Jury Trial, *Ibrahim Turkmen, et al. v. John Ashcroft, et al.*, CV-02-2307 (E.D.N.Y. Apr. 17, 2002), http://news. findlaw.com/hdocs/docs/terrorism/turkmenash41702cmp.pdf (last visited Nov. 13, 2009).

40. *Estelle v. Gamble*, 429 U.S. 97 (1976).

41. UN Economic and Social Council, *Standard Minimum Rules for the Treatment of Prisoners*, Res. 663 C, July 31, 1957.

42. *Estelle v. Gamble*, 429 U.S. at 102.

43. Fyodor Dostoevsky (1821–1881).

44. See Mayer, *Dark Side*, p. 153.

45. See Bybee, memo regarding interrogation; Yoo, memorandum regarding treaty application.

46. 18 U.S.C. 114.

47. The Convention defines torture as: "any act by which severe pain or suffering, whether physical or mental, is intentionally inflicted on a person for such purposes as obtaining from him or a third person information or a confession, punishing him for an act he or a third person has committed or is suspected of having committed, or intimidating him or a third person, or for any reason based on discrimination of any kind, when such pain or suffering is inflicted by or at the instigation of or with the consent or acquiescence of a public official or other person acting in an official capacity." *Convention Against Torture*, pt. I, art. 1. Cf. Jay S. Bybee, memorandum to Alberto Gonzales regarding the definition of torture, Aug. 1, 2002, http://www.gwu.edu/~nsarchiv/NSAEBB/ NSAEBB127/02.08.01.pdf (last visited Nov. 10, 2009).

48. Deborah Solomon, "Questions for John Yoo," *New York Times Magazine*, Dec. 29, 2010, http://www.nytimes.com/2010/01/03/magazine/03fob-q4-t.html (last visited Jan. 6, 2010).

49. See *Convention Relative to the Treatment of Prisoners of War* (*Geneva Convention III*), art. 17, 130, Aug. 12, 1949; *Convention Relative to the Protection of Civilian Persons in Time of War* (*Geneva Convention IV*), art. 32, 283, Aug. 12, 1949.

50. *Hamdan v. Rumsfeld*, 548 U.S. 557 (2006).

51. See Jan Crawford Greenburg, Howard L. Rosenburg, and Ariane de Vogue, "Bush Aware of Advisers' Interrogation Talks," *ABC News*, Apr. 11, 2008, http://abcnews.go.com/TheLaw/LawPolitics/story?id=4635175&page=1 (last visited Nov. 10, 2009).

52. Richard Cheney, interview with *ABC News*, Dec. 15, 2008, http://abcnews. go.com/Politics/story?id=6464697&page=1&page=1 (last visited Nov. 10, 2009).

53. Jon Ward, "Cheney Defends War on Terror's Morality," *Washington Times*, Dec. 18, 2008, http://www.washingtontimes.com/news/2008/dec/18/cheney-defends-morality-of-war-on-terror/?page=2 (last visited Nov. 16, 2009).

54. "Bush Unrepentant," *Daily News; New Plymouth, NZ*, June 4, 2010.

55. U.S. Senate Armed Services Committee, *Inquiry Into the Treatment of Detainees in U.S. Custody*, p. xii, http://levin.senate.gov/newsroom/supporting/2008/Detainees. 121108.pdf (last visited Nov. 11, 2009).

56. U.S. Constitution, art. II, § 1.

57. See Phillip Rucker, "Leahy Proposes Panel to Investigate Bush Era," *Washington Post*, Feb. 10, 2009, http://www.washingtonpost.com/wp-dyn/content/article/2009/02/09/AR2009020903221.html (last visited Nov. 11, 2009).

58. See also *International Covenant on Civil and Political Rights*, art. 7, G.A. res. 2200A (XXI), 21 U.N. GAOR Supp. (No. 16) at 52, U.N. Doc A/6316 (1966), 999 U.N.T.S. 171; U.N. Human Rights Comm., General Comment No. 20, Concerning the Prohibition of Torture and Cruel, Inhuman or Degrading Treatment or Punishment (Article 7), U.N. Doc. A/47/40 (1992).

59. 18 U.S.C. 2340 *et seq.*

60. Although beyond the scope of this book, it bears mention that there are civil statutes that can be used to hold corporations and individuals liable for their participation in torture committed in foreign countries. The Alien Tort Statute, 28 U.S.C. 1350, provides a cause of action in U.S. courts for an alien who is the victim of a tort committed in violation of the law of nations (customary international law) or a U.S. treaty. In *Filartiga v. Peña-Irala*, 630 F.2d 876 (2d Cir. 1980), the Court of Appeals held that torture committed by a state official in Paraguay against one in detention violated the law of nations and thus U.S. law. See *Doe v. Unocal*, 395 F.3d 932 (9th Cir. 2002), *vacated pending rehearing en banc and settled*, 403 F.3d 708 (9th Cir. 2005), and *Sosa v. Alvarez-Machain*, 542 U.S. 692 (2004). The Torture Victim Protection Act, 28 U.S.C. 1350, provides a cause of action for U.S. citizens and non-citizens against those who commit acts of torture under color of foreign law. See *Wiwa v. Royal Dutch Petroleum Co.*, 226 F.3d 88 (2d Cir. 2000) *cert. denied*, 532 U.S. 941 (2001).

61. See Dan Froomlin, "General Accuses WH of War Crimes," *Washington Post*, June 18, 2008, http://www.washingtonpost.com/wp-dyn/content/blog/2008/06/18/BL2008061801546.html (last visited Nov. 11, 2009).

62. See *United States v. Altstoetter* ("The Justice Case"), reprinted in *Trials of War Criminals Before the Nuremberg Military Tribunals Under Control Council Law*, vol. 3, no. 10: p. 1058 (Washington, DC: U.S. Government Printing Office, 1951).

63. See Ayaz Nanji, "Report: 108 Died in U.S. Custody," *CBS News*, Mar. 16, 2005, http://www.cbsnews.com/stories/2005/03/16/terror/main680658.shtml (last visited Nov. 11, 2009).

64. See Daniel Levin, memorandum for James B. Comey regarding "Legal Standards Applicable Under 18 U.S.C. §§ 2340–2340A," Dec. 30, 2004, http://fl1.findlaw.com/news.findlaw.com/hdocs/docs/terrorism/dojtorture123004mem.pdf (last visited Nov. 11, 2009).

65. The Supreme Court agreed with the Obama administration, and denied review of a D.C. Circuit Court of Appeals decision that had rejected the claims of the detainees. See *Rasul, et al., v. Myers, et al.*, 09-227, "Order List: 558 U.S.," Dec. 14, 2009, p. 3, http://www.supremecourtus.gov/orders/courtorders/121409zor.pdf (last visited Jan. 6, 2010).

PART I

The History and Character of Torture

1

Mind Maze

The CIA's Pursuit of

Psychological Torture

ALFRED W. MCCOY

O n April 28, 2004, American viewers were stunned when CBS Television broadcast those now-notorious photographs from Iraq's Abu Ghraib prison, with hooded Iraqis stripped naked while American soldiers stood by smiling. As this scandal grabbed headlines around the globe, U.S. Defense Secretary Donald Rumsfeld insisted that the abuses were "perpetrated by a small number of U.S. military,"[1] whom the conservative *New York Times'* columnist William Safire branded "creeps."[2]

That iconic photo of a hooded Iraqi with wires hanging from his extended arms showed not the sadism of a few "creeps," but instead the two key trademarks of CIA psychological torture. The hood was for sensory deprivation. The arms were extended for self-inflicted pain. Indeed, the same two techniques recur in most of the 1,600 still-classified photos that the U.S. Army's Criminal Investigation Command collected from the Abu Ghraib crime scene.

Nor were these methods a recent innovation. Tracking the trail of these distinctive tortures through declassified documents reveals an extraordinary institutional continuity, from Cold War past to present-day counterterrorism operations. From 1951 to 1962, the Central Intelligence Agency (CIA) led a secret effort to crack the code of human consciousness, a veritable Manhattan Project of the mind with costs that reached at peak a billion dollars a year, developing thereby a distinctive method of psychological torture.[3] For the next 30 years, the CIA disseminated these techniques among allied security agencies. After a brief hiatus following the collapse of the Soviet Union, Washington revived the agency's psychological methods for its current war on Islamic terrorists. Over the past 60 years, the CIA's pursuit of psychological torture has passed through four successive phases—discovery, propagation, perfection, and, most recently, legalization. Thus, this Cold War past is both prologue and precedent for the U.S. use of torture in the "Global War on Terror."

Discovery

Throughout the Cold War, U.S. foreign policy was driven by what we might call a convenient contradiction between its humane principles and a realpolitik policy toward torture. At the end of World War II, Washington played a lead role in drafting the Geneva Conventions and the UN Universal Declaration of Human Rights, which contained specific prohibitions against torture. At the start of the Cold War in the late 1940s, however, communist states in Eastern Europe staged show trials that featured automaton-like confessions by protestant pastors and a Catholic prelate.[4] Concerned that the Soviets had somehow learned to manipulate human consciousness, Washington launched a massive, often misdirected mind-control effort that reflected the era's rudimentary knowledge of cognitive science. Announcing his agency's battle against communist "brain warfare," CIA director Allen Dulles told Princeton alumni in 1953 that the Soviet Union was using powerful combinations of drugs and electroshock for "the perversion of the minds of selected individuals who are subjected to such treatment so that they are deprived of the ability to state their own thoughts."[5]

Starting in 1951, the CIA led the U.S. intelligence community in developing a top-secret "Special Interrogation Program" whose working hypothesis was, to quote an agency memo: "Medical science . . . has developed various techniques by means of which some external control can be imposed on the mind/or will of an individual, such as drugs, hypnosis, electric shock and neurosurgery."[6] In a later investigation of this "secret, 25-year, $25 million effort by the CIA to learn how to control the human mind," the *New York Times* reported that the agency "was able to assemble an extensive network of non-government scientists" for experiments the CIA's own inspector general "considered to be professionally unethical and in some instances border on the illegal."[7] In contrast to the

Soviet Union's command-economy model for scientific mobilization, the agency employed financial incentives and collegial manipulation by a few leading researchers to effect a subtle, secret redirection of the cognitive science community.

The exploration of both hypnosis and drugs proved chimerical—a failure illustrated by a hidden chapter in the otherwise distinguished career of Dr. Henry K. Beecher, honored today as the father of modern clinical ethics. In 1947, the chief of the army's Medical Intelligence Branch sent Beecher a captured German report, compiled by Dr. Kurt Plötner, detailing 30 mescaline experiments on Nazi concentration camp inmates done "to eliminate the will of the person examined . . . by the Gestapo." In enticing words, Plötner concluded: "If the Messkalin had an effect on the mental state of the P.E.'s, the examining person succeeded in every case in drawing even the most intimate secrets from the P.E. when the questions were cleverly put." Apparently inspired by this report, Beecher would spend the next decade in a quest for such a "truth serum."[8]

In 1951, Dr. Beecher traveled across Europe seeking colleagues in his search for a drug that could unlock the mind for interrogation. Although the chief U.S. Army surgeon for Europe considered Beecher's research as potentially criminal, meetings at the European Command's interrogation center at Oberursel, Germany, where U.S. military intelligence conducted inhumane interrogations of suspected Soviet agents, were more productive. There, the chief inquisitor, Captain Malcolm Hilty, advised Beecher, "It would be desirable for me to return, perhaps in a year, when we know better the signs and symptoms of the newer derivatives of mescaline and lysergic acid [LSD]."

In the interim, they recommended he work with a Dr. Schreiber, their former staff doctor, whom Beecher described as "a physician and former German general who . . . is intelligent and helpful." This was, in fact, General Walter Schreiber, the Wehrmacht medical chief who had presided over deadly concentration camp medical experiments. Moving on to Berlin, Beecher met with a U.S. Military Intelligence officer and "Mr. Peter Sichel, C.I.A." to discuss his plans "to interrogate as many high-level escapees as possible as to the presence of significant signs and symptoms [of drugs] during periods of interrogation." When Beecher's report on his dark voyage reached the Pentagon in October 1951, it was, at his recommendation, stamped "TOP SECRET" and not declassified until 1977.[9]

After mescaline apparently proved disappointing, Beecher focused on a more dangerous drug: Lysergic acid diethylamide, or LSD. The army sent

Beecher reports from the Swiss Sandoz Company warning that its new drug LSD induced a "tendency to pathological reactions (hysterical attacks, trances, epileptic fits)." Apparently intrigued, Beecher won a classified military contract to test heavy LSD doses on unwitting human subjects at Massachusetts General Hospital in 1953–54—a clear violation of the Nuremberg medical code.[10] So deep is our collective ignorance about the extent of scientific complicity in this mind-control research that today Harvard Medical School awards the annual Henry K. Beecher Prize for medical ethics.

Although such drug research was pursued vigorously at CIA headquarters and a half-dozen university research hospitals for a decade, this agency experimentation led to nowhere except lawsuits. By contrast, obscure CIA-funded behavioral experiments, outsourced to leading universities, produced findings that contributed to the development of a distinctly American form of torture: psychological torture. This behavioral approach was given real impetus by an American-British-Canadian research effort that began in 1951 when Sir Henry T. Tizard, the senior scientist at the U.K. Ministry of Defense, visited Montreal to mobilize behavioral scientists for mind warfare against the Soviet Union.[11]

In 1986, a Canadian government inquiry by George Cooper, Q.C., reported that "a high-level meeting took place at the Ritz Carlton Hotel in Montreal on June 1, 1951" attended by Dr. Omond Solandt, head of Canada's Defense Research Board, Dr. Donald O. Hebb, head of the Board's Behavioral Research and chair of Psychology at McGill, and two Americans identified as "CIA," Dr. Caryl Haskins and Commander R. J. Williams. Indicative of CIA penetration of the U.S. scientific establishment, Haskins later became president of the influential Carnegie Institution. As noted in the Canadian minutes of this meeting, "Dr. Hebb suggested that an approach based upon the situation of sensory isolation might lead to some clues" to answering "the central problem," specifically, "'confession,' 'menticide,' 'intervention in the individual mind,'—together with methods concerned in psychological coercion."[12] Consequently, in 1951 Canada's Defense Research Board gave Hebb a "confidential" grant to pursue this secret agenda.[13]

Within just a few years, this Allied mind-control effort would include a British "intelligence research unit" at Maresfield, Sussex, a secret Anglo-American facility near Frankfurt for lethal experiments on captured Soviet-bloc "expendables," CIA-funded psychology research at U.S. universities, periodic conferences to exchange results, and classified Canadian studies of sensory deprivation at McGill University.[14]

All this research produced two discoveries which would prove foundational for the CIA's psychological torture paradigm. Most fundamentally, Hebb found that he could induce virtual psychosis in just 48 hours. What had the doctor done—drugs, hypnosis, electroshock?

For two days, student volunteers at McGill University, where Hebb was chair of the Department of Psychology, simply sat in a comfortable cubicle deprived of sensory stimulation by goggles, gloves, and earmuffs, inducing extreme hallucinations similar to the effect of the drug mescaline.[15] In contrast to the modest impact anticipated, Hebb noted in a classified 1952 report that "motivational disturbance appears great," and among the 22 subjects "four remarked spontaneously that being in the apparatus was a form of torture"—findings that were, he advised, "of both theoretical and practical significance."[16]

Hebb himself later admitted that he was not prepared for the strong hallucinations. As he recalled in 1985, "we found that . . . the subjects, some of them, were seeing things in the experimental conditions, and feeling things. One felt his head was disconnected from his body, another had two bodies." Hebb was shocked at the devastating impact of his experiments: "It scared the hell out of us to see how completely dependent the mind is on a close connection with the ordinary sensory environment, and how disorganizing to be cut off from that support."[17] Only four years after Hebb began releasing results in 1954, over 230 articles on sensory deprivation would appear in peer-reviewed journals, demonstrating the effectiveness of the CIA's manipulation of the cognitive science community.[18]

During the 1950s as well, two neurologists working for the CIA at Cornell Medical Center found, in a second significant discovery, that the KGB's most devastating torture technique involved simply forcing victims to stand for days at a time while the legs swelled, the skin erupted in suppurating lesions, and hallucinations began—all incredibly painful. These procedures became integral to the CIA's psychological paradigm and are now called "stress positions."[19]

Although the main aim of this mind-control research was originally for offense, there was a renewed interest about its defensive uses in 1954–55 with news of the "brain washing" of American prisoners in North Korea.[20] After a year-long military inquiry, President Dwight Eisenhower ordered that every soldier at risk of capture should be given "specific training and instruction designed to better equip him to . . . withstand all enemy efforts against him." Consequently, the Air Force developed its SERE program (Survival, Evasion, Resistance, Escape) to train its pilots to resist psychological torture.[21]

As the military consulted psychologists and psychiatrists to diagnose past prisoner of war treatment in Korea, there thus developed two intertwined strands in mind-control research—offensive for CIA interrogation of communist agents and defensive for training American troops to resist enemy interrogators. The most famous of these defensive studies by Air Force sociologist Albert D. Biderman contained a chart of eight basic communist interrogation techniques and concluded that enforced standing was the most "excruciating" since the "immediate source of pain is not the interrogator but the victim himself," thus turning the "individual against himself." Indicative of how completely offensive and defensive research merged into a single inquiry, Biderman's major publication, *The Manipulation of Human Behavior* (1961), collected studies funded by two CIA conduits to explore, not resistance techniques, but "interrogation . . . for the purposes of intelligence."[22]

In 1963, the CIA distilled this decade of secret mind-control research into the "KUBARK Counter-intelligence Interrogation" manual delineating its discovery of psychological torture. Citing "experiments conducted at McGill University," KUBARK explained that sensory deprivation was effective because "the calculated provision of stimuli during interrogation tends to make the regressed subject view the interrogator as a father-figure . . . strengthening . . . the subject's tendencies toward compliance."[23]

If genius is the discovery of the obvious, then the CIA's development of this "no-touch torture" was the first real revolution in the cruel science of pain in centuries. Through 2,000 years of Western judicial torture, the same problem had persisted—the strong defied pain while the weak blurted out whatever was necessary to stop it. In the third century A.D., when scourging witnesses was a requisite of Roman law, the jurist Ulpian noted the "deceptive" nature of torture: "For many persons have such strength of body and soul that they heed pain very little . . . while others are so susceptible to pain that they will tell any lie rather than suffer it."[24]

By contrast, the CIA's psychological paradigm fused two new methods—the sensory disorientation discovered by Hebb and the self-inflicted pain documented by Biderman and the Cornell researchers—in a combination that would, in theory, cause victims to feel responsible for their own suffering and capitulate more readily to their torturers. Refined over the next 40 years, the CIA's method came to rely on a mix of sensory overload and sensory deprivation via deceptively banal procedures—heat and cold, light and dark, noise and silence, feast and famine—all meant to attack six essential sensory pathways into the human mind.

In its clandestine journey across continents and decades, this American form of psychological torture would prove elusive, resilient, adaptable, powerfully seductive, and devastatingly destructive. Since these attributes have allowed CIA psychological torture to persist to the present and perhaps into the future, we must review each.

First, *Elusive.* Unlike its physical variant, psychological torture lacks clear signs of abuse, greatly complicating any investigation, prosecution, or attempt at prohibition. After being trained in this doctrine by British intelligence, the Royal Ulster Constabulary used these psychological methods on Irish Republic Army suspects at Belfast in 1971 through the "five techniques": enforced wall standing, hooding, blaring music, sleep deprivation, and dietary manipulation. After articles in the British press stirred controversy, an inquiry by Lord Parker of Waddington found that these psychological methods greatly complicated any determination of torture. "Where," Lord Parker asked, "does hardship and discomfort end and for instance humiliating treatment begin, and where does the latter end and torture begin?" The answer, he said in prescient words, turns on "words of definition" and thus "opinions will inevitably differ."[25]

Similarly, when General Randall Schmidt investigated conditions at Guantánamo for the Pentagon in 2005, he found that the standards for physical "torture" were clear but "anything else beyond that was fairly vague"—adding that "something might be degrading but not necessarily torture." In reviewing treatment of the camp's star prisoner, Mohamed al-Kahtani, the general "felt that the cumulative effect of simultaneous applications of numerous authorized techniques had an abusive and degrading impact on the detainee"—a finding rejected, significantly, by higher echelons.[26]

Next, *Resilient.* Psychological torture is shrouded in a scientific patina that appeals to policy makers and avoids the obvious physical brutality that is so unpalatable to the American public. Even though *New York Times* headlines in early 2009 warned "Memos Spell Out Brutal C.I.A. Mode of Interrogation," the public seemed nonplused by the release of Justice Department documents from 2005 detailing, in sanitized medico-legal language, the CIA's use of beatings, stress positions, and waterboarding. Yet the White House refused to release photographs of similar interrogations, apparently aware that these graphic images could arouse anger at home and abroad.[27]

Third, *Adaptable.* In the 40 years since its discovery, the CIA's psychological paradigm has proved surprisingly supple, with each sustained application producing, as we will see below, innovation.

Fourth, *Seductive.* For both the perpetrators and the powerful who command them, torture has a multifaceted psychological appeal, ranging from a sense of empowerment to a darkly erotic dimension. In 1956, cognitive scientists working for the CIA described torture's lure for the Soviet leadership in words with universal implications:

> When feelings of insecurity develop within those holding power, they [the Soviet leaders] become increasingly suspicious and put great pressures upon the secret police to obtain arrests and confessions. At such times police officials are inclined to condone anything which produces a speedy "confession," and brutality may become widespread.[28]

Even when the abuse is initially intended for only a few, it soon spreads in two directions—rapid proliferation to the torture of many and an inexorable escalation in brutality. So seductive is torture's allure that the powerful, whether in the Kremlin or the White House, will often concoct rationales to preserve their prerogative of torture in defiance of strong evidence of its ineffectiveness and its high political costs.

Fifth and finally, *Destructive.* Although seemingly less brutal than physical methods, psychological torture leaves lasting emotional trauma. In early 2007, a half-century after the CIA codified these methods, researchers published clear clinical evidence that psychological torture is just as traumatic as its physical variant. "Ill treatment during captivity, such as psychological manipulations . . . and forced stress positions," Dr. Metin Basoglu reported in the *Archives of General Psychiatry* after interviews with 279 Bosnian victims, "does not seem to be substantially different from physical torture in terms of the severity of mental suffering."[29] In a subsequent study of 432 survivors, Basoglu concluded that "inhuman and degrading treatment" were the "major determinants of lasting psychological damage in detainees," indicating the need for a "broader definition" beyond "a rather stereotypical image of torture as involving only certain atrocious acts of physical violence."[30]

Propagation

After codification in the 1963 KUBARK manual, the CIA spent the next 30 years propagating these torture techniques among anti-communist allies across Asia and Latin America. During the Vietnam War, the CIA applied them in South Vietnam under the Phoenix program with methods that became brutally physical, producing more than 40,000 extrajudicial executions. Moreover, from 1966 to 1991, the U.S. Army's Military Intelligence ran "Project X" to transmit the counterinsurgency lessons from South Vietnam to Latin America via Spanish-language manuals, interrogation curricula, and field training programs.[31]

As part of this "resurgence of interest in teaching interrogation techniques" during the 1980s, the CIA conducted the Human Resources Exploitation (HRE) program which was, as reported by the agency's inspector general, "designed to train foreign liaison services on interrogation techniques."[32] In a 1983 HRE manual for the Honduran military, the CIA taught interrogators that they should "manipulate the subject's environment . . . to disrupt patterns of time, space, and sensory perception"— in short, to assault the sensory pathways to human consciousness.[33] Significantly, the techniques in this 1983 program seem strikingly similar to those outlined 20 years *earlier* in the KUBARK manual and those that would be used 20 years *later* at Abu Ghraib.

When the Cold War ended, Washington retracted its torture training and resumed its advocacy of human rights. After an internal CIA investigation of "misconduct" that killed a detainee, and some negative publicity about human rights abuse in Central America, the agency ended its HRE training programs in 1986. In a parallel process inside the Defense Department, the assistant secretary for intelligence oversight advised Secretary Dick Cheney in a March 1992 memo that seven counterinsurgency and interrogation manuals, compiled during the 1980s for Project X, contained "material . . . not to be consistent with U.S. policy." Interviews with army personnel who used these manuals found they believed incorrectly that U.S. regulations on "legal and proper" interrogation "did not apply to the training of foreign personnel." As a corrective, the Defense Department tried to recover the documents from Latin American governments and ordered that, except for a file copy, all those recovered "should be destroyed"—an experience that may have contributed to Cheney's knowledge of these dark arts.[34]

Most importantly, in 1994 the Clinton administration ratified the UN Convention Against Torture (CAT), apparently resolving the tension between Washington's anti-torture principles and its torture practices. Yet when Clinton sent this convention to Congress, he included exculpatory language drafted by the State Department for the Reagan administration, with four detailed diplomatic "reservations" focused on just one word in the convention's 26 printed pages. That word was "mental." Instead of CAT's broad language about "severe pain or suffering," these reservations narrowed the standard for psychological torture by requiring "prolonged mental harm" caused by just four specific acts: "(1) the intentional infliction or threatened infliction of severe physical pain or suffering; (2) the administration . . . of mind-altering substances . . . ; (3) the threat of imminent death; or (4) the threat that another person will imminently be subjected to death."[35] In effect, these reservations redefined mental torture to exclude sensory deprivation and self-inflicted pain—the very techniques the CIA had propagated for the past 40 years. Moreover, this definition was reproduced verbatim when the Clinton administration enacted complementary domestic legislation, first in Section 2340 of the U.S. Federal Code and later in the War Crimes Act of 1996.[36]

But above all it was this little known law, Section 2340, that opened a loophole in CAT's language to allow the CIA's use of psychological torture after September 2001. Under Article 1, CAT defined "torture" as "any act by which severe pain or suffering, whether physical or mental, is *intentionally inflicted* on a person for such purposes as obtaining . . . information." Instead of the UN's more inclusive use of the passive voice in the phrase "intentionally inflicted," this U.S. law limited torture to an "act committed by a person . . . *specifically intended* to inflict severe physical or mental pain or suffering." If any pain inflicted through CIA techniques proved incidental to the pursuit of information and thus was not "specifically" intentional—and intentionality was now situated subjectively in the mind of the torturer, not objectively in the nature of his actions—then, under this U.S. law, psychological torture was not torture.[37]

Through this legal legerdemain, Washington split the UN convention, banning physical torture but exempting the CIA's psychological methods. For seven years following the start of the Clinton administration's covert campaign against al-Qaeda in 1995, the CIA avoided direct involvement in torture by sending some 70 terror suspects to Middle East allies notorious for brutal, physical torture.[38] This practice, called "extraordinary rendition," is explicitly banned under CAT's Article 3. By failing to repudiate the CIA's use of torture, while adopting a UN convention that condemned its practice, the United States left this contradiction buried like a political land mine ready to detonate with such phenomenal force just ten years later in the Abu Ghraib scandal.

Perfection

Right after his address to a shaken nation on September 11, 2001, President Bush gave his staff secret orders for torture, saying: "I don't care what the international lawyers say, we are going to kick some ass."[39] In the months that followed, administration attorneys translated their president's forceful but otherwise unlawful orders into U.S. policy through three controversial, neoconservative legal doctrines: (1) the president is above the law, (2) torture is legally acceptable, and (3) the U.S. Navy base at Guantánamo is not subject to U.S. laws. Reflecting these findings, in February 2002 the president ordered that "none of the provisions of Geneva apply to our conflict with al Qaeda," thereby removing requirements of "minimum standards for humane treatment."[40]

Though the gloves were off, interrogators still had to be taught how to hit. According to the CIA Inspector General's 2004 report, the "Agency had discontinued virtually all involvement in interrogations after encountering difficult issues" in Central America and the Middle East, leaving "almost no foundation" for reviving interrogation. Compounding the problem, the CIA "lacked adequate linguists" and "had very little hard knowledge" about al-Qaeda's leaders, denying the Agency any metric for assessing the effectiveness of its interrogation techniques. In the ten-year hiatus since the end of the Cold War, the only agency that had preserved an institutional memory of harsh methods, either defensive or offensive, was the Pentagon's SERE program which was still training U.S. troops to withstand "sensory deprivation, sleep disruption, stress positions, waterboarding, and slapping." Starting in early 2002, several SERE psychologists, using Biderman's 1957 chart of communist techniques, advised both Defense and the CIA about ways to "reverse engineer" these defensive methods for effective interrogation. In later Senate testimony, CIA director Michael Hayden admitted using waterboarding, while an assistant attorney general stated that the agency's technique was "adapted from the SERE training program."[41]

Almost from the start, however, revival of the CIA's psychological paradigm through this prism proved problematic. As the Senate Armed Services Committee later pointed out, the SERE methods were derived, in part, from "coercive methods used by the Chinese Communist dictatorship to elicit *false confessions* from U.S. POWs during the Korean War"—not to gather accurate intelligence.[42]

In response to White House inquiry about the legality of such techniques, Assistant Attorney General Jay Bybee and his subordinate John Yoo found grounds in their August 2002 memo for exculpating any CIA interrogator who tortured but later claimed his intention was information, not pain. Moreover, by parsing Section 2340's already restrictive definition, they argued that "physical pain amounting to torture must be equivalent in intensity to the pain accompanying serious physical injury such as organ failure"—allowing abuse that stopped just short of death. "For purely mental pain or suffering to amount to torture," the memo continued, "it must result in significant psychological harm . . . lasting for months or even years"—expansive language reflecting both the permissive standard of Section 2340 and the elusive character of psychological torture.[43]

Further up the chain of command, Condoleezza Rice, then National Security Adviser, later recalled that, after the "CIA sought policy approval from the National Security Counsel (NSC) to begin an interrogation program for high-level al-Qaida terrorists," she "convened a series of meetings of NSC principals in 2002 and 2003." After watching CIA operatives mime "certain physical and psychological interrogation techniques," this group—including Vice President Cheney, Attorney General John Ashcroft, Secretary of State Colin Powell, and CIA director George Tenet—repeatedly authorized extreme psychological techniques stiffened by hitting, walling, and waterboarding.[44]

During one of these meetings, Ashcroft asked aloud: "Why are we talking about this in the White House? History will not judge this kindly." Yet, according to CIA records, Ashcroft approved "expanded use" of enhanced techniques at meetings in July and September 2003, even when "informed that the waterboard had been used 119 times on an individual."[45] Even after the broadcast of the Abu Ghraib photos, these principals still met to consider the continued use of CIA torture techniques. Despite concerns about the damage Abu Ghraib was doing to America's reputation, which were shared by Colin Powell, Condoleezza Rice coldly commanded the agency officials: "This is your baby. Go do it."[46] These recommendations were delivered to President Bush, who told ABC News in April 2008: "Yes, I'm aware our national security team met on this issue. And I approved."[47] So seductive is torture's allure for the powerful, whether presidents or party secretaries, that they can often seem oblivious to evidence of its high political costs.

Operating under this broad White House protocol, in December 2002 Defense Secretary Rumsfeld approved the use of fifteen aggressive interrogation techniques for the military prison at Guantánamo, amplifying stress positions in a handwritten note: "I stand for 8–10 hours a day. Why is standing limited to 4 hours?" In developing its expansive interrogation protocol, the Pentagon relied on the senior counsel at CIA's Counterterrorism Center, Jonathan M. Fredman, who echoed the Bybee-Yoo August 2002 memo to advise that the legal definition of torture was "written vaguely" and "is basically subject to perception" by the perpetrator. Hence, he concluded that U.S. law had no real restraints on interrogation, saying: "If the detainee dies, you're doing it wrong."[48]

Simultaneously, Rumsfeld appointed General Geoffrey Miller to command Guantánamo with a wide latitude for interrogation, making this prison an ad hoc behavioral science laboratory. Under General Miller, Guantánamo's interrogators stiffened the psychological assault by exploring Arab "cultural sensitivity" to sexuality, gender identity, and fear of dogs. Miller also formed Behavioral Science Consultation Teams of military psychologists who probed each detainee for individual phobias, such as fear of dark or attachment to mother.[49] Through this three-phase attack on sensory receptors, cultural identity, and individual psyche, Guantánamo perfected the CIA's psychological paradigm, thereby creating an interrogation protocol that the International Red Cross deemed "tantamount to torture."[50] Sustained application of the CIA's psychological methods had once again produced innovation.

These techniques then escalated virally. After Rumsfeld ordered harsh interrogation at Guantánamo, word spread rapidly down the chain of command. Within weeks, intelligence officers at Bagram prison in Afghanistan were shown "a power point presentation listing the aggressive techniques that had been authorized by the Secretary"—encouraging a harsh climate that allowed guards to beat shackled detainees "with virtual impunity."[51] According to the New York Times, Special Operations forces operated five field interrogation centers across Iraq in 2004–05 where detainees were subjected to sensory deprivation, beating, burning, electric shock, and waterboarding. Among the thousand soldiers in these

elite units, 34 were later convicted of abuse and many more escaped prosecution only because records were officially "lost."[52]

After a visit from the Guantánamo chief General Miller in September 2003, the U.S. commander for Iraq, General Ricardo Sanchez,
issued orders for abusive interrogation at Abu Ghraib prison using these
enhanced psychological techniques—sensory disorientation, self-inflicted
pain, and cultural humiliation:

X. Isolation: Isolating the detainee from other detainees . . . for 30
days.

Y. Presence of Military Working Dogs: Exploits Arab fear of dogs
while maintaining security during interrogations . . .

AA. Yelling, Loud Music, and Light Control: Used to create fear,
disorient detainee and prolong capture shock . . .

CC. Stress Positions: Use of physical posturing (sitting, standing,
kneeling, prone, etc.)[53]

Indeed, my own review of the 1,600 still-classified photos collected by
the army's Criminal Investigation Command from Abu Ghraib reveals,
not random acts by those putative "creeps," but just three psychological
torture techniques repeated *ad nauseam*: first, hooding for sensory deprivation; second, shackling and enforced standing for self-inflicted pain;
and, third, nudity, sexual humiliation, and dogs for exploitation of Arab
cultural sensitivities. It is no accident that Private Lynndie England was
famously photographed leading an Iraqi detainee leashed like a dog.

Through this same tangled decision-making, the White House also
authorized the CIA to build a global network of prisons, airplanes, and
allied agents that could seize suspects from sovereign states and levitate
them into a supranational gulag. Between 2002 and 2006, the agency
operated two dozen jet aircraft that made thousands of secret flights fer-
rying detainees between the U.S. base at Guantánamo, allied prisons from
Morocco to Uzbekistan, and some eight CIA "black sites" from Thailand
to Poland. Moreover, the Bush administration gave the CIA primary control over al-Qaeda captives, ending the FBI's lead role in U.S. counterintelligence that it had held since 1940, because the agency, unlike the bureau,
had an institutional history of utilizing torture.[54]

In the months following the 9/11 attacks, Bush also allowed the CIA
to implement ten "enhanced" interrogation methods designed by "agency
psychologists," including "waterboarding," that represented an intensifica-

tion of the CIA's psychological paradigm. Among these ten techniques, three showed clear continuity from the agency's Cold War counterintelligence methods—"cramped confinement" in a dark box for sensory deprivation, the "stress positions" originally copied from the Soviet KGB, and "wall standing" used by British intelligence at Belfast in 1971. In a secret memo dated August 2002, the Justice Department approved the agency's use of these techniques "in some sort of escalating fashion, culminating with the waterboard."[55] Of the 94 detainees in CIA custody by mid-2005, about 28 would be subjected to some combination of these "enhanced techniques."[56]

During the first year of this CIA program, early 2002 to mid-2003, the absence of guidelines or supervision made its black sites a lurid *Grand-Guignol* of what the agency itself later called "unauthorized, improvised, inhumane, and undocumented . . . interrogation techniques."[57] Reflecting torture's inexorable escalation in brutality, the CIA Inspector General's 2004 report found that these "improvised actions" ranged from cruel to possibly criminal, including strangling with both hands "to restrict the detainee's carotid artery," staging "mock executions" by brandishing or firing handguns, confining a detainee "in a cold room, shackled and naked," racking "an unloaded semi-automatic . . . once or twice," revving a "power drill" close to a detainee's head, threatening, through an Arabic interpreter, to begin "sexually abusing female relatives in front of the detainee," telling a high-level prisoner "we're going to kill your children," and beating an Afghan detainee to death "with a large metal flashlight." When asked about some of this abuse, one CIA interrogator replied with an empowered arrogance, "How cold is cold?"[58] Even though these death threats clearly violated U.S. law, including the Torture Statute[59] and the War Crimes Act,[60] Bush's Justice Department decided, symbolically on September 11, 2003, not to prosecute any interrogators.[61]

After CIA headquarters issued clear "guidelines" in January 2003, such improvisation slowly ended and interrogation inside the Agency's secret prisons began to follow a uniform roster of standard and enhanced techniques.[62] As described in the agency's classified 2004 *Background Paper on CIA's Combined Use of Interrogation Techniques*, each detainee was transported to an agency black site while "deprived of sight and sound through the use of blindfolds, earmuffs, and hoods." Once inside, he was reduced to "a baseline dependent state" through "nudity, sleep deprivation (with shackling . . .), and dietary manipulation." For "more physical and psychological stress," CIA inquisitors used coercive measures such as "an insult slap or abdominal slap," and then "walling," which involved slamming the detainee's head against a cell wall. If these failed, interrogators escalated to waterboarding, which the Bush Justice Department called "the most intense of CIA interrogation techniques."[63]

The Waterboard

This medieval technique, called "Standard Gallic Torture" in a 1541 French judicial handbook, would now become what CIA director Porter Goss baptized, in March 2005, a "professional interrogation technique."[64] Indeed, so seductive was this torture that both CIA field operatives and Langley officials violated the agency's own guidelines to increase both its frequency and intensity. In 2004, the CIA inspector general reported that "the waterboard was used with far greater frequency" and "in a different manner" than that approved by the Justice Department. Whereas SERE trainers disrupted airflow by a brief, carefully supervised "application of a damp cloth over the air passages," actual agency interrogators "applied large volumes of water to a cloth that covered the detainee's mouth and nose."[65]

In defiance of sound procedures, this extreme method was applied to al-Qaeda captive Abu Zubaydah "at least 83 times during August 2002" and to Khalid Sheikh Mohammad 183 times in March 2003[66]—an excess best explained by the sado-erotic appeal of psychological torture. Significantly, agency investigators concluded that "there was no *a priori* reason to believe that applying the waterboard with the frequency and intensity with which it was used by the psychologist/interrogators was either efficacious or medically safe."[67]

Although Bush Justice Department lawyers had cited SERE training to advise the CIA in August 2002 that waterboarding was not torture and thus perfectly legal, their conclusions are questionable.[68] After French paratroopers tortured him with this technique during the Battle of Algiers in 1957, journalist Henri Alleg wrote a moving description in a book that turned France against the Algerian War. "I tried, by contracting my throat," he wrote, "to take in as little water as possible ... But I couldn't hold on for more than a few moments. I had the impression of drowning, and a terrible agony, that of death itself, took possession of me."[69]

Let us think about the deeper meaning of Alleg's sparse words: "a terrible agony, that of death itself." Although written decades before discovery of this cognitive phenomenon, Alleg's description was an eerily accurate adumbration of the "mammalian diving reflex"—a deep-seated fear of drowning hard wired in the human brain that allows infants to survive drowning in cold water for up to 20 minutes without brain damage. As waterboarding blocks air to the lungs, this diving reflex responds and the brain is wracked by terrifying panic signals that produce the most extreme pain imaginable—the ultimate fear, the one fear none of us can ever conquer, the visceral fear of death itself. Significantly, the International Committee of the Red Cross (ICRC) reported in 2006, from extended interviews with 14 "high value detainees" after their transfer from agency black sites to Guantánamo, that the "ill-treatment to which they were subjected while held in the CIA program . . . constituted torture."[70]

Legalization

Confronted by anger over detainee abuse at Abu Ghraib, the Bush White House fought back by defending CIA torture and endless detention as presidential prerogatives necessary for the War on Terror. But in June 2006, in a dramatic rebuke of the president's position, the Supreme Court ruled in *Hamdan v. Rumsfeld* that Bush's military commissions were illegal because they did not meet the Geneva Conventions' requirement that Guantánamo detainees be tried with "all the judicial guarantees . . . recognized as indispensable by civilized peoples."[71]

Thus, on September 6, 2006, in a dramatic bid to legalize his now-illegal policies, Bush announced that he was transferring 14 top al-Qaeda captives from the secret CIA prisons to Guantánamo Bay. To allow the "CIA program" with its "alternative set of procedures" to go forward, Bush was sending legislation to Congress that would legalize these same presidential prerogatives.[72]

After negotiations within Vice President Cheney's Senate office on September 21, 2006, Republican partisans drafted legislation that sailed through Congress without amendment to become the Military Commissions Act of 2006.[73] Significantly, this law provided CIA interrogators both legal immunity for past physical abuse and ample latitude for future psychological torture. Buried in 38 pages of dense print, this law defines "serious physical pain" as the "significant loss or impairment of the function of a bodily member, organ, or mental faculty"—a paraphrase of that iconic definition of physical torture as pain "equivalent in intensity to . . .

organ failure" in the August 2002 Bybee-Yoo torture memo already repudiated by the Justice Department.[74]

Moreover, by using verbatim the narrow definition of "severe mental pain" that the U.S. first adopted under Section 2340 back in 1994, this legislation immunized CIA interrogators for future use of these "enhanced" techniques. By focusing on the means rather than the end result, both Section 2340 and the Military Commissions Act limited the crime of inflicting "severe mental pain" to just four specific actions: (1) drug injection, (2) death threats, (3) threats against another, and (4) extreme physical pain.[75] Beyond these acts, all of the CIA's many psychological torture techniques developed since 1951 are not "severe mental pain" and are thus legalized.

This law's permissive intent was confirmed nine months later when President Bush, as provided in the act, issued new guidelines for CIA interrogation, restraining the range of temperature modulation and restricting waterboarding. But the president's order remained classified, masking many of its provisions, and still denied the ICRC access to agency prisoners. Most importantly, Bush's concessions were a presidential prerogative and could be rescinded at any time for a resumption of waterboarding and other tortures.[76] Through this process, Bush had resolved that convenient contradiction between U.S. anti-torture principles and torture practices dating back to the Cold War. But he did so not by banning torture, but instead by legitimating CIA psychological methods as a lawful instrument of American power.

In the transition from the Bush to the Obama administration, Washington continued its reversion to this contradictory Cold War torture policy: publicly advocating human rights while covertly outsourcing torture to allied intelligence agencies. In retrospect, the real aberration of the Bush years lay not in torture policies per se, but in the president's orders that the CIA should operate its own torture prisons and agents should dirty their own hands with waterboarding and walling. The advantage of the bipartisan torture consensus of the Cold War era was, of course, that it insulated Washington from the taint of torture, even when it was widely practiced.

In this reversion to status quo ante Bush, the Obama administration introduced some significant reforms—closing the CIA's secret prisons and barring its coercive methods in January 2009, as well as stripping the agency of its lead role in counter-terror interrogation and transferring that responsibility back to the FBI. Simultaneously, Attorney General Eric Holder, who had "reacted with disgust when he recently read graphic accounts" of abuse in the CIA Inspector General's 2004 report, overruled the Bush-era exoneration and appointed a special prosecutor to investigate possible war crimes, albeit with a narrow mandate. Yet there were also clear signs of a shift to outsourcing interrogation, much as Washington had done during the Cold War. Since the last months of Bush's presidency in mid-2008, U.S. intelligence captured a half dozen al-Qaeda suspects and, instead of shipping them to CIA secret prisons, had them interrogated by allied agencies in the Middle East. Showing that this policy is again bipartisan, Obama's new CIA director Leon Panetta announced that his agency would continue to engage in the rendition of terror suspects to allies like Egypt, Jordan, or Pakistan where we can, of course, "rely on diplomatic assurances of good treatment."[77]

Although Obama has ordered the CIA to comply with the Army Field Manual's non-coercive methods, in August 2009 his interrogation task force recommended against any changes to this document which had been revised by the Bush administration to permit harsh psychological techniques. In the future, both the CIA and military intelligence can employ stress positions, environmental manipulation, protracted sleep deprivation, and limitless solitary confinement—techniques whose synergy could constitute inhumane treatment or torture under the Geneva Conventions.[78]

Legacy of Torture

In retrospect, this recourse to CIA psychological torture has corrupted U.S. intelligence and compromised America's international standing. CIA director George Tenet has claimed that these enhanced techniques were "extremely valuable in obtaining . . . critical threat information." But a careful review by the CIA's Inspector General found, "effectiveness . . . cannot be so easily measured," since there is no means to "determine . . . the totality of the intelligence the detainee actually possesses," or whether waterboarding versus simple "length of detention" was the "catalyst" for eventual compliance.[79] While the utility of these methods for intelligence gathering is still unclear, evidence has been building slowly since 2004 that the Bush administration used torture, not to extract accurate intelligence, but to fabricate evidence of an alliance between Saddam Hussein and al-Qaeda. A CIA report had earlier indicated that, during interrogations started in 2002, the first al-Qaeda captive, Ibn al-Shaykh al-Libi, stated that Saddam Hussein's regime had "provided unspecified chemical or biological weapons training for two al-Qa'ida associates."[80] Based on such intelligence, Secretary Colin Powell told the UN Security Council in February 2003 that "this detainee describes . . . Iraq offering chemical or biological weapons training for two al-Qaida associates."[81]

A year later, in January 2004, however, al-Libi admitted to CIA investigators that he had "fabricated information while in U.S. custody" when threatened with torture and forced to sleep on a cold floor. To get socks and a bed, he claimed full membership in al-Qaeda though really only a minor employee, and rattled off all the names he knew. Following his transfer to Egyptian intelligence, al-Libi was asked about "al-Qaida's connections with Iraq," and first "said he knew nothing." But after 17 hours in a "small box" and being "punched for 15 minutes," suddenly "he came up with a story that three al-Qai'ida members went to Iraq to learn about nuclear weapons." This story "pleased his interrogators, who directed that al-Libi be . . . given food."[82] In May 2009, Secretary Powell's former military aide, Col. Lawrence B. Wilkerson, charged that Vice President Cheney ordered the torture of al-Libi to extract false intelligence about contacts between Saddam Hussein and al-Qaeda. The colonel recalled:

> So furious was this effort, even when the interrogation team had reported to Cheney's office that their detainee "was compliant" (meaning the team recommended no more torture), the VP's office ordered them to continue the enhanced methods. . . . This ceased only after Ibn al-Shaykh al-Libi, under waterboarding in Egypt, "revealed" such contacts.[83]

With just some socks, a wood box, and a wet rag, the CIA and its allies fabricated convincing intelligence that dazzled the U.S. Senate and persuaded the UN Security Council—illustrating the extraordinary power of torture to force false confessions and compromise the intelligence process.

More immediately, torture has done enormous damage to U.S. prestige among its closest allies. In 2006, prompted by "press reports about prisoner transfers by the CIA," the Council of Europe's Secretary General called for "stronger supervision over the activities of national secret services" with closer controls "in respect of foreign services."[84] A few months later, Italy launched the trial of 25 CIA agents in absentia for the Milan kidnapping of a Muslim cleric who was flown to Egypt for months of torture—an extraordinary rupture in covert relations.[85] Thus, the web of international intelligence collaboration, central to CIA operations in Europe for more than half a century, now appeared ripped beyond repair.

If history repeats itself not as tragedy but as farce, then this revival of CIA Cold War torture for the War on Terror has been so unnecessary that it was almost farcical. Just as the CIA's psychological protocol has become a distinctively American form of torture, so there is an alternative American approach that we might call empathetic interrogation. During World War II, the Marine Corps interrogator, Major Sherwood F. Moran, a former missionary fluent in Japanese, used empathy to establish "intellectual and spiritual" rapport with Japanese prisoners, prompting the U.S. Navy to train a corps of like interrogators who got quick, accurate order-of-battle intelligence from supposedly fanatical Japanese soldiers on islands across the Pacific.[86]

From 1940 to 2002, the FBI controlled all U.S. counter-intelligence operations and used this same method quite successfully to investigate threats to domestic security. After the bombings of U.S. embassies in East Africa in 1998, FBI teams used empathic methods to gain some of our best intelligence on al-Qaeda and win convictions of the accused in federal courts. But in early 2002, President Bush transferred control of all al-Qaeda captives from the FBI to the CIA because the agency, unlike the bureau, could and would torture. For the next six years, experienced FBI interrogators from Cuba to Afghanistan would complain bitterly to their headquarters that the CIA's extreme methods were blocking effective interrogation of detainees.[87]

No matter what position Washington might adopt toward CIA interrogation, this tangled history has one clear lesson worth remembering. As a powerfully symbolic state practice synonymous with brutal autocrats throughout the ages, torture—even of the few, even of just one—raises profound moral issues about the quality of America's justice, the character of its civilization, and the legitimacy of its global leadership.

NOTES

1. See U.S. Congress, Senate and House Armed Services Committees, *Testimony of Secretary of Defense Donald H. Rumsfeld*, May 7, 2004, http://www.defenselink.mil/speeches/speech.aspx?speechid=118 (last visited Aug. 25, 2009).

2. William Safire, "Hold Fast, Idealists," *New York Times*, May 12, 2004, http://www.nytimes.com/2004/05/12/opinion/12SAFI.html?scp=1&sq=safire%20 2004%20creeps&st=cse (last visited Sept. 25, 2009).

3. Christopher Simpson, *Science of Coercion: Communication Research & Psychological Warfare, 1945–1960* (New York: Oxford Univ. Press, 1994), 8–9.

4. Irving L. Janis, *Are the Cominform Countries Using Hypnotic Techniques to Elicit Confessions in Public Trials?* (Santa Monica: Rand Corp., 1949), 1, 3, 6–7, 16–20; Walter Bowart, *Operation Mind Control* (New York: Dell, 1978), 67–71, 109–10.

5. CIA, Summary of Remarks by Mr. Allen W. Dulles at the National Alumni Conference of the Graduate Council of Princeton University, Hot Springs, VA, Apr. 10, 1953, File: Artichoke Docs: 362–388, Box 5, CIA Behavior Control Experiments Collection, National Security Archive, Washington, DC.

6. CIA, *Proposed Study on Special Interrogation Methods*, Feb. 14, 1952, CIA Behavior Control Experiments Collection (John Marks Donation), National Security Archive, Washington, DC.

7. "Private Institutions Used in C.I.A. Effort to Control Behavior; 25-Year, $25 Million Project," *New York Times*, Aug. 2, 1977.

8. John Marks, *The Search for the "Manchurian Candidate": The CIA and Mind Control* (New York: Times Books, 1979), 4–6; U.S. Naval Technical Mission to Europe, *German Aviation Medical Research at the Dachau Concentration Camp*, Technical Report no. 3331-45, Harvard Medical Library, Oct. 1945, H MS c64, Box 11, f.75; Arthur M. Turner, MD, letter to Dr. Henry K. Beecher, Feb. 7, 1947, Box 6, CIA Behavior Control Experiments Collection (John Marks Donation), National Security Archive, Washington, DC.

9. Henry K. Beecher, letter to the Surgeon General, Oct. 21, 1951, Box 16, RG 319, U.S. National Archives & Research Admin. (NARA).

10. Henry K. Beecher, letter to Col. William S. Stone, Aug. 29, 1950; Henry K. Beecher, letter regarding "Information from Europe Related to the Ego-Depressants, 6 August to 29 August 1952," Sept. 4, 1952; Ernst Rothlin, letter regarding d-Lysergic acid diethylamide (LSD 25); Arthur R. Lund, letter, May 26, 1951; Henry K. Beecher, "Final Report: Response of Normal Men to Lysergic Acid Derivatives," in *Project Title: Neuropsychiatry and Stress*, Dec. 31 1954; CIA, *Behavior Control Experiments Collection* (John Marks Donation), National Security Archive, Washington, DC; Sharon Perley, et al., "The Nuremberg Code: an International Overview," in *The Nazi Doctors and the Nuremberg Code: Human Rights in Human Experimentation*, ed. George J. Annas and Michael A. Grodin (New York: Oxford Univ. Press, 1992), 149–68.

11. Ronald W. Clark, *Tizard* (London: Methuen, 1965), 386–402.

12. See Canadian Dept. of Justice (DOJ), ed., *Opinion of George Cooper, Q.C., Regarding Canadian Government Funding of the Allan Memorial Institute in the 1950's and 1960's* (Ottawa: Minister of Supply and Services Canada, 1986), appendix 21.

13. See D. O. Hebb, W. Heron, and W. H. Bexton, "Annual Report, Contract DRB-X38, Experimental Studies of Attitude," in *Opinion of George Cooper, Q.C.,* Canadian DOJ, ed., Appendix 22.

14. Harvey M. Weinstein, *Psychiatry and the CIA: Victims of Mind Control* (Washington, DC: American Psychiatric Press, 1990), 274; James Meek, "Nobody Is Talking," *The Guardian,* Feb. 18, 2005; Marks, *The Search for the "Manchurian Candidate,"* 32–33; Michael Ignatieff, "What Did the C.I.A. Do to His Father?" *New York Times Magazine,* Apr. 1, 2001, 60.

15. Woodburn Heron, "The Pathology of Boredom," *Scientific American* 196 (1957):52–56.

16. See Hebb, Heron, and Bexton, "Annual Report, Contract DRB-X38," in *Opinion of George Cooper, Q.C.,* Canadian DOJ, ed., Appendix 22.

17. D. O. Hebb, *This Is How It Was,* Canadian Psychological Association, ca. 1980 (Copy provided by Mary Ellen Hebb).

18. For citations of these 230 articles, see Philip Solomon, et al., eds., *Sensory Deprivation: A Symposium Held at Harvard Medical School* (Cambridge, MA: Harvard Univ. Press, 1961), 239–57.

19. Lawrence E. Hinkle, Jr., *A Consideration of the Circumstances Under Which Men May Be Interrogated, and the Effects That These May Have Upon the Function of the Brain* (n.d., ca. 1958), 1, 5, 6, 11–14, 18, File: Hinkle, Box 7, CIA Behavior Control Experiments Collection (John Marks Donation), National Security Archive, Washington, DC; Lawrence E. Hinkle, Jr. and Harold G. Wolff, "Communist Interrogation and Indoctrination of 'Enemies of the States': Analysis of Methods Used by the Communist State Police (A Special Report)," *Archives of Neurology and Psychiatry* 76 (1956):115–74.

20. Associated Press, "Psychiatrist Aids 'Germ'Confessor," *New York Times,* March 10, 1954; Elie Abel, "Eisenhower Gives View on Schwable," *New York Times,* March 11, 1954; Edgar H. Schein, "Patterns of Reactions to Severe Chronic Stress in American Army Prisoners of War of the Chinese," *Journal of Social Issues* 13 (1957):253–69; Louis J. West, "United States Air Force Prisoners of the Chinese Communists," in *Symposium No. 4. Methods of Forceful Indoctrination: Observations and Interviews* (New York: Group of the Advancement of Psychiatry, 1957), 270–84.

21. Joseph Marguilies, *Guantánamo and the Abuse of Presidential Power* (New York: Simon & Schuster, 2006), 120–25; UP, "Officers to Study 'Brainwash' Issue," *New York Times,* August 23, 1954; Anthony Leviero, "For the Brainwashed: Pity or Punishment," *New York Times Sunday Magazine,* August 14, 1954; Russell Baker, "Eisenhower Pen Activates Code," *New York Times,* August 18, 1955; Dwight D. Eisenhower, *Executive Order 10631: Code of Conduct for Members of the Armed Forces of the United States,* Aug. 17, 1955, American Presidency Project, Univ. of California at Santa Barbara.

22. UP, "Training Is Ordered on New P.O.W. Code," *New York Times*, August 20, 1955; UP, "'Brainwash' Course Backed by Marines," *New York Times*, September 15, 1955; UP, "U.S. Orders Review of Torture School," *New York Times*, September 17, 1955; Special to the *New York Times*, "The Air Force Suspends Its 'Brainwash Course,'" *New York Times*, December 14, 1955; Albert D. Biderman, "Communist Attempts to Elicit False Confessions from Air Force Prisoners of War," *Bulletin of the New York Academy of Medicine* 33, no. 9 (1957): 618–22; Albert D. Biderman and Herbert Zimmer, "Introduction," in *The Manipulation of Human Behavior*, ed. Albert D. Biderman and Herbert Zimmer (New York: John Wiley, 1961), 1, 10; Lawrence E. Hinkle, Jr., "The Physiological State of the Interrogation Subject as it Affects Brain Function," in Biderman and Zimmer, *The Manipulation of Human Behavior*, 19–20, 43. Four of the seven essays in the volume were funded by two CIA conduits, the Office of Naval Research and the Society for the Investigation of Human Ecology.

23. CIA, *KUBARK Counterintelligence Interrogation*, July 1963, pp. 87–90, http://www.gwu.edu/~nsarchiv/NSAEBB/NSAEBB122/#kubark (last visited Sept. 12, 2009).

24. Edward Peters, *Torture* (Philadelphia: Univ. of Pennsylvania Press, 1996), 1, 14–18, 25–33, 35.

25. *The Times* (London), Mar. 3, 1972; Lord Parker of Waddington, *Report of the Committee of Privy Counsellors Appointed to Consider Authorised Procedures for the Interrogation of Persons Suspected of Terrorism* (London: Stationery Office, Cmnd. 4901, 1972), 3–17.

26. U.S. Dept. of Defense, *Army Regulation 15-6: Final Report: Investigation into FBI Allegation of Detainee Abuse at Guantánamo Bay, Cuba Detention Facility* (Apr. 1, 2005; amended June 9, 2005), 1; U.S. Senate Armed Services Committee, "Hearing on Guantánamo Bay Detainee Treatment" (July 13, 2005), 19, 20, 35, 55.

27. Scott Shane and Mark Mazzetti, "Memos Spell Out Brutal C.I.A. Mode of Interrogation," *New York Times*, Apr. 17, 2009; Editorial, "The Torturers' Manifesto," *New York Times*, Apr. 19, 2009; Jeff Zeleny and Thom Shanker, "Obama Moves to Bar Release of Detainee Abuse Photos," *New York Times*, May 14, 2009.

28. Hinkle and Wolff, "Communist Interrogation and Indoctrination," *Archives of Neurology and Psychiatry*, 135.

29. Metin Basoglu, Maria Livanou, and Cvetana Crnobaric, "Torture vs Other Cruel, Inhuman, and Degrading Treatment: Is the Distinction Real or Apparent?" *Archives of General Psychiatry* 64, no. 3 (2007):277–85.

30. Metin Basoglu, "A Multivariate Contextual Analysis of Torture and Cruel, Inhuman, and Degrading Treatments: Implications for an Evidence-Based Definition of Torture," *American Journal of Orthopsychiatry* 79, no. 2 (2009):135–45.

31. See Alfred W. McCoy, *A Question of Torture: CIA Interrogation, From the Cold War to the War on Terror* (New York: Metropolitan Books, 2006), ch. 3.

32. Steven G. Bradbury, memorandum for John A. Rizzo regarding "Application of United States Obligations Under Article 16 of the Convention Against Torture to Certain Techniques That May be Used in the Interrogation of High Value al Qaeda Detainees," May 30, 2005, 32.

33. CIA, Human Resources Exploitation Training Manual, 1983, Box 1, CIA Training Manuals, National Security Archive, Washington, DC.

34. Werner E. Michel, memorandum regarding "Improper Material in Spanish-Language Intelligence Training Manuals," Mar. 10, 1992, Box 2, Intelligence Training Source Manuals, Folder: Untitled, National Security Archive, Washington, DC.

35. U.S. Senate, Committee on Foreign Relations, Convention Against Torture: Hearing Before the Committee on Foreign Relations, 101st Cong., 2d sess. (Washington, DC: Government Printing Office, 1990), 1, 12–18, 34, 35, 40–43, 66–69, 70–71.

36. U.S. Congress, Proceedings and Debates, 103rd Cong., 2nd sess., vol. 140, pt. I (Washington, DC: Government Printing Office, 1994), Feb. 2, 1994, 827; U.S. Congress, War Crimes Act of 1996, 104th Cong., 2nd sess., H.R. 3680 (1994); 18 U.S.C. § 2340–2340A.

37. 18 U.S.C. § 2340.

38. Douglas Jehl and David Johnston, "Rule Change Lets C.I.A. Freely Send Suspects Abroad to Jails," *New York Times*, Mar. 6, 2005; Jane Mayer, "Outsourcing Torture: The Secret History of America's 'Extraordinary Rendition' Program," in this book.

39. Richard A. Clarke, *Against All Enemies: Inside America's War on Terror* (New York: Free Press, 2004), 24.

40. U.S. Senate, Committee on Armed Services, Inquiry into the Treatment of Detainees in U.S. Custody, 110th Cong., 2nd sess., 2008, xiii; George W. Bush, memorandum to the Vice President regarding "Humane Treatment of Taliban and al Qaeda Detainees," Feb. 7, 2002.

41. U.S. Senate, Inquiry into the Treatment of Detainees, xiv–xvi.

42. Ibid. at xiii, xx; emphasis added.

43. Jay S. Bybee, memorandum to Alberto R. Gonzales regarding "Standards of Conduct for Interrogation under 18 U.S.C. §§ 2340–2340A," Aug. 1, 2002, 1; U.S. Senate, Inquiry into the Treatment of Detainees, xv–xvi, xxi.

44. U.S. Senate, Inquiry into the Treatment of Detainees, xv, xx–xxi, 16–17.

45. CIA, Counterterrorism Detention, 44–45.

46. Jan Crawford Greenburg, Howard L. Rosenberg, and Ariane de Vogue, "Sources: Top Bush Advisors Approved 'Enhanced Interrogation,'" *ABC News*, Apr. 9, 2008, http://abcnews.go.com/TheLaw/LawPolitics/story?id=4583256&page=1 (last visited Aug. 25, 2009).

47. Jan Crawford Greenburg, Howard L. Rosenberg, and Ariane de Vogue, "Bush Aware of Advisers' Interrogation Talks," *ABC News*, Apr. 11, 2008, http://abcnews.go.com/TheLaw/LawPolitics/story?id=4635175&page=1 (last visited Aug. 25, 2009).

48. U.S. Senate, Inquiry into the Treatment of Detainees, xix; William J. Haynes II, memorandum for Secretary of Defense regarding "Counter-Resistance Techniques," Nov. 27, 2002; Mark Mazzetti and Scott Shane, "Notes Show Confusion on Interrogation Methods," *New York Times*, June 18, 2008.

49. M. Gregg Bloche and Jonathan H. Marks, "Doctors and Interrogators at Guantánamo Bay," *New England Journal of Medicine* 353, no. 1 (2005):7; Jonathan H. Marks, "The Silence of the Doctors," *The Nation*, Dec. 7, 2005.

50. Neil A. Lewis, "Red Cross Finds Detainee Abuse in Guantanamo," *New York Times*, Nov. 30, 2004, http://www.nytimes.com/2004/11/30/politics/30gitmo.html (last visited Aug. 26, 2009).

51. U.S. Senate, Inquiry into the Treatment of Detainees, xxii. See Tim Golden, "Army Faltered in Investigating Detainee Abuse," *New York Times*, Mar. 4, 2003, http://www.nytimes.com/2005/05/22/international/asia/22abuse.html (last visited Aug. 31, 2009); Tim Golden, "In U.S. Report, Brutal Details of 2 Afghan Inmates' Deaths," *New York Times*, May 20, 2005, http://www.nytimes.com/2005/05/20/international/asia/20abuse.html (last visited Aug. 31, 2009).

52. Eric Schmitt and Carolyn Marshall, "In Secret Unit's 'Black Room,' a Grim Portrait of U.S. Abuse," *New York Times*, Mar. 19, 2006, http://www.nytimes.com/2006/03/19/international/middleeast/19abuse.html?pagewanted=1&_r=1 (last visited Aug. 26, 2009).

53. Ricardo S. Sanchez, memorandum for Combined Joint Task Force Seven regarding "CJTF-7 Interrogation and Counter-Resistance Policy," Sept. 14, 2003; Ricardo S. Sanchez, memorandum for Combined Joint Task Force Seven regarding "CJTF-7 Interrogation and Counter-Resistance Policy," Oct. 12, 2003.

54. See Stephen Grey, *Ghost Plane: The True Story of the CIA Torture Program* (New York: St. Martin's Press, 2006), 87, 181, 227, 269–308; see also Scott Shane, Stephen Grey, and Margot Williams, "C.I.A. Expanding Terror Battle Under Guise of Charter Flights," *New York Times*, May 31, 2005, http://www.nytimes.com/2005/05/31/national/31planes.html?pagewanted=all (last visited Aug. 26, 2009).

55. See Douglas Jehl, "Report Warned C.I.A. on Tactics in Interrogation," *New York Times*, Nov. 9, 2005, http://www.nytimes.com/2005/11/09/politics/09detain.html?pagewanted=print (last visited Aug. 26, 2009); CIA, Counterterrorism Detention, 14–15, 20.

56. Bradbury, memorandum regarding "Application of the Convention Against Torture," 5.

57. CIA, Counterterrorism Detention, 102-103.

58. Ibid. at 41–43, 69–71, 75–79.

59. 18 U.S.C. § 2340, 2340A.

60. 18 U.S.C. § 2441.

61. CIA, Counterterrorism Detention, 42.

62. Ibid. at 6–7.

63. Steven G. Bradbury, memorandum for John A. Rizzo regarding "Application of 18 U.S.C. §§ 2340–2340A to the Combined Use of Certain Techniques in the Interrogation of High Value al Qaeda Detainees," May 10, 2005, 53–56.

64. Joannes Millacus, *Praxis Criminis Persequendi* (Paris: Prostant and Simonem Colinacum, 1541); Douglas Jehl, "Questions Left By C.I.A. Chief on Torture Use," *New York Times*, March 18, 2005.

65. CIA, Counterterrorism Detention, 37.

66. Ibid. at 36, 91.

67. Ibid. at 21–22.

68. Jay S. Bybee, memorandum for John Rizzo regarding "Interrogation of al Qaeda Operative," Aug. 1, 2002, 5–6, 11.

69. Henri Alleg, *The Question* (New York: G. Braziller, 1958), 61.

70. International Committee of the Red Cross, *ICRC Report on the Treatment of Fourteen "High Value Detainees" in CIA Custody*, Feb. 14, 2007, p. 26.

71. *Hamdan v. Rumsfeld*, 548 U.S. 557, 559–60, 562 (2006); see David Stout, "C.I.A. Detainees Sent to Guantanamo," *New York Times*, June 30, 2006, http://www.nytimes.com/2006/09/06/washington/06cnd-bush.html (last visited Aug. 26, 2009).

72. George W. Bush, "President Discusses Creation of Military Commissions to Try Suspected Terrorists" (White House, Washington, DC, Sept. 6, 2006).

73. U.S. Congress, *Military Commissions Act of 2006*, H.R. 6166, 109th Cong., 2d sess., Sept. 25, 2006.

74. Bybee, memorandum regarding "Standards of Conduct for Interrogation," 5–7; U.S. Congress, *Military Commissions Act*, 29, 35.

75. U.S. Congress, *Military Commissios Act*, 28.

76. Mark Mazzetti, "Rules Lay Out C.I.A.'s Tactics in Questioning," *New York Times*, July 21, 2007, http://www.nytimes.com/2007/07/21/washington/21intel.html (last visited Aug. 26, 2009); Karen De Young, "Bush Approves New CIA Methods," *Washington Post*, July 21, 2007, http://www.washingtonpost.com/wpdyn/content/article/2007/07/20/AR2007072001264.html (last visited Aug. 26, 2009).

77. Charlie Savage, "Obama's War on Terror May Resemble Bush's in Some Areas," *New York Times*, Feb. 18, 2009, http://www.nytimes.com/2009/02/18/us/politics/18policy.html (last visited Aug. 31, 2009); David Johnston, "U.S. Says Rendition to Continue, But With More Oversight," *New York Times*, May 24, 2009, http://www.nytimes.com/2009/08/25/us/politics/25rendition.html (last visited Aug. 31, 2009); David Johnston, "For Holder, Inquiry on Interrogation Poses Tough Choice," *New York Times*, July 21, 2009, http://www.nytimes.com/2009/07/22/us/22holder.html (last visited Sept. 13, 2009).

78. Scott Shane, "Obama Orders Secret Prisons and Detention Camp Closed," *New York Times*, Sept. 23, 2009, http://www.nytimes.com/2009/01/23/us/politics/23GITMOCND.html, accessed Jan. 23, 2010; Matthew Alexander, "Torture's Loopholes," *New York Times*, Jan. 21, 2010.

79. CIA, *Counterterrorism Detention*, 85–91, 100.

80. See U.S. Senate, Select Committee of Intelligence, *Postwar Findings About Iraq's WMD Programs and Links to Terrorism and How They Compare with Prewar Assessments*, 109th Cong., 2nd sess., Sept. 8, 2006, 106–8.

81. Colin L. Powell, "Remarks to the United Nations Security Council," New York, Feb. 5, 2003, http://www.informationclearinghouse.info/article3710.htm (last visited Aug. 26, 2003).

82. See U.S. Senate, *Postwar Findings About Iraq's WMD Programs*, 79–82, 106–8.

83. Lawrence B. Wilkerson, "The Truth About Richard Bruce Cheney," *The Washington Note*, May 13, 2009.

84. Council of Europe, Secretary General, *Report by the Secretary General under Article 52 ECHR on the Question of the Secret Detention and Transport of Detainees Suspected of Terrorist Acts, Notably by or at the Instigation of Foreign Agencies*, SG/Inf (2006) 5, Feb. 28, 2006, http://www.globalsecurity.org/intell/library/reports/2006/secret-detentions-transport_ce-sg_060228.htm (last visited Aug. 26, 2009), 8, 10–11.

85. See Ian Fisher and Elisabetta Povoledo, "Italy Seeks Indictment of C.I.A. Operatives in Egyptian's Abduction," *New York Times*, Jul. 6, 2006, http://www.nytimes.com/2006/12/06/world/europe/06italy. html (last visited Aug. 26, 2009).

86. Stephen Budiansky, "Intelligence: Truth Extraction," *The Atlantic Monthly*, June 2005, 32–35.

87. See Jane Mayer, "Outsourcing Torture: The Secret History of America's 'Extraordinary Rendition' Program," in this book.

2

Torture and Human Rights Abuses at the School of Americas-WHINSEC

BILL QUIGLEY[1]

On June 28, 2009, former students of a U.S. Army School in Georgia known for teaching torture and graduating human rights abusers led a military coup that overthrew the democratically elected government of Honduras. Honduran General Romeo Vasquez, the leader of the coup, was trained at the U.S. Army School of the Americas (SOA), now renamed the Western Hemisphere Institute for Security Cooperation (WHINSEC). Other leaders of the 2009 coup were also trained by the U.S. Army.[2]

General Vasquez is the third graduate of the SOA to overthrow governments in Honduras. A previous graduate, General Juan Melgar Castro, tortured and executed two priests and several peasants in the 1970s by baking them alive in bread ovens and then throwing their bodies in a well. Melgar was toppled by yet another brutal SOA grad, General Paz Garcia, who formed his own military death squad that worked closely with the CIA targeting leftists in Honduras in the 1980s.[3]

In fact, graduates of SOA have been implicated in many of the worst human rights atrocities in the Western Hemisphere, including the assassination of bishops, labor leaders, women, children, priests, nuns, community workers, and in the massacres of entire communities. Numerous murders and human rights violations by alumni have been documented in Bolivia, Chile, Colombia, El Salvador, Guatemala, Honduras, and Paraguay among others.[4] Moreover, the following techniques have been advocated in training manuals used at SOA: motivation by fear, payment of bounties for enemy dead, false imprisonment, use of truth serum, torture, execution, extortion, kidnapping and arresting a target's family members.[5]

As a result, Amnesty International USA has directly condemned the school's techniques, demanding that the school be shut down and a truth commission established to chronicle its crimes since 2002. Though SOA no longer denies that it taught military leaders how to employ illegal measures to suppress dissent and democracy, including torture,[6] the U.S. government continues to resist any accountability of its graduates.

Amnesty featured the school as a prominent example of troubling human rights problems in the United States in its report, *Unmatched Power, Unmet Principles: The Human Rights Dimensions of U.S. Training of Foreign Military and Police Forces* (hereafter "Amnesty Report").[7]

The Amnesty Report pointed out:

> Throughout the decade of the 1990s, the record of one U.S. military training institution, in particular, attracted public scrutiny in the United States. The U.S. Army's School of the Americas offered training and education to Latin American soldiers, some of whom went on to commit human rights violations, including the 1989 murder in El Salvador of six Jesuit priests, their housekeeper and her daughter. Then, in 1996, it came to light that, in the 1980s and early 1990s, the School of the Americas had used manuals that advocated practices such as torture, extortion, kidnapping and execution.[8]

The report also contained several strong recommendations to the U.S. government to remedy the human rights violations occurring at SOA-WHINSEC, including the following:

- The U.S. government should take immediate steps to establish an independent commission to investigate the past activities of the SOA and its graduates, particularly the use of these torture manuals in SOA training and the impact of such training;
- Pending the publication of the findings of the independent commission of inquiry, training at the WHINSEC-SOA should be suspended; and
- The independent commission of inquiry should recommend appropriate reparations for any violations of human rights to which training at SOA contributed, including criminal prosecutions, redress for victims and their families, and a public apology.[9]

What Is the SOA-WHINSEC?

Originally established in Panama in 1946 to train Latin American military forces, the school was named the U.S. Army School of Americas in 1963. Because of a conflict between the United States and Panama, the SOA was moved to Fort Benning, Georgia in 1984. Together these schools have trained more than 60,000 members of the military from 22 Central and South American countries.[10]

The nations that send students to the school are generally high-level recipients of U.S. military assistance. For example, during the 1980s, when the United States was providing large amounts of aid to El Salvador's military, about one-third of the students at SOA came from El Salvador.[11] In the 1990s, half of the students hailed from just five countries: Colombia, El Salvador, Nicaragua, Peru, and Panama. Since 2000, Colombia, Chile, and El Salvador have had the largest number of students at the school.[12]

Because of the history of human rights abuses in its teaching and by its graduates, several legislative attempts have been made to close the SOA. In 1999, the U.S. House of Representatives voted 230-197 for an amendment that would have eliminated funds for training officers at SOA. In 2000, a resolution to close the SOA failed to pass in the House of Representatives by a 214 to 204 vote. As a result, there was a cosmetic renaming of the School of Americas as WHINSEC and a revised legal charter.[13]

WHINSEC now operates in the same building as the SOA, training the same soldiers with the same goal, creating only an artificial distinction between the two schools. The U.S. government and the Army have tried mightily to equate the superficial transformation to a permanent closure of the SOA, but few outside Army apologists are persuaded.

As Amnesty International noted:

> Although the United States Army claims that it has closed the School of the Americas (SOA) and established the Western Hemisphere Institute for Security Cooperation (WHINSEC) as an entirely new institution that happens to be located in the same physical place, WHINSEC is essentially the same school as SOA, with the same primary mission—conveying military skills to members of Latin American armed forces.[14]

SOA graduates have played key roles in nearly every coup and major human rights violation in Latin America over the past 50 years. In fact, Latin American nations with the worst human rights records have consistently sent the most soldiers to the SOA. Martin Meehand, a Congressman from Massachusetts, has noted, "[I]f the SOA held an alumni association meeting, it would bring together some of the most unsavory thugs in the hemisphere."[15]

Did the School Actually Teach Torture?

Yes. The school taught the systematic use of torture and executions to neutralize dissidents. After years of refusals to acknowledge that torture was being taught, the Pentagon finally admitted in 1996 that seven training manuals used for nearly ten years at the SOA advocated execution, torture, blackmail, and other forms of coercion.[16] Dana Priest of the *Washington Post* reported:

> Used in courses at the U.S. Army's School of the Americas, the [training] manual says that to recruit and control informants, counterintelligence agents could use "fear, payment of bounties for enemy dead, beatings, false imprisonment, executions and the use of truth serum," according to a secret Defense Department summary of the manuals compiled during a 1992 investigation of the instructional material.[17]

Priest refers to a memo dated March 10, 1992, stamped "secret," sent to then-Secretary of Defense Richard Cheney which details an investigation by Werner E. Michel, Assistant to the U.S. Secretary, into "Improper Material in Spanish-Language Intelligence Training Materials."[18]

The Department of Defense (DOD) admitted that "five of the seven manuals contained language and statements in violation of legal, regulatory or policy prohibitions . . ." These manuals are: Handling of Sources, Revolutionary War and Communist Ideology, Terrorism and the Urban Guerilla, Interrogation, and Combat Intelligence.[19]

Who were the targets of this torture? The manuals identified insurgents, including religious workers, labor organizers, student groups, and others in sympathy with the poor. The manuals also contained instructions for "neutralizing," which the Pentagon admitted was a euphemism for execution, of governmental officials, political leaders, and members of the infrastructure.[20]

But actual torture manuals, as bad as they are, are only part of the story. It is very important to note that the torture manuals were compiled from materials already in use as lesson plans for years at the School of the Americas since 1982.[21]

The DOD memo states that lesson plans at the SOA that were later used to create the manuals were based on materials used in the Vietnam war in the 1960s from the Army's Foreign Intelligence Assistance Programs, entitled "Project X." The existence of the actual manuals is evidence of only a part of the teaching of torture by the school.[22]

As many as 1,000 of the manuals were used in the training at the School of the Americas of students from the militaries of Bolivia, Colombia, Costa Rica, Dominican Republic, Ecuador, Guatemala, Honduras, Mexico, Peru, and Venezuela.[23]

U.S. Army Major Joseph Blair, an instructor at the SOA and a recipient of five meritorious service medals and a Bronze Star, began speaking out against the SOA in 1993. At that time, the U.S. Army and officials of the school still denied any knowledge of the atrocities and murders that the graduates went on to commit in Latin America. Major Blair told *Progressive* magazine in 1997:

> When I was at the school, we routinely had Latin American students who were known human rights abusers, and it didn't make any difference to us. I sat next to Major Victor Theiss who created and taught the entire course, which included seven torture manuals and 382 hours of instruction. He taught primarily using manuals which we used during the Vietnam War in our intelligence-gathering techniques. The techniques included murder, assassination, torture, extortion, false imprisonment. . . . Literally thousands of those manuals were passed out. The officers who ran the intelligence courses used lesson plans that included the worse material contained in the seven manuals. Now they say that there were only eighteen to twenty passages in those manuals in clear violation of U.S. law. In fact, those same passages were at the heart of the intelligence instruction.[24]

How Extensive Are Human Rights Abuses of SOA-WHINSEC Graduates?

The Amnesty Report documents the most well-known example of torture that graduates of SOA-WHINSEC participated in—the murder of six Jesuit priests in El Salvador:

On the morning of November 16, 1989, Salvadoran soldiers made their way into the Pastoral Center at the Central American University in San Salvador. They ordered five Jesuit priests to go outside and lie face down on the ground, where they were subsequently shot and killed. A sixth priest, the housekeeper and her 16-year-old daughter were then murdered inside the residence. The Jesuits had been labeled "subversives" by the Salvadoran government for speaking out against the socioeconomic structure of Salvadoran society. Of the twenty-six soldiers subsequently implicated in the murders of the Jesuit priests and women in El Salvador, nineteen had received training at the School of the Americas.[25]

The catalogue of human rights violations by graduates spans most of the countries in Central and South America. Below are examples of some of the worst graduates of the SOA:[26]

- General Leopoldo Galtieri headed the military junta in Argentina during the time of the "dirty war" when 30,000 people were killed or disappeared.[27]
- Bolivian General Hugo Banzer, who took power through a violent coup in 1971 and ruled until his downfall in 1978, was a SOA graduate. His penchant for brutality and his anti-democratic inclinations were probably not acquired when, as a young captain, he took a short course in 1956 to prepare him for duty as a driver. Banzer was, however, a long-time friend of the United States, and he so impressed the Army in his later career that it inducted him into the School's Hall of Fame in 1988.[28]
- Ten of 30 Chilean officers against whom a Spanish judge sought indictments for crimes of terror, torture, and disappearance.[29] Most of the Chilean military who overthrew the democratically elected government of Salvador Allende on September 11, 1973, attended the SOA.[30]
- One hundred twenty-three of the 247 Colombian army officers cited in "El Terrorismo de Estado en Colombia," a 1992 study of human rights abuses in Colombia.[31]
- In El Salvador, SOA grads have been implicated in the murder of Archbishop Oscar Romero, in addition to the killing of the Jesuit priests and their housekeeper and her 16-year-old daughter. They executed numerous massacres, rapes, and murders, including the multiple rapes and murder of a French nurse.[32]

- On March 24, 1980, Monsignor Oscar Romero was shot dead by a sniper as he celebrated mass in the Chapel of the Hospital de la Divina Providencia. During his funeral, a bomb went off outside San Salvador Cathedral. The panic-stricken crowd, estimated at 50,000 people, was machine-gunned, leaving approximately 27 to 40 people dead and more than 200 wounded. Two of the three officers cited in the assassination are graduates on the SOA, including the founder of the Salvadoran death squads, Roberto D'Aubuisson.[33]

- U.S. Army Special Forces were training members of the Atlacatl battalion in El Salvador in the days before and after members of the battalion killed a woman, her daughter, and six Jesuit priests in November 1989. Three of the four Atlacatl officers implicated had received training while attending the Salvadoran cadet course at the School of the Americas—two officers in 1982 and one in 1988. Overall, 19 of the 26 soldiers linked to the murder had taken some training at the SOA. One of them had also attended the Special Forces Officer Course at Fort Bragg during late 1988 and early 1989.[34]

- On December 2, 1980, four U.S. church women were arrested by the National Guard after they left the airport in El Salvador and were never heard from again.[35] Three of the five officers cited in the murders of these women were graduates of the SOA.[36]

- The massacre of El Mozote, in December 1981, took the lives of over 750 civilians, including 382 children under the age of 18.[37] Of the 245 cartridge cases recovered from the massacre site, 184 had discernible markings identifying the ammunition as manufactured for the U.S. government at Lake City, Missouri. Thirty-four cartridges were sufficiently preserved for analysis of individual and class characteristics. Of these, all except one appeared to have been fired from M-16 rifles manufactured in the United States.[38] Coincidentally, ten of the twelve officers cited as responsible for the massacre at El Mozote were graduates of the SOA.[39]

- The UN Truth Commission Report on El Salvador listed the names of more than 60 Salvadoran officers most responsible for the worst atrocities.[40] More than two-thirds of those officers were alumni of the SOA.[41]

- General Romeo Lucas Garcia was the dictator of Guatemala from 1978 to 1982, a period marked with 5,000 political murders and up to 25,000 other civilian deaths.[42]

- Army General Héctor Gramajo, also of Guatemala, was found personally responsible for "acts of gruesome violence inflicted by military personnel under his direct command," in a federal court of Massachusetts in 1995 and ordered to pay $42 million in damages.[43]
- More than 300 Mayan victims have filed suit against SOA graduate General Efrain Rios Montt, another former Guatemalan dictator, for genocidal actions taken in attempts to wipe out their villages.[44]
- Juan López Grijalba of Honduras stands accused in U.S. District Court of heading up a special military unit responsible for the disappearances of over 150 persons.[45]
- More soldiers from Nicaragua attended SOA than from any other country in the period of 1947–1979. Many were in the Somoza National Guard, which terrorized Nicaraguan peasants in the 1970s.[46]
- The most infamous Panamanian graduate of the SOA is Manuel Noriega, Panama's former dictator, who was arrested and forcibly extradited by U.S. military forces on drug trafficking charges in 1989.[47]
- In April 2002, Army Commander in Chief Efrain Vasquez and General Ramirez-Poveda helped lead a failed coup against the democratically elected government of Venezuela.[48]

Accountability for Torture and Human Rights Abuses at SOA-WHINSEC

The 1992 DOD memo documenting the teaching of torture and the publication of torture manuals at SOA concluded:

> It is incredible that the use of the lesson plans since 1982, and the manuals since 1987, evaded the established system of doctrinal controls. Nevertheless, we could find no evidence that this was a deliberate and orchestrated attempt to violate DoD or Army policies.[49]

There has been no accountability for the teaching of torture at the SOA. There has been no full public investigation into the school. There has been no apology. There have been no reparations for the victims. No one has been censured. No one has been prosecuted. No one has been sanctioned. No one has been demoted or fired. No one.[50]

• • •

As Amnesty International says:

> [T]he failure of the U.S. Army to hold anyone accountable for the preparation, dissemination and use of training manuals advocating torture . . . sends a signal to other militaries that impunity for violations [of the international laws on human rights, humanitarian law and civil military relations] is acceptable. It may also communicate that violations are only a problem when they receive public attention.[51]

Protesting Torture at SOA-WHINSEC

Despite the refusal of the U.S. government to hold anyone accountable, there has been a growing movement of people who are standing up against the teaching of torture and human rights abuses at SOA-WHINSEC.

Since the early 1980s, there have been regular teach-ins, protests, prayer vigils, lobbying sessions, and incidents of civil disobedience at Fort Benning, Georgia. The protests began after the assassination of Archbishop Oscar Romero in El Salvador in 1980.[52]

In 1983, Father Roy Bourgeois, a Maryknoll Catholic priest who was a purple heart Vietnam veteran before he became a priest and who had later spent time in Latin America, discovered that hundreds of Salvadoran soldiers were being trained at Fort Benning. Bourgeois and two others bought Army uniforms and walked onto the base at night. In the darkness, and carrying a large portable sound system, they climbed a pine tree outside of the barracks where the Salvadoran soldiers lived.[53]

Bourgeois and the others turned on the boom box and blasted a sermon from Archbishop Romero into the still night directly down at the barracks of the sleeping soldiers. In this taped sermon, Romero made a direct appeal to the soldiers of El Salvador to stop killing their brothers and sisters, and to disobey any military orders to do so: "Thou shalt not kill. . . . In the name of God, and in the name of this suffering people, whose laments rise to heaven each day more tumultuous, I beg you, I beseech you, I order you in the name of God: Stop the repression."[54] The three in the tree kept playing it over and over until they were forcibly removed. As a result of their civil disobedience, all three were charged with trespass and impersonating an officer. They were convicted and sentenced to 18 months in federal prison.[55]

After the massacre of the Jesuits, protests and civil disobedience erupted across the United States.[56] A congressional task force headed by Rep. Joseph Moakley (D-MA) investigated and concluded that those responsible for these murders were also trained at the SOA.[57]

In November 1990, a year after the Jesuit murders, Father Bourgeois, Charles Liteky, a Congressional Medal of Honor winner, and Patrick Liteky, a Vietnam vet who trained at Fort Benning, entered the SOA and poured several baby bottles of human blood on photographs of Salvadoran soldiers who graduated from SOA. They were convicted in 1991 of willful violation of federal property in violation of 18 U.S.C. 1361. The Liteky brothers each served 9 months in prison; Bourgeois served 14 months.[58]

The protest developed into an annual event. By 2008, the number protesting at the gates to Fort Benning had risen to nearly 20,000 from just a handful of people when the demonstrations began. Tens of thousands have made the trip to Fort Benning to protest SOA-WHINSEC.

Hundreds have been arrested on federal and state charges over the years, often spending months in federal prison. Thousands more have come to Washington, DC to lobby Congress.[59] These protests, as well as international attention to SOA-WHINSEC, have not yet closed the school. But, in recent years, Argentina, Bolivia, Costa Rica, Uruguay, and Venezuela have announced they will no longer send people to WHINSEC. The usefulness of the school for the U.S. Army is waning.[60]

Conclusion

Training militaries in torture and human rights abuses is illegal, immoral, and un-American. Until the U.S. government admits what it has done in the SOA-WHINSEC schools, allows an independent investigation, and accepts responsibility for the consequences, the human rights abuses and coups by graduates of SOA-WHINSEC will continue. With growing resistance in the United States and Latin America, the torture school must be closed. Every day the school remains open belies the United States' promise of a commitment to human rights.

Yet there is hope. Amnesty International USA has condemned SOA-WHINSEC. Increasing numbers of Latin American countries are refusing to allow their soldiers to train there. In the United States, a growing movement is working to close the school and to hold the U.S. Army accountable for its misdeeds. Every day, more and more U.S. citizens and global allies are learning about the school and organizing, protesting, lobbying, speaking out, and resisting through School of Americas Watch. Join them.

NOTES

1. Bill Quigley is the Legal Director of the Center for Constitutional Rights and a law professor at Loyola University New Orleans. He has represented many of the people protesting against torture and human rights abuses at the School of the Americas-WHINSEC.

2. Mark Weisbrot, "U.S. Leaves Honduras to its Fate: Washington is Unwilling to Take the Side of Democracy in Honduras by Opposing the Coup Leaders it Helped Train," *Guardian*, July 8, 2009, http://www.guardian.co.uk/commentis-free/cifamerica/2009/jul/08/honduras-coup-washington-zelaya (last visited July 9, 2009).

3. See Linda Cooper and James Hodge, "Honduran Coup Leader a Two-time SOA Graduate," *National Catholic Reporter*, June 29, 2009, http://ncronline.org/news/global/honduran-coup-leader-two-time-soa-graduate (last visited July 9, 2009).

4. See Timothy J. Kepner, "Torture 101: The Case Against the United States for Atrocities Committed by School of Americas Alumni," 19 *Dickinson Journal of International Law* 475, 480–86 (2001). See also 2002 Amnesty International report on SOA discussed below; and Jack Nelson-Pallmeyer, *School of Assassins: Guns, Greed, and Globalization* (Maryknoll, NY: Orbis, 2001). For details of what appears to be the most murders in one incident, over 700, in which 10 of the 12 officers in charge were graduates of the School of the Americas, see Mark Danner, *The Massacre at El Mozote* (New York: Vintage, 2004).

5. Amnesty International, *Unmatched Power, Unmet Principles: The Human Rights Dimensions of U.S. Training of Foreign Military and Police Forces*, 10 (2002) (internal citations omitted), http://www.amnestyusa.org/stoptorture/msp.pdf (last visited July 11, 2009).

6. See Dana Priest, "U.S. Instructed Latins on Executions, Torture; Manuals Used 1982–1991, Pentagon Reveals," *Washington Post*, Sept. 21, 1996.

7. Amnesty, *Unmatched Power, Unmet Principles*, 5.

8. Ibid. at iii.

9. Ibid. at v, 55–56.

10. U.S. General Accounting Office (GAO), *School of the Americas: U.S. Military Training for Latin American Countries*, Letter Report from General Accounting Office to U.S. Congress, August 8, 1996, GAO/NSIAD-96-178, http://www.fas.org/asmp/resources/govern/gao96178.pdf (last visited July 11, 2009). The U.S. Army website for WHINSEC says that over 61,000 soldiers were trained by the School of the Americas. https://www.infantry.army.mil/WHINSEC/about.asp?id=37 (last visited July 11, 2009).

11. U.S. GAO, *School of the Americas*, 8–9.

12. Center for International Policy, *Western Hemisphere Institute for Security Cooperation (Successor to School of the Americas) Fort Benning, Georgia* (2006), http://www.ciponline.org/facts/soa.htm (last visited July 11, 2009).

13. Amnesty, *Unmatched Power, Unmet Principles*, 37. The legislation creating the Western Hemisphere Institute on Security Cooperation can be found at 10 U.S.C. § 2166. John Donnelly, "Army's Tainted School of the Americas to Close, Reopen with New Name," *The Boston Globe*, Dec. 15, 2000.

14. Amnesty, *Unmatched Power, Unmet Principles*, at 55.

15. See Kepner, *Torture 101*, 475, 476–77.

16. United Nations (UN), *Report of the U.N. Truth Commission on El Salvador* (hereafter *Truth Commission Report*), S/25500, 28 (1993), http://www.derechos.org/nizkor/salvador/informes/truth.html (last visited July 11, 2009).

17. Priest, "U.S. Instructed Latins."

18. This memo was declassified in 1996 after nine attachments were removed. Michel E. Werner, Assistant to the Secretary of Defense (Intelligence Oversight), Memo to Secretary of Defense Cheney Regarding "Improper Material in Spanish-Language Intelligence Training Manuals" (hereafter *Torture Memo*), March 10, 1992, http://www.gwu.edu/~nsarchiv/NSAEBB/NSAEBB122/920310%20Imporper%20Material%20in%20Spanish-Language%20Intelligence%20Training%20Manuals.pdf (last visited July 27, 2009). The National Security Archive of George Washington University has posted this memo as part of their report "Prisoner Abuse: Patterns from the Past," *National Security Archive Electronic Briefing Book*, No. 122, http://www.gwu.edu/~nsarchiv/NSAEBB/NSAEBB122/ (last visited July 11, 2009).

19. Ibid. at 2–3, "Analysis of the Manuals."

20. See Gail Lumet Buckley, "Left, Right, Center," *America*, May 9, 1998; See also Kepner, *Torture 101*, 486–87; Priest, "U.S. Instructed Latins."

21. Werner, *Torture Memo*, 1–2, "Evolution of the Manuals." "In 1987, Army military intelligence (MI) officers in Panama had compiled the manuals from lesson plans used at an MI course at USASOA since 1982." Ibid. The National Security Archive of George Washington University describes

Project X as "a military effort to create training guides drawn from counterinsurgency experience in Vietnam." See "Prisoner Abuse: Patterns from the Past," *National Security Archive Electronic Briefing Book*, No. 122, http://www.gwu.edu/~nsarchiv/NSAEBB/NSAEBB122/ (last visited July 11, 2009).

22. Werner, *Torture Memo*, 1, "Evolution of the Manuals." According to a 1999 article:

> Project X [was] a 1965 army program to train military, police, and paramilitary forces throughout Southeast Asia and Latin America. Project X was a direct precursor to Operation Phoenix in Vietnam and Operation Condor in South America—notorious programs that resulted in the deaths of tens of thousands of civilians. Project X was halted under the Carter administration, but its essentials were reinstated in 1982 under President Ronald Reagan.

Bob Harris, "Guatemala: Clinton's Latest Damn-Near Apology," *Humanist*, May 1, 1999.

23. Werner, *Torture Memo*, 2, "USASOA."

24. See Barbara Jentzsch, "School of the Americas Critic," *The Progressive*, July 1, 1997.

25. Amnesty, *Unmatched Power, Unmet Principles*, 4.

26. For more detailed breakdowns of SOA graduates country by country, see the School of Americas Watch website, www.soaw.org.

27. Nelson-Pallmeyer, *School of Assassins*, 3. See also *To Close the United States Army School of the Americas*, H.R. 732, 106th Cong., 1st sess., section 1.5 (G); Amnesty, *Unmatched Power, Unmet Principles*, 35–36, 44.

28. Lesley Gill, *The School of Americas: Military Training and Political Violence in the Americas*, 78 (Durham, NC: Duke Univ. Press, 2004).

29. Amnesty, *Unmatched Power, Unmet Principles*, 35–36.

30. Gill, *School of Americas*, 2.

31. Amnesty, *Unmatched Power, Unmet Principles*, 35–36.

32. U.N., *Truth Commission Report*, 28. Romero was forcefully speaking out against the violence of the government and calling for peace in the civil war in El Salvador.

33. Nelson-Pallmeyer, *School of Assassins*, 33.

34. Amnesty, *Unmatched Power, Unmet Principles*, at 35–36, 43.

35. UN, *Truth Commission Report*, 62–67.

36. Nelson-Pallmeyer, *School of Assassins*, 32.

37. See Danner, *Massacre at El Mozote*. A list of the victims and their ages, as compiled by the Human Rights Office of the Archbishop of El Salvador, can be found at pages 280–304.

38. UN, *Truth Commission Report*, 119.

39. Nelson-Pallmeyer, *School of Assassins*, 32.

40. UN, *Truth Commission Report*, 32.

41. Nelson-Pallmeyer, *School of Assassins*, 27.

42. Kepner, *Torture 101*, 483.

43. *Xuncax v. Gramajo*, 886 F. Supp. 162 (D. Mass. 1995). See also Dianna Ortiz, *The Blindfold's Eyes: My Journey from Torture to Truth* (Maryknoll, NY: Orbis, 2002).

44. T. Christian Miller, "The Americas," *Newsday*, June 9, 2001.

45. A federal civil lawsuit has been filed in the United States against López Grijalba by the Center for Justice and Accountability on behalf of six former Honduran citizens who were victimized by these actions. The Center for Justice and Accountability, *Honduras: Juan Lopez Grijalba*, 1 (2009), http://www.cja.org/cases/grijalba.shtml (last visited July 11, 2009).

46. Cecilia Menjivar and Nestor Rodriguez, *When States Kill: Latin America, the U.S., and Technologies of Terror*, 66 (Austin: Univ. of Texas Press, 2005).

47. Amnesty, *Unmatched Power, Unmet Principles*, 35–36.

48. Doug Ireland, "Teaching Torture in the USA," *Human Quest*, Sept. 1, 2004, http://findarticles.com/p/articles/mi_qa3861/is_200409/ai_n9441138/?tag=content;col1 (last visited May 24, 2010).

49. Werner, *Torture Memo*, 3, "Approval and Delivery Process" (emphasis added).

50. There have been in-house studies and overview reports on the school, but never a full-ranging investigation. See for example, the 1996 G.A.O. report on the School of the Americas, in which the authors of the report admit on page 16, "We did not independently verify the accuracy of the data reported to us." U.S. GAO, *School of the Americas*, 16.

51. Amnesty, *Unmatched Power, Unmet Principles*, 37.

52. For details on the organized gatherings that have occurred throughout the past few decades, visit www.soaw.org.

53. See Virginia Anderson, "Civil Disobedience: Priest Ready for Prison," *Atlanta Journal-Constitution*, June 20, 1996.

54. See Thomas Bokenhotter, *Church and Revolution: Catholics in the Struggle for Democracy and Social Justice*, 528 (New York: Doubleday, 1998).

55. See Anderson, "Civil Disobedience."

56. See Hector Tobar, "Civil War Turmoil from El Salvador Spills Over to LA Demonstrations," *Los Angeles Times*, Nov. 25, 1989 (more than a dozen demonstrations in southern California alone). See also Rosalind Bentley and Gary Harvey, "Saying a Prayer for Peace: Hunger Strikers Confront Roach on El Salvador," *Tribune Newspaper of Twin Cities*, Nov. 24, 1989; Associated Press, "LA Protest

Results in 66 Arrests," *Orange County Register*, Nov. 23, 1989; Dale Simmons, "Local Protest Against Aid to El Salvador Set," *Austin American Statesman*, Nov. 22, 1989; Joe Gyan, Jr., "Berrigan, 15 Others Convicted in Anti-war Protest," *Baton Rouge Advocate*, Feb. 13, 1990.

57. See Susan Benesch, "US Needs a Dose of Truth about El Salvador," *St. Petersburg Times*, March 17, 1993.

58. See Mark Curriden, "3 Sentenced for Bloody Protest," *Atlanta Journal Constitution*, June 22, 1991; Associated Press, "La. Priest Sentenced for Bloody Protest," *Baton Rouge Advocate*, June 23, 1991; *U.S. v Liteky*, 114 S. Ct. 1147 (1994). See also *U.S. v Liteky*, 973 F.2d 910 (11th cir. 1992).

59. People who want to learn more about the organizing, protests, lobbying, and civil disobedience campaigns can visit the website of SOA Watch, www.soaw.org.

60. See Joao Da Silva, "Bolivian Military Withdraws from Controversial U.S. Army Training School," 1 (2008), http://www.commondreams.org/news2008/0219-04.htm (last reviewed July 11, 2009).

3

U.S. Foreign Policy, Deniability, and the Political "Utility" of State Terror

The Case of El Salvador

TERRY LYNN KARL[1]

Neris Gonzalez had been on the stand all morning, testifying in the case known as Romagoza v. Garcia,[2] against the former heads of the Salvadoran military for the torture she suffered in 1979. Having been repeatedly burnt with cigarettes, cut with a razor, shocked with electricity, partially asphyxiated, pushed down stairs, forced to sit in ice water and compelled to witness the murder and torture of others—all while being eight months pregnant—the reality of describing to a jury these and other far worse moments specifically targeting her unborn child had brought on an intense headache. As I massaged her head, neck and face to give her some relief, I mentioned that one side of her jaw was very different from the other. "Oh, they pulled out my teeth on that side—one by one," she said, touching her mouth. This was not in her testimony in the trial. Having lost her baby to torture and seen a boy eviscerated before her eyes, it did not seem important enough to mention.

State terror, including torture, is widely used for both interrogation and social control. Its purpose is to destroy the voice, the self, the reality, and the existence of its victims, their families, friends, and supporters and to instill fear in opposition movements. Citizens of democracies tend to rest comfortably in the belief that liberal democratic states use repression and torture against their own citizens much less often than other states. But democracies have not only tortured, as the Bush administration's orders and practices in Abu Ghraib and Guantánamo so vividly demonstrate, but those with colonial histories or expansive ambitions have set the international standard in the development of the doctrines and techniques of repression.[3] In fact, some democracies have taken the lead in pioneering and exporting methods of torture that "leave no marks" as well as theories of "limited war" that can sweep away civilian protections. Not only have they trained other military and state authorities in the science of coercive interrogation, but they and their allies have also used methods of torture and repression extensively in foreign wars. Take, for example, the French in Algeria, the British in Northern Ireland, and the Americans in Vietnam.

These practices pose an enormous dilemma for the conduct of foreign policy in democracies that extend themselves abroad, especially the United States. On the one hand, U.S. foreign policy is embedded in notions of American exceptionalism, with the concomitant belief that actions abroad should reflect the self-image of a people who stand for freedom everywhere. Although most governments (even dictatorships)[4] attribute some sort of virtue to their actions abroad, the United States sees itself as blessed by a unique goodness. This strong moral streak in political culture, perhaps best captured by the oft-cited vision of a "city on a hill," as well as the desire to serve as a model to the world, would seem to preclude the adoption of policies that can be widely perceived as morally deficient.[5]

Yet from its first efforts to establish dominance beyond its borders to its newer status as the sole superpower, the United States has developed a template for its operations abroad that conflicts with this self-image. Beginning with its efforts to assert control over the Philippines in 1899, government rhetoric and reality have clashed. In the Philippines, some U.S. troops tortured prisoners of war (most frequently with the "water cure" currently known as waterboarding) and some commanders "took no prisoners" even if this meant killing every male capable of bearing arms (which one general defined as males over ten years old).[6] In Vietnam, tiger cages, waterboarding, electric shocks, assassinations, abuses, kidnap-pings, and the summary executions in the Phoenix program of more than 20,000 suspected Viet Cong operatives without trial or due process[7] were prominent features of a war that the American public eventually repudi-ated for its brutality.[8] These same practices migrated to Latin America, largely through the teachings of U.S. advisers, where they helped keep military dictatorships in power.[9] Yet, in every case, public revelations about the actions of the United States in supporting these types of allies caused repeated uproars as stories of abuses accumulated. Each time this resulted in a public relations disaster, the eventual loss of congressional support for administration policy, a series of official investigations, sig-nificant foreign policy reforms, and even a few (very few) prosecutions.[10]

For the United States, making palatable its support for the often-unpal-atable actions of its own officials or its allies has been a central problem from Vietnam to the current conflicts in the Middle East. Presidents Johnson and Nixon learned to their peril that they would lose domestic support if they depended upon a foreign policy that was widely perceived to be immoral—a lesson that was not lost on subsequent administrations. Thus, every U.S. president since has made rhetorical support for human rights and/or democratization a cornerstone of foreign policy—even when their partners abroad are anything but rights-respecting or demo-cratic. However reassuring and popular this rhetoric, it seldom stands up against the primary goal of defending certain visions of national security. Nor is it ever enough in situations where allies or even some rogue U.S. officials and advisers might be running amok. Under these circumstances, the temptation to dissemble is not only enormous, it also can appear vital for protecting what an administration chooses to define as the "national interest."

Deniability is a collusive business. Allies use "deniability" to hide or downplay (as much as possible) the extent of human rights violations. U.S. officials, in turn, use deceptive rhetoric to "reshape" their allies into "freedom fighters" in order to win and retain support from U.S. citizens. Together, their actions produce a form of "double deniability." But as pub-lic opinion has grown more skeptical about the costs and probabilities of success in what U.S. officials call "nation-building,"[11] this long-standing practice of dissembling to achieve acquiescence for involvement in for-eign conflicts has become increasingly difficult to sustain. When it is no longer possible to hide, blame others for, or simply downplay the extent of abuses, an administration may employ its knowledge of these very abuses against its own ally to demonstrate its concern for reform (and show its own goodness), while at the same time failing to fully break with that ally. This action has the advantage of preserving the notion that the United States is indeed different and that it can spread its own "civilizing" influence. Thus, deniability has increasingly taken a different form: a cyclical (and cynical) swing between deception and denunciation that is largely driven by U.S. domestic concerns. This is what I call the fluctuating political "utility" of state terror.

This chapter discusses the relationship between counterinsurgency and deniability in the United States in order to show the logic of this deception. After demonstrating why counterinsurgency wars are especially subject to deniability, it presents the case of El Salvador. Not only is El Salvador the United States' most prolonged and (prior to the Persian Gulf conflicts) most costly military involvement since Vietnam, but it has been touted as a model for other conflicts, most notably through the "Salvador option" in Iraq. The line against "terrorist aggression" was supposed to be drawn in El Salvador by a military victory over the rebel Farabundo Marti Liberation Front (FMLN).

But the partners of the United States, the Salvadoran Armed Forces, scarcely fit the image of a virtuous ally in the conduct of moral foreign policy. Its officer corps directed widespread torture and murder, killing moderate leaders of all center and left-of-center parties, priests, nuns, and thousands of peasants. Officers not only kidnapped the children of the oligarchy for profit, but also invented "ghost soldiers" and other mechanisms to steal U.S. military assistance—all with complete impunity and with the aim of furthering their own political and pecuniary advantage.[12] By the time the U.S. Congress succeeded in cutting military aid to El Salvador after 12 years of war, thus ending any lingering administration aspirations for a military victory over the rebels, the Salvadoran Armed Forces had failed to inflict significant defeats on the FMLN and was forced to accept the political solution its high command had so relentlessly tried to block: the removal of the entire top echelons and the reform of the military and security forces. In the meantime, at least 75,000 unarmed men, women, and children died, with an estimated 85 percent of these deaths attributed to the military and security forces that were the partners of the United States.[13] Thousands more were detained and/or tortured, almost a million people were displaced, and one-fifth of the population fled the country.

Building on previous scholarship, especially the excellent work of Cynthia Arnson and Mark Danner,[14] this chapter illustrates the logic of "double" deniability by drawing upon evidence gleaned from thousands of declassified documents used in preparation for two trials, *Romagoza v. Garcia* and *Chavez v Carranza*.[15] In the first trial, a West Palm Beach jury (convened in Florida where the defendants lived) found the two highest ranking Salvadoran generals who oversaw the worst period of human rights abuses from 1979 to 1989—Minister of Defense Jose Guillermo Garcia and National Guard Commander then Minister of Defense Carlos Eugenio Vides Casanova—responsible for torture. They awarded $54.6 million to Neris Gonzalez, the church worker whose torture was partially recounted above, and two other plaintiffs—Juan Romagoza, a medical doctor, and Carlos Mauricio, a professor.[16] The second trial resulted in a $6 million judgment against Memphis resident Colonel Nicolas Carranza, the former Vice Minister of Defense of El Salvador and head of the Treasury Police, for the torture and extrajudicial killings suffered by four Salvadoran plaintiffs and their families.[17]

Counterinsurgency and Double Deniability

Deniability is built into situations where counterinsurgency tactics are used. Because counterinsurgency necessitates partnering with and strengthening existing (and usually) repressive governments, all U.S. administrations from Johnson to Obama have been faced with the problem of explaining and justifying why the United States has "friends like these." Counterinsurgency doctrine does not adequately address this dilemma. To the contrary, successful counterinsurgency relies upon the ability of an ally's military, intelligence, and security forces to win the allegiance of the population. According to a U.S. Army Field Circular: "The [host] government must clearly demonstrate that it is a better choice than the insurgent organization."[18] Doctrinal statements further emphasize the imperative of reforming existing political, social, and economic institutions to improve the quality of life and strengthen the links between the government and the population. Indeed, this reform is the theoretical centerpiece of counterinsurgency assessments in military thinking since Vietnam.[19]

Even if counterinsurgency operations were to function as military theories suggest (and they generally do not), the limited war template makes a critical assumption about the nature of the government being assisted—namely that enhancing the power of the government will make the population less likely to support rebellion. But what if this very same government and its military and security forces are the source of the problem and the catalyst for insurgency? What if enhancing their capabilities simply strengthens their repressive capacity? And what if transforming or removing these government armed forces is the core of any solution? Studies of different insurgencies have repeatedly shown that the repressive and reactionary nature of a government and its military and security forces have often given rise to rebellion in the first place, and allies of this sort are unlikely to embrace reform. Thus, counterinsurgency theory and practice collide.[20]

The results are predictable. Counterinsurgency first involves clearing an area of rebels, then instigating control measures to ensure they do not come back, and finally, focusing on building institutions that encourage the population to embrace its government and reject revolutionary efforts. Especially given this sequence, the reliance on an already repressive ally is disastrous. Because success in counterinsurgency warfare is measured by the ability to disconnect rebels from their unarmed supporters, which in turn is supposed to bring with it an upsurge in the flow of intelligence regarding the location of other insurgents, the separation of "fish from the sea" will most likely be achieved by widespread brutality. Since repressive forces must employ widespread interrogation for intelligence aimed at locating and annihilating guerrillas, they rely on torture to get information and often the punishment of entire communities to serve as warnings to others to refrain from supporting any opposition forces. This does not win "hearts and minds" but instead creates powerful incentives to swell the ranks of the rebels and makes them even more difficult to defeat. In this respect, the interests of a repressive ally that wants to block reform and forego restraint against civilians do not mesh with a doctrine that insists on controlled military behavior coupled with gradual efforts at reform. Rather than transforming its ally, the United States may find itself held hostage to the practices of its partner, self-corrupted, and complicit in human rights abuses.

When allies or their U.S. advisers disregard the laws of war, practice torture to get "intelligence," do not see restraint as a military ideal, do not view unarmed civilians as "innocents" but rather as the necessary infrastructure for rebel subsistence, and accept high civilian casualties as a necessary and even normatively desirable strategic dimension of conflict, they risk losing external political support and thus economic and military assistance. This is a critical factor that the doctrine generally does not address but that politicians fully understand. Thus, to avoid U.S. opposition, deception about these abuses occurs at two levels: allies dissemble to U.S. officials, on the one hand, and the U.S. officials dissemble to their public, on the other.

This double deniability has a consistent pattern, both between allies and between U.S. government officials and the public, with phases that may occur in a visible sequence but more often overlap or happen simultaneously:[21]

- Phase One: Denial that violations occurred. This is the simple assertion that "nothing happened," that is, the torture did not happen, the massacre did not occur. This requires attacking the objectivity or credibility of the observer or reporter of violations and, in its most terrible form, the trustworthiness of the victim, for example, "He was not 'disappeared' but ran off with another woman."

- Phase Two: Admission that violations occurred, but downplaying their gravity. This can involve "playing the numbers game," that is, deniability consists of arguing that the number of abuses is exaggerated. Since exact figures on human rights violations are impossible to obtain in the context of war, it is easy to cast doubt on the credibility of human rights sources. Downplaying also occurs through the strategic use of euphemisms, for example, torture becomes "enhanced interrogation techniques" or civilian deaths become "collateral damage."

- Phase Three: Admission that the violations occurred, but denying responsibility for them. When irrefutable evidence is presented that massacres, tortures, and other human rights violations have occurred, responses take the form of "blaming the other side" or, when that does not work, blaming "unknown groups" for what is actually state-sponsored terror. Thus, responsibility can be assigned to "shadowy" forces that cannot be controlled. Another form of deniability exploits the "fog of war" argument, that is, that violations are the result of chaos, accident, or the unintentional consequences of crossfire rather than the intentional acts of repressive forces.

- Phase Four: Admission that violations occurred and the government is responsible, coupled with assertions that "reformers" do not (yet) have the power to stop them. Officials claim that "others" in the government, military, or political party are responsible and are too influential to stop. They may also claim that investigations will be carried out to the best of their (very limited) capacity.

◦ Phase Five: Admission that violations occurred, the government is responsible, and some changes will be made. As pressure builds to do more to stop abuses, cosmetic reforms are often carried out, for example, political prisoners may be released, low-level egregious violators may be removed from their positions, and some punishment of minor violators may occur.

◦ Phase Six: Real Reform and/or Justification. This moment presents a fork in the road of deniability. Either deniability ends because significant reform occurs, for example, purging violators from their institutions, holding trials, abolition of especially repressive forces, etc., or deniability stops because powerful perpetrators openly justify the necessity and righteousness of their actions against a legitimate (that is, "not innocent") enemy, whether civilian or military. In other words, they openly vilify and dehumanize their opponents as unworthy of any protections whatsoever.

In most of these phases, while there is often clear pressure on allies (or their advisers) to change their behavior, a type of complicity sets in. Allies are told, even threatened, to change, and they promise they will, but both partners understand that they need each other to effectuate a shared vision of national security, thus the consequences of forestalling reform do not appear to be high. Therefore, double deniability can operate simultaneously and reiteratively.

Deniability in El Salvador[22]

Deniability never seemed to be a problem for El Salvador's military leaders—once they learned that it was necessary. Initially, Ministers of Defense Garcia and Vides Casanova and Vice Minister Carranza, the top commanders during the period of the worst repression, did not appear to understand its value. But when repeatedly confronted with human rights abuses, all three followed the classic deniability script—acting as if the violations had not occurred, were carried out by the FMLN, or were due to the general chaos of the time. None admitted to any organized effort at state terror or systematic torture in the military and security forces despite being presented with an enormous amount of evidence to the contrary. All three repeatedly insisted that they did not have the power to stop human rights abuses—even though they had the absolute *de jure* and *de facto* authority necessary to exercise both operational and administrative control of their troops.[23] Instead, military leaders used their "inability" to stop repression to try to redefine the armed forces (the source of greatest repression) as "centrists" and "reformists" besieged by both a phantom right-wing and the guerrilla left. Another favorite argument of the military leadership was to plead poverty in the military institution (despite its being the richest entity in the country), claiming that this made human rights training difficult, and then ask for more military aid so that abuses could be addressed.[24] In this they were successful: U.S. aid totals in the two years of greatest repression (1980–1981) were far greater than the total for the previous 33 years.

The rhetoric of Garcia and Carranza serves as classic examples of deniability. Reports of conversations involving U.S. officials in early cables demonstrate a palpable disdain for the rights and protection of unarmed civilians coupled with an initial lack of understanding that the ministers were supposed to hide these attitudes from U.S. officials. For example, when the top leadership of the civilian opposition to military rule, the Democratic Revolutionary Front (FDR), was kidnapped, tortured, and killed by elements of the security forces, thus ending any hope of a peacefully negotiated regime transition, Garcia and Carranza indicated their approval, saying that they supported the "line of thinking" of the individuals who carried out these murders.[25] Later, when it became clear that the Carter administration did not welcome this degree of honesty, the defendants changed tack and began denying that human rights violations occurred at all or that they had knowledge of such violations. In addition, they claimed that stories of violations were propaganda from the other side.[26]

The massacre at El Mozote, so movingly described by Mark Danner, is indicative of this pattern. On December 10, 1981, units of the Atlacatl Battalion and the Third Infantry Brigade detained between 500 and 900 people in the village of El Mozote and the surrounding area, then executed them in groups, first the men, and then the women and children. They killed the entire civilian population found in the village, with one overlooked exception. Despite the fact that these events were reported in both the *New York Times* and the *Washington Post* and that there was an eyewitness account of the massacre, Garcia vehemently denied that any massacre had taken place. "I will deny it and prove it was a fabrication," he told the U.S. ambassador.[27] Calling international press stories a "plot to discredit the armed forces," and attributing reports of the mass killings to enemy propaganda, Garcia refused to identify the units involved in the massacre, saying he did not know where his forces operated—a claim that was easily refuted.[28] Garcia's refusal to admit that a massacre had taken place was effective in the short run. Not only did the slaughter at El Mozote fail to influence an important debate to cut off military aid that was occurring at the same time in Congress, but also it took the report of a 1992 forensic team, whose work at one part of the site uncovered the remains of at least 131 children under the age of 12, to finally "prove" that the massacre occurred.[29] "Were it not for the children's skeletons at El Mozote," the Truth Commission concluded, "some people would still be disputing that such massacres took place."[30]

Eventually the central purpose behind this deniability—protecting the absolute impunity of armed forces—came to be understood by some U.S. officials based in El Salvador. A cable sent by former Ambassador Robert E. White explained:

> There is something of an Alice in Wonderland air to conversations with top military officers here. Garcia and Carranza know perfectly well that some middle and low level members of the military are involved in death squads and other right wing violence, and yet . . . there is almost no way to break through the pose, the pose Garcia and company have adopted.

White's successor, Edwin Corr, described the rationale behind the military's "code of silence," and stated the reasons for deniability even more bluntly:

> The officer corps . . . circles its wagons when faced with human rights scrutiny. In part from a skeleton-in-the-closet syndrome that keeps one officer from tattling on another for fear that each accused will become an accuser until all the long-buried secrets are unearthed. The skeletons not only include human rights abuses but corruption.[31]

Subsequent military leaders became savvier in their deniability. Realizing that public denials of what were obviously military abuses frustrated some American officials and that simply dismissing facts was not a sufficient response,[32] the defense ministers that followed Garcia instead privately admitted their knowledge of abuses but argued to U.S. officials that these were Salvadoran cultural "idiosyncrasies," confined to only "one percent" of the armed forces. They insisted it would be politically unwise to discuss these matters publicly.[33] While carefully hiding their own opinions of these violations and their own past histories as perpetrators, and sometimes even ordering "investigations" to enhance their own status as "reformers," each of these top commanders demonstrated their support for a strategy of repression by ordering, protecting, and/or promoting the commanders in charge of the troops carrying out atrocities.[34]

Deniability in the United States

Deniability was not as easy for U.S. officials as it was for the Salvadoran high command. The firmly entrenched history of committing atrocities, most notoriously during the 1932 matanza,[35] was known to U.S. advisers as early as the 1960s, even if most of the U.S. public had scarcely heard of El Salvador. U.S. intelligence agencies had helped set up an intelligence apparatus (ANSESAL) and a network of informants (ORDEN) that ultimately became the root of death squad activity and the training ground for El Salvador's most influential rightist terrorists.[36] The results were evident to observers even before the outbreak of the civil war: the 1977 threat to "kill all Jesuit priests if they did not leave the country" had been the focus of congressional investigations, and internal documents repeatedly warned that the military and security forces were committing widespread atrocities aimed at killing the very forces that could bring about a peaceful resolution to the country's internal disputes.[37] Given that the post-Vietnam public had no appetite for involvement in Central America, much less to support a repressive military, the Reagan administration's decision to "draw the line" against communism meant that it would have to use new forms of deniability to deflect attention from the brutality of its allies.[38]

While it employed a combination of outright denial, "blaming the other side," and downplaying the extent of violence, the crux of Reagan administration efforts was the creation of a sophisticated apparatus aimed at reshaping public attitudes about Central American operations, similar to a CIA covert operation. Eventually establishing a Central America Public Diplomacy Task Force and later an Office of Public Diplomacy as a sort of Ministry of Information,[39] administration officials planted stories in U.S. newspapers, launched misleading campaigns to convince the public that the "other side" was worse,[40] targeted leading congressional critics, and intimidated journalists and academics whose findings proved inconvenient. In one of the best-known examples, Reagan officials pressured the *New York Times* to fire the reporter who had broken the El Mozote story.[41] But in a pattern that was to be repeated over and over in subsequent years, the administration's interpretations were consistently challenged in the House of Representatives, the only branch that was not controlled by President Reagan's own party. Arguing in congressional testimony that the security forces were responsible for the deaths of thousands and thousands of young people, executed on the mere suspicion that they might sympathize with leftists, former Ambassador White asked the question that the administration sought to deflect:

> The real issue is how do you supply military assistance to a force that is going to use that military assistance to assassinate, to kill, in a totally uncontrolled way? Do you want to associate the United States with the type of killing that has been going on down there in El Salvador?[42]

This question not only lay at the heart of the debate over El Salvador, but it also formed the core of a pattern of deniability. Once the Reagan administration declared its unconditional alliance with a murderous military, it was compelled to demonstrate that this military was the lesser of two evils. The pattern that emerges in declassified documents is characterized by:[43]

- ⊕ The false assignment of responsibility for the majority of political violence to the rebels even though the overwhelming responsibility for this violence lay with the Salvadoran government. This misattribution depended on dismissing any information to the contrary as either unreliable or as the propaganda of guerrilla sympathizers;
- ⊕ The false attribution of government violence to ultra-rightist forces, especially death squads acting "independently of the armed forces," thus absolving the government of responsibility. This was coupled with the creation of the impression of a centrist "democratic" and "civilian" Salvadoran government caught between two extremes rather than one that had little or no control over its military; and
- ⊕ The public "break" with some military figures as a scapegoat when other forms of deniability failed and when atrocities could no longer be denied, coupled with the public "anointing" of a new reformer, thus absolving the military as an institution for persistent human rights abuses.

Contrary to the near unanimity of non-governmental sources about the primary source of violence, U.S. officials repeatedly went along with these fabrications and insisted that the armed left was primarily responsible for the majority of violence in El Salvador—long after their own sources told them differently.[44] President Reagan himself told a group of school-children that murders attributed to rightist death squads might actually be the work of leftist guerrillas masquerading as soldiers.[45] The military government was portrayed as generally blameless. According to the 1980 testimony of Deputy Secretary of State for Inter-American Affairs, John Bushnell, "I think there is some misperception by those who follow the press that the government is itself repressive in El Salvador."[46]

This position was consistently repeated by the State Department during the period when thousands of civilians were being killed by the armed forces: "We are aware of no evidence that General Garcia, General Gutierrez or their associates are responsible for atrocities," another report stated. "On the contrary, the leaders of the armed forces are attempting to bring an end to violence against non-combatants."[47] To sustain these claims, officials argued that the information of human rights groups was "distorted," exaggerated, and biased.[48] In some cases, like the well-documented massacres of hundreds of civilians at El Mozote and Rio Sumpul, official reports talked only of an "alleged" massacre, "not backed by first-hand accounts."[49]

But, like their Salvadoran counterparts, U.S. officials eventually discovered that outright deception was not effective, especially in a context where Congress insisted that President Reagan personally certify progress in human rights in El Salvador. When members of the National Guard murdered four U.S. churchwomen, the suggestion by Secretary of State Haig, Jeanne Kirkpatrick, and other Reagan officials that these victims were somehow responsible for their own deaths (by running a blockade and exchanging fire with the military) caused an uproar. Faced with evidence by Amnesty International, the ACLU, and Americas Watch charging the Salvadoran government with "about 200 politically motivated murders a week," and the widespread use of torture by all branches of the nation's security forces,[50] officials publicly maintained that it was next to impossible to determine who was doing the killing—even though their own CIA cables were identifying the perpetrators. These same officials were privately warning the Salvadoran military to stop killing civilians.[51] Denials of the El Mozote massacre by Assistant Secretary Thomas Enders were repeated by Assistant Secretary of State for Human Rights and Humanitarian Affairs Elliott Abrams,[52] and Lt. Gen. Wallace Nutting,[53] even though embassy personnel were reporting that in El Mozote, "something bad had happened." The net result was to increase congressional incredulity: military aid to El Salvador was frozen at 1981 levels in 1982, and for the next two years it appeared that aid would soon be cut.

Not surprisingly under these circumstances, officials learned to do better. Adopting what Secretary Enders called a "two track strategy" of combining political reform (including elections) and military victory, instead of the search for military victory alone, officials increasingly sought to paint the Salvadoran government and its top military commanders as reformers who, though besieged from both sides, were successfully curbing abuses from a small minority of its own military. Coupled with this notion of a besieged "reformist center," officials for the first time acknowledged the brutality of the ultra-right (though not the government) as terrorist. The government's inability to fully control the actions of the military and security forces was also acknowledged, though officials insisted that progress was being made but "not yet complete."[54]

El Salvador's notorious death squads played a significant role in this deniability. While the clandestine nature of their activity facilitated concealment of the state's role in formation and support of these squads, U.S. officials were able to concentrate on ending death squad violence and deflect attention from the main source of murder: the military and security forces. Death squads were repeatedly referred to as a "spontaneous phenomenon" without a center—one that lacked a headquarters that could give orders or be contained.[55] Assistant Secretary Abrams expressed deep skepticism about the security forces' involvement in death squads, publicly arguing that this accusation "might be right, though I suspect it isn't right."[56] But death squads owed their very existence to the intelligence sections (S-II) of the military and security forces, and some had benefitted from U.S. training. This information was reported to the State Department and CIA as early as May 1980 but somehow escaped the attention of those testifying in Congress two years later.[57] Indeed, early intelligence reported death squads operating out of the intelligence sections (G-II) of the National Guard,[58] the National Police,[59] and the Treasury Police, as well as the Air Force and the regular armed forces, especially the San Salvador-based First Brigade, though this was never made public by the administration. Instead, information about the death squads and their links to the CIA was withheld from the House of Representatives during its investigation, perhaps because Nicolas Carranza, Vice Minister of

Defense, former Director of the Treasury Police, and a notorious human rights abuser, was a paid CIA asset (which he subsequently admitted in his 2005 trial).[60]

Emphasizing the notion of a besieged "center" trying to build democracy—though usually a winning strategy in Congress—was unconvincing as long as the obviously repressive Salvadoran military was directly in power. Thus, for the first time, officials turned to denunciations of their allies. In November 1983, Vice President George H. W. Bush held a private meeting with the high command in El Salvador and handed over a list naming specific active-duty death squad participants that had to be sent out of the country before Congress reconvened in January. While privately promising a huge increase in military and economic assistance as an explicit quid pro quo for transferring some ultra-rightists and lowering the levels of violence against civilians, Bush's public message made no mention of increased aid to the military and instead reinforced the notion of a moral United States: "These cowardly death-squad terrorists are just as repugnant to me, to President Reagan, to the U.S. Congress, and to the American people as the terrorists of the Left," he said. "If these death squad murders continue, you will lose the support of the American people."[61] The visit signaled a new understanding: If the Salvadoran officer corps would keep its violence against civilians at an "acceptable" level, punish its most egregious perpetrators of rights violations (especially in cases involving U.S. citizens), and accept reformist civilian leaders, it would be substantially rewarded and congressional opposition could be contained. Vice President Quayle repeated a similar message in his February 1989 visit.

The administration had finally found an acceptable deniability formula—a "reformist" military in a democratizing setting that would commit smaller numbers of abuses and (eventually) accept elections as a mechanism to choose the country's leader. Despite the fact that the high command did not keep its side of the bargain (only two Salvadoran officers were transferred abroad and a lieutenant accused of complicity in the murder of Archbishop Oscar Romero was reportedly dismissed from the army), U.S. assistance increased in tandem with military impunity. Privately, U.S. intelligence reports were derisive on the issue of military reform, but in the public realm a pattern emerged of repudiating outgoing military and civilian leaders and greeting their replacements as great transformers in order to keep alive the myth of a restructured military and security forces and progress in building democracy. Thus, Garcia's replacement, Defense Minister Vides Casanova, was heralded as the man to lead change even though he personally promoted a number of the ultra-rightists on Bush's list and appointed an investigative team to examine armed forces' abuses headed by a leader of a death squad that specialized in killing priests.[62] One later minister of defense was derisively heralded in a Rand Corporation study as "the expectancy and rose of the fair state."[63]

The Disutility of Double Deniability

This formula of deniability on both sides—top military leaders pretending to be reformers and top U.S. officials claiming to believe them—lasted for years with repeated rounds of denial and denunciation. This double deniability helped to prolong the war until the murders of six Jesuit priests by the U.S.-trained Atlacatl Brigade finally exploded the myth of a reformed and competent military.

El Salvador was once viewed as an "ideal testing ground"[64] for demonstrating the effectiveness of low-intensity conflict, especially its key elements of counterinsurgency and "terrorism counteraction." Double deniability was its necessary accompaniment. But did it work? Despite over $6 billion of U.S. aid aimed at defeating the rebels and "professionalizing" the military, and despite the occasional claim by former officials that U.S. policy was a success,[65] the reality proved quite different. The U.S. government did not achieve the military reform it claimed to advocate, in part because it lost credibility through repeated empty threats that lacked any real consequences for its Salvadoran allies. Instead, as a Rand Corporation study noted toward the end of the war: "It is precisely the young aggressive, U.S. trained officers who are most intoxicated by the extreme right's vision and most resentful of America's influence over the conduct of the war and who commit many of the worst atrocities."[66] Furthermore, rather than defeat what were originally small groups of poorly armed guerrillas, the United States witnessed the transformation of the FMLN into the best-trained and best-organized rebel movement ever seen in Latin America—one whose growth was fueled largely by the atrocities committed by the Salvadoran Armed Forces.

In the end, faced with a dismayed public, a Congress that shut off the aid spigot after the shocking 1989 murder of six Jesuit priests, their housekeeper, and her young daughter, and the end of the Cold War that removed any sort of rationality for "friends like these," the George H.W.

Bush administration broke with its military allies and supported a UN-sponsored political settlement—the same type of negotiations that Republican administrations had previously spurned. This settlement included the purging of the officer corps that the Salvadoran High Command and its U.S. allies had spent more than a decade effectively blocking.[67]

If the original policy goals were not achieved, political learning has also proved to be haphazard. As we have seen, policy makers were able to adjust their deniability tactics to different circumstances and thus move from outright denial of atrocities to promises of reform. But some also became prisoners of their own false understandings. Years later, among some of the very same officials who were deeply involved in different aspects of Central America policy and who had risen to influential positions in the George W. Bush administration, including Richard Cheney, Elliot Abrams, John Negroponte, and Otto Reich, the so-called Salvador Option for Iraq would surface. This was a reputed Pentagon plan to employ official and quasi-official death squads based on the "successful" Salvador model to counter resistance to the U.S. occupation. Trained by the former commander of the U.S. military group in El Salvador, Colonel James Steele, based in the Ministry of Interior and deployed first in Mosul, where evidence of at least 150 summary executions soon appeared, their introduction around the country was accompanied by an orgy of torture and murder.[68] Secretary of Defense Donald Rumsfeld dismissed reports of their activities as "unverified comments," despite the fact that U.S. troops had uncovered at least one of their clandestine torture chambers.[69]

More important, the Secretary of Defense sought to undercut one of the main lessons from U.S. involvement in the Salvadoran civil war by maintaining that "the United States does not have a responsibility" to do anything about the police forces it established and trained except "report" their crimes. This irresponsible (and potentially illegal) position was quickly repudiated by his own Chairman of the Joint Chiefs of Staff, Peter Pace: "It is absolutely the responsibility of every U.S. service member, if they see inhumane treatment being conducted, to intervene to stop it," Pace insisted.[70] But just as the scale of atrocities by U.S.-trained forces contributed to a legacy of violence and shadowy paramilitaries that still plague El Salvador today, the besieged Iraqi government is inheriting a similar bequest and a damaged social fabric that will take generations to restore. In effect, U.S. officials never really looked at the central lesson from El Salvador: alliances with corrupt and repressive forces to carry out counterinsurgency wars are not only reprehensible; such partnerships are also unlikely to work.

Deniability is the abuse of democracy. By deforming the public debate and rationalizing away systematic patterns of murder and torture, the lies at its core and the way these lies eventually trap the administration initiating them (and those that follow) is a central explanation for the repetition of misguided and ultimately disastrous political decisions in choosing allies from Vietnam to Iraq. In the process, the U.S. position as a moral force in the world is tainted. The necessary learning that should take place simply does not occur. This is why General Trombitas, the effective head of the American Iraq Special Operations Forces (ISOF), can say that he is "very proud of what was done in El Salvador," and that training missions in Latin America are "extremely transferable" to Iraq. Failing to mention the horrific consequences for some 75,000 unarmed civilians, and millions of others, in what proved to be a deliberate policy of state terror, he notes that the Salvadoran Special Forces have even helped to train Iraqi Special Forces: "It's a world of coalitions. The longer we work together, the more alike we are. When we share our values and our experiences with other armies, we make them the same."[71] But sharing is a two-way street: as El Salvador, Abu Ghraib, and accounts of an "executive assassination ring" reporting directly to the Vice President of the United States demonstrate,[72] these same partnerships can make some U.S. politicians and some military and intelligence authorities embrace death squads, assassination, and torture in the heart of democracy.

The ultimate target of double deniability is the U.S. public. Driven by the fear of disclosure and the way in which revelations of abuses resonate in the political culture of the United States, deniability is a perverse response to several features specific to American democracy: an independent and competitive press, a congress with investigative power that is not entirely dependent on the executive branch, an independent judiciary, and the great variety of advocacy groups that defend human rights. Double deniability reflects the reality that the domestic pressures on allies are different. Faced with strong and active protest, the U.S. government will denounce its partner if necessary, but a repressive ally faces no such pressure. The actual or intended victims of repression cannot be the target of dissembling; to the contrary, state terror depends on the calculation that the local population knows exactly what is happening and who is doing it. But as juries in *Romagoza v. Garcia* and *Chavez v. Carranza* have shown, when U.S. citizens do learn that the "utility" of deniability is built on hundreds of thousands of stories like that of Neris Gonzalez, and when they are confronted with the terrible reality of state-sponsored murder and torture by U.S. allies, they can accept no excuse for this treatment.

NOTES

1. Terry Lynn Karl is the Gildred Professor of Latin American Studies and Professor of Political Science at Stanford University. She served as an expert witness in a series of human rights cases, including *Chavez v. Carranza*, 559 F.3d 486 (6th Cir. 2009), and *Romagoza v. Garcia*, 434 F.3d 1254 (11th Cir. 2006), discussed in this chapter. The author wishes to thank the plaintiffs in these cases, Philippe Schmitter, and her (former and current) student assistants, especially Gina Bateson, Alexei Dunaway, Thad Dunning, Emily Flynn, Mason Flink, and Jenais Zarlin.

2. *Romagoza v. Garcia*, 434 F.3d 1254 (11th Cir. 2006).

3. Some of these same methods were used against marginalized groups, especially prisoners, minorities, and non-citizens within their own territories. See Darius Rejali, *Torture and Democracy* (Princeton, NJ: Princeton Univ. Press, 2007). On the Bush administration, see Jane Mayer, *The Dark Side: The Inside Story of How the War on Terror Turned into a War on American Ideals* (New York: Doubleday, 2008); and Philippe Sands, *Torture Team: Rumsfeld's Memo and the Betrayal of American Values* (New York: Palgrave Mcmillan, 2008), as well as their chapters in this book.

4. Saddam Hussein, for example, apparently believed that invasions of his neighbors were justified as a mechanism that could redraw the unfair colonial boundaries left by British occupiers.

5. See, for example, Richard Rosencrance, *America as an Ordinary Country: U.S. Foreign Policy and the Future*, (Ithaca, NY: Cornell Univ. Press, 1976); and Arthur Schlesinger, Jr., "Human Rights and the American Tradition," *Foreign Affairs* 57, no. 3 (1978): 403–536.

6. On the Philippines and other examples, see John T. Parry, "Torture Nation, Torture Law," *Georgetown Law Journal* 97 (2008): 1001–56.

7. Rejali, citing one study, concludes that "the most optimistic scenario is that about 4.7 innocent persons were killed for every Vietcong agent," while an intermediate scenario has more than 10 civilians killed for every rebel participant. See Rejali, *Torture and Democracy*, 471.

8. The Winter Soldier hearings of 1971, the Dellums War Crimes Hearings, and the 22 hearings of the Senate Foreign Relations Committee, chaired by William Fulbright, document U.S. actions in Vietnam. By the end of 1971, partially as a result of making this information public, support for the war dropped to about 28 percent. See Parry, "Torture Nation," 1011–14.

9. See Bill Quigley, "Torture and Human Rights Abuses at the School of America-WHINSEC," in this book.

10. On these dynamics, see David P. Forsythe, *Human Rights and U.S. Foreign Policy: Congress Reconsidered* (Gainsville: Univ. Press of Florida, 1988); and an earlier work by Lars Schoultz, *Human Rights and United States Policy Toward Latin America* (Princeton, NJ: Princeton Univ. Press, 1981).

11. Especially interesting on this issue is Bruce W. Jentleson, "The Pretty Prudent Public: Post Post-Vietnam American Opinion on the Use of Military Force," *Intl. Studies Quarterly* 36, no. 1 (1992): 49–73.

12. The Rand Corporation's especially damning report notes:

> [T]he greed and apparent tactical incompetence of Salvadoran military officers has so exasperated American experts posted in El Salvador that all the individuals interviewed for this report . . . believe that the Salvadoran military does not wish to win the war because in doing so it would lose the American aid that has enriched it for the past decade.

See Benjamin C. Schwarz, *American Counterinsurgency Doctrine and El Salvador: The Frustrations of Reform and the Illusions of Nation Building* (Santa Monica, CA: RAND, 1991), p. 21. See also Joel Millman, "El Salvador's Army: A Force Unto Itself," *New York Times*, Dec. 10, 1989, which demonstrates how ghost soldiers, that is, non-existent soldiers, were put on a military roster by officials of the armed forces so that their salaries could be collected and shared by officers. Also see William Stanley, *The Protection Racket State: Elite Politics, Military Extortion, and Civil War in El Salvador* (Philadelphia: Temple Univ. Press, 1996).

13. See United Nations (UN), Commission on the Truth for El Salvador, *From Madness to Hope: The 12-Year War in El Salvador* (hereafter *Truth Commission Report*), Mar. 15, 1993. Specifically, of the 22,000 "grave acts" it investigated, the Truth Commission found that the armed forces were accused in 60 percent, the security forces in 25 percent, paramilitary and civil defense forces in 20 percent, and death squads in 10 percent. The FMLN was accused in only 5 percent of the cases. The numbers do not add up to 100 because forces involved in these acts often were combined.

14. See Cynthia J. Arnson, *Crossroads: Congress, the President, and Central America, 1976–1993* (University Park: Pennsylvania State Univ. Press, 1993); and Mark Danner, *The Massacre of El Mozote* (New York: Vintage Press, 1993).

15. These were civil trials, in which I served as the expert witness for the plaintiffs, held under the Alien Torts Claims Act (28 U.S.C. §1350) and the Torture Victim Protection Act (Pub. L. 102-56, 102nd Cong., 2nd sess., Mar. 12, 1992). The declassified documents were released by the Clinton administration in 1993. See George Washington Univ., *The National Security Archive*, http://www.gwu.edu/~nsarchiv/ (last visited Sept. 9, 2009).

16. This case was originally filed by the Center for Justice and Accountability on behalf of three Salvadoran plaintiffs in 1999. In July 2006, with the judgment final after appeal, Defendant Vides Casanova was forced to relinquish over $300,000 of his own funds to the plaintiffs, a collection that represents one of the first human rights cases in U.S. history in which survivors have recovered money from those found responsible for abuse. For a full collection of transcripts, see Center for Justice and Accountability (CJA), *Romagoza v. Garcia and Vides Casanova: Trial Transcripts*, http://www.cja.org/cases/Romagoza_Docs/Romagoza_Trial_Transcripts.shtml (last visited Sept. 9, 2009).

17. On March 17, 2009, the U.S. Court of Appeals for the Sixth Circuit affirmed the November 2005 jury verdict, which represents the first time a U.S. jury has found a commander liable for crimes against humanity in a contested case. For the full transcript, see CJA, *Chavez v. Carranza: Trial Transcripts*, http://www.cja.org/cases/cases.shtml#ElSalvador (last visited Sept. 9, 2009).

18. 1986 Xerox copy provided by U.S. Embassy in El Salvador, p. 3.

19. For an excellent review of reform in counterinsurgency doctrine, see Schwarz, *American Counterinsurgency*, 5–10.

20. See Daniel L. Byman, *Going to War with the Allies You Have: Allies, Counterinsurgency, and the War on Terrorism* (Carlisle, PA: Strategic Studies Institute, 2005), http://www.brookings.edu/views/papers/fellows/byman_nov2005.pdf (last visited Sept. 9, 2009).

21. These patterns of deniability were developed from my own study of the responses of human rights violators in South Africa, South America, and Central America and are a reworking of my testimony in *Romagoza v. Garcia*. They are also part of a different study (Karl, forthcoming).

22. In this section I am drawing on my own interviews conducted in El Salvador in 1983, reports of conversations with top military leaders quoted in U.S. declassified government documents, and the testimonies of the three top military leaders during the period of greatest repression in that country (1980–1983), Ministers of Defense Guillermo Garcia and Carlos Eugenio Vides Casanova, and Vice Minister of Defense and Head of the Treasury Police, Nicolas Carranza, in the trials cited above.

23. Evidence of the power of all three of these men, both legal and *de facto*, was presented extensively in the trials, especially in the testimonies of this author and Latin American military expert Col. Jose Garcia. See CGA, *Romagoza Transcripts*.

24. Commanders of the Salvadoran Armed Forces have repeatedly claimed that they could not curb abuses because they lacked equipment and funds. For example, a 1983 CIA report quoted Col. Francisco Moran as saying, "at least seven of his officers are guilty of serious abuses but that he cannot afford to bring them up on charges." See CIA, *El Salvador—Situation # 14—Truth Commission I*, Mar. 16, 1983, http://www.faqs.org/cia/docs/30/0000049403/EL-SAL-VADOR—-SITUATION-REPORT- (last visited Sept. 9, 2009). Such claims were especially unbelievable coming from Moran, who had a reputation as one of the worst human rights abusers in security forces.

25. The cable reads as follows:

> Most military officers were highly pleased with the assassination of the six FDR leaders. These officers believe that other leaders and members of the FDR should be eliminated in a similar fashion whenever possible. These feelings were expressed by several middle level Army officers on the 28 November 1980 in the presence of Colonel Guillermo Jose Garcia Merino, Minister of Defense, and Nicholas Carranza, sub-Minister of Defense, and both Garcia and Carranza indicated that they supported this line of thinking. From the comments of all those present during this conversation, it was clear that Garcia, Carranza, and the other officers present accepted as fact that the military services were responsible for the assassination of the six FDR leaders.

CIA, cable, Dec. 1, 1980.

26. The military also denied that it was responsible for the deaths of 300–600 civilians in the Rio Sumpul massacre, and then later argued that the number of massacred villagers was "exaggerated." In another example, it blamed the execution of 12 peasants in San Francisco Guajoyo on a "subversive attack." These denials occurred repeatedly. See the descriptions of these and other massacres in UN, *Truth Commission Report*. The statement of Ambassador Corr is taken from a deposition on March 16, 2001.

27. U.S. Dept. of State, cable, Feb. 2, 1982.

28. On February 21, 1982, Ambassador Hinton asked his Milgroup commander if "it were possible High Command did not know where and when their field forces operated. No, it was not, he told me." See Mark Danner, "The Truth of El Mozote," *New Yorker*, Dec. 6, 1993, p. 9, http://globetrotter.berkeley.edu/people/Danner/1993/truthelmozo1.html (last visited Sept. 9, 2009).

29. In a building adjacent to the church, called the convent, noted forensic experts uncovered the remains of at least 143 people, most of them minors, and they identified at least 131 children under the age of 12. The total number of dead children is believed to be 280. The average age of the victims was approximately

six years. See Aurore Schmitt, Eugénia Cunha, and João Pinheiro, eds., *Forensic Anthropology and Medicine: Complementary Sciences from Recovery to Cause of Death* (Totowa, NJ: Humana Press, 2006), p. 421.

30. See UN, *Truth Commission Report*, 126.

31. For a citation to the quote by Ambassador Edwin Corr to U.S. Secretary of State on June 29, 1988, see CJA, *Romagoza v. Garcia and Vides Casanova: Brief of Appellants-Appellees*, p. 23, http://www.cja.org/cases/Romagoza_Docs/romagoza%20-%20new%20appeal%20brief_v2.pdf (last visited Sept. 9, 2009).

32. On February 10, 1982, for example, Ambassador Hinton reported a new massacre in San Salvador of 17 persons and said, "While García talks a good game, I no longer believe him . . . García should be read the riot act while in Washington." See William Deane Stanley, *The Protection Racket State: Elite Politics, Military Extortion, and Civil War in El Salvador* (Philadelphia: Temple Univ. Press, 1996), p. 226; Elinor J. Brecher, "Envoy Wrote of Salvador Abuses," *Miami Herald*, Oct. 31, 200, http://www.latinamericanstudies.org/elsalvador/cables.htm (last visited Sept. 9, 2009).

33. For example, a June 17, 1983, U.S. government cable reported that Minister of Defense Vides Casanova preferred that a well-documented massacre at Las Hojas be forgotten due to negative publicity that the incident would cause for El Salvador. See CJA, *Romagoza Transcripts*, 238, 251.

34. Ministers Garcia and Vides Casanova promoted the Commanding Officer, the Chief of Operations, and Company Commander of the El Mozote massacre to higher ranks—an example that was followed by all other top commanders. Examples are plentiful. In the 1988 San Sebastian massacre, contrary to direct insistence by Vice President Quayle to the High Command that the responsible officers be brought to justice, the Commander, Col. Jose Emilio Chavez Caceres, was never arrested and continued to command troops despite the evidence of his involvement. Indeed, until 1990, no Salvadoran military officer was ever charged or convicted of wrongdoing in human rights cases.

35. This was a brief, peasant-led rebellion that occurred on January 2, 1932, in the western departments of El Salvador, and was brutally suppressed by government troops, led by Maximiliano Hernández Martínez—who eventually became a hero to the armed forces. The death toll is estimated at 10,000 to 40,000 peasants, mostly indigenous people. This event is central to the memory and thinking of the armed forces. As one highly respected colonel explained to me in an interview in June 1983, "We killed 30,000 peasants in 1932, and they were quiet for 50 years. We want another 50 years."

36. Green Berets began the establishment of this network with the Salva-dorans starting in 1963. Military advisers worked with the two chief lieutenants of Medrano, the leader of the ultra-right at the time, Roberto D'Aubuisson and Nicolas Carranza. See Allan Nairn, "Behind the Death Squads," *The Progressive*, May 1984, 20–28. Also see Cynthia Arnson, "Window on the Past: A Declassi-fied History of Death Squads in El Salvador," in *Death Squads in Global Perspec-tive: Murder with Deniability*, ed. Bruce B. Campbell and Arthur D. Brenner (New York: Palgrave MacMillan, 2000).

37. Ambassador Robert White's cables repeatedly warned of the dangers of the military and security forces. The CIA also documented how the "ultra right has a long history of using violence as a political tool," since 1932. See CIA, *El Salvador: The Right Wing*, Mar. 18, 1981.

38. "Drawing the line" in El Salvador was a phrase first utilized by Secretary of State Alexander Haig.

39. See Robert Parry and Peter Kornbluh, "Iran-Contra's Untold Story," *For-eign Policy*, Fall 1988, no. 72, pp. 3–30.

40. Attempting to tie the FMLN to an international communist conspiracy, officials released a White Paper, entitled "Communist Interference in El Salva-dor," which claimed to present "definitive evidence" of foreign military support for the Salvadoran guerrillas. However, the evidence actually showed the oppo-site, and several months passed before a more balanced assessment seeped out. One reporter quotes the author of the White Paper as saying it is "misleading." See U.S. Dept. of State, *White Paper: Communist Interference in El Salvador*, Feb. 1981; Jonathan Kwitney, "Apparent Errors Cloud U.S. White Paper on Reds in El Salvador," *Wall Street Journal*, June 8, 1981.

41. Strongly criticized by the editorial page of the *Wall Street Journal*, Accuracy In Media, and officials for reporting the story of the massacre, and pressured to pull reporter Raymond Bonner from the Central American Desk, then-managing editor Abe Rosenthal moved Bonner, and Bonner resigned. He returned to the *Times* in 1992 after details of the massacre were verified, where he was nominated for a Pulitzer for his coverage of the genocide in Rwanda.

42. See Arnson, *Crossroads*, 58–59.

43. These characteristics are drawn from my own study of thousands of declassified documents, but they are similar to those found in a congressional study, ordered in the wake of the Truth Commission revelations, and found in Congressional Research Service. See U.S. Congress, House Committee on Foreign Affairs, *Comparison of U.S. Administration Testimony and Reports with 1993 U.N. Truth Commission Report on El Salvador* (Washington, DC: GPO, 1993).

44. By the end of their ambassadorial terms, Ambassadors White, Hinton, Corr, Pickering, and Walker had warned of right-wing terrorism inside the military and security forces.

45. Parry and Kornbluh, "Iran-Contra's Untold Story," 6.

46. See U.S. Senate, Committee on Appropriations, Subcommittee on Foreign Operations, *Hearings on Foreign Assistance and Related Programs Appropriations of 1981*, and Related Programs (Washington, DC: GPO, 1980).

47. See U.S. Dept. of State, *Reply to Senator Percy's Written Questions*, cited in Congressional Research Committee (1993), p. 10.

48. U.S. Congress, *Comparison of U.S. Administration Testimony and Reports*, 11.

49. Ibid. at 35.

50. Americas Watch Committee and American Civil Liberties Union, *Report on Human Rights in El Salvador* (New York: Vintage Books, 1982).

51. This difference between the public and private official position is illustrated by the dual role of Ambassador Hinton. On the one hand, his January 25, 1982 cable claimed: "The killers of the majority are in fact the true phantoms of this struggle. Responsibility for the overwhelming number of deaths . . . cannot be fixed in the majority of cases." On the other hand, Hinton warned privately inside El Salvador of "serious excesses" by the government that could reduce aid. Speaking of human rights, he added: "There is a limit, and at times this government has treaded dangerously close to that limit." See Joanne Omang, "U.S. Envoy Warns El Salvador of Excesses," *Washington Post*, Feb. 12, 1982; Christopher Dickey, "Hinton Attacks Salvadorans for 'Silence' About Murders," *Washington Post*, July 14, 1983.

52. Arnson reports that the Embassy officer sent close to El Mozote said he informed Ambassador Deane Hinton of his impression that non-combatants had been killed. Hinton then discarded the possibility of a massacre in a January 31, 1982, cable to the State Department, which later served as the basis for Enders's and Abrams's congressional testimony. See Arnson, *Crossroads*, 90.

53. "There has been no evidence to support periodic guerrilla accusations of large scale massacres allegedly committing by government forces." See the testimony of Commander Nutting in U.S. Senate, Committee on Foreign Relations, *Presidential Certifications on Conditions in El Salvador*, 97th Cong., 2nd sess., Aug. 3, 1982.

54. The tone of State Department's reply to Senator Pell's written questions, for example, is in sharp contrast to the answers to Senator Percy a year and a half earlier. See U.S. Senate, Committee on Foreign Relations, *Central America Policy: Progress on Certification in El Salvador*, 98th Cong., 1st sess., Aug. 4, 1983.

55. See the testimony of Thomas Enders in U.S. Senate, *Presidential Certifications on Progress in El Salvador.*

56. See U.S. House of Representatives, Committee on Foreign Affairs, *The Situation in El Salvador: Hearings Before the Subcommittees on Human Rights and International Organizations and Western Hemisphere Affairs*, 98th Cong., 2nd sess., Jan. 26, 1984, Feb. 6, 1984, p. 296.

57. This is when rightist extremists led by Roberto D'Aubuisson were arrested for plotting a coup. Two dozen active duty and retired military personnel were present and evidence linked some of these plotters to the murder of Archbishop Romero in March 1980. See CIA, *El Salvador: The Right Wing.*

58. This was headed by Major Mario Denis Moran, identified by the CIA as the director of the White Warriors Union, a death squad specializing in the murder of Catholic priests. Moran incurred the ire of the United States for his involvement in the assassination of the director of the land reform agency and two U.S. advisers, who were gunned down in a Sheraton Hotel dining room. Other than cable traffic, the best description of this event and other death squad activities can be found in two intelligence documents. See CIA, Directorate of Intelligence, *El Salvador: Dealing with Death Squads*, Jan. 20, 1984; and CIA, *Briefing Paper on Right-Wing Terrorism in el Salvador*, Oct. 27, 1983.

59. Headed by Aristides Marquez, a lieutenant colonel and chief of intelligence, the CIA reported this squad operating as early as 1979. Members of this death squad ran a "kidnap for profit" ring between 1982 and 1986. See ibid.

60. Col. Roberto Santivanez, former chief of the Salvadoran Army's special military intelligence unit, named Carranza as a principal organizer of death squads and paid CIA informer. Documents that would have confirmed this were withheld from a House Intelligence Committee investigation, which ultimately concluded that the CIA did not directly encourage or support death squad killings. The report added that "some intelligence relationships with individuals connected with death squads may have given the impression that the CIA condoned, because it was aware of, some death squad killings." See U.S. Senate, Select Committee on Intelligence, *Recent Political Violence in El Salvador*, 98th Cong., 2nd sess., Oct. 5, 1984.

61. See Mark Peceny, *Democracy at the Point of Bayonets* (University Park: Pennsylvania State Univ. Press, 1999), p. 143; "Death Squads, Truth Squads," *National Review*, Jan. 27, 1984.

62. According to a 1984 report by the CIA:

We believe efforts by the civilian government and the military high command to crack down on rightwing violence have made little progress and have been aimed almost exclusively at placating Washington...Since December, the response of the government and military leaders to the problem of rightwing violence has been mainly verbal.

In continuing, the report names notorious right-wing extremists that had been given prestigious commands by Vides, including Colonels Moran, Zepeda, Zacapa, Ponce, and Staben. See CIA *El Salvador: Dealing with Death Squads*.

63. See Schwarz, *American Counterinsurgency*, 23.

64. Lewis Tambs and Lt. Cdr. Frank Aker referred to El Salvador as an "ideal testing ground" for low-intensity conflict. See Lewis A. Tambs and Frank Aker, "Shattering the Vietnam Syndrome: A Scenario for Success in El Salvador," *Conflict* 4, no. 1 (1983): 1–20.

65. Edwin Corr, Ambassador to El Salvador from August 1985 to 1988, writes that the achievement of a UN-sponsored peace agreement between the government and the FMLN "vindicates" U.S. support for the Salvadoran government, ignoring that a negotiated settlement was not the goal or intention of U.S. policy until the Congress cut aid. See Edwin G. Corr, "Societal Transformation for Peace in El Salvador," *Annals of the American Academy of Political and Social Science* 541, no. 1 (1995): 144–56. Corr served as the expert witness on behalf of two Salvadoran ministers of defense, subsequently found liable for torture in *Romagoza v. Garcia*.

66. See Schwarz, *American Counterinsurgency*, vi.

67. See Terry Lynn Karl, "El Salvador's Negotiated Revolution," *Foreign Affairs* 71, no. 2 (1992): 147–65.

68. In Baghdad, this started with the deaths of 14 young men, many of whom had their right eye gouged out. They were subsequently identified as a group of farmers who had been detained at a vegetable market. See Nicolas J. S. Davies, "Evidence of an American Dirty War in Iraq" *Peace Review* 19, no. 3 (2007): 435–43.

69. Editorial, "Iraq's Death Squads," *Washington Post*, Dec. 4, 2005, http://www.washingtonpost.com/wp-dyn/content/article/2005/12/03/AR2005120300881.html (last visited Sept. 10, 2009).

70. Ibid.

71. See Shane Bauer, "Iraq's New Death Squad," *The Nation*, June 22, 2009, http://www.thenation.com/doc/20090622/bauer (last visited Sept. 10, 2009).

72. Seymour Hirsch first raised this issue, which was subsequently widely reported and is being investigated by the House Intelligence Committee. See Sam Stein, "Was The CIA Hiding Cheney's 'Executive Assassination Ring'?" *Huffington Post*, July 9, 2009, http://www.huffingtonpost.com/2009/07/09/was-the-cia-hiding-cheney_n_228864.html (last visited Sept. 10, 2009).

4

Fundamental Human Rights and the Coercive Interrogation of Terrorists in an Extreme Emergency

JOHN W. LANGO

The main question of this chapter is as follows: Even though it is our right as human beings not to be subjected to torture or to other cruel, inhuman, or degrading treatment or punishment, should this human right be set aside in an extreme emergency to allow such acts as means of extracting information from terrorists?[1] Utilizing a nuclear-weapon case as a counterexample, I challenge an absolute moral prohibition of such coercive interrogations. In reply to a slippery-slope objection, I propose some moral constraints on them. Seemingly paradoxically, I argue that the absolute legal prohibition of such acts in the Convention against Torture and Other Cruel, Inhuman or Degrading Treatment or Punishment ("Convention against Torture")[2] should be retained and enforced. For, even when the stated right is set aside, it still (in a sense to be explained) holds. The question presupposes a conception of moral conflict in an extreme emergency. In the course of answering it, I answer another question. What is the nature of this moral conflict?

My writing of this chapter is occasioned by revelations about the abusive treatment of prisoners and detainees by U.S. personnel in Iraq and elsewhere, and the countenancing of such treatment by U.S. governmental officials. To avoid any misunderstanding at the outset, I want to declare emphatically my belief that these individuals have violated the Convention against Torture. One of my aims in this chapter is to show why the idea of extreme emergencies should not be used to justify or excuse those violations. Because the United States is presently the champion of a worldwide campaign against terrorism, I make remarks particularly about that country, but my generalizations are meant to apply also to other countries.

For brevity, I use the term *torment* to mean any act of torture or any other act that amounts to cruel, inhuman, or degrading treatment or punishment. The point is to have a single term for the range of acts that the Convention against Torture prohibits.

Two objections need to be considered, one absolutist and the other realist. According to the absolutist objection, to allow any exception whatsoever to the moral prohibition of torment is to create an inescapable slippery slope into immoral practices. With this cogent objection in mind, I formulate strong moral constraints on the extreme-emergency practice of torment, ones that should help to keep practitioners and officials who countenance the practice securely on top of the slope. However, I also anticipate the realist objection that these moral constraints are too strong, and that they would prevent acts of torment that are necessary to combat terrorism. To avoid again any misunderstanding, I want to declare equally emphatically my belief that morality trumps political or military necessity. I would be happy if the moral constraints would prevent almost all if not all acts of torment.

There is a third objection: the only counterexamples to moral absolutism about torment are fanciful or artificial.[3] Hence, it is important to determine whether there are acceptable real-world counterexamples. A widely held opinion about contemporary terrorism is summarized thus: "We have certainly known since Sept. 11, if not before, that terrorism poses the gravest and most immediate threat to the United States."[4] Admittedly, the threat of terrorism thus characterized might constitute (in an ordinary sense of the word) an emergency. However, to constitute (in the special sense of the term) an extreme emergency, a threat must be proven to be both imminent and extremely dangerous, and so it must be characterized far more specifically.

Let us imagine what could be such a terrorist threat, with the caveat that it is insufficiently narrated: There is a proven danger of an imminent attack by a group of terrorists who are armed with a nuclear weapon, and the only chance of thwarting the attack is by tormenting a member of the group.[5] I am inclined to accept this nuclear-weapon case, once it is sufficiently narrated, as a real-world counterexample to moral absolutism about torment. I discuss below how it should be sufficiently narrated.

At present, I want to respond briefly to an objection: The attack is imminent, there is very little time to thwart it. But considerably more time is needed to extract pertinent information from the captured terrorist by means of torment. Therefore, the nuclear-weapon case is a "fantasy," as are ticking-bomb cases generally.[6] However, for a ticking bomb to be an imminent danger, the amount of time before detonation does not have to be very brief. The bomb is an imminent danger because it is ticking, even if the amount of time before detonation is fairly long. Accordingly, to circumvent the objection, I augment the case as follows: The attack is imminent, in that it might happen at any time—this minute, this hour, today, tomorrow, the next day, or even later. By chance, pertinent information might be extracted from the captured terrorist by means of torment in time to thwart the attack; but also, by chance, it might not.

Hedged in now by the word "inclined," I accept this nuclear-weapon case eventually, but only in a special usage of the term "counterexample." For, seemingly paradoxically, I am also inclined to accept the absolutist objection. In answering the question about the nature of moral conflict in an extreme emergency, I try to reconcile these discordant inclinations. Hence, it is important to realize that my procedure in this chapter is dialectical. Initially, it might seem that I am endorsing the claim that there are (in a more usual sense) exceptions to the moral prohibition of torment, but eventually it should become evident that I am not.

With the aim of making the moral prohibition of torment more effective, I suggest how it should be fortified by a protocol to the Convention against Torture. For brevity, I focus on that Convention, but my chief moral claims about torment pertain to international law generally (e.g., the Geneva Conventions and the Rome Statute for the International Criminal Court). However, the Convention against Torture states, "No exceptional circumstances whatsoever, whether a state of war or a threat of war, internal political instability or any other public emergency, may be invoked as a justification of torture" (article 2).[7] To avoid yet again any misunderstanding, I also want to declare emphatically my belief that this absolute legal prohibition of torture—and also the legal prohibition of other cruel, inhuman, or degrading treatment or punishment[8]—should be retained and enforced.[9]

Torture and Torment

In article 1 of the Convention against Torture, the term *torture* is defined as follows.[10] (I have inserted numbers in this quotation to divide it into four parts.)

> [T]he term "torture" means [1] any act by which severe pain or suffering, whether physical or mental, is intentionally inflicted on a person [2] for such purposes as obtaining from him or a third person information or a confession, punishing him for an act he or a third person has committed or is suspected of having committed, or intimidating or coercing him or a third person, or for any reason based on discrimination of any kind, [3] when such pain or suffering is inflicted by or at the instigation of or with the consent or acquiescence of a public official or other person acting in an official capacity. [4] It does not include pain or suffering arising only from, inherent in or incidental to lawful sanctions.

Drawing upon the first part, I use the term torture to mean any act by which severe pain or suffering, whether physical or mental, is intentionally inflicted on a person. The second part lists some of the purposes of torture. The third part, which lists ways in which torture can be countenanced by different sorts of officials, can be abbreviated thus: "when such pain or suffering is officially countenanced." The fourth part excludes acts by which pain or suffering is intentionally inflicted that are not unlawful. Drawing upon all four parts, I use the term *informational torture* to mean any act by which severe pain or suffering, whether physical or mental, is intentionally inflicted on a person *for the purpose of obtaining information* from him or a third person, when such pain or suffering is both unlawful and officially countenanced.

The qualification expressed by the term *severe* is crucial. Although the Convention prohibits "acts of torture,"[11] it permits some acts by which *non-severe* pain or suffering is intentionally inflicted. Although there certainly is no bright line here, the term severe marks an imprecise threshold: roughly speaking, pain or suffering above this *severity threshold* is prohibited by the Convention and pain or suffering below it is sometimes permitted.

In addition to prohibiting acts of torture, the Convention states that:

> Each State Party shall undertake to prevent in any territory under its jurisdiction other acts of cruel, inhuman or degrading treatment or punishment which do not amount to torture as defined in article 1, when such acts are committed by or at the instigation of or with the consent or acquiescence of a public official or other person acting in an official capacity.[12]

Note that, whereas the term "torture" is defined in the Convention, the terms "cruel," "inhuman," and "degrading" are not.[13]

Furthermore, in this chapter, I presuppose a *nonmaleficence principle*: it is morally wrong to intentionally harm other persons.[14] Of course, any such principle is controversial. Throughout this chapter, I make other claims involving normative ethics or ethical theory that are controversial. Since there is insufficient space to enter into controversies about them, they have to remain presuppositions.

The nonmaleficence principle prohibits many different kinds and degrees of intentionally harmful acts that are (in ordinary senses of the terms) cruel, inhuman, or degrading. But when is an act so intentionally harmful that it amounts to (in the legal usages in the Convention) cruel, inhuman, or degrading treatment or punishment? That this question is sometimes difficult to answer indicates that other imprecise *torment thresholds* are implicit in the Convention.

Generalizing the term "informational torture," I use the term *informational torment* to mean any act of tormenting a person *for the purpose of obtaining information* from him or a third person, when such an act is both unlawful and officially countenanced.

Accordingly, the main question of this chapter can be restated as follows: Should the human right not to be tormented be set aside in an extreme emergency to allow informational torment of terrorists?

In contrast, I use the term *terroristic torment* to mean any act of torment that has as its purpose intimidating or terrifying.[15] In the nuclear-weapon case, informational torment is a last resort. However, I do not think that there are acceptable real-world counterexamples to moral absolutism about torment in which terroristic torment is a last resort. Terrorism can never warrant terroristic torment.

Torment or Genocide?

Characteristically, in a work in philosophy, much of the effort is devoted to clarifying the questions to be answered. The main question of this chapter presupposes a conception of setting aside a human right, and it also presupposes a conception of moral conflict in an extreme emergency. In the course of answering this question, I also answer the following interrelated questions. What is the nature of this moral conflict? What is meant by the term "set aside"?

It is our right as human beings not to be tormented. This human right is among those stated in the Universal Declaration of Human Rights: "No one shall be subjected to torture or to cruel, inhuman or degrading treatment or punishment."[16] The Universal Declaration is part of customary international law, and the human rights stated in it are moral rights.[17]

It is also our right as human beings not to be killed. This human right is also among the human rights stated in the Universal Declaration: "Everyone has the right to life, liberty and security of person."[18] The most important specification of this human right is stated in the Convention on the Prevention and Punishment of the Crime of Genocide ("Genocide Convention"): "genocide means any of the following acts committed with intent to destroy, in whole or in part, a national, ethnical, racial or religious group, as such"; and the first of the listed acts is "Killing members of the group."[19] It is our right as human beings not to be victims of genocide.

In answering the main question of this chapter, I focus on a kind of extreme emergency that is particularly clear-cut: the danger of an imminent act of genocide. For an illustration, let me augment the nuclear-weapon case. The group of terrorists would use their nuclear weapon with the intent to kill hundreds of thousands of U.S. citizens. Such an act of mass killing would violate the right of U.S. citizens not to be victims of genocide. (The above meaning of the term "genocide" includes any act committed with intent to destroy *in part* a *national* group as such. If a narrower usage of the term genocide is preferred, my discussion would not be substantially affected by substituting the following claim. It is our right as human beings not to be victims of extremely large-scale mass killings.) And the only chance of preventing this violation of that human right is by informational torment of a captured terrorist. In this extreme emergency, should the human right not to be tormented be set aside?

Clearly, in this extreme emergency, the two human rights are in conflict. We cannot prevent the right not to be the victim of genocide from being violated without violating the right not to be tormented. This conflict between human rights is a moral conflict between moral rights. In other words, one human right is opposed to another human right. In contrast, in Michael Walzer's ethics of supreme emergencies, "a rights normality" is opposed to a "utilitarianism of extremity."[20] Thomas Nagel's comparable moral dilemma about the conduct of war is produced by conflicting "utilitarian" and "absolutist" categories.[21]

A widespread view is that moral conflict should be resolved through a process of weighing or balancing. I accept this view, but with the proviso that the idea of weighing or balancing needs to be critically examined. With regard to the nuclear-weapon case, it is crucial to understand that what should be weighed are two *moral* requirements—namely, the two human rights. Recall my claim that morality trumps political or military necessity. Indeed, when the right not to be tormented is weighed merely against the practical necessity of torment, the former trumps the latter. However, when the right not to be tormented is weighed against the right not to be the victim of genocide—and also the practical necessity of informational torment to prevent genocide—we are confronted with a problematic question of moral conflict. Which right trumps?

I reject the following answer. There is a morally relevant difference between doing and allowing: a moral duty not to do harm usually outweighs a moral requirement to prevent harm from occurring. Therefore, because the act of torment is so dehumanizing, the moral duty not to torment is morally absolute, always outweighing any conflicting moral requirement to prevent harm. Instead, my view is that, because being the victim of genocide also is so dehumanizing, we also have the moral duty to prevent genocide. Such a duty is embodied in the Genocide Convention: "The Contracting Parties confirm that genocide, whether committed in time of peace or in time of war, is a crime under international law which they undertake to prevent and to punish."[22] A main point is that the above moral conflict between human rights is embodied in international treaties, and so is the above problematic question. In an extreme emergency—one in which genocide cannot be prevented without informational torment—which should trump, the contractual obligation to prevent genocide (in the Genocide Convention) or the contractual obligation not to torment (in the Convention against Torture)?[23]

When the lives of hundreds of thousands of U.S. citizens are so seriously threatened, why should the well-being of a few captured terrorists matter? Why does the right not to be tormented have substantial weight? To answer these questions, we might consult the just war principle of noncombatant immunity.[24] Understood as a specification of the nonmaleficence principle (which morally prohibits *intentional* harm), the noncombatant-immunity principle mandates (very roughly) that noncombatants not be *intentionally* killed in the conduct of war.[25] Analogously, the right not to be tormented might be grounded on a specification of the nonmaleficence principle: we must not *intentionally* inflict severe pain or suffering on a person or otherwise *intentionally* treat or punish him cruelly, inhumanely, or degradingly. It is a presupposition of this chapter that intention matters in ethics. There is a morally relevant difference between harm that is caused intentionally and harm that is not intended.

According to the noncombatant immunity principle, an enemy's aggression can never justify terror bombing, but tactical bombing can sometimes be justified. Analogously, my belief is that an enemy's terrorism can never warrant terroristic torment, but I am asking whether informational torment can sometimes be warranted. As a consequence of tactical bombing, a truly innocent noncombatant might suffer far worse harm than might a truly guilty terrorist, as a consequence of informational torment. However, for tactical bombing to be morally permissible, noncombatants cannot be intentionally killed or injured, although they sometimes may be knowingly killed or injured. In contrast, informational torment is an act by which great harm is caused intentionally. I presuppose that this difference between intentionally performing an action and knowingly bringing about a consequence is morally relevant. Presumably, such a difference is embodied in international law: whereas the laws of war permit some civilian casualties, informational torment is absolutely legally prohibited.

Why, then, does the right not to be tormented have substantial weight? I assume that this question can be answered satisfactorily, if not in the way sketched in the preceding two paragraphs, then in some comparable way that features the idea of intention. This is one of my two most disputable presuppositions. Since space will not permit me to enter into relevant controversies among ethical theorists, it has to remain a presupposition.

Two Types of Moral Conflict

Correlative to the nonmaleficence principle's obligation, there is a right. It is our right as human beings not to be intentionally harmed. To illustrate another problematic question of moral conflict, one that counterposes this human right and the human right not to be killed, let us imagine a different case. There is a proven danger of an imminent attack by a group of terrorists who are armed with a conventional bomb. The group of terrorists would use their conventional bomb with the intent to kill hundreds of persons. And the only chance of thwarting the attack is by intentionally harming a member of the group. However, to interrogate this terrorist effectively, it would not be necessary to cross the severity threshold, and it would not be necessary to cross any other torment threshold. Clearly, in this case of emergency, the two human rights are in conflict. We cannot prevent the right not to be killed from being violated without violating the right not to be intentionally harmed.

With regard to this conventional-bomb case, it is crucial once again to understand that what should be weighed are two *moral* requirements—namely, the two human rights. Indeed, when the right not to be intentionally harmed is weighed merely against the practical necessity of torment, the former trumps the latter. However, when the right not to be intentionally harmed is weighed against the right not to be killed—and also the practical necessity of intentional harm to prevent killing—we also are confronted with a problematic question of moral conflict. Which right trumps? In the present section, my purpose is to show how this type of moral conflict—harm or killing?—is morally relevantly different from the type of moral conflict—torment or genocide?—discussed in the preceding section.

How should a moral conflict of the former type be resolved? Admittedly, in the conventional-bomb case, the captured terrorist has the right not to be harmed, even by means of a coercive interrogation technique that only intentionally inflicts pain or suffering that is not severe (and is neither cruel nor inhuman nor degrading). However, because such harm would not cross the severity threshold (and because there would be no cruel, inhuman, or degrading treatment), this right is clearly and definitely outweighed by the right of the hundreds of persons not to be killed. Having weighed the two rights, we decide that the former right may be overridden. But what is implied by the term *overridden?* When we override the former right, we are no longer bound by it. We no longer have to observe or respect it. Therefore, our conclusion is that it is morally wrong *not* to save the lives, but it is *not* morally wrong to thus harm the terrorist. We would be morally blameworthy for failing to try to save the lives, but we would not be morally blameworthy for thus harming the terrorist. The moral conflict has been resolved.

How should a moral conflict of the latter type be resolved? The brief answer is that it cannot be resolved. To illustrate this answer, let us return to the nuclear-weapon case. The captured terrorist has the right not to be tormented. This human right is so substantial—it has so much weight—that it counterbalances the right of the hundreds of thousands of persons not to be victims of genocide. Having weighed the two rights, we decide that we are bound by both rights. They must both be observed or respected. Therefore, our conclusion is that not saving the lives and tormenting the terrorist are both morally wrong. We would be morally blameworthy both for failing to try to save the lives and for tormenting the terrorist. We are trapped in an irresolvable moral dilemma.

To review, there is a morally relevant difference between the two types of moral conflict. Moral conflicts of the former type are resolvable, whereas moral conflicts of the latter type are not.[26] The second of my two most disputable presuppositions is, I think, that there are such irresolvable moral dilemmas. Since it would require too much space to engage in controversy about the nature of moral dilemmas, this also has to remain a presupposition. My discussion of the subject of moral conflicts is strongly influenced by two somewhat independent streams of literature: writings in political philosophy about the problem of "dirty hands" and writings in ethical theory about the "logic" of moral dilemmas.[27] Regarding different theories of the nature of moral dilemmas, we may distinguish different problems of dirty hands. In accordance with some of those theories, and utilizing the language of moral obligation, there is in the nuclear-weapon case (roughly) the following moral dilemma. We are morally obligated to save the lives and we are morally obligated not to torment the terrorist and we cannot save the lives without tormenting the terrorist. My contention is that this conflict of moral obligations is irresolvable.[28]

For those who contend that all moral conflicts are resolvable, much of my discussion in the remainder of this chapter would not be significantly affected if something like the following presupposition were made instead. Some morally conflicting moral requirements are so stringent that the moral conflict between them cannot be resolved in the stated way. Instead, when the moral conflict is resolved, both moral requirements remain in force. We are still bound by both of them. And so, if we do right by acting in accordance with one of them, we do wrong by failing to act in accordance with the other. We remain trapped, in that we cannot avoid wrongdoing.

Even though we cannot resolve a moral conflict of the latter type, we still have to act. In the nuclear-weapon case, either we torment the terrorist (thereby violating the right not to be tormented) or we do not (thereby violating the right not to be the victim of genocide). There is no third alternative. We have to perform one of these two actions. How, then, do we decide between the two alternative actions? To answer this question, it is presupposed that numbers matter. There is a morally relevant difference between large-scale harm and small-scale harm. Therefore, by comparing the harms resulting from the two alternative actions, we decide which of them to perform: we decide to torment the terrorist. Although our decision is warranted by the presupposition that numbers matter, we have not thereby resolved the moral conflict between the two human rights, for we are still bound by both of them. Despite our warranted decision to torment the terrorist, we remain trapped in an irresolvable moral dilemma.

Those who contend that all moral conflicts are resolvable might object that the warranting of this decision constitutes a sort of resolution of the moral conflict. Rather than quarrel about the term "resolution," my reply is that what is essential is that the two human rights remain in force. We are still bound by both of them. We remain trapped, in that we have to do wrong, we cannot escape being blameworthy.

Let us return to the main question of this chapter: Should the human right not to be tormented be set aside in the nuclear-weapon case to allow informational torment of the captured terrorist? If the term *set aside* means *overridden* (in the above sense of the latter term), the answer is that, because the moral dilemma is irresolvable, the human right cannot be set aside. However, let us understand the term *set aside* differently. Having compared the harms resulting from the two alternative actions, our decision is to torment the terrorist. Nonetheless, the moral conflict between the two human rights is not resolved by this decision. Although we act in accordance with the right not to be the victim of genocide, we are still bound by the right not to be tormented. Thus, in a different sense of the term *set aside*, we have set aside the human right not to be tormented, but we have not overridden it. Indeed, we have set aside this human right, but we are still bound by it. Torment is still morally prohibited.

Additionally, other ethical terms have correspondingly different senses. Consider, in particular, the term *counterexample*: a counterexample that warrants rejecting a moral principle can be distinguished from a counterexample that warrants setting aside a moral principle. It is in the latter sense that I am inclined to accept the nuclear-weapon case as a counterexample to the human right not to be tormented.

It might be objected that there also are intermediate types of moral conflict, in which the conflicting human rights have different degrees of moral force, and thus are counterposed in intermediate ways. If this objection is correct, my answer needs to be qualified. Let us suppose that the moral conflict between the right not to be the victim of genocide and the right not to be tormented is of such an intermediate type, and that the former right has somewhat greater moral force than the latter right.

My presupposition is that we are still bound by the latter right, and that it retains sufficient moral force to ground an absolute legal right not to be tormented.[29]

Moral Constraints

Moreover, it might be objected that my answer creates an inescapable slippery slope into morally disastrous practices. In reply to this objection, I propose some strong moral constraints on the extreme-emergency practice of informational torment. In doing this, I presuppose analogues of the just war principles of just cause, right authority, proportionality, and last resort. Such torment must have a just cause, and it must be rightly authorized, proportionate, and a last resort.

Just war theories are often based on a moral presumption against war. When legitimate agents deliberate about whether to resort to war, they ought to make the moral presumption that they must not. To override this moral presumption, they have the burden of proving that relevant just war principles are satisfied.[30] As James Childress remarked, this burden of proof should be "heavy."[31] There should be a stringent standard of evidence—for instance, a standard of clear and convincing evidence. Analogously, in order to morally constrain the extreme-emergency practice of informational torment, there has to be a moral presumption against it. Because of this moral presumption, we have the burden of proving that the human right not to be tormented should be set aside. Additionally, there is the heavy burden of proving that the above four ancillary principles are satisfied.

What could be a just cause for informational torment? In the absence of a just cause, the attempt to justify torment through an appeal to political or military necessity is morally empty. In imposing his tyrannical rule on Germany, it would have been absurd for Hitler to try to morally justify torment through its practical necessity, for there was no just cause. In the nuclear-weapon case, the just cause is preventing the genocidal killing of U.S. citizens. In general, a just cause for informational torment is the prevention of genocide. It is presupposed that the burden of proving that there is such a just cause can be satisfied readily. Are there other just causes? If we answer, for instance, that another just cause is preventing a wide spectrum of mass killings that do not amount to genocide, we have the burden of proving that there is such a just cause, but this burden is much more difficult to satisfy, if it can be satisfied at all. My purpose here is to illustrate how the ideas of moral presumption and burden of proof serve to secure us on the top of a slippery slope. For lack of space, I cannot attempt to provide a typology of just causes.

To satisfy the just war principle of right authority, a war must be declared and controlled by persons who are legally authorized to do so. Analogously, to satisfy the corresponding ancillary principle, any extreme-emergency act of informational torment must be regulated correctly by legally authorized persons. And there is the burden of proving that it is so regulated. Within any state, there must be a hierarchy of legal authority with the head (or heads) of state at the apex. If there is uncertainty about whether a head of state (or a subordinate official) has regulated such an act of torment correctly, we should presume that he has not. He has the burden of proving that he has regulated it correctly.

The ancillary principle of proportionality requires (roughly) that the benefits resulting from an extreme-emergency act of informational torment must outweigh the harms. It is essential to weigh not just harms to the victims of such torment but also a far broader range of harms, including harms to the international human rights regime. Presumably, there is a threshold above which benefits outweigh harms, but this proportionality threshold is very imprecise. There can be great uncertainty about whether the benefits of a projected act of torment outweigh the harms. In the face of such uncertainty, we might believe that prudence requires us to presume that the proportionality principle is satisfied. It is such beliefs about thresholds that lubricate slippery slopes. Instead, because of the moral presumption against torment, morality requires us to presume that the proportionality principle is *not* satisfied. It is our burden to prove that the principle is satisfied. When we are not reasonably certain that benefits outweigh harms, we have not fulfilled this burden of proof. The prudential presumption eases slippage, whereas the moral presumption hampers it.

Similarly, utilizing these ideas of moral presumption and burden of proof, the severity threshold could be made more precise. In the face of uncertainty about whether an interrogation practice would inflict pain or suffering that is severe, we might believe that political or military necessity requires us to presume that it would not. Instead, because of the moral presumption against torment, we must presume that it would. It is our burden to prove that it would not. We have the burden of proving that we would not cross the severity threshold. For the other torment thresholds, there are similar burdens of proof.

The ancillary last-resort principle mandates (roughly) that measures other than torment must be attempted first.[32] In the nuclear-weapon case, the only chance of thwarting the attack is by informational torment. However, in most real-world cases of extreme emergency where captured terrorists are interrogated, it is doubtful that torment would prove a last resort. Because of the moral presumption against torment, the interrogators and the officials who countenance their interrogations have the burden of proving that torment is a last resort. They have the burden of proving that measures other than torment would not be successful, a burden that would be, in most real-world cases of extreme emergency, very difficult to satisfy.

Let us raise again the question of whether there are acceptable real-world counterexamples to moral absolutism about torment. Because of the moral presumption against torment, we have to presume that there are not. It is our burden to prove that a proposed counterexample actually is a counterexample. Accordingly, if the sketch of the nuclear-weapon case is to be an acceptable counterexample, it has to be made far more specific. In particular, we have to provide full accounts of how all of the above burdens of proof are satisfied. For instance, to narrate it sufficiently, the benefits and harms of informational torment of the captured terrorist have to be detailed, the process of weighing them has to be related, and the proof that the proportionality principle is satisfied has to be given. Similar remarks apply to the just cause, right authority, and last resort principles.

It should now be clear why the detainee in this case is called a "terrorist" and not a "suspected terrorist." Because of the moral presumption against torment, we have to presume that he does not possess relevant information. It is our burden to prove that he does possess relevant information. If we only suspect that he is a terrorist who is a member of the terrorist group, we have not satisfied this burden of proof. A primary goal of these moral constraints should be to thwart the morally disastrous practice of "fishing expeditions."

To strongly morally constrain the extreme-emergency practice of informational torment, it is crucial that the term *extreme emergency* be adequately understood. Evidently, the component term *extreme* marks yet another imprecise threshold. In the nuclear-weapon case, there is a proven danger of imminent genocide. In general, for an emergency to be an extreme one, it must be both imminent and exceptionally dangerous.[33] And, because of our moral presumption against torment, we have the burden of proving that it is both imminent and exceptionally dangerous. It is our burden to prove that the extremity threshold has been crossed. A main point is that, in order to satisfy this burden of proof, we have to be highly specific. We have to detail how the emergency is both imminent and exceptionally dangerous. We have to be highly specific about how the just cause, right authority, proportionality, and last resort principles are satisfied. In particular, concerning the last resort principle, we have to prove very specifically that informational torment is truly necessary.

Is informational torment a necessity in the U.S. campaign against terrorism? One answer to this question can be found in a U.S. Department of Justice memorandum about the subject of detainee interrogations, which has been dubbed "The Torture Memo":[34]

> Indeed, al Qaida's plans apparently include efforts to develop and deploy chemical, biological, and nuclear weapons of mass destruction. Under these circumstances, a detainee may possess information that could enable the United States to prevent attacks that potentially could equal or surpass the September 11 attacks in their magnitude.

Therefore, even if a method of interrogation is prohibited by U.S. law, the memorandum argues, it could nonetheless be justified by a "necessity defense."

In contrast to my nuclear-weapon case (when sufficiently narrated), the emergency stated in this memorandum is not very specific. The memorandum states that apparently a terrorist group is planning to deploy weapons of mass destruction. But it does not prove that there is such a danger, nor does it prove that the danger is imminent. It states that a detainee *may* possess information that *could* enable the prevention of an attack with weapons of mass destruction. However, such a suspicion, which could hover over any captured terrorist, cannot warrant setting aside the human right not to be tormented. For, because of the moral presumption against torment, we must presume that a detainee does not possess such information. And we must presume that, even if a detainee does possess the information, obtaining the information by torment is not a last resort. In general, the memorandum does not state how the above burdens of proof are satisfied.

Toward a Protocol

In review, the main question of this chapter was illustrated as follows. Should the human right not to be tormented be set aside in the nuclear-weapon case to allow informational torment of the captured terrorist? Given that the nuclear-weapon case has been narrated sufficiently, we are trapped in an irresolvable moral dilemma. Even if we set aside the human right not to be tormented, we are still bound by it. Torment is still morally prohibited. In this final section, I suggest how this moral prohibition of torment should be fortified by a protocol to the Convention against Torture (henceforth, the "Protocol").

In conducting the U.S. campaign against terrorism, some U.S. governmental officials might continue to have fierce incentives to authorize harsh interrogation techniques. To evade charges of wrongdoing, they might continue to want to cloak interrogations of suspected terrorists in a mantle of secrecy. And, to have the guise of legality, they might continue to misuse the excuse of national emergency. To obstruct such deviousness by governmental officials, who often wield immense powers, the human right not to be tormented ought to be embodied in the suggested Protocol as an absolute legal right not to be tormented.[35]

The Protocol should not contain provisions in terms of which a person who is guilty of the extreme-emergency practice of informational torment could avoid or escape punishment. There should not be provisions for justifying or excusing informational torment. Such a guilty person must always be punished, and never exonerated. In contrast, Oren Gross has advocated a "mechanism of extralegal action" that would allow not only punishment but also clemency, pardon, reward, and commendation.[36] My view is that any procedure countenancing informational torment outside the law would violate the spirit if not the letter of the Convention against Torture, and would be especially subject to abuse.

Similarly, in comparing justifying torture and justifying civil disobedience, Henry Shue remarked that a justified "act of torture ought to remain illegal."[37] However, in a comparable analogy with civil disobedience, which includes the idea of acceptance of punishment, Michael Walzer observed (in 1973) that "there seems no way to establish or enforce the punishment."[38] In the several decades since, we have experienced the growth of a global human rights movement, international laws embodying those rights (e.g., the Convention against Torture), and institutions for enforcing them (e.g., the International Criminal Court). My hope is that now we need not be so pessimistic.

How, then, should the moral prohibition of torment be fortified by the Protocol? Similarly to the Convention against Torture, the Protocol should be implemented internationally (e.g., by the International Criminal Court), and it should be implemented in national legislation.[39] According to article 4 of the Convention against Torture, "Each State Party shall ensure that all acts of torture are offences under its criminal law." To make explicit what is only implicit, the Protocol should supplement article 4 as follows: "Each State Party shall ensure that all acts that amount to cruel, inhuman or degrading treatment or punishment are offences under its criminal law." Consequently, U.S. criminal law should absolutely prohibit torment.

Furthermore, the Protocol should function to hinder a necessity defense.[40] In using such a defense, the aim of a defendant is to avoid or escape criminal liability, thereby avoiding or escaping punishment.[41] In the Model Penal Code of the American Law Institute (ALI), the concept of an affirmative defense of necessity is formulated as a general principle of justification involving a choice of evils:[42]

Conduct which the actor believes to be necessary to avoid a harm or evil to himself or another is justifiable, provided that:
 (a) the harm or evil sought to be avoided by such conduct is greater than that sought to be prevented by the law defining the offense charged; and
 (b) neither the Code nor other law defining the offense provides exceptions or defenses dealing with the specific situation involved; and
 (c) a legislative purpose to exclude the justification claimed does not otherwise plainly appear.

The purpose to exclude such a justification of torture plainly appears in article 2 of the Convention: "No exceptional circumstances whatsoever [. . .] may be invoked as a justification of torture." The Protocol should supplement article 2 roughly as follows: "No exceptional circumstances whatsoever [. . .] may be invoked as a justification of cruel, inhuman or degrading treatment or punishment."

Furthermore, according to the U.S. Constitution, "all Treaties made, or which shall be made, under the Authority of the United States, shall be the supreme Law of the Land."[43] However, when consenting to ratification of the Convention, the U.S. Senate stated the following reservation:

"That the United States declares that the provisions of articles 1 through 16 of the Convention are not self-executing." What this means is that these provisions do not become legally binding in the United States until the U.S. Congress implements them through legislation.[44] Consequently, it might be argued that article 2 of the Convention is not self-executing, that the provisions in it do not plainly appear in U.S. law, and that a necessity defense of torture is therefore allowed in U.S. courts.[45] To obstruct such U.S. exceptionalism, and comparable hypocrisy by other countries, the Protocol should supplement the Convention roughly as follows: "Each State Party shall ensure that the criminal offense of torture cannot be justified (or excused or pardoned) by a necessity defense."

Unfortunately, the purpose to exclude such a justification of other forms of cruel, inhuman, or degrading treatment or punishment does not plainly appear in the Convention. Therefore, the Protocol should supplement the Convention roughly as follows: "The obligations contained in all of the articles about torture in the Convention shall apply with the substitution for references to torture of references to other forms of cruel, inhuman or degrading treatment or punishment."[46] Moreover, the Protocol should say roughly the following: "Each State Party shall ensure that the criminal offenses of cruel, inhuman or degrading treatment or punishment cannot be justified (or excused or pardoned) by a necessity defense."

Finally, provisions prohibiting the mitigation of punishment should plainly appear in the Protocol.[47] For, in the absence of such provisions, it might be argued that the mitigation of punishment should be allowed by the sort of general balancing of harms or evils expressed by clause (a) of the ALI Model Penal Code's necessity defense.

Despite real-world counterexamples to moral absolutism about informational torment, torture and other cruel, inhuman, or degrading treatment or punishment must be legally prohibited absolutely.

NOTES

1. Some writings with discussions of this sort of question are Fritz Allhoff, "Terrorism and Torture," *International Journal of Applied Philosophy* 17 (2003), pp. 121–34; Bob Brecher, *Torture and the Ticking Bomb* (Oxford: Blackwell, 2007); Alan M. Dershowitz, *Why Terrorism Works: Understanding the Threat, Responding to the Challenge* (New Haven: Yale Univ. Press, 2002); Karen J. Greenberg, ed., *The Torture Debate in America* (Cambridge: Cambridge Univ. Press, 2006); Michael Ignatieff, *The Lesser Evil: Political Ethics in an Age of Terror* (Princeton: Princeton

Univ. Press, 2004); Sanford Levinson, ed., *Torture: A Collection* (Oxford: Oxford Univ. Press, 2004); Larry May, "Torturing Detainees During Interrogation," *International Journal of Applied Philosophy* 19 (2005), pp. 193–208; Seumas Miller, "Is Torture Ever Morally Justifiable? " *International Journal of Applied Philosophy* 19 (2005), pp. 179–92; and Christopher W. Tindale, "Tragic Choices: Reaffirming Absolutes in the Torture Debate," *International Journal of Applied Philosophy* 19 (2005), pp. 179–92. A classic philosophical writing about the subject of torture is Henry Shue, "Torture," *Philosophy & Public Affairs* 7 (1978), pp. 124–43 (an abridgement of which is included in Levinson, ed., *Torture*).

2. Convention against Torture and Other Cruel, Inhuman or Degrading Treatment or Punishment, G.A. res. 39/46, annex, 39 U.N. GAOR Supp. (No. 51) at 197, U.N. Doc. A/39/51 (1984), *entered into force* June 26, 1987 (hereinafter "Convention against Torture").

3. For such an objection about torture, see Brecher, *Torture and the Ticking Bomb*, pp. 14–39; Shue, "Torture"; and Christopher W. Tindale, "The Logic of Torture: A Critical Examination," *Social Theory and Practice* 22 (1996), pp. 349–74.

4. Bob Herbert, "Waking Up to the War," Op-Ed piece, *New York Times*, July 2, 2004, p. A19.

5. For some reasons why such a case is not fanciful or artificial, see Graham Allison, *Nuclear Terrorism: The Ultimate Preventable Catastrophe* (New York: Henry Holt, 2004).

6. For such an objection, see Brecher, *Torture and the Ticking Bomb*, p. 16. For a debunking of ticking-bomb scenarios, see David Luban, "Liberalism, Torture, and the Ticking Bomb," in Greenberg, ed., *The Torture Debate*, pp. 44–47. But note that in an endnote Luban admits "that the catastrophic case can actually occur," and describes how a "ticking bomb case might occur" (ibid., p. 76 n. 40).

7. Convention against Torture, art. 2.

8. Arguably, this prohibition is not absolute, so I suggest that there should be provisions in the protocol ensuring that it is absolute.

9. Similarly, Oren Gross, while endorsing the relevance of catastrophic cases, advocates an absolute legal prohibition. See his "The Prohibition on Torture and the Limits of the Law," in Levinson, ed., *Torture*, pp. 229–31. Later, I note how our views are different.

10. Concerning article 1, consult J. Herman Burgers and Hans Danelius, *The United Nations Convention against Torture: A Handbook on the Convention against Torture and Other Cruel, Inhuman or Degrading Treatment or Punishment* (Dordrecht: Martinus Nijhoff, 1988), pp. 41–47, 114–23.

11. Convention against Torture, art. 2.

12. Ibid., art. 16.

13. Concerning article 16, see Burgers and Danelius, *The United Nations Convention against Torture*, pp. 2, 47, 70–71, 148–50.

14. My presupposition is influenced by W. D. Ross, *The Right and the Good* (Indianapolis, Hackett, 1988), pp. 21–22.

15. Cf. Shue, "Torture," pp. 132–33.

16. Universal Declaration of Human Rights, G.A. res. 217 A(III), U.N. Doc. A/810 at 71 (1948), art. 5 (hereinafter "Universal Declaration").

17. See *Filartiga v. Pena-Irala*, 630 F.2d 876, 882 (1980): "[A]lthough there is no universal agreement as to the precise extent of the 'human rights and fundamental freedoms' guaranteed to all by the [United Nations] Charter, there is at present no dissent from the view that the guarantees include, at a bare minimum, the right to be free from torture. This prohibition has become part of customary international law, as evidenced and defined by the Universal Declaration of Human Rights . . . which states, in the plainest of terms, 'no one shall be subjected to torture.' The General Assembly has declared that the Charter precepts embodied in this Universal Declaration 'constitute basic principles of international law.' G.A. Res. 2625 (XXV) (Oct. 24, 1970)." See also Jordan J. Paust, *International Law as Law of the United States*, 2nd ed. (Durham, NC: Carolina Academic Press, 2003), p. 207.

18. Universal Declaration, art. 3.

19. Convention on the Prevention and Punishment of the Crime of Genocide, 78 U.N.T.S. 277, *entered into force* Dec. 9, 1948, art. 2 (hereinafter "Genocide Convention").

20. See Michael Walzer, "Emergency Ethics," in *Arguing about War* (New Haven: Yale Univ. Press, 2004), p. 40.

21. Thomas Nagel, "War and Massacre," in *Mortal Questions* (Cambridge: Cambridge Univ. Press, 1979), p. 54 (italics removed).

22. Genocide Convention, art. 1.

23. The prohibition against torture, like slavery and genocide, is a *jus cogens* norm, which means that no state can violate it, regardless of consent. See Jack Goldsmith and Daryl Levinson, "Law for States: International Law, Constitutional Law, Public Law," 122 *Harvard Law Review* 122 (2009): 1791.

24. See John W. Lango, "Generalizing and Temporalizing Just War Principles: Illustrated by the Principle of Just Cause," in *Rethinking the Just War Tradition*, ed. Michael Brough, John W. Lango, and Harry van der Linden, pp. 75–95 (Albany: State Univ. of New York Press, 2007).

25. My conception of the specification of a moral principle is influenced by the discussion of specification in bioethics in Tom L. Beauchamp and James F. Childress, *Principles of Biomedical Ethics*, 6th ed. (New York: Oxford University Press, 2009).

26. In contrast, the view that moral conflicts between the "right not to be tortured" and "innocents' rights to not be killed unjustly" are resolvable is defended by Allhoff, "Terrorism and Torture," pp. 125–27.

27. Archetypical of the former is Michael Walzer, "Political Action: The Problem of Dirty Hands," *Philosophy and Public & Affairs* 2 (Winter 1973). Representative of the latter is Bas C. Van Fraassen, "Values and the Heart's Command," *The Journal of Philosophy* 70 (1973), pp. 5–19. Very roughly, the problem of dirty hands is this: sometimes in politics we cannot achieve a good end without using immoral means, thereby dirtying our hands.

28. For an extensive discussion of the logic of such irresolvable moral dilemmas, see Walter Sinnott-Armstrong, *Moral Dilemmas* (New York, Blackwell, 1988).

29. Cf. the "third position" espoused by Ignatieff, *The Lesser Evil*, p. 8. His definition of torture is limited to "the deliberate infliction of physical cruelty and pain" (p. 136). But the nonphysical coercion that he thinks is permissible (pp. 138, 141) could sometimes violate the Convention against Torture. Accordingly, I would summarize his position thus: although physical torture must always be legally prohibited, mental torment could sometimes be the lesser evil.

30. Concerning the role of the ideas of moral presumption and burden of proof in just war theory, see James F. Childress, *Moral Responsibility in Conflicts: Essays on Nonviolence, War, and Conscience* (Baton Rouge: Louisiana State Univ. Press, 1982), pp. 64–73.

31. Ibid., p. 71.

32. Concerning the idea of last resort, see John W. Lango, "The Just War Principle of Last Resort: The Question of Reasonableness Standards," *Asteriskos: Journal of International and Peace Studies* 1:1–2 (2006), pp. 7–23, http://www.igesip.org/asteriskos/1_2/galego/art1.pdf.

33. See the closely similar "two criteria" for a supreme emergency in Michael Walzer, *Just and Unjust Wars: A Moral Argument with Historical Illustrations*, 4th ed. (New York: Basic Books, 2006), p. 252. For a recent discussion of this conception of supreme emergency, see Henry Shue, "Liberalism: The Impossibility of Justifying Weapons of Mass Destruction," in *Ethics and Weapons of Mass Destruction*, ed. Sohail H. Hashmi and Steven P. Lee (Cambridge: Cambridge Univ. Press, 2004).

34. Jay S. Bybee, Assistant Attorney General, Office of Legal Counsel, U.S. Department of Justice, "Memorandum for Alberto R. Gonzales, Counsel to the President, RE: Standards of Conduct for Interrogation Under 18 U.S.C. §§ 2340–2340A," reprinted in Greenberg, ed., *The Torture Debate in America*, p. 352.

35. For some pragmatic reasons for an absolute legal prohibition, see Gross, "The Prohibition on Torture and the Limits of the Law," pp. 234–36.

36. Ibid., pp. 240–41.

37. Shue, "Torture," p. 143.

38. Walzer, "Political Action: The Problem of Dirty Hands," p. 179.

39. For a discussion of the importance of such national implementation particularly within a democracy, see Oona A. Hathaway, "The Promise and Limits of the International Law of Torture," in Levinson, ed., *Torture.*

40. For a relevant discussion of the idea of a necessity defense, see Luban, "Liberalism, Torture, and the Ticking Bomb," pp. 65–67.

41. Necessity defenses are permitted in Supreme Court of Israel, "Judgment Concerning the Legality of the General Security Service's Interrogation Methods (September 6, 1999)," in (but abridged) Levinson, ed., *Torture,* p. 178. For a discussion of this court decision and also the nature of a necessity defense, see Miriam Gur-Arye, "Can the War against Terror Justify the Use of Force in Interrogations?: Reflections in Light of the Israeli Experience," in Levinson, ed., *Torture,* pp. 183–98.

42. *Model Penal Code* (Philadelphia: American Law Institute, 1962), Section 3.02. I have not quoted a sentence that disallows the justification when the defendant has been reckless or negligent in a specified way.

43. U.S. Constitution, art. VI, cl. 2.

44. Under article 18 of the Vienna Convention on the Law of Treaties, a reservation that violates the object and purpose of a treaty is void *ab initio.* 1155 U.N.T.S. 331; 1969 U.N.J.Y.B. 140; 1980 U.K.T.S. 58, Cmnd. 7964, *entered into force* 27 January 1988. A non-self-executing reservation would violate the object and purpose of a treaty by conditioning its obligations on the enactment of legislation.

45. For a writing that is very supportive of the legal prohibition of torture, but that would allow a sort of necessity defense, see Philip B. Heymann, *Terrorism, Freedom, and Security: Winning without War* (Cambridge, MA: MIT Press, 2003), pp. 110–11.

46. This sentence uses the language of article 16 of the Convention. Article 16 says this only about articles 10, 11, 12, and 13.

47. Concerning such mitigation of punishment, see Nigel S. Rodley, *The Treatment of Prisoners under International Law,* 2nd ed. (Oxford: Oxford University Press, 1999), pp. 78–84.

5

Torture, War, and the
Limits of Liberal Legality

RICHARD FALK

Returning a year ago from my fifth visit to Vietnam, I was struck by the strong unacknowledged links between the ongoing torture debate in the United States that has resulted from the treatment of suspected terrorists after 9/11 during the Bush presidency, and the wider legacy of one-sided warfare, especially as waged against the darker peoples of Third World countries. In June 1968, when I first visited Hanoi in the midst of the Vietnam War, I was deeply impressed by the bravery and tenderness of the Vietnamese people in the face of the high-tech military onslaught inflicted daily upon the country. I was, at the time, appalled by the cruel realities of modern warfare being waged against a defenseless society that was basically at a pre-industrial stage of development, and by the related realization that this war was being planned and executed in distant Washington by the liberal elite of America ("the best and the brightest") in air-conditioned ascendancy during the presidencies of John F. Kennedy and Lyndon Baynes Johnson. It was a war, especially in what was then North Vietnam, in which total command of air and sea meant that death and destruction could be imposed at will on Vietnam without ever worrying about any kind of retaliation.

Prior to this direct experience of the Vietnam War over 40 years ago, nothing I had read or heard had really prepared me for this encounter with one-sided warfare, and this unawareness is part of a continuing problem of great magnitude, most recently evident in the attacks launched by Israel on a helpless Gaza, and carried on for 22 days, between December 27, 2008 and January 18, 2009.[1] My experience of one-sided warfare in Vietnam had a transforming effect on my attitude toward that particular war and with regard to my own government's level of responsibility. Before the visit, I had actively, yet abstractly, opposed the war as unlawful and as an ill-advised and historically regressive colonialist venture. While in Vietnam, and subsequently, I came to identify existentially with the emancipatory struggle of the Vietnamese who were being massively victimized by these American war policies. For me, this shift from intellectual critic to citizen/partisan made an enormous psychological and political difference, deepening my anti-war engagement and creating a kind of solidarity with the Vietnamese heroic effort to achieve self-determination by way of political independence.[2]

Returning to the United States from Vietnam in 1968, I was frequently interviewed by mainstream news and television journalists who were interested in my meetings with high government officials in Hanoi, especially the Prime Minister of North Vietnam, and by proposals for ending the war that had been entrusted to me for delivery due to the absence of intergovernmental contact at the time. I was thankful for the attention given my central diplomatic message that peace was in all likelihood attainable by way of diplomacy. It is of more than passing interest that these proposals set forth by Hanoi in 1968 turned out to be more favorable to U.S. political objectives than the arrangements negotiated four years and tens of thousands of casualties later by Henry Kissinger (for which he received a Nobel Peace Prize that he accepted, but was more honorably refused by his able negotiating partner, Xuan Thuy). Washington dismissed the proposals I was asked to convey, clearly continuing to wrongly believe that its war strategy would eventually yield positive results, and be vindicated.

But what struck me most at the time was the total disinterest of the mainstream media and most of my friends in those aspects of my Vietnamese experience that touched on the one-sided nature of the war and its horribly inhumane effects on a poor peasant society of the sort that existed in Vietnam. This disinterest was as true for journalists who seemed clearly critical of the war, such as Hedrick Smith of the *New York Times* and Charles Collingwood of CBS, as it was for more conservative and hostile pro-war journalists I encountered, such as Pat Buchanan and William F. Buckley. My liberal academic colleagues at Princeton and elsewhere were eager to hear about my contact with Vietnamese leaders, but not about my observations on the fundamentally unacceptable character of such an unequal encounter. Their anti-war concerns were focused on the imprudence, costs, and failure of American policies in Vietnam, but they seemed completely disinterested in the logic and implementation of one-sided warfare that was devastating North Vietnam while leaving the United States free from any risk of retaliation. Of course, this legacy of indifference has far deeper roots, going back to the strategic bombing patterns of the latter stages of World War II, especially the use of atomic bombs against Hiroshima and Nagasaki.[3] And perhaps more revealingly, in the overall Euro-American approach to race and imperial rule in Africa, Asia, and Latin America powerfully depicted in important books by Sven Lindquist and Vinay Prashad.[4]

This indifference was perplexing to me then, and remains so now, but it also bears on what is a most dangerous and unacceptable disconnect between condemning a reliance on torture while silently accommodating, or at least not vigorously protesting, the tactics and actualities of one-sided warfare of the sort that has plagued Iraq since 2003, exhibited in the Gulf War in 1991, as well as in the NATO Kosovo War of 1999. These same tactics have been at the core of Israel's approach to occupied Palestine since the Second Intifada (2000), especially evident in Israeli practice of targeted assassinations, the Lebanon War of 2006, the Gaza blockade established in 2007, and the Gaza War of 2008–2009.[5] In fact, the Vietnam experience temporarily complicated the American war discourse, not because of its deeply abusive character, but because it ended in defeat, resulted in more than 58,000 American combat deaths, exposed the deceptions and deceits of a wartime government, and alerted the country for a while to the immense dangers of an imperial presidency. But the 1990s overcame the so-called Vietnam syndrome, that is, the name given to the post-Vietnam reluctance to use force in Third World settings. What overcame the Vietnam syndrome were the easy, that is, one-sided victories in the First Gulf War (1991) and Kosovo War (1999). Indeed, after the NATO victory in Kosovo without a single combat casualty, American militarists were talking about the real prospect of zero-casualty warfare in the future. Of course, the Iraqi ordeal has put a temporary stop to this ultra-militarist variant of triumphalism, and there is now talk of an "Iraq syndrome" that policy makers in Washington fear may inhibit future American interventions. What never became problematic in assessing the lessons of the Vietnam War, and in my view should have been the most troubling reflection, was the magnitude of Vietnamese casualties (estimated to be 3–5 million) and the ratio of loss on the two sides. Among the many retrospective insider accounts of the Vietnam War, including the moralizing memoir of Robert McNamara, was the utter insensitivity to these concerns of mine.[6]

But the disturbing underlying problem persists. The United States, and some of its allies, rely on and seek to sustain and enhance a posture of military dominance enabling the pursuit of political goals throughout the world. And this dominance basically relies upon American technological superiority in warfare that enables it to inflict limitless devastation on a foreign country anywhere on earth without fearing retaliation at home. It is an accepted idea in national defense planning in all countries to develop the most effective weaponry that is technologically and financially feasible. This disposition is reinforced by strategic thinking about how to inflict maximal damage in battlefield situations and as an instrument of coercive diplomacy. The U.S. government, without any serious domestic challenge, has carried this image of national security to absurd limits, currently with an annual military budget about equal to that of the entire rest of the world. Such budgetary excess is needed to pay the costs of maintaining a network of about 1,000 overseas bases, navies in every ocean, and a multibillion-dollar investment in the militarization of space. The purpose of this rampant militarism is to further a grand strategy that is so overwhelming as to undermine the will of adversaries to offer resistance.[7] It is notable that none of the main candidates for the U.S. presidency in 2008 ever questioned this orientation toward war and over-investment in a militarized conception of security, which has huge opportunity costs given the challenges of global warming, poverty, the AIDS pandemic, negative trade balances, economic crisis, and a huge national debt. The liberal elite completely ignore this massive waste of resources associated with maintaining this American military machine, or believe that it would be political suicide to question reliance on this dysfunctional and grossly immoral militarism.

If this pattern of liberal acquiescence is a more or less accurate postulate, then how can we explain the liberal sense of moral outrage about the revelations of torture at Guantánamo and Abu Ghraib during the Bush presidency? I am arguing that torture is an individualized and personalized instance of one-sided violence in which the perpetrator inflicts unspeakable pain while facing no risk of retaliation and is generally insulated from accountability under law. It is, in my view, this contrast between the helplessness of the victim and the total control of the perpetrator that properly causes such moral revulsion. There is also a lesser pragmatic form of objection that questions the effectiveness of torture as a means of acquiring reliable information and repudiates torture because of its assault on the professionalism and morale of the military.[8] I am more concerned here with the principled objections that have led torture to be *unconditionally* prohibited, and verbally repudiated even by its most vigorous advocates in the Bush presidency.[9] In effect, those American leaders who have authorized torture to gain information have resorted to euphemisms such as "an alternative set of procedures" or "enhanced interrogation techniques," the nature of which could not be disclosed. Such sleazy acknowledgments of "torture" in close proximity to a denial are, in effect, recognition of the ethical/legal hegemony of the anti-torture consensus. That is, even those anti-liberals who authorize torture feel obliged by the general climate of opinion to reassure the public that they do not engage in torture, a truly Orwellian conundrum.[10]

Of course, for liberal legalists this official posture of evasion, associated with the denials of Bush, Cheney, Rumsfeld, and Tenet, since 9/11 is, as it should be the case, totally unacceptable.[11] The prohibition on torture, embodied in the 1984 Convention Against Torture, is probably the most important international agreement in the field of human rights and deserves to be respected, and not cynically manipulated to provide rationalizations for engaging in the very behavior that has been prohibited. John Yoo, David Addington, Alberto Gonzales, Jay Bybee, Stephen Bradbury, and a series of lesser legal mercenaries have worked hard since 9/11 to put a legalistic mask on the criminal tactics employed by the U.S. government in its war on terror. But we must still ask ourselves why the liberal consensus that is so impressively mobilized in defense of the anti-torture norm should not show comparable interest in the gross moral outrages associated with one-sided warfare that impact far more lives, indeed, entire societies. Liberal legalists could argue plausibly that one-sided warfare remains lawful so long as military targets are selected in a manner that respects civilian innocence, and even here the legal prohibitions are somewhat controversial when it comes to application. The prohibitions are embodied in international humanitarian law and the customary law of war on the basis of rather vague abstractions about "discrimination," "proportionality," and "necessity." In contrast, the anti-torture norm seems direct and specific, and constitutes a deliberate practice that is clearly separated from "the fog of war."[12]

A realist answer regarding the neglect of one-sided war by liberals might suggest that underlying issues of war, peace, and security are beyond the current reach of effective law and morality, and that it is in the nature of sovereign states to be as successful as possible in wartime, inflicting maximum damage on their enemy, and doing their best to limit damage and casualties to themselves to the extent possible. Furthermore, it is to be expected, given the strength of nationalism and sovereignty, that during a war an almost absolute value would be placed on the lives of one's own citizens, while regarding the lives of civilians in the enemy state as of virtually no consequence, except possibly with respect to public relations. This indifference to enemy civilian casualties is revealing, and is evidenced by the Pentagon's refusal to keep statistics on such losses in the ongoing Iraq War. What information on Iraqi civilian casualties is available depends on information collected by reliable civil society actors, such as the British health NGO Lancet and the online site, antiwar.com.[13] These responses to the challenges posed by one-sided warfare, attributed to anti-torture liberals are unsatisfactory, and move us only a small and somewhat arbitrary step back from the attitudes and behavior of the apologists for torture in the debate on detainee treatment and interrogation methods.

What is at stake here is the whole attitude of the political culture toward the use of violence against vulnerable people, whether singly as in torture situations or collectively as in instances of one-sided warfare. My contention is that there exists a self-serving split consciousness associated with liberal legality that is properly sensitive to abuses directed at individuals while being morally far less concerned with the abusive structure of warfare, which inflicts collective punishment on a massive scale, especially as between rivals of grossly unequal technological capabilities. This split explains the absence of mainstream political debate surrounding the defense budget, reliance on nuclear weaponry, and the way force is used against distant, darker peoples. This split is particularly glaring in the post-9/11 world with its focus on counter-terrorism. In effect, one-sided warfare combines the worst features of torture and terrorism, if the latter is associated, as it should be, with the use and scale of political violence against the innocent. The doctrine of "total war," which became operative for both sides in World War II, provided the rationale for massive and repeated indiscriminate bombing of German and Japanese cities, and was deliberately and unabashedly aimed at terrorizing the civilian population in enemy societies so as to demoralize the society to the extent of abandoning the war effort.

The concern over one-sidedness was disguised to some slight extent in the context of the major wars of the past century: World Wars I and II, and the Cold War. In these three instances, the level of technological sophistication on the two sides seemed roughly equal, at least at the outset of the conflict. Yet the absence of serious moral questioning of policies that deliberately sought to inflict massive death on the civilian population in World War II is notable, even granting the hypothesis that the victors fought a necessary war consistent with the postulates of the just war doctrine, at least with respect to recourse to war (*jus ad bellum*) if not the conduct of the war (*jus in bello*).[14] There is no doubt that World War II remains widely regarded as a just war, an indispensable war to defeat Nazism and Japanese imperialism. This helps explain the reluctance to raise questions about the moral and legal status of the tactics used by the victors.[15] But it was in the course of this war that the ethos of one-sidedness became mainstream, with little objection raised at the time or later to the deliberate targeting of helpless civilian populations in the urban centers of Germany and Japan. Occasional assertions of lament, as in Robert McNamara's passing observation that had the United States lost the war to Japan, he and Curtis LeMay, a strategic air commander, would have been subject to prosecution for war crimes, are noted, but pass quickly into the societal unconscious of victors. The horror of Hiroshima and Nagasaki has raised some critical comment, mainly in retrospect and by more radical social critics, but at the time was widely lauded as a means to bring a just war to a rapid end.[16] Putting aside the controversy about facts, whether Japan would have surrendered in any event and whether a similar effect might have been achieved by demonstrating the destructiveness of an atomic bomb by detonating it in an uninhabited area, there was little notable dissent then or later. This gross insensitivity was reinforced by the outlook associated with "victors' justice" that scrutinizes and passes moral/legal judgment on the behavior of losers while granting a comprehensive exemption from accountability to the victors. Perversely, this has generally meant that the perpetrators of one-sided warfare enjoy impunity while the leaders of victim states may be subject to criminal prosecution. For instance, in relation to Iraq, Saddam Hussein and his lieutenants are prosecuted and punished, while George W. Bush and entourage possess an unchallengeable impunity.[17]

During the Cold War, a central role for weaponry of mass destruction was formalized, and became the mainstay of strategic doctrine, "mutual assured destruction." E. P. Thompson aptly condemned this willingness to use such weapons on urban population as an "exterminist logic," but it was not seriously criticized by the liberal establishment.[18] There are two issues intertwined here, both of which relate to the torture debate: first, one-sidedness and non-reciprocity; second, victimizing the innocent. At the latter stages of World War II both issues were raised, while the Cold War raised mainly the issue of civilian innocence and omnicidal war. In the torture context, the one-sidedness is integral to the situation, while those who are mainly innocent of involvement with terrorism are swept up in the wide net of detention, and seem to be the overwhelming majority of the victims of unfounded suspicion who are flagrantly denied a presumption of innocence. By introducing the issue of innocence, there is of course no implication that it is permissible to torture anyone, however certain their connection with prohibited activity. That is the whole purpose of an unconditional prohibition, a rule that is not subject to exception.[19] In these respects, one-sided war is different than torture. War can under certain conditions be lawful, and in very rare circumstances, moral (as in the war against fascism or in certain wars of liberation), and international law is deficient in its failure to condemn one-sided war directly. It does condemn partially, if ineffectually, and indirectly, through the general rules of customary international law that prohibit the use of force against civilians and non-military targets. But deference to "military necessity" is so strong in war settings as to make these restraints virtually irrelevant. Beyond this, the self-defense loophole in relation to war, combined with the veto power of the permanent members of the UN Security Council, effectively grants an exemption from the law of the Charter with respect to war-making by geopolitical actors, and in the present historical setting, especially to the United States. If this was not enough, there is no effort whatsoever to regulate one-sided warfare, and effectively, international law and morality do not challenge or even debate the acquisition or reliance upon one-sided military superiority. Such issues never arose in the public discussion of either "successful" recent instance of one-sided warfare: Gulf War I or Kosovo War. Indeed, the American commentary on such one-sidedness is generally celebratory in tone, an attitude inscribed in Western political consciousness in colonialist settings where greatly outnumbered European troops prevailed over the indigenous masses in Asia, Africa, and the Americas, compiling favorable casualty ratios of anywhere from 1:100 to 1:1,000. What I am arguing here is that the prohibition of "torture" has been benevolently inscribed in the political mentality of liberal legality, but the reliance on one-sided warfare stirs no comparable moral concern. Is this a reflection of the *legalist* side of a political consciousness that reacts so strongly to torture because there exists a valid, widely endorsed legal norm? Or is this better understood as an expression of the *liberal* side of the political consciousness that defers to political realism when it comes to matters of war and security? It would seem that both elements are to varying degrees present, allowing such cognitive dissonance to pass virtually unnoticed.

When apologists for post-9/11 torture are challenged about reliance upon "alternate" procedures, they fall back in one way or another on rationalization about the need to make America secure, or more vividly, to save American lives.[20] This was very much a motif of Bush's September 6 wordplay, simultaneously repudiating and acknowledging torture. If we think back, asking ourselves, "Where have we heard this before?" the answer is, "In the aftermath of Hiroshima and Nagasaki." This was the mask worn by American leaders to hide one of the worst of modern atrocities, and one that was generally accepted by the liberal mainstream; indeed, it was Harry Truman who lent his authority to such a rationalization of criminality. The main line of revisionist critique of the atomic bombings was to produce evidence that the attacks had hidden motives (to warn the Soviets, to ensure American control of the Pacific, to satisfy the thirst for vengeance) or that it was not needed (Japan was ready to surrender).[21] The use of such a weapon against an essentially defenseless civilian population was not made a centerpiece of the critique. Even those who decried the ensuing suffering and were disgusted by the wrongfulness of such an attack did not connect their concerns with the manner with which modern warfare has evolved. There were concerns about the future implications for humanity of such weaponry, unlocking the apocalyptic imagination, shifting discussion to preventing such a catastrophe in the future. In the end, even this appeal to elemental species survival went unheeded. It became obvious that biological prudence as a cultural commitment was no match for the lure of technological mastery in relation to war. Put differently, prevailing views about the links between national security and military capabilities were so strongly entrenched in bureaucratic structures and ideological commitments to governmental survival that the political risks and moral costs of relying on and being targeted by exterminist threats never became a public issue for debate in democratic societies.

I would not want to minimize the conceptual and operational difficulties associated with the repudiation of one-sided warfare. It is almost impossible to comprehend how a government in an established sovereign state would continue to prepare for war without seeking to take full advantage of its technological capabilities to improve its prospects of success. Further, the definition of "one-sided" is relational, and the implementation of a posture of renunciation would depend on self-restraint and voluntary compliance in a variety of circumstances. At the same time, significant inroads on one-sided warfare could be made by a more conscientious adherence to international humanitarian law and by the unconditional repudiation of geopolitical "wars of choice," that is, non-defensive wars.[22] The abuses mentioned above, including the use of atomic bombs, would have been avoided if the United States had exhibited respect for the customary international law of war and the United Nations Charter. Almost every instance of one-sided warfare in the Third World involves non-defensive wars and unlawful recourse to force.[23]

There is a further dimension that is relevant here. The normative incoherence of the liberal repudiation of torture combined with an acquiescence in nuclearism and one-sided warfare is perceived understandably by much of public opinion as either inexplicable or as a display of hypocrisy. In contrast, militarists and conservatives who accept the postulates of sovereignty as the foundation of security are free from such ambiguity. They enjoy the benefits of normative coherence. If it is okay to bomb cities, adopt a doctrine of "total war," and celebrate victories in one-sided wars, then it is surely acceptable to "torture" for the sake of avoiding that omni-present ticking bomb or to save American lives. And to the extent that liberal energies are devoted to showing that there will never be a ticking bomb or that such tactics do not save American lives, it often becomes a losing game. If the argument against torture is made to rest ultimately on facts and contextual interpretation rather than on the unconditional moral authority of the norm, it can never be won, *except verbally*, and we have seen that this doesn't count for much. And once torture is allowed for exceptional instances, the exception slides naturally until it becomes the operative rule. If torture can potentially extract life-saving information, who knows whether any captured or detained person possesses such information. Every person may know of a ticking bomb!

In conclusion, there are several interdependent arguments being made: (1) the ethical resemblance between one-sided warfare and torture should be acknowledged, and addressed; (2) the moral impossibility of effectively repudiating torture without also rejecting one-sided warfare needs to be confronted; (3) the difficulty of rejecting one-sided warfare without drawing into question the primacy of national sovereignty and state survival in conceiving of "security" also requires analysis and assessment; (4) the further difficulty of isolating one-sided warfare from warfare in general must be faced.

Such a formidable agenda is daunting, but to evade the challenge is to succumb to a political culture that implicitly endorses torture and terrorism on a massive and unrestricted scale so long as it is labeled "war." The historical record demonstrates that one-sided warfare has been consistently and frequently waged for centuries, especially against the darker peoples of the Third World, as well as against indigenous peoples everywhere. The position taken here is not meant to weaken the important campaign against post-9/11 torture, but rather to expand and deepen that struggle, and implicitly to offer an alternative approach to state violence to that taken by liberal legalists.

NOTES

1. At least in the Vietnamese setting, the victimized side had some capacity to shoot the planes down, and on land to mount punishing ambush and surprise attacks on the superior American ground forces. In Gaza, the resisting forces under the command of Hamas had no capacity to neutralize Israeli weaponry, and were able to respond only by launching primitive rockets that did little damage, and what damage was done violated international humanitarian law because the rockets were aimed at Israeli civilian targets. The threat of such attacks upon Israelis in southern Israel should not be minimized despite the small level of actual harm inflicted, but it did not alter the one-sidedness of the military encounter, or the moral questions raised thereby. See Richard Falk, "Israeli War Crimes: Why It Matters," *Le Monde Diplomatique* (March 2009): 12–13.

2. By citizen/partisan I refer to an orientation toward conflict based on *conscience* and *sympathy* rather than national affiliation. Although I am loyal to the ideals of America, I reject the postulates of *tribal patriotism*, unquestioning loyalty to the state. For this reason, also, I would favor the repudiation of treason as a crime.

3. An intriguing alternative mode of moral reasoning involves reflections on the use of the atomic bomb in 1945 and the Holocaust. See Robert Jay Lifton and Eric Makusen, *The Genocidal Mentality: Nazi Holocaust and Nuclear Threat* (New York: Basic Books, 1988).

4. See Sven Lindquist, *"Exterminate All the Brutes": One Man's Odyssey into the Heart of Darkness and the Origins of European Genocide* (New York: New Press, 1996), and Vijay Prashad, *The Darker Nations: A People's History of the Third World* (New York: New Press, 2007).

5. Whether the terminology of war should even be used given this absence of reciprocity seems like a serious issue. The whole idea of war is of an encounter between opposed armed forces, not necessarily equal, but with a mutual capacity to inflict serious harm on the adversary. In this sense, war is a contest of wills *and* capabilities. In a one-sided conflict, the encounter is ended either when the side with capabilities decides to stop or the side without capabilities gives up its posture of resistance, and surrenders. As the Vietnam War illustrated, the militarily dominant side can still lose the war because in the end, the contest of wills proved more decisive than defeat or comparative losses on the battlefield. In the Gaza War of 2008–2009, critics of the military operation were instinctively reluctant to call it a war, and instead referred to the undertaking as "a massacre" or simply as "slaughter" or "atrocity."

6. See Robert S. McNamara (with Brian VanDeMark), *In Retrospect: The Tragedy and Lessons of Vietnam* (New York: Vintage, 1996).

7. Of course, this kind of thinking is anachronistic insofar as the main security threats come from actors other than territorial states. This military megamachine is virtually useless against such threats as are associated with transnational terrorism and international piracy.

8. These issues are vividly explored by Jane Mayer, *The Dark Side* (New York: Doubleday, 2008).

9. The approach taken to deny torture while affirming the security rationale for practices that are generally regarded to be torture is most fully described in a speech by President George W. Bush. "President Discusses Creation of Military Commissions to Try Suspected Terrorists" (speech, White House, Washington, DC, Sept. 6, 2006); other American leaders endorsed this approach, including Dick Cheney, Donald Rumsfeld, and the head of the CIA, George Tenet. Government lawyers reinforced this way of evading the torture norm, most notably, John Yoo, David Addington, Alberto Gonzales, Stephen Bradbury, and Jay Bybee. The torture norm is considered universally binding as a matter of customary international law, but it is also embodied in a 1984 treaty ratified by the United States. UN General Assembly, *Convention Against Torture and Other Cruel Inhuman or Degrading Treatment or Punishment*, Resolution 39/46, 1984.

10. Only a few advocates of torture are brazen enough to call a spade a spade. The most notorious advocate, in this vein, is undoubtedly Alan Dershowitz. See Alan Dershowitz, "The Torture Warrant: A Response to Professor Strauss," *New York Law School Law Review* 48 (2004): 275–94; Alan Dershowitz, "Tortured Reasoning," in *Torture: A Collection*, ed. Sanford Levinson, 257–80 (New York: Oxford Univ. Press, 2004).

11. For an excellent overview of the torture debate, with treatment of its historical antecedents, see Lisa Hajjar, "Does Torture Work?" *Annual Review of Law and Social Science* 5 (2009) 311–45; for the most comprehensive treatment of torture as a political practice see Darius Rejali, *Torture and Democracy* (Princeton, NJ: Princeton Univ. Press, 2007).

12. For comparison of the torture prohibition with attitudes toward war see Henry Shue, "Torture," in *Torture: A Collection* (see note 10), 47–60.

13. According to Lancet reports, the number of Iraqi civilian deaths attributable to the U.S. invasion and occupation between March 2003 and October 2006 was 655,000. Gilbert Burnham et al., "Mortality After the 2003 Invasion of Iraq: A Cross-sectional Cluster Sample Survey," *The Lancet* 368, no. 9545 (Oct. 2006): 1421–28. More recent figures estimate a total of 1,366,350 Iraqi deaths due to the war. Just Foreign Policy, "Iraq Deaths," http://www.justforeignpolicy.org/iraq (last visited May 21, 2010).

This appalling statistic does not include the number injured. Also, the costs of war need to take account of the more than 5 million displaced Iraqis, as well as the extensive physical damage and destruction of cultural heritage. Lisa Schlein, "Displaced Iraqis Find Difficult to Return Home," *Voice of America*, April 13, 2008, http://www.voanews.com/english/archive/2008-04/2008-04-13-voa13.cfm?moddate=2008-04-13 (last visited July 28, 2009).

14. There is a large body of literature addressing these issues. One of the most influential texts written from a liberal legalist perspective, with strong realist sympathies, is Michael Walzer, *Just and Unjust Wars*, 3rd ed. (New York: Basic Books, 2000). For a wider and imaginative inquiry that looks at the history of bombing through the prism of one-sidedness, see Sven Lindqvist, *A History of Bombing* (New York: New Press, 2001).

15. For a critique of the war crimes trials after World War II that prosecuted surviving Japanese military and political leaders, while exempting American leaders from comparable scrutiny, see Richard H. Minear, *Victors' Justice: The Tokyo War Crimes Tribunal* (Princeton, NJ: Princeton Univ. Press, 1971); see also the dissent at Tokyo by the Indian judge who challenged the basic charge of aggression made against the Japanese defendants. Radhabinod Pal, *International Military Tribunal for the Far East: Dissentient Judgement* (Calcutta, India: Sanyal, 1953).

16. Perhaps the most notable feature of President Obama's April 5, 2009, speech on nuclear weapons in Prague was an acknowledgment of a special responsibility due to past behavior: "As a nuclear power—as the only nuclear power to have used a nuclear weapon—the United States has a moral responsibility to act." It is interesting that the *Wall Street Journal* in an angry editorial entitled "The Nuclear Illusionist" picked out the same sentence, derisively

declaring, "[t]hat barely concealed apology for Hiroshima is an insult to memory of Harry Truman, who saved a million lives by ending World War II without a bloody invasion of Japan." "The Nuclear Illusionist," *Wall Street Journal*, April 7, 2009.

17. Small inroads were laid on the impunity by some foreign national courts claiming so-called universal jurisdiction to prosecute even such individuals if their physical presence can be obtained by way of extradition or detention. The Pinochet litigation in Britain gave rise to an expanded interest in the potential role of universal jurisdiction in strengthening international criminal law. For a thorough exploration of these issues, see Stephen Macedo, ed., *Universal Jurisdiction* (Philadelphia: Univ. of Pennsylvania Press, 2004). Even without actual prosecution, the threat of extradition or detention alters travel plans, and implies at least potential accountability. On a more symbolic level, certain civil society initiatives have organized citizen tribunals to consider evidence of individual responsibility for war crimes and other crimes of state, and may shape the legitimacy climate that could be conducive to the establishment of boycotts or calls for divestment, as occurred in the anti-apartheid movement. For a notable attempt along these lines, see Müge Gürsöy Sökmen, ed., *World Tribunal on Iraq* (Northampton, MA: Interlink, 2008). The initial effort was prompted by the Vietnam War, initiated by the British philosopher Bertrand Russell, and known as "the Russell Tribunal." For the record compiled, see John Duffett, ed., *Against the Crimes of Silence: Proceedings of the International Russell War Crimes Tribunal* (Flanders, NJ: O'Hare, 1968).

18. See Edward Thompson, "Notes on Exterminism: The Last Stage of Civilization," in *Beyond the Cold War: A New Approach to the Arms Race and Nuclear Armageddon*, ed. Edward Thompson, 41–79 (New York: Pantheon, 1982); for a more characteristic liberal view based on living with nuclear weapons, see Joseph S. Nye, *Nuclear Ethics* (New York: Free Press, 1986).

19. See David Luban, "Unthinking the Ticking Bomb," Georgetown Public Law Research Paper No. 1154202, http://papers.ssrn.com/sol3/papes. cfm?abstract_id=1154202; also Kim Scheppele, "Hypothetical Torture in the 'War on Torture," *Journal of National Security Policy and Law* 1 (2005): 285–340.

20. See Bush, "President Discusses Creation of Military Commissions."

21. See, e.g., Gar Alperovitz, *Atomic Diplomacy: Hiroshima and Potsdam: The Use of the Atomic Bomb and the American Confrontation with Soviet Power*, 2nd ed. (London: Pluto, 1994).

22. See Richard Falk, "Renouncing Wars of Choice: Toward a Geopolitics of Nonviolence," in *The Ameican Empire and the Commonwealth of God*, ed. David Ray Griffin et al., 69–85 (Louisville, KY: Westminster John Knox Press, 2006).

23. An arguable exception was the Gulf War of 1991, which did proceed as a result of a mandate from the UN Security Council and was legally validated as a defensive response to Iraq's invasion and annexation of Kuwait. Even here there are legal/moral ambiguities in the failure to give diplomacy an adequate opportunity to restore Kuwaiti sovereignty and by the targeting of the civilian infrastructure of Iraq in a manner that would foreseeably cause widespread civilian casualties.

PART II

Torture and Cruel Treatment of Prisoners in U.S. Custody

6

Outsourcing Torture

The Secret History of America's
"Extraordinary Rendition" Program

JANE MAYER

On January 27, 2005, President George W. Bush, in an interview with the *New York Times,* assured the world that "torture is never acceptable, nor do we hand over people to countries that do torture."[1] Maher Arar, a Canadian engineer who was born in Syria, was surprised to learn of Bush's statement. Two and a half years earlier, American officials, suspecting Arar of being a terrorist, apprehended him in New York and sent him back to Syria, where he endured months of brutal interrogation, including torture. When Arar described his experience in a phone interview, he invoked an Arabic expression. The pain was so unbearable, he said, that, "you forget the milk that you have been fed from the breast of your mother."

Arar, a 34-year-old graduate of McGill University whose family emigrated to Canada when he was a teenager, was arrested on September 26, 2002, at John F. Kennedy Airport in New York. He was changing planes; he had been on vacation with his family in Tunisia, and was returning to Canada. Arar was detained because his name had been placed on the United States Watch List of terrorist suspects. He was held for the next 13 days, as American officials questioned him about possible links to another suspected terrorist. Arar said that he barely knew the suspect, although he had worked with the man's brother. Arar, who was not formally charged, was placed in handcuffs and leg irons by plainclothes officials and transferred to an executive jet. The plane flew to Washington, continued to Portland, Maine, stopped in Rome, Italy, then landed in Amman, Jordan.

During the flight, Arar said, he heard the pilots and crew identify themselves in radio communications as members of "the Special Removal Unit." The Americans, he learned, planned to take him next to Syria. Having been told by his parents about the barbaric practices of the police in Syria, Arar begged crew members not to send him there, arguing that he would surely be tortured. His captors did not respond to his request; instead, they invited him to watch a spy thriller that was aired on board.

Ten hours after landing in Jordan, Arar was driven to Syria, where interrogators, after a day of threats, "just began beating on me." They whipped his hands repeatedly with two-inch-thick electrical cables, and kept him in a windowless underground cell that he likened to a grave. "Not even animals could withstand it," he said. Although he initially tried to assert his innocence, Arar eventually confessed to anything his tormentors wanted him to say. "You just give up," he said. "You become like an animal."

One year later, in October 2003, Arar was released without charges after the Canadian government took up his cause. Imad Moustapha, the Syrian Ambassador in Washington, announced that his country had found no links between Arar and terrorism. Arar, it turned out, had been sent to Syria on orders from the U.S. government, under a secretive program known as "extraordinary rendition." This program had been devised as a means of extraditing terrorism suspects from one foreign state to another for interrogation and prosecution. Critics contend that the unstated purpose of such renditions is to subject the suspects to aggressive methods of persuasion that are illegal in America—including torture.

Rendition was originally carried out on a limited basis, but after September 11, what began as a program aimed at a small, discrete set of suspects—people against whom there were outstanding foreign arrest warrants—came to include a wide and ill-defined population that the Bush administration termed "illegal enemy combatants." Many of them have never been publicly charged with any crime.

Scott Horton, an expert on international law who helped prepare a report on renditions issued by NYU Law School and the New York City Bar Association, estimates that 150 people have been rendered since 2001. Representative Ed Markey, a Democrat from Massachusetts and a member of the Select Committee on Homeland Security, said that a more precise number was impossible to obtain. "I've asked people at the CIA for numbers," he said. "They refuse to answer. All they will say is that they're in compliance with the law."

Although the full scope of the extraordinary rendition program is unknown, several recent cases have come to light that may well violate U.S. law. In 1998, Congress passed legislation declaring that:

> [It is] the policy of the United States not to expel, extradite, or otherwise effect the involuntary return of any person to a country in which there are substantial grounds for believing the person would be in danger of being subjected to torture, regardless of whether the person is physically present in the United States.[2]

The Bush administration, however, argued that the threat posed by stateless terrorists who draw no distinction between military and civilian targets is so dire that it requires tough new rules of engagement. This shift in perspective, labeled the New Paradigm in a memo written by Alberto Gonzales, then the White House counsel, "places a high premium on . . . the ability to quickly obtain information from captured terrorists and their sponsors in order to avoid further atrocities against American civilians," giving less weight to the rights of suspects.[3]

It also questions many international laws of war.

Five days after al-Qaeda's attacks on the World Trade Center and the Pentagon, Vice President Dick Cheney, reflecting the new outlook, argued in an appearance on the NBC show *Meet the Press* that the government needed to "work through, sort of, the dark side." Cheney continued:

> A lot of what needs to be done here will have to be done quietly, without any discussion, using sources and methods that are available to our intelligence agencies if we're going to be successful. That's the world these folks operate in. And so it's going to be vital for us to use any means at our disposal, basically, to achieve our objective.[4]

The extraordinary rendition program bears little relation to the system of due process afforded suspects of crimes in America. Terrorism suspects in Europe, Africa, Asia, and the Middle East have often been abducted by hooded or masked American agents, then forced onto a Gulfstream V jet, like the one described by Arar. This jet, which has been registered to a series of dummy American corporations, such as Bayard Foreign Marketing, of Portland, Oregon, has clearance to land at U.S. military bases. Upon arriving in foreign countries, rendered suspects often vanish. Detainees are not provided with lawyers, and families often are not informed of their whereabouts.

The most common destinations for rendered suspects were Egypt, Morocco, Syria, and Jordan, all of which have been cited for human rights violations by the State Department, and are known to torture suspects. To justify sending detainees to these countries, the Bush administration appears to have relied on a very fine reading of an imprecise clause in the *Convention Against Torture* (which the U.S. ratified in 1994), requiring "substantial grounds for believing" that a detainee will be tortured abroad.[5] Martin Lederman, a lawyer who left the Justice Department's Office of Legal Counsel in 2002, after eight years, said, "The Convention only applies when you know a suspect is more likely than not to be tortured, but what if you kind of know? That's not enough. So there are ways to get around it."

Rendition was just one element of the Bush administration's New Paradigm. The CIA itself held dozens of "high-value" terrorist suspects outside of the territorial jurisdiction of the United States, in addition to the estimated 750 detainees in Guantánamo Bay, Cuba. The administration confirmed the identities of at least ten of these suspects to the 9/11 Commission—including Khalid Sheikh Mohammed, a top al-Qaeda operative, and Ramzi bin al-Shibh, a chief planner of the September 11 attacks—but refused to allow commission members to interview the men, and would not say where they were being held. Reports have suggested that CIA prisons were being operated in Thailand, Qatar, and Afghanistan, among other countries.

At the request of the CIA, Secretary of Defense Donald Rumsfeld personally ordered that a prisoner in Iraq be hidden from Red Cross officials for several months,[6] and Army General Paul Kern told Congress that the CIA may have hidden up to a hundred detainees.[7] The *Geneva Conventions of 1949*, which established norms on the treatment of soldiers and civilians captured in war, require the prompt registration of detainees so that their treatment can be monitored.[8] However, the Bush administration argued that al-Qaeda members and supporters, who were not part of a state-sponsored military, are not covered by the Conventions.[9]

The Bush administration's departure from international norms has been justified in intellectual terms by elite lawyers like Gonzales, a graduate of Harvard Law School. Gonzales, who served as Attorney General from 2005 to 2007, argued during his confirmation proceedings that the *Convention Against Torture's* ban on "cruel, inhuman, and degrading treatment" of terrorist suspects did not apply to American interrogations of foreigners overseas.[10] Perhaps surprisingly, the fiercest internal resistance to this thinking came from people who have been directly involved in interrogation, including veteran FBI and CIA agents.

Their concerns are as much practical as ideological. Years of experience in interrogation have led them to doubt the effectiveness of physical coercion as a means of extracting reliable information. They also warn that the Bush administration, having taken so many prisoners outside the realm of the law, may not be able to bring them back in. By holding detainees indefinitely, without counsel, without charges of wrongdoing, and under circumstances that could, in legal parlance, "shock the conscience" of a court, the administration jeopardized its chances of convicting hundreds of suspected terrorists, or even of using them as witnesses in almost any court in the world.

"It's a big problem," Jamie Gorelick, a former deputy attorney general and a member of the 9/11 Commission, said. "In criminal justice, you either prosecute the suspects or let them go. But if you've treated them in ways that won't *allow* you to prosecute them you're in this no man's land. What do you do with these people?"

The criminal prosecution of terrorist suspects was not a priority for the Bush administration, which focused, rather, on preventing additional attacks. But some people who have been fighting terrorism for many years are concerned about unintended consequences of the radical legal measures employed. Among these critics is Michael Scheuer, a former CIA counter-terrorism expert who helped establish the practice of rendition. Scheuer left the agency in 2004, and has written two acerbic critiques of the government's fight against Islamic terrorism under the pseudonym Anonymous, the most recent of which, *Imperial Hubris*,[11] was a bestseller.

Not long ago, Scheuer, who lives in northern Virginia, spoke openly for the first time about how he and several other top CIA officials set up the program in the mid-nineties. "It was begun in desperation," he told me. At the time, he was the head of the CIA's Islamic-militant unit, whose job was to "detect, disrupt, and dismantle" terrorist operations. His unit spent much of 1996 studying how al-Qaeda operated; by the next year, Scheuer said, its mission was to try to capture Osama bin Laden and his associates. He recalled, "We went to the White House"—which was then occupied by the Clinton administration—"and they said, 'Do it.'" He added that

Richard Clarke, who was in charge of counter-terrorism for the National Security Council, offered no advice. "He told me, 'Figure it out by yourselves,'" Scheuer said. (Clarke did not respond to a request for comment.)

Scheuer sought the counsel of Mary Jo White, the former U.S. Attorney for the Southern District of New York, who, along with a small group of FBI agents, was pursuing the 1993 World Trade Center bombing case. In 1998, White's team obtained an indictment against bin Laden, authorizing U.S. agents to bring him and his associates to the United States to stand trial. From the start, though, the CIA was wary of granting terrorism suspects the due process afforded by American law. The agency did not want to divulge secrets about its intelligence sources and methods, and American courts demand transparency. Even establishing the chain of custody of key evidence—such as a laptop computer—could easily pose a significant problem: foreign governments might refuse to testify in U.S. courts about how they had obtained the evidence, for fear of having their secret cooperation exposed. (Foreign governments often worried about retaliation from their own Muslim populations.)

The CIA also felt that other agencies sometimes stood in its way. In 1996, for example, the State Department stymied a joint effort by the CIA and the FBI to question one of bin Laden's cousins in America because he had a diplomatic passport, which protects the holder from U.S. law enforcement. Describing the CIA's frustration, Scheuer said, "We were turning into voyeurs. We knew where these people were, but we couldn't capture them because we had nowhere to take them." The agency realized that "we had to come up with a third party."

The obvious choice, Scheuer said, was Egypt. The largest recipient of U.S. foreign aid after Israel, Egypt was a key strategic ally, and its secret police force, the Mukhabarat, had a reputation for brutality. Egypt had been cited frequently by the State Department for torture of prisoners. According to a 2002 report:

> [Detainees were] stripped and blindfolded; suspended from a ceiling or doorframe with feet just touching the floor; beaten with fists, metal rods, or other objects; doused with hot or cold water; flogged on the back; burned with cigarettes; and subjected to electrical shocks. Some victims . . . [were] forced to strip and threatened with rape.[12]

Hosni Mubarak, Egypt's leader, who came to office in 1981 after President Anwar Sadat was assassinated by Islamist extremists, was determined to crack down on terrorism. His prime political enemies were radical Islamists, hundreds of whom had fled the country and joined al-Qaeda. Among these was Ayman al-Zawahiri, a physician from Cairo, who went to Afghanistan and eventually became bin Laden's deputy.

In 1995, Scheuer said, American agents proposed the rendition program to Egypt, making clear that it had the resources to track, capture, and transport terrorist suspects globally—including access to a small fleet of aircraft. Egypt embraced the idea. "What was clever was that some of the senior people in al-Qaeda were Egyptian," Scheuer said. "It served American purposes to get these people arrested, and Egyptian purposes to get these people back, where they could be interrogated." Technically, U.S. law requires the CIA to seek "assurances" from foreign governments that rendered suspects will not be tortured.[13] Scheuer told me that this was done, but he was "not sure" if any documents confirming the arrangement were signed.

A series of spectacular covert operations followed from this secret pact. On September 13, 1995, U.S. agents helped kidnap Talaat Fouad Qassem, one of Egypt's most wanted terrorists, in Croatia. Qassem had fled to Europe after being linked by Egypt to the assassination of Sadat; he had been sentenced to death in absentia. Croatian police seized Qassem in Zagreb and handed him over to U.S. agents, who interrogated him aboard a ship cruising the Adriatic Sea and then took him back to Egypt. Once there, Qassem disappeared. There is no record that he was put on trial. Hossam el-Hamalawy, an Egyptian journalist who covers human rights issues, said, "We believe he was executed."

A more elaborate operation was staged in Tirana, Albania, in the summer of 1998. According to the *Wall Street Journal*, the CIA provided the Albanian intelligence service with equipment to wiretap the phones of suspected Muslim militants. Tapes of the conversations were translated into English, and U.S. agents discovered that they contained lengthy discussions with Zawahiri, bin Laden's deputy. The U.S. pressured Egypt for assistance; in June, Egypt issued an arrest warrant for Shawki Salama Attiya, one of the militants.[14]

Over the next few months, according to the article, Albanian security forces, working with U.S. agents, killed one suspect and captured Attiya and four others. These men were bound, blindfolded, and taken to an abandoned airbase, then flown by jet to Cairo for interrogation. Attiya later alleged that he suffered electrical shocks to his genitals, was hung from his limbs, and was kept in a cell in filthy water up to his knees. Two other suspects, who had been sentenced to death in absentia, were hanged.[15]

On August 5, 1998, an Arab-language newspaper in London published a letter from the International Islamic Front for Jihad, in which it threatened retaliation against the United States for the Albanian operation—in a "language they will understand." Two days later, the U.S. Embassies in Kenya and Tanzania were blown up, killing 224 people.

Eventually, the United States began rendering terror suspects to other countries, though Egypt remained the most common destination. The partnership between the American and the Egyptian intelligence services was extraordinarily close: the Americans could give the Egyptian interrogators questions they wanted put to the detainees in the morning, Scheuer said, and get answers by the evening. The Americans asked to question suspects directly themselves, but, Scheuer said, the Egyptians refused. "We were never in the same room at the same time."

Scheuer claimed that "there was a legal process," undergirding these early renditions. Every suspect who was apprehended, he said, had been convicted in absentia. Before a suspect was captured, a dossier was prepared containing the equivalent of a rap sheet. The CIA's legal counsel signed off on every proposed operation. Scheuer said that this system prevented innocent people from being subjected to rendition. "Langley would never let us proceed unless there was substance," he said.

Moreover, Scheuer emphasized, renditions were pursued out of expedience—"not out of thinking it was the best policy."

Since September 11, as the number of renditions has grown, and hundreds of terrorist suspects have been deposited indefinitely in places like Guantánamo Bay, the shortcomings of this approach have become manifest. "Are we going to hold these people forever?" Scheuer asked. "The policymakers hadn't thought what to do with them, and what would happen when it was found out that we were turning them over to governments that the human-rights world reviled." Once a detainee's rights have been violated, he says, "you absolutely can't" reinstate him into the court system. "You can't kill him, either," he added. "All we've done is create a nightmare."

On a bleak winter day in Trenton, New Jersey, Dan Coleman, an ex-FBI agent who had retired in 2004 because of asthma, scoffed at the idea that a CIA agent was now having compunctions about renditions. The CIA, Coleman said, liked rendition from the start. "They loved that these guys would just disappear off the books, and never be heard of again," he said. "They were proud of it."

For ten years, Coleman worked closely with the CIA on counter-terrorism cases, including the Embassy attacks in Kenya and Tanzania. His methodical style of detective work, in which interrogations were aimed at forging relationships with detainees, became unfashionable after September 11, in part because the government was intent on extracting information as quickly as possible, in order to prevent future attacks. Yet the more patient approach used by Coleman and other agents had yielded major successes.

In the Embassy-bombings case, they helped convict four al-Qaeda operatives on 302 criminal counts; all four men pleaded guilty to serious terrorism charges. The confessions the FBI agents elicited, and the trial itself, which ended in May 2001, created an invaluable public record about al-Qaeda, including details about its funding mechanisms, its internal structure, and its intention to obtain weapons of mass destruction. (The political leadership in Washington, unfortunately, did not pay sufficient attention.)

Coleman is a political nonpartisan with a law-and-order mentality. His eldest son is a former Army Ranger who served in Afghanistan. Yet Coleman was troubled by the Bush administration's New Paradigm. Torture, he said, "has become bureaucratized." Bad as the policy of rendition was before September 11, Coleman said, "afterward, it really went out of control." He explained, "Now, instead of just sending people to third countries, we're holding them ourselves. We're taking people, and keeping them in our own custody in third countries. That's an enormous problem." Egypt, he pointed out, at least had an established legal system, however harsh. "There was a process there," Coleman said. "But what's our process? We have no method over there other than our laws—and we've decided to ignore them. What are we now, the Huns? If you don't talk to us, we'll kill you?"

From the beginning of the rendition program, Coleman said, there was no doubt that Egypt engaged in torture. He recalled the case of a suspect in the first World Trade Center bombing who fled to Egypt. The United States requested his return, and the Egyptians handed him over—wrapped head to toe in duct tape, like a mummy. In another incident, an Egyptian with links to al-Qaeda who had cooperated with the U.S. government in a terrorism trial was picked up in Cairo and imprisoned by Egyptian authorities until U.S. diplomats secured his release. For days, he had been chained to a toilet, where guards had urinated on him.

Under such circumstances, it might seem difficult for the U.S. government to legally justify dispatching suspects to Egypt. But Coleman said that since September 11, the CIA "has seemed to think it's operating under different rules, that it has extralegal abilities outside the U.S." Agents, he said, have "told me that they have their own enormous office of general counsel that rarely tells them no. Whatever they do is all right. It all takes place overseas."

Coleman was angry that lawyers in Washington were redefining the parameters of counter-terrorism interrogations. "Have any of these guys ever tried to talk to someone who's been deprived of his clothes?" he asked. "He's going to be ashamed, and humiliated, and cold. He'll tell you anything you want to hear to get his clothes back. There's no value in it." Coleman said that he had learned to treat even the most despicable suspects as if there were "a personal relationship, even if you can't stand them." He said that many of the suspects he had interrogated expected to be tortured, and were stunned to learn that they had rights under the American system.

Due process made detainees more compliant, not less, Coleman said. He had also found that a defendant's right to legal counsel was beneficial not only to suspects but also to law enforcement officers. Defense lawyers frequently persuaded detainees to cooperate with prosecutors, in exchange for plea agreements. "The lawyers show these guys there's a way out," Coleman said. "It's human nature. People don't cooperate with you unless they have some reason to." He added, "Brutalization doesn't work. We know that. Besides, you lose your soul."

The Bush administration's redefinition of the standards of interrogation took place almost entirely out of public view. One of the first officials to offer hints of the shift in approach was Cofer Black, who was then in charge of counter-terrorism at the CIA. On September 26, 2002, he addressed the House and Senate Intelligence Committees, and stated that the arrest and detention of terrorists was "a highly classified area." He added, "All I want to say is that there was 'before' 9/11 and 'after' 9/11. After 9/11, the gloves come off."[16]

Laying the foundation for this shift was a now famous set of internal legal memos—some were leaked, others were made public by groups such as the NYU Center for Law and National Security. Most of these documents were generated by a small, hawkish group of politically appointed lawyers in the Justice Department's Office of Legal Counsel and in the office of Alberto Gonzales, the White House counsel. Chief among the authors was John C. Yoo, the deputy assistant attorney general at the time. (A Yale Law School graduate and a former clerk to Justice Clarence Thomas, Yoo now teaches law at the University of California at Berkeley.)

Taken together, the memos advised the president that he had almost unfettered latitude in his prosecution of the war on terror. Soon after September 11, Yoo and other administration lawyers began advising President Bush that he did not have to comply with the *Geneva Conventions* in handling detainees in the war on terror. The lawyers classified these detainees not as civilians or prisoners of war—two categories of individuals protected by the Conventions—but as "illegal enemy combatants." The rubric included not only al-Qaeda members and supporters but the entire Taliban, because, Yoo and other lawyers argued, the country was a "failed state." Eric Lewis, an expert in international law who represents several Guantánamo detainees, said, "The Administration's lawyers created a third category and cast them outside the law."

The State Department, determined to uphold the *Geneva Conventions*, fought against Bush's lawyers and lost. In a 40-page memo to Yoo, dated January 11, 2002 (which was eventually released to the public), William Taft IV, the State Department legal adviser, argued that Yoo's analysis was "seriously flawed." Taft told Yoo that his contention that the president could disregard the *Geneva Conventions* was "untenable," "incorrect," and "confused." Taft disputed Yoo's argument that Afghanistan, as a "failed state," was not covered by the Conventions. "The official U.S. position before, during and after the emergence of the Taliban, was that Afghanistan constituted a state," he wrote.[17]

Taft also warned Yoo that if the United States took the war on terrorism outside the *Geneva Conventions*, not only could U.S. soldiers be denied the protections of the Conventions—and therefore be prosecuted for crimes, including murder—but President Bush could be accused of a "grave breach" by other countries, and be prosecuted for war crimes.[18] Taft sent a copy of his memo to Gonzales, hoping that his dissent would reach the president. Within days, Yoo sent Taft a lengthy rebuttal, which remains classified as of this writing.

Others in the administration worried that the president's lawyers were wayward. "Lawyers have to be the voice of reason and sometimes have to put the brakes on, no matter how much the client wants to hear something else," the former State Department lawyer said. "Our job is to keep the train on the tracks. It's not to tell the President, 'Here are the ways to avoid the law.'" He went on, "There is no such thing as a non-covered person under the *Geneva Conventions*. It's nonsense. The protocols cover fighters in everything from world wars to local rebellions."

The lawyer said that Taft urged Yoo and Gonzales to warn President Bush that he would "be seen as a war criminal by the rest of the world," but Taft was ignored. This may be because President Bush had already made up his mind. According to top State Department officials, Bush decided to suspend the *Geneva Conventions* on January 8, 2002, three days before Taft sent his memo to Yoo.

The legal pronouncements from Washington about the status of detainees were painstakingly constructed to include numerous loopholes. For example, in February 2002, President Bush issued a written directive stating that, even though he had determined that the *Geneva Conventions* did not apply to the war on terror, all detainees should be treated "humanely."[19] A close reading of the directive, however, revealed that it referred only to military interrogators—not to CIA officials. This exemption allowed the CIA to continue using interrogation methods, including rendition that stopped just short of torture.

Further, an August 2002 memo written largely by Yoo but signed by Assistant Attorney General Jay S. Bybee argued that torture required the intent to inflict suffering "equivalent in intensity to the pain accompanying serious physical injury, such as organ failure, impairment of bodily function, or even death."[20] In April 2009, the Justice Department released a series of memos in which Bush administration lawyers authorized the CIA to use novel interrogation methods—including "waterboarding," where a suspect is bound and immersed in water until he nearly drowns.[21] Dr. Allen Keller, the director of the Bellevue/NYU Program for Survivors of Torture, told me that he had treated a number of people who had been subjected to such forms of near-asphyxiation, and he argued that it was indeed torture. Some victims were still traumatized years later, he said. One patient couldn't take showers, and panicked when it rained. "The fear of being killed is a terrifying experience," he said.

The administration's justification of the rough treatment of detainees appears to have passed down the chain of command. In late 2003, at Abu Ghraib prison, in Iraq, photographs were taken that documented prisoners being subjected to grotesque abuse by U.S. soldiers. After the scandal became public, the Justice Department revised the narrow definition of torture outlined in the Bybee memo, using language that more strongly prohibited physical abuse during interrogations. But the Bush administration fought hard against legislative efforts to rein in the CIA.

Republican leaders, at the White House's urging, have blocked two attempts in the Senate to ban the CIA from using cruel and inhuman interrogation methods. An attempt in the House to outlaw extraordinary rendition, led by Representative Markey, also failed.[22] Two days after he was inaugurated, President Obama signed an executive order outlawing torture,[23] and has since confirmed his resolution that "America does not torture."[24]

In a 2005 phone interview, Yoo was soft-spoken and resolute:

Why is it so hard for people to understand that there is a category of behavior not covered by the legal system? . . . What were pirates? They weren't fighting on behalf of any nation. What were slave traders? Historically, there were people so bad that they were not given protection of the laws. There were no specific provisions for their trial, or imprisonment. If you were an illegal combatant, you didn't deserve the protection of the laws of war.

Yoo also cited precedents for his position. "The Lincoln assassins were treated this way, too," he said. "They were tried in a military court, and executed." The point, he said, was that the *Geneva Conventions'* "simple binary classification of civilian or soldier isn't accurate."

Yoo also argued that the U.S. Constitution granted the president plenary powers to override the *Convention Against Torture* when acting in the nation's defense—a position that has drawn dissent from many scholars. As Yoo saw it, Congress doesn't have the power to "tie the President's hands in regard to torture as an interrogation technique." He continued, "It's the core of the Commander-in-Chief function. They can't prevent the President from ordering torture." If the president were to abuse his powers as Commander-in-Chief, Yoo said, the constitutional remedy was impeachment. He went on to suggest that President Bush's victory in the 2004 election, along with the relatively mild challenge to Gonzales mounted by the Democrats in Congress, was "proof that the debate is over." He said, "The issue is dying out. The public has had its referendum."

A few months after September 11, the U.S. gained custody of its first high-ranking al-Qaeda figure, Ibn al-Sheikh al-Libi. He had run bin Laden's terrorist training camp in Khalden, Afghanistan, and was detained in Pakistan. Zacarias Moussaoui, who was already in U.S. custody, and Richard Reid, the Shoe Bomber, had both spent time at the Khalden camp. At the FBI's field office in New York, Jack Cloonan, an officer who had worked for the agency since 1972, struggled to maintain control of the legal process in Afghanistan. CIA and FBI agents were vying to take possession of Libi. Cloonan, who worked with Dan Coleman on anti-terrorism cases for many years, said he felt that "neither the Moussaoui case nor the Reid case was a slam dunk."

He became intent on securing Libi's testimony as a witness against them. He advised his FBI colleagues in Afghanistan to question Libi respectfully, "and handle this like it was being done right here, in my office in New York." He recalled:

> I remember talking on a secure line to them. I told them, "Do yourself a favor, read the guy his rights. It may be old-fashioned, but this will come out if we don't. It may take ten years, but it will hurt you, and the bureau's reputation, if you don't. Have it stand as a shining example of what we feel is right."

Cloonan's FBI colleagues advised Libi of his rights and took turns with CIA agents in questioning him. After a few days, FBI officials felt that they were developing a good rapport with him. The CIA agents, however, felt that he was lying to them, and needed tougher interrogation.

To Cloonan's dismay, the CIA reportedly rendered Libi to Egypt. He was seen boarding a plane in Afghanistan, restrained by handcuffs and ankle cuffs, his mouth covered by duct tape. Cloonan, who retired from the FBI in 2002, said, "At least we got information in ways that wouldn't shock the conscience of the court. And no one will have to seek revenge for what I did." He added, "We need to show the world that we can lead, and not just by military might."

After Libi was taken to Egypt, the FBI lost track of him. Yet he evidently played a crucial background role in Secretary of State Colin Powell's momentous address to the United Nations Security Council in February 2003, which argued the case for a preemptive war against Iraq. In his speech, Powell did not refer to Libi by name, but he announced to the world that "a senior terrorist operative" who "was responsible for one of Al Qaeda's training camps in Afghanistan" had told U.S. authorities that Saddam Hussein had offered to train two al-Qaeda operatives in the use of "chemical or biological weapons."[25]

However, *Newsweek* later reported that Libi, who was eventually transferred from Egypt to Guantánamo Bay, was the source of the incendiary charge cited by Powell, and that he had recanted.[26] By then, the first anniversary of the U.S. invasion of Iraq had passed and the 9/11 Commission had declared that there was no credible evidence of a working relationship between Saddam and al-Qaeda.[27] Dan Coleman was disgusted when he heard about Libi's false confession:

> It was ridiculous for interrogators to think Libi would have known anything about Iraq. I could have told them that. He ran a training camp. He wouldn't have had anything to do with Iraq. Administration officials were always pushing us to come up with links, but there weren't any. The reason they got bad information is that they beat it out of him. You never get good information from someone that way.

Most authorities on interrogation, in and out of government, agree that torture and lesser forms of physical coercion succeed in producing confessions. The problem is that these confessions are not necessarily true. Three of the Guantánamo detainees released by the United States to Great Britain, for example, had confessed that they had appeared in a blurry video obtained by American investigators that documented a group of acolytes meeting with bin Laden in Afghanistan. As reported in the London *Observer*, British intelligence officials arrived at Guantánamo with evidence that the accused men had been living in England at the time the video was made. The detainees told British authorities that they had been coerced into making false confessions.[28]

Craig Murray, the former British Ambassador to Uzbekistan, told me that "the U.S. accepts quite a lot of intelligence from the Uzbeks," that has been extracted from suspects who have been tortured. This information was, he said, "largely rubbish." He said he knew of "at least three" instances where the United States had rendered suspected militants from Afghanistan to Uzbekistan. Although Murray does not know the fate of the three men, he said, "They almost certainly would have been tortured." In Uzbekistan, he said, "partial boiling of a hand or an arm is quite common." He also knew of two cases in which prisoners had been boiled to death.

In 2002, Murray, concerned that America was complicit with such a regime, asked his deputy to discuss the problem with the CIA's station chief in Tashkent. He said that the station chief did not dispute that intelligence was being obtained under torture. But the CIA did not consider this a problem. "There was no reason to think they were perturbed," Murray told me.

Scientific research on the efficacy of torture and rough interrogation is limited, because of the moral and legal impediments to experimentation. Tom Parker, a former officer for M.I.5, the British intelligence agency, who teaches at Yale, argued that, whether or not forceful interrogations yield accurate information from terrorist suspects, a larger problem is that many detainees "have nothing to tell." For many years, he said, British authorities subjected members of the Irish Republican Army to forceful interrogations, but, in the end, the government concluded that "detainees aren't valuable." A more effective strategy, Parker said, was "being creative" about human intelligence gathering, such as infiltration and eavesdropping. "The U.S. is doing what the British did in the nineteen-seventies, detaining people and violating their civil liberties," he said. "It did nothing but exacerbate the situation. Most of those interned went back to terrorism. You'll end up radicalizing the entire population."

Although the Bush administration tried to keep the details of extraordinary renditions secret, several accounts have surfaced that reveal how the program operates. On December 18, 2001, at Stockholm's Bromma Airport, a half-dozen hooded security officials ushered two Egyptian asylum seekers, Muhammad Zery and Ahmed Agiza, into an empty office. They cut off the Egyptians' clothes with scissors, forcibly administered sedatives by suppository, swaddled them in diapers, and dressed them in orange jumpsuits. As was reported by "Kalla Fakta," a Swedish television news program, the suspects were blindfolded, placed in handcuffs and leg irons; according to a declassified Swedish government report, the men were then flown to Cairo on a U.S.-registered Gulfstream V jet.[29]

Swedish officials have claimed they received assurances from the Egyptians that Zery and Agiza would be treated humanely. But both suspects have said, through lawyers and family members, that they were tortured with electrical charges to their genitals. (Zery said that he was also forced to lie on an electrified bed frame.) After spending two years in an Egyptian prison, Zery was released. Agiza, a physician who had once been an ally of Zawahiri but later renounced him and terrorism, was convicted on terrorism charges by Egypt's Supreme Military Court. He was sentenced to 25 years in prison.

Another case suggests that the Bush administration authorized the rendition of suspects for whom it has little evidence of guilt. Mamdouh Habib, an Egyptian-born citizen of Australia, was apprehended in Pakistan in October 2001. According to his wife, Habib, a radical Muslim with four children, was visiting the country to tour religious schools and determine whether his family should move to Pakistan. A spokesman at the Pentagon claimed that Habib—who expressed support for Islamist causes—spent most of his trip in Afghanistan, and was "either supporting hostile forces or on the battlefield fighting illegally against the U.S." In January 2005, after a three-year ordeal, Habib was released without charges.

Habib is one of a handful of people subjected to rendition who are being represented pro bono by human rights lawyers. According to a document released in 2005 and prepared by Joseph Margulies,[30] a lawyer affiliated with the MacArthur Justice Center at the University of Chicago Law School, Habib said that he was first interrogated in Pakistan for three weeks, in part at a facility in Islamabad, where he said he was brutalized. Some of his interrogators, he claimed, spoke English with American accents. (Having lived in Australia for years, Habib is comfortable in English.) He was then placed in the custody of Americans, two of whom wore black short-sleeved shirts and had distinctive tattoos: one depicted an American flag attached to a flagpole shaped like a finger, the other a large cross. The Americans took him to an airfield, cut his clothes off with scissors, dressed him in a jumpsuit, covered his eyes with opaque goggles, and placed him aboard a private plane. He was flown to Egypt.[31]

According to Margulies, Habib was held and interrogated for six months. "Never, to my knowledge, did he make an appearance in any court," Margulies told me. Margulies was also unaware of any evidence suggesting that the United States sought a promise from Egypt that Habib would not be tortured. For his part, Habib claimed to have been subjected to horrific conditions. He said that he was beaten frequently with blunt instruments, including an object that he likened to an electric "cattle prod." And he was told that if he didn't confess to belonging to al-Qaeda, he would be anally raped by specially trained dogs. (Hossam el-Hamalawy said that Egyptian security forces train German shepherds for police work, and that other prisoners have also been threatened with rape by trained dogs, although he knows of no one who has been assaulted in this way.)

Habib said that he was shackled and forced to stand in three torture chambers: one room was filled with water up to his chin, requiring him to stand on tiptoe for hours; another chamber, filled with water up to his knees, had a ceiling so low that he was forced into a prolonged, painful stoop; in the third, he stood in water up to his ankles, and within sight of an electric switch and a generator, which his jailers said would be used to electrocute him if he didn't confess. Habib's lawyer said that he submitted to his interrogators' demands and made multiple confessions, all of them false. (Egyptian authorities have described such allegations of torture as "mythology.")

After his imprisonment in Egypt, Habib said that he was returned to U.S. custody and was flown to Bagram Air Force Base, in Afghanistan, and then on to Guantánamo Bay, where he was detained until he was released in 2005. On January 11, a few days after the *Washington Post* published an article on Habib's case, the Pentagon, offering virtually no explanation, agreed to release him into the custody of the Australian government. "Habib was released because he was hopelessly embarrassing," Eric Freedman, a professor at Hofstra Law School, who has been involved in the detainees' legal defense, says. "It's a large crack in the wall in a house of cards that is midway through tumbling down." In a prepared statement, Lt. Cdr. Flex Plexico, a Pentagon spokesman, said there was "no evidence" that Habib "was tortured or abused" while he was in U.S. custody. He also said that Habib had received "Al Qaeda training," which included instruction in making false abuse allegations. Habib's claims, he suggested, "fit the standard operating procedure."

The U.S. government has not responded directly to Habib's charge that he was rendered to Egypt. However, several other men who were released from Guantánamo reported that Habib told them about it. Jamal al-Harith, a British detainee who was sent home to Manchester, England, last March, told me in a phone interview that at one point he had been placed in a cage across from Habib. "He said that he had been in Egypt for about six months, and they had injected him with drugs, and hung him from the ceiling, and beaten him very, very badly," Harith recalled. "He seemed to be in pain. He was haggard-looking. I never saw him walk. He always had to be held up."

Another piece of evidence that may support Habib's story is a set of flight logs documenting the travels of a white Gulfstream V jet—the plane that seems to have been used for renditions by the U.S. government. These logs show that on April 9, 2002, the jet left Dulles Airport, in Washington, and landed in Cairo. According to Habib's attorney, this was around the same time that Habib said he was released by the Egyptians in Cairo, and returned to U.S. custody. The flight logs were obtained by Stephen Grey, a British journalist who has written a number of stories on renditions for British publications, including the London *Sunday Times.* Grey's logs are incomplete, but they chronicle some 300 flights over three years by the 14-seat jet, which was marked on its tail with the code N379P. (It was later changed, to N8068V.) All the flights originated from Dulles Airport, and many of them landed at restricted U.S. military bases.[32]

Even if Habib is a terrorist aligned with al-Qaeda, as Pentagon officials have claimed, it seems unlikely that prosecutors would ever be able to build a strong case against him, given the treatment that he allegedly received in Egypt. John Radsan, a law professor at William Mitchell College of Law, in St. Paul, Minnesota, who worked in the general counsel's office of the CIA until last year, said, "I don't think anyone's thought through what we do with these people."

Similar problems complicated the case of Khalid Sheikh Mohammed, who was captured in Pakistan in March 2003. Mohammed was "waterboarded" multiple times during interrogations. Thus, Radsan said:

It would be almost impossible to take him into a criminal trial. Any evidence derived from his interrogation could be seen as fruit from the poisonous tree. I think the government is considering some sort of military tribunal somewhere down the line. But, even there, there are still constitutional requirements that you can't bring in involuntary confessions.

The trial of Zacarias Moussaoui, in Alexandria, Virginia—the only U.S. criminal trial of a suspect linked to the September 11 attacks—was stalled for months. The case was held up by Moussaoui's demand—and the Bush administration's refusal—to let him call as witnesses al-Qaeda members held in government custody, including Ramzi bin al-Shibh and Khalid Sheikh Mohammed. (Bin al-Shibh is thought to have been tortured.) Government attorneys argued that producing the witnesses would disrupt the interrogation process.[33] Eventually, in 2006, more than four years after Attorney General John Ashcroft called Moussaoui's indictment "a chronicle of evil,"[34] he was convicted and sentenced to life in prison without parole.[35]

In fact, the Bush Justice Department admitted that it had something to hide in relation to Maher Arar, the Canadian engineer. The government invoked the rarely used "state secrets privilege" in a motion to dismiss a lawsuit brought by Arar's lawyers against the U.S. government. To go forward in an open court, the government said, would jeopardize the "intelligence, foreign policy and national security interests of the United States."[36] Barbara Olshansky, who was the assistant legal director of the

Center for Constitutional Rights, which is representing Arar, stated that government lawyers "are saying this case can't be tried, and the classified information on which they're basing this argument can't even be shared with the opposing lawyers. It's the height of arrogance—they think they can do anything they want in the name of the global war on terrorism."

Nadja Dizdarevic is a 30-year-old mother of four who lives in Sarajevo. On October 21, 2001, her husband, Hadj Boudella, a Muslim of Algerian descent, and five other Algerians living in Bosnia were arrested after U.S. authorities tipped off the Bosnian government to an alleged plot by the group to blow up the American and British Embassies in Sarajevo. One of the suspects reportedly placed some 70 phone calls to the al-Qaeda leader Abu Zubaydah in the days after September 11. Boudella and his wife, however, maintain that neither he nor several of the other defendants knew the man who had allegedly contacted Zubaydah. And an investigation by the Bosnian government turned up no confirmation that the calls to Zubaydah were made at all, according to the men's American lawyers, Rob Kirsch and Stephen Oleskey.

At the request of the United States, the Bosnian government held all six men for three months, but was unable to substantiate any criminal charges against them. On January 17, 2002, the Bosnian Supreme Court ruled that they should be released. Instead, as the men left prison, they were handcuffed, forced to put on surgical masks with nose clips, covered in hoods, and herded into waiting unmarked cars by masked figures, some of whom appeared to be members of the Bosnian special forces. Boudella's wife had come to the prison to meet her husband, and she recalled that she recognized him, despite the hood, because he was wearing a new suit that she had brought him the day before.

"I will never forget that night," she said. "It was snowing. I was screaming for someone to help." A crowd gathered, and tried to block the convoy, but it sped off. The suspects were taken to a military airbase and kept in a freezing hangar for hours; one member of the group later claimed that he saw one of the abductors remove his Bosnian uniform, revealing that he was in fact American. The U.S. government has neither confirmed nor denied its role in the operation.

Six days after the abduction, Boudella's wife received word that her husband and the other men had been sent to Guantánamo. One man in the group has alleged that two of his fingers were broken by U.S. soldiers.

Boudella's wife said that she was astounded that her husband could be seized without charge or trial, at home during peacetime and after his own government had exonerated him. The term "enemy combatant" perplexed her. "He is an enemy of whom?" she asked. "In combat where?" She said that her view of America had changed. "I have not changed my opinion about its people, but unfortunately I have changed my opinion about its respect for human rights," she said. "It is no longer the leader in the world. It has become the leader in the violation of human rights."

In October, Boudella attempted to plead his innocence before the Pentagon's Combatant Status Review Tribunal. The CSRT is the Pentagon's answer to the Supreme Court's ruling in 2004, over the Bush administration's objections, that detainees in Guantánamo had a right to challenge their imprisonment. Boudella was not allowed to bring a lawyer to the proceeding. And the tribunal said that it was "unable to locate" a copy of the Bosnian Supreme Court's verdict freeing him, which he had requested that it read. Transcripts show that Boudella stated, "I am against any terrorist acts," and asked, "How could I be part of an organization that I strongly believe has harmed my people?" The tribunal rejected his plea, as it has rejected 387 of the 399 pleas it has heard.

Upon learning this, Boudella's wife sent the following letter to her husband's American lawyers:

> Dear Friends, I am so shocked by this information that it seems as if my blood froze in my veins, I can't breathe and I wish I was dead. I can't believe these things can happen, that they can come and take your husband away, overnight and without reason, destroy your family, ruin your dreams after three years of fight. . . . Please, tell me, what can I still do for him? . . . Is this decision final, what are the legal remedies? Help me to understand because, as far as I know the law, this is insane, contrary to all possible laws and human rights. Please help me, I don't want to lose him.

Despite efforts by the Bush administration to preserve a right to hold detainees in custody indefinitely, a recent U.S. Supreme Court decision finally guaranteed all prisoners a right to *habeas corpus*. Thus, in *Boumediene v. Bush*, even detainees designated as enemy combatants and held overseas have the right to know the charges against them and receive a meaningful opportunity to be heard.[37] How the court's opinion will be translated into action is a work still in progress.

John Radsan, the former CIA lawyer, offered a reply of sorts. "As a society, we haven't figured out what the rough rules are yet," he said. "There are hardly any rules for illegal enemy combatants. It's the law of the jungle. And right now we happen to be the strongest animal."

NOTES

This chapter first appeared in the February 14, 2005, issue of the *New Yorker*. Reprinted with permission from the author.

1. See Elisabeth Bumiller, David E. Sanger, and Richard W. Stevenson, "Bush Says Iraqi Leaders Will Want U.S. Forces to Stay to Help," *New York Times*, Jan. 28, 2005, http://www.nytimes.com/2005/01/28/politics/28prexy.html?_r=1&pagewanted=all&position= (last visited Aug. 13, 2009).

2. U.S. Congress, *Foreign Affairs Reform and Restructuring Act of 1998*, H.R. 1757, 105th Cong. 2nd sess., 1998, §1242(a), p. 65.

3. Alberto Gonzales, memo to President Bush regarding "Application of Geneva Convention on Prisoners of War to the Conflict with Al Qaeda and the Taliban," Jan. 25, 2002, 2, http://www.gwu.edu/~nsarchiv/NSAEBB/NSAEBB127/02.01.25.pdf (last visited Aug. 13, 2009).

4. See "Meet the Press" transcript for March 30, 2008, 1, http://www.msnbc.msn.com/id/23866794/page/4/ (last visited Aug. 13, 2009).

5. United Nations (UN), *Convention Against Torture and Other Cruel, Inhuman or Degrading Treatment or Punishment*, A/RES/39/46, Dec. 10, 1984, Part I, art. 3.

6. Eric Schmitt and Thom Shanker, "Rumsfeld Issued an Order to Hide Detainee in Iraq," *New York Times*, June 17, 2004, http://www.nytimes.com/2004/06/17/politics/17abuse.html?pagewanted=2 (last visited Aug. 13, 2009).

7. Dana Priest, "Memo Lets CIA Take Detainees Out of Iraq," *Washington Post*, Oct. 24, 2004, http://www.washingtonpost.com/wp-dyn/articles/A57363-2004Oct23.html (last visited Aug. 13, 2009).

8. Intl. Committee of the Red Cross, *Geneva Conventions of 1949*, Aug. 12, 1949; see *Convention III*, art. 17.

9. Nonetheless, the U.S. Supreme Court held that the *Geneva Conventions*, including the writ of *habeas corpus*, apply to all prisoners. *Boumediene v. Bush* 28 S.Ct. 2229 (2008).

10. See the transcript for the U.S. Senate Judiciary Committee hearing on the nomination of Alberto Gonzales to be U.S. Attorney General, Jan. 6, 2005, http://www.washingtonpost.com/wp-dyn/articles/A53883-2005Jan6_5.html (last visited Aug. 13, 2009).

11. See Michael Scheuer, *Imperial Hubris: Why the West Is Losing the War on Terror* (Dulles, VA: Brassey's, 2004).

12. U.S. Dept. of State, Bureau of Democracy, Human Rights, and Labor, *Egypt: Country Reports on Human Rights Practices*, Feb. 23, 2001, http://www.state.gov/g/drl/rls/hrrpt/2000/nea/784.htm (last visited Aug. 13, 2009).

13. See U.S. Congress, *Foreign Affairs Reform and Restructuring Act of 1998*, §1242(a); UN, *Convention Against Torture*, art. 3.

14. See Andrew Higgins and Christopher Cooper, "CIA-Backed Team Used Brutal Means to Break Up Terrorist Cell in Albania," *Wall Street Journal*, Nov. 20, 2001.

15. Ibid.

16. U.S. Congress, Senate Intelligence Committee, Testimony of Cofer Black, 107th Cong., 2nd sess., Sept. 26, 2002, http://intelligence.senate.gov/020926/black.pdf (last visited Aug. 19, 2009).

17. See William H. Taft, IV, memo to John C. Yoo regarding application of the *Geneva Conventions*, Jan. 11, 2002, 1–2, 7, http://www.scribd.com/doc/12822068/Memo-From-William-Taft-to-John-Yoo-January-11-2002 (last visited Aug. 13, 2009).

18. Ibid. at 2, 28–29.

19. George W. Bush, memo to White House staff regarding "Humane Treatment of Taliban and al Qaeda Detainees," Feb. 7, 2002, www.pegc.us/archive/White_House/bush_memo_20020207_ed.pdf (last visited Aug. 14, 2009).

20. Jay S. Bybee, memo to Alberto R. Gonzales regarding the definition of torture, Aug. 1, 2002, 5–6, http://www.gwu.edu/~nsarchiv/NSAEBB/NSAEBB127/ (last visited Aug. 14, 2009).

21. See, e.g., Jay S. Bybee, memo to John A. Rizzo regarding "Interrogation of al Qaeda Operative," Aug. 1, 2002, 3–4. This memo and three others are available at: http://www.aclu.org/safefree/general/olc_memos.html (last visited Aug. 14, 2009).

22. See "Markey Bill to End Administration's Egregious Practice of Outsourcing Torture," March 6, 2007, http://markey.house.gov/index.php?option=content&task=view&id=2650&Itemid=125 (last visited Aug. 14, 2009).

23. See President Obama, "Executive Orders," Jan. 22, 2009, http://www.whitehouse.gov/briefing_room/executive_orders/ (last visited Aug. 14, 2009).

24. See Barack Obama, Address to Joint Sessions of Congress, Feb. 24, 2009, http://www.whitehouse.gov/the_press_office/remarks-of-president-barack-obama-address-to-joint-session-of-congress/ (last visited Aug. 19, 2009).

25. See Colin Powell, Remarks to the United Nations Security Council, New York, Feb. 5, 2003, http://www.globalsecurity.org/wmd/library/news/iraq/2003/iraq-030205-powell-un-17300pf.htm (last visited Aug. 19, 2009).

26. See Michael Isikoff, "The Missing Terrorist," *Newsweek*, May 28, 2007, http://www.newsweek.com/id/183629 (last visited Aug. 14, 2009).

27. National Commission on Terrorist Attacks on the United States, *The 9/11 Commission Report*, 61–66, http://www.911commission.gov/report/911Report.pdf (last visited Aug. 14, 2009).

28. See David Rose, "How We Survived Jail Hell," *The Observer*, Mar. 14, 2004, http://www.guardian.co.uk/uk/2004/mar/14/terrorism.afghanistan (last visited Aug. 19, 2009).

29. See U.S. Congress, Committees on Foreign Affairs and the Judiciary, *Rendition to Torture: The Case of Maher Arar* (Washington, DC: U.S. Government Printing Office, 2007), 20, www.fas.org/irp/congress/2007_hr/arar.pdf (last visited Aug. 14, 2009).

30. See Joseph Margulies, *Guantanamo and the Abuse of Presidential Power* (New York: Simon & Schuster, 2006), 193–94.

31. See Dana Priest and Dan Eggen, "Terror Suspect Alleges Torture," *Washington Post*, Jan. 6, 2005, A01, http://www.washingtonpost.com/wp-dyn/articles/A51726200sJan5.html (last visited Aug. 14, 2009).

32. See, e.g., Stephen Grey, "U.S. Accused of 'Torture Flights,' " *Sunday Times*, Nov. 14, 2004, http://www.timesonline.co.uk/tol/news/world/article390989.ece (last visited Aug. 19, 2009).

33. See Chris Hawke, "9/11 Death Penalty Trial Delayed," *CBS News*, Nov. 15, 2005, http://www.cbsnews.com/stories/2005/11/15/terror/main1044135.shtml (last visited Aug. 18, 2009).

34. John Ashcroft, Attorney General Transcript, News Conference regarding Zacarias Moussaoui, Dec. 11, 2001, DOJ Conference Center, http://www.usdoj.gov/archive/ag/speeches/2001/agcrisisremarks12_11.htm (last visited Aug. 18, 2009).

35. See Jerry Markon and Timothy Dwyer, "Jurors Reject Death Penalty for Moussaoui," *Washington Post*, May 4, 2006, http://www.washingtonpost.com/wpdyn/content/article/2006/05/03/AR2006050300324.html (last visited Aug. 18, 2009).

36. Documents submitted by the government in *Arar v. Ashcroft*, 414 F.Supp.2d 250 (E.D. N.Y. 2006), are available at http://www.fas.org/sgp/jud/statesec/index.html (last visited Aug. 19, 2009). See *Declaration of James B. Comey* and *Memorandum in Support of the United States' Assertion of State Secrets Privilege*, Jan. 18, 2005.

37. See *Boumediene v. Bush* 28 S.Ct. 2229 (2008).

7

This Is To Whom It
May Concern

A Guantánamo Narrative

MARC D. FALKOFF[1]

November 19, 2004. I am sitting in an interview cell—really, a retrofitted storage container—in Camp Echo at Guantánamo Bay. Across the table, Adnan sits with his arms crossed and his head down. The guards have removed his handcuffs, but when he shifts his weight his leg irons clang and echo in the bare room. The irons are chained to an eyebolt on the floor. Guards are stationed outside the door, and I can see a video camera in the corner.

Adnan is a small, thin man with a scraggly beard. He looks pale. He looks weak. He is dressed in a pullover shirt and cotton pants that are dyed iconic, Gitmo orange.

"I see they're keeping you shackled," I say, shaking my head, trying to communicate that the precaution is unnecessary. My interpreter translates my words into Arabic.

Adnan looks up and smiles briefly, acknowledging the obvious. But he does not meet my eyes.

Adnan has been in this prison for nearly three years, since January 2002. He is only 30, but he looks much older. He bows his head and stares at his ankle cuffs again. *He doesn't trust me*, I write in my notebook.

I have been Adnan's lawyer for several months, although Adnan himself does not know this until our first meeting. One of my tasks is to explain to him how I came to be his lawyer, and how he and a group of Yemeni detainees ended up suing the President of the United States.

I tell him of the recent Supreme Court case, *Rasul v. Bush*,[2] which held that the detainees were entitled to their day in court. I tell him of our difficulties in learning the names of the prisoners, since the military has kept their identities secret for three years. We had learned the names of our Yemeni clients, I explain, only when their families showed up at a human rights conference in Sana'a, the capital of Yemen, seeking help. I explain to Adnan that initially the Pentagon refused to allow lawyers even to visit Guantánamo, and then agreed only if our client meetings could be monitored and videotaped. I tell him that we convinced a judge that such an intrusion would be a gross violation of the attorney-client privilege, and that eventually we were given the green light to meet with our clients, unmonitored.

We both look up at the video camera in the corner of the interview cell. "They assured me it's off," I say, and we both chuckle.

Finally, I tell Adnan that the government claimed the right to hold him in Guantánamo, without charge or trial, for the duration of the "war on terrorism." Because this "war" is against an inchoate idea, it could go on indefinitely. For Adnan that means he could be held in this prison forever.

Neither of us is laughing now.

TO: Personal Representative
FROM: [Officer in Charge, CSRT]
SUBJECT: Summary of Evidence for Combatant Status Review Tribunal – ALLAL, [Adnan] Ab-Aljallil

The U.S. government has previously determined that the detainee is an enemy combatant. This determination is based on information possessed by the United States that indicated he was a fighter for al-Qaida who engaged in hostilities against the United States or its coalition partners.

    a. The detainee is an al-Qaida fighter:

        1. In the year 2000 the detainee reportedly traveled from Yemen to Afghanistan.

        2. The detainee reportedly received training at the al-Farouq training camp.

    b. The detainee engaged in hostilities:

        1. In April 2001 the detainee reportedly returned to Afghanistan.

        2. The detainee reportedly went to the front lines in Kabul.

After I finish speaking, Adnan talks to me. He tells me that during his first three years in Guantánamo, he has been interrogated hundreds of times. No charges, no hearings before a judge, only endless interrogations. Then, a month ago, he was brought before a "status" hearing, at which the government accused him for the first time of being an al-Qaida fighter and of manning the front lines against the Northern Alliance, America's newest ally.

I tell Adnan that I saw the "charges" a few weeks earlier, after we successfully asked the court to order the government to explain why it was holding him captive. I tell him that when I first saw the accusations, I thought they looked serious. But that when I looked at the government's evidence, I was amazed. There was nothing there. Nothing at all trustworthy. Nothing that could be admitted into evidence in a court of law. Nothing that was remotely persuasive, even leaving legal niceties aside.

"*I* haven't seen any of the evidence," Adnan says. "How can I begin to refute it?" He is right. He has never been allowed to see the evidence against him, paltry as it is. Like all but a handful of the approximately 800 detainees who have been held at Guantánamo, Adnan has never been charged with a crime.

The only hearing Adnan ever received was his "status" hearing, which occurred three years into his imprisonment and about six weeks before I first met with him. The hearing, officially called a "Combatant Status Review Tribunal," took place before a military panel that was convened to decide whether or not Adnan was an "enemy combatant"—a term with scant legal pedigree and no anchor in the *Geneva Conventions*.[3]

Adnan saw none of the evidence against him. He was not given the names of witnesses whose statements would be used against him. He was not allowed to challenge witness statements on grounds of hearsay, or to question whether their statements had been tortured out of them. And I am not allowed to show him the evidence either, even though I have seen it. All I can do is learn his story, in his own words.

"My case is very clear," Adnan begins. He was in an automobile accident in 1994, he explains. The accident caused serious head trauma, leaving him with inner ear problems and persistent head pain. For the next half-dozen years, he found himself roaming from hospital to hospital and country to country, seeking inexpensive medical care.

Yemen, Jordan, Pakistan.

Eventually, an acquaintance told him about the health care office of a Pakistani aid worker living in Afghanistan. Adnan, a man from the desert, considered himself strong and self-sufficient. But his family was poor and his medical needs were serious. He accepted the Pakistani's charity, and thus found himself in Afghanistan in late 2001.

Then history caught up to him. The 9/11 tragedies. The American bombing runs against the Taliban. Like all Arabs caught in Afghanistan, Adnan fled for the border.

Adnan becomes more animated and more frustrated as he narrates his story. "I've told this story hundreds of times to the interrogators. Why don't they listen?"

UNCLASSIFIED SUMMARY OF BASIS FOR TRIBUNAL DECISION

Summarized Sworn Detainee Statement

DETAINEE: Why have I been here for three years? Why have I been away from my home and family for three years?

TRIBUNAL PRESIDENT: That is what we are trying to determine today.

DETAINEE: Why did you come after three years? Why wasn't it done much sooner after my arrest?

TRIBUNAL PRESIDENT: I cannot answer to what has happened in the past. I was asked to come here now, and I came.

DETAINEE: Why am I not allowed my freedom here?

TRIBUNAL PRESIDENT: Because you have been classified as an enemy combatant.

DETAINEE: How can they classify me an enemy combatant? You don't have the right documents.

TRIBUNAL PRESIDENT: That is what we are here to determine.

DETAINEE: For three years I haven't been treated very well because of wrong information. Would you let that happen to you? What will be your position if you find out what happened to me was based on wrong information and I am innocent?

TRIBUNAL PRESIDENT: Your current conduct is unacceptable. If you keep interrupting the proceedings, you will be removed and the hearing will continue without you.

Adnan breaks into metaphor. He describes himself as a caged bird. He sits silent for a moment, then suddenly his sentences fly out from him in hasty bursts. His words themselves are like caged birds, tumbling out from him in a flapping frenzy.

"Why doesn't the military check my hospital records? Where is the evidence that I ever held a gun in Afghanistan? Why don't they find the medical documents?"

MEMORANDUM

FROM: Legal Advisor

TO: Director, Combatant Status Review Tribunal

SUBJ: Legal Sufficiency Review of Combatant Status Review Tribunal for Detainee ISN # [156]

During the hearing, the detainee requested that the Tribunal President obtain medical records from a hospital in Jordan. He alleged the records would support his story that he went to Afghanistan for medical treatment.

The Tribunal President denied the request. He determined that, since the detainee failed to provide specific information about the documents when he previously met with his Personal Representative, the request was untimely and the evidence was not reasonably available. After reviewing the evidence in the course of the Tribunal, the Tribunal President further determined that even if the medical records did exist and contained the information described by the detainee, the information was not relevant to the issue of whether the detainee is properly classified as an enemy combatant.

The proceedings and decision of the Tribunal are legally sufficient and no corrective action is required.

The tribunal was not interested in Adnan's medical documents, but I was. His brother sent them to us, and they provided strong support for his explanation of his presence in Afghanistan.

From the Islamic Hospital in Amman, Jordan:

The patient was admitted under my supervision to the Islamic hospital on 07/09/1994 following a head injury. He was suffering from aches and a headache. A clinical test showed blood concentration and hemorrhage above the left eye, and a hole in the left eardrum. The x-ray test showed a broken skull but no brain injury.

From the Yemen Ministry of Defense's "Military Medical Decision Form," dated July 10, 1995: "Diagnosis: 1. Loss of sight in the left eye as a result of eye nerve damage. 2. Loss of hearing in the ears."

From the Al-Thawra General Hospital's Medical Report, to the Yemen Ministry of Public Health, dated August 18, 1999:

> The above-named is hard of hearing. Upon examination, a wide circular hole was detected in his left eardrum. The attached audiography revealed a hearing loss in the left ear. We recommend that he return to the previous center outside for more tests and therapeutic and surgical procedures at his own expense. This is to whom it may concern.

Adnan and I discuss his Combatant Status Review Tribunal, and we agree it had been a farce. Though he did not know it at the time, I was already his lawyer in October 2004 when the hearing took place. But I was not allowed to attend. Instead, Adnan was given the assistance of a "Personal Representative." By regulation, the Personal Representative was to be a military officer and could not be a lawyer. If a Personal Representative had any legal training, he would be disqualified from helping Adnan.

Adnan would have been better off without him. After meeting with him for just 85 minutes in preparation for the status hearing, the Personal Representative wrote an unsolicited letter to the status review tribunal. Adnan was never told of this letter. He was never given a chance to rebut the unflattering portrait that his own (quasi-) lawyer painted of him.

DETAINEE ELECTION FORM
DATE: 27 Sep 04
START TIME: 12:55
END TIME: 14:20
ISN# [156]
PERSONAL REPRESENTATIVE: Lt. Col. [redacted]

Personal Representative Comments:

No witnesses. Rambles for long periods and does not answer questions. He has clearly been trained to ramble as a resistance technique and considered the initial [interview] as an interrogation. This detainee is likely to be disruptive during the Tribunal. Wanted witnesses and documents but is evasive and failed to provide names, addresses, or phone numbers.

Perhaps if Adnan had been represented by a real lawyer at his hearing—one who had not acted as an unsworn witness against his own client—he would have received a fair hearing. As it turned out, the panel was unwilling to even make sure that Adnan understood the charges against him.

UNCLASSIFIED SUMMARY OF BASIS FOR TRIBUNAL DECISION

Summarized Sworn Detainee Statement

TRIBUNAL PRESIDENT: Personal Representative[,] tell us what the Detainee told you yesterday.

PERSONAL REPRESENTATIVE: . . . He said he did not live in al-Qaida. This is a case of mistaken identity. . . .

DETAINEE: That is not correct. . . . I am from Orday City in Yemen, not a city in al-Qaida. My city is very far from the city of al-Qaida. . . . [That is] not the city I am from.

TRIBUNAL PRESIDENT: al-Qaida is not a city. It is the name of an organization.

DETAINEE: Whether it is a city or an organization, I am not from al-Qaida. I am from Orday City.

TRIBUNAL PRESIDENT: Are you from Yemen?

DETAINEE: Yes, I am from Orday.

I tell Adnan that back in October, when I had first read the unclassified transcript of his Combatant Status Review Tribunal, I was confused by the discussion of "al-Qaida City." I had opened an atlas and looked up cities in Yemen. Sure enough, there it was—in the Baladiyat Adan region of Yemen at about 14 degrees north latitude and 44 degrees east longitude. I tell Adnan that I had understood. Al-Qaida is pretty darned far from Orday City.

I ask Adnan how he was taken captive. He tells me that he was trying to get to the border of Pakistan so that he could make his way to the Yemeni embassy and, from there, back home. With bombs dropping everywhere, Afghanistan was dangerous for everyone. But it was especially dangerous for Adnan, as he was told, because the Americans were on the lookout for any Arabs in the country.

Adnan arrived at the border town of Khost and made his way through the rough terrain into Pakistan. Almost immediately, however, Pakistani forces picked him up, along with about 30 other men who looked Arab. Most turned out to be Yemenis. He eventually learned that each of them had been sold to the U.S. military for a bounty of $5,000.

A British historian, Andy Worthington, would later explain to me how the Pakistanis ended up detaining these 30 men. Hundreds of al-Qaida fighters, he tells me, escaped from their position in the Tora Bora Mountains after the Americans began a long-distance bombing campaign against them. However, American military intelligence was unaware that there were two routes out of Tora Bora—one down to Khost and the other across the White Mountains.

The Americans were focused on the Khost road, oblivious to the actual escape route of the fighters. So when the Pakistanis seized the 30 Arabs— mostly civilian—passing through Khost, the Americans touted the capture as a successful roundup of al-Qaida soldiers. In fact, the hundreds of al-Qaida forces from Tora Bora had escaped clean through the mountains.

Adnan tells me that he and the other Yemenis were treated harshly by the Pakistanis after being captured, but that they were soon turned over to the Americans. At least, Adnan thought at the time, the abuse would stop now that he was in American custody. He was wrong.

"This is an island of hell," Adnan tells me, when I ask him to explain what life is like in Guantánamo. He tells me about his arrival in Cuba. After deplaning, he was chained hand and foot while still wearing blackout goggles and ear muffs. Soldiers kicked him and hit him, dislocating his shoulder.

He spent his first weeks in Camp X-Ray, where he was kept in an open-air cage, exposed to the tropical sun. There was little shade and no shelter from the wind, which buffeted him with sand and pebbles. His only amenities were a bucket for water and another for urine and feces. During one of his first interrogations at Guantánamo, he was questioned with a gun to his head.

Adnan then explains to me some of the punishments for disobeying the arbitrary disciplinary rules inside the wire, like the rule against squirreling away some food from your lunch: solitary confinement, no comfort items, no mattress, no pants.

"No pants?" I ask. "What do you mean?"

"They take away your pants," he explains, "and leave you wearing only shorts. This is to prevent the brothers from praying. It would be immodest to pray uncovered. They do it to humiliate us."

I get it now, and I find it chilling. The punishment makes no sense except as a religious humiliation. Another typical punishment was shaving detainees' beards, also a form of religious humiliation.

November 20, 2004. At my second meeting with Adnan, the leitmotif of our conversation is the uselessness of lawyers. Yesterday, I had left Adnan with a folder clearly marked "Attorney-Detainee Materials. Privileged & Confidential." I told him that the guards were not allowed to read any of the documents inside, but that he in turn was obligated to keep nothing but legal papers in the envelope. He said he understood and placed his notes from our meeting in the envelope.

Today, Adnan tells me that the guards confiscated his folder. He believes they have read all the documents inside. He wants to know what use I can be to him if I cannot even prevent the military from reading his privileged materials.

This will not be the first time that Adnan's legal materials will be confiscated during the years I represent him. In June 2006, three detainees will commit suicide. In response, the military will proceed to confiscate every document from nearly every detainee in the camp, looking for evidence, in part, that the lawyers had something to do with facilitating the suicides. All of Adnan's legal papers will be confiscated. As of the publication of this piece, they have yet to be returned to him.

I tell Adnan that we will make sure the guards understand the rules and, if necessary, we will seek judicial intervention. But I know—and I tell Adnan—that judges are rarely willing to interfere in the day-to-day management of a prison, and that we must choose our battles wisely.

Sometime during our second day together, I begin to feel that Adnan and I have connected. He is still skeptical of my value to him and refuses—for now—to sign the document letting the Department of Justice know that he wants my firm to represent him.

But we are developing a rapport. We are engaged in a spirited back and forth about the rule of law, and he is downing a remarkable number of the "Filet-o-Fish" sandwiches that I brought him from the Guantánamo McDonald's. The fast food is a welcome change from his bland diet of overcooked chicken and rice, barely ripe fruit, and inedible vegetables, which he has grown used to over the past three years.

I tell Adnan that I am surprised the military let us bring in food. He tells me that it is not unheard of, as interrogators sometimes give out McDonald's food as a reward for cooperating during interrogations. As our discussion turns to the separation of powers and the role of the courts in the United States, Adnan pauses and asks to borrow my notepad. In flowing Arabic script, he begins composing a lengthy letter.

I watch and wait for him to finish. Something about the way he leans over the paper seems odd but familiar. Then I figure it out. Adnan is right-handed, and in order to keep the ink from smearing his Arabic text, which is written from right to left, he has to contort his body. "So, what's that?" I ask finally, nodding at the paper. He smiles and tells me to have it translated when I return to the States.

Several weeks later, I am in the "Secure Facility" in Arlington, Virginia. This is where, by court order, our clients' letters and the notes from our meetings are stored. The military convinced the court that anything our clients communicate to us could pose a potential national security threat.

A linguist translates Adnan's letter for me. In it, Adnan thanks me for volunteering to represent him and tells me that God will reward me. He also suggests that I convert to Islam, as a safeguard against the hellfire. I cannot help but smile at this last part, but I am moved by the trust he has placed in me.

January 26, 2005. Today I am scheduled to visit with Adnan. Just two days ago, the Department of Justice refused our request to bring a doctor down to Guantánamo to evaluate the health of our clients, almost all of whom have lost significant weight while at the camp. According to them:

> Detainees at GTMO are provided competent, more than adequate medical care, in most cases exceeding the level of care a detainee may have received prior to his capture. . . . Allegations of inadequate care are untrue, perhaps the result of misunderstanding or miscommunication.

I enter the interview cell. Adnan is slouched in his folding chair. He is painfully thin. His eyes are rheumy and he can barely speak. When I ask, he tells me in a weak and scratchy voice that he has been spitting up blood, has problems hearing, and has suffered from an excruciating headache for weeks. He gets no rest because they have confiscated his mattress, leaving him to sleep on the steel of his bunk. Adnan had apparently violated some disciplinary rule, but he waves off my questions about it.

I call the guards on the intercom and ask them to come to the interview cell. They arrive and ask if I am okay. I say that I am, but that my client needs to be taken to the infirmary at once. Their faces immediately turn to stone.

"A corpsman visits regularly, sir," one of the soldiers tells me. He spits out the *sir* like an insult. A corpsman, I learn, is a soldier who has been given some rudimentary medical training. Not a nurse, and certainly not a doctor.

I insist that Adnan be seen by medical personnel at the infirmary immediately. They refuse, so I try to work my way up the chain of command at Guantánamo. That does not work, so I call our law office in Washington, and they call the Department of Justice, and someone from Justice must have called someone at Defense who called back down to Guantánamo, because the soldiers finally agree to take Adnan to the infirmary.

April 9, 2005. I'm visiting Adnan again, this time accompanied by another lawyer, Jason Knott. The topic for the day: What will happen if and when Adnan is transferred back to Yemen?

We talk about the likelihood of transfer to a Yemeni prison. We talk about the U.S. State Department's annual reports on Yemen, and about the country's sketchy human rights record.

Adnan asks us about reports that the United States may move most of the detainees to Saudi Arabia, so that President Bush could get rid of his Guantánamo problem. He has also heard that men might be moved to places like Jordan or Syria to be interrogated through torture. He feels he can handle anything that the Yemeni government's thuggish Political Security Organization is likely to mete out, but he is concerned about the treatment he would receive in a third country.

We explain that the judge has ordered the government to give us 30 days' advance notice before Adnan or any of our other clients are transferred out of Guantánamo. We explain that we proved to the judge's satisfaction that we had legitimate and well-founded fears that the United States might render our clients to other countries to be tortured. Our notice order would provide Adnan protection and enough time for us to get to the courts in case the government tried anything like that.

Everything starts to feel topsy-turvy as I am talking to Adnan. I have just explained to a man from Yemen that we have credible evidence that my government has considered sending some of its prisoners to be tortured, and that a judge has agreed with me that the threat is substantial.

June 18, 2005. I have been coming down to Guantánamo frequently, mostly to keep Adnan and the rest of our clients sane. They have no access to the outside world, no newspapers, television, or radio. They are allowed to send and receive infrequent letters to family via the International Committee of the Red Cross, but the military uses the family letters as leverage to try to get the detainees to talk. Most of the men have stopped writing as a result.

We are not allowed to bring our clients news from the outside either, unless it "directly relates" to their cases. The detainees' lawyers have a different understanding from the military about what the term "directly relates" means. The military, for instance, believes that news of Supreme Court cases dealing with the rights of Guantánamo detainees does not "directly relate" to any particular detainee's case. Remarkable. We just make our own good-faith determinations and continue to do our jobs.

On this trip, Adnan complains about the water. Many people in the camp, he says, are sick from it. It is difficult to know whether his claim is true, of course. All sorts of stories go around in a prison environment. It is good to maintain a healthy skepticism when you are talking with someone who has been incarcerated for a long time. During this trip, I gather two sealed bottles of water from my other clients, and bring them back to New York. Both have bugs floating in them.

October 21, 2005. My colleague, David Remes, visits with Adnan. Adnan tells David, "This prison is like a hideous ghost. The situation is beyond human comprehension. This place is a vicious jungle, without law or justice."

April 15, 2006. We have won some legal victories, and we thought we would finally get our day in court. Then, in December, Congress stripped the detainees of their *habeas corpus* rights.[4] I have come to Guantánamo to discuss these legal developments with Adnan. "I've lost hope of being released," he tells me in a weak voice.

I listen, but it is difficult to concentrate. Adnan looks like he has just been in a car accident. One eye is swollen shut; the other is a sickly black-blue. There are cuts on his head and contusions all over his body. He is slumped in his chair and can barely keep his head up. He cannot swallow. He can talk, but it hurts and he has to stop frequently.

Three days ago, he explains, he had been visited by an "Immediate Reaction Force" team. A half-dozen men in body armor, carrying shields and batons, forcibly extracted him from his cell. His offense? He had stepped over a line, painted on the floor of his cell, while his lunch was being passed through the food slot of his door.

Suddenly the riot police came. No one in the cell block knew who for. They closed all the windows except mine. A female soldier came in with a big can of pepper spray. Eventually I figured out they were coming for me. She sprayed me. I couldn't breathe. I fell down. I put a mattress over my head. I thought I was dying.

They opened the door. I was lying on the bed but they were kicking and hitting me with the shields. They put my head in the toilet. They put me on a stretcher and carried me away.

He'd stepped over the line, you see.

"Perhaps you can kill yourself without realizing it," Adnan says quietly, as if to himself. "If you don't realize what you're doing, maybe you won't end up in hell."

THREE GUANTANAMO BAY DETAINEES DIE OF APPARENT SUICIDE

By Sgt. Sara Wood, USA

American Forces Press Service

WASHINGTON, June 10, 2006
Three detainees at U.S. Naval Station Guantanamo Bay, Cuba, died of apparent suicides early this morning, military officials reported today. . . .

[Navy Rear Adm. Harry B. Harris] said the joint suicides were clearly planned by the detainees as a way to advance their cause in the war on terror.

"I believe this was not an act of desperation, but an act of asymmetric warfare aimed at us here at Guantanamo," he said. "We have men here who are committed jihadists. They are dangerous men and they will do anything they can to advance their cause."

September 7, 2006. I have been collecting poems from the Guantánamo detainees, and now the University of Iowa Press is interested in publishing them as a book. For months now, Adnan has included poems in his letters to us. The Pentagon has mostly refused to declassify them, including one called *The Shout of Death*. But for some reason, they cleared his poem about the hunger strikers, which I decide to include in the volume. This is part of Adnan's *Hunger Strike Poem*:

They are artists of torture,
They are artists of pain and fatigue,
They are artists of insults and humiliation.

* * *

Where is the world to save us from torture?
Where is the world to save us from the fire and sadness?
Where is the world to save the hunger strikers?

But we are content, on the side of justice and right,
Worshipping the Almighty.
And our motto on this island is, *salaam.*

February 27, 2007. Adnan has been on a hunger strike for more than a month. In keeping with their Orwellian tendencies, the military refers to the hunger strike as a "voluntary fast." Long ago, the military redefined suicide attempts as "manipulative self-injurious behavior" and "hanging gestures."

Twice a day, soldiers force-feed Adnan a liquid nutrient by inserting a tube up his nose and into his stomach. His arms and legs are strapped to a special restraint chair during the feedings. His head is immobilized.

Another of my colleagues, Brent Starks, visits with Adnan for the first time. In his notes from the meeting, he writes, "Still on hunger strike. Incredibly thin. Looks incredibly weak and broken. Horrible." Later, he observes scars on Adnan's wrists.

FROM: [Department of Justice]
SENT: Monday, March 26, 2007
TO: Marc Falkoff
SUBJECT: RE: Allal ab Aljallil Abd al Rahman Abd, ISN 156

We have raised with DoD your request that a psychiatrist of your choosing be permitted to visit petitioner [Adnan] Abd with you to assess Mr. Abd's mental and physical condition and encourage him to take medication. . . Guantanamo is not in a position to accede to your request for intervention by an outside medical professional.

May 14, 2007. Adnan tells me he has now been on a hunger strike for four and a half months and that he has been force-fed for three months. The force-feeding, he says, "is like having a dagger shoved down your throat." The United Nations Commission on Human Rights calls this torture.[5]

Sitting across the table, shackled as always, Adnan seems more sedate than usual. Or maybe, I think, he has simply been sedated. I wonder whether the military has silently slipped some sedatives into the liquid nutrient they force-feed him.

Of course, there is no way for me to know if they are sedating him or feeding him antipsychotics or antidepressants, since the military refuses to share his medical records. We could try to go to court, but Congress has taken away judges' power to intervene. And the Justice Department is right—the courts do not like to micromanage our prison camps.

Maybe, I think to myself, it is for the best that they are feeding and medicating Adnan by any means necessary. Maybe this will keep him from trying to escape from Guantánamo by the only way that seems possible to him. It is growing difficult for me to keep his faith in our legal system alive. Right now, it is hard for me to keep my faith in the legal system alive.

As I prepare to leave, Adnan has one last thing to say. "Death," he tells me, "would be more merciful than life here."

NOTES

A similar version of this chapter was first published in the *DePaul Journal for Social Justice* (2008, v.1).

1. Assistant Professor of Law, Northern Illinois University College of Law; J.D., Columbia Law School; Ph.D., Brandeis University; M.A., University of Michigan, Ann Arbor; B.A., University of Pennsylvania. Professor Falkoff represents 16 Yemeni prisoners, most of whom have been detained at Guantánamo for more than six years. He is the editor of *Poems From Guantánamo: The Detainees Speak* (University of Iowa Press, 2007). The litigation documents that are quoted are all on file with the author and are available upon request. None of the information in this piece is classified.

2. *Rasul v. Bush*, 542 U.S. 466 (2004).

3. Intl. Committee of the Red Cross, *Geneva Conventions of 1949*, Aug. 12, 1949.

4. See U.S. Congress, *Detainee Treatment Act of 2005*, H.R. 2863, Title X, 109th Cong., 1st sess., Dec. 2005, § 1005(e).

5. See U.N. Commission on Human Rights, *Situation of Detainees at Guantanamo Bay*, E/CN.4/2006/120, Feb. 15, 2006, http://news.bbc.co.uk/2/shared/bsp/hi/pdfs/16_02_06_un_guantanamo.pdf (last visited Aug. 17, 2009).

8

Psychologists, Torture, and Civil Society

Complicity, Institutional Failure, and the Struggle for Professional Transformation

STEPHEN SOLDZ

As the public record, as well as the chapters in this book, attest, post-9/11 torture, also known as "harsh interrogation techniques," or "enhanced interrogations techniques," was authorized by President George W. Bush based on bogus legal doctrines purposely created by a bevy of lawyers from the Vice President's Office and the Justice Department's Office of Legal Counsel (OLC), as well as the President's Counsel, Alberto Gonzales. Somewhat less well known, but central to the OLC memos, is that, in addition to the lawyers, another group of professionals played a key role in the development of this program—psychologists.

Psychological Assessment as Legal Protection

The roles of psychologists in the U.S. torture program appear to be central and multifold. One of these roles flowed directly from the "torture" memos issued by the OLC[1] in 2002 and 2005. The Department of Justice's definition of torture requires that interrogators possess the "specific intent" to cause "severe physical and mental suffering." Moreover, "severe mental pain and suffering," the memo explains, requires that the harm inflicted must not only be severe but must also be "prolonged," that is, "lasting months or even years after the acts were inflicted upon the prisoner."[2]

One of the August 1, 2002, memos reassured interrogators and their superiors that a "good faith belief" that the techniques would not cause severe mental suffering was sufficient to bar prosecution for torture, regardless of the outcome. Here is where the psychologists come in. This memo states:

> [T]he psychological impact of a course of conduct must be assessed with reference to the subject's psychological history and current mental health status. The healthier the individual, the less likely that the use of any one procedure or set of procedures will result in prolonged mental harm.[3]

The 2005 OLC memos, publicly released in April 2009, placed an even greater emphasis on the monitoring role of psychologists and other health professionals.[4] By 2005, monitoring was standardized through continual assessments by staff from the CIA's Office of Medical Services (OMS). As reported in one of the 2005 memos, the CIA provided the OLC with the following background information to aid legal analysis:

> [T]echnique-specific advance approval is required for all "enhanced" measures and is conditional on on-site medical and psychological personnel confirming from direct detainee examination that the enhanced technique(s) is not expected to produce "physical or mental pain or suffering."[5]

This OLC memo describes the continual monitoring and evaluations throughout the interrogation process as follows:

> Medical and psychological personnel are on-scene throughout (and, as detailed below, physically present or otherwise observing during the application of many techniques, including all techniques involving physical contact with detainees) and, "[d]aily physical and psychological evaluations are continued throughout the period of [enhanced interrogation technique] use."[6]

That is, psychologists or other mental health professionals are essential for deciding how much abuse an individual can endure before suffering prolonged mental harm, which would officially constitute illegal torture. A simple statement by a psychologist that a prisoner would not suffer prolonged harm, that an interrogation was *safe* for the prisoner, would likely be sufficient defense against any claim that the interrogator "intended" mental harm, thus keeping the interrogation "safe and ethical" for the interrogator.

In short, psychologists helped to define what constitutes "torture" in general terms of detainee breaking points. They then assessed the breaking points of specific detainees, to subject them to the "safe and ethical" amount of abuse, and, at the same time, protected interrogators and their superiors from war crimes charges. Thus, psychologists became critical components of a before-the-fact amnesty for future investigations.

In addition to the obvious ethical issues here, it should be noted that the CIA's claim that psychologists could predict future psychological harm flies in the face of well-founded experience and research in the field. Such predictability is even less reliable in a domain, such as "enhanced interrogations," where very little research or clinical experience exists. If the CIA and OLC were truly seeking an assessment of the potential negative consequences of their interrogation techniques, they would have consulted the research and clinical literature on the psychological effects of torture and similar abuse.[7]

Survival, Evasion, Resistance, and Escape

Psychologists, however, were not just monitors of abuse—a role they shared with other health professionals. They were also the designers and trainers, via the military's Survival, Evasion, Resistance, and Escape (SERE) program. SERE was designed to teach pilots, Special Forces, and others likely to be captured how to resist breaking and cooperating if detained and tortured by a country that does not obey the Geneva Conventions.

During SERE training, service members are subjected to torture over several days, including sleep deprivation, beatings, sexual humiliation, confinement in tiny spaces, and, in some cases, waterboarding.[8] An interesting feature of SERE was the prominent role of psychologists in the program.[9] Psychologists were present to supervise the abuse of our troops and evaluate how much stress an individual could tolerate. It was these psychologists on whom the government relied, when it "reverse engineered" SERE techniques to design "counterresistance techniques" to break down detainees.

As was initially reported in *Vanity Fair*,[10] the *New Yorker*,[11] and *Salon. com*,[12] when the CIA brought torture in-house at its secret "black sites," it contacted former SERE psychologists James Mitchell and Bruce Jessen of Mitchell, Jessen, and Associates to design their interrogation program. Detainee Abu Zubaydah was initially questioned by the Federal Bureau of Investigation (FBI) using the FBI's standard rapport-building techniques. He revealed that Khalid Sheikh Mohammed was the architect of 9/11 and described the planning for the attack. However, the CIA was not satisfied with the FBI's methodology and sent a team that included psychologist James Mitchell to obtain further information by employing a systematic attack on Zubaydah's sense of self. *Vanity Fair* reporter Katherine Eban quoted a knowledgeable source as stating, "the basic approach was to break down [the detainees] through isolation, white noise, completely take away their ability to predict the future, create dependence on inter-rogators."[13]

Their approach was similar to the CIA's Debility, Dependency, Dread (DDD) paradigm of psychological torture, developed in the 1950s. How-ever, it appears that Mitchell and Jessen may have independently redis-covered much of this DDD work, based this time upon psychologist Martin Seligman's theory of *learned helplessness*. This theory was devel-oped from research in which dogs were shocked in conditions where they were unable to escape the torment. Seligman noted that they eventually appeared to give up hope, no longer attempting to escape even when escape could be easily accomplished. Seligman postulated that learned helplessness might provide a model for clinical depression.

In May 2002, while trying to figure out what to do with Abu Zubaydah, the CIA invited Seligman to speak on learned helplessness at the Navy SERE school in San Diego.[14] While Seligman denies any knowledge that his talk might aid the CIA in its development of the "enhanced interroga-tion" program,[15] he admits that Mitchell and Jessen were in the audience.[16] In her *New Yorker* article, Jane Mayer reports that Mitchell and Jessen were enamored with learned helplessness and quotes sources as saying that Mitchell's approach to detainee interrogations was based upon this theory.

We now know that part of the Mitchell-Jessen CIA "program" included waterboarding, a paradigmatic torture involving interrupted drown-ing, as well as throwing detainees against walls, multiple days of "sleep deprivation" induced by painful shackling to the ceiling, and semi-star-vation, among many other techniques designed to induce helplessness.[17]

We know that these tortures were videotaped and that the tapes were destroyed, probably to prevent public release. We also now know that this torture was micromanaged out of the White House with presidential approval by the so-called Principals Committee of Condoleezza Rice, Richard Cheney, Colin Powell, George Tenet, and Alberto Gonzales.[18]

The Defense Department Office of the Inspector General (OIG) report and Senate Armed Services Committee (SASC) hearings and report[19] document further how SERE staff trained the Behavioral Science Consultation Teams (BSCTs) at Guantánamo, which originally consisted of psychologists and psychiatrists and later primarily psychologists, in these counter-resistance techniques. BSCTs were granted authority to apply SERE-type techniques to Guantánamo detainees, including "stress positions, removal of clothing, use of phobias (such as fear of dogs), and deprivation of light and auditory stimuli."[20]

Col. Morgan Banks, who had been appointed a member of the American Psychological Association's (APA) Psychological Ethics and National Security (PENS) ethics task force, was reportedly opposed to the use of some of the most brutal SERE-based interrogation techniques, those described as *physical pressures*, as opposed to the *psychological pressures* he apparently advocated. Nonetheless, he arranged training in both physical and psychological pressures for Guantánamo BSCT members, as well as other Guantánamo staff at Fort Bragg in September 2002.[21]

One psychologist, Maj. John Leso, a member of the BSCT, was present during the torture of Mohamed al Qahtani, who was believed to be the "20th hijacker" in the 9/11 terrorist attacks. Leso's participation in the interrogation, which utilized both physical and psychological abusive techniques, is revealed by a leaked interrogation log obtained by *Time* magazine.[22] Bioethicist Steven Miles summarizes the harsh process:

> For eleven days, beginning November 23, al-Qahtani was interrogated for twenty hours each day by interrogators working in shifts. He was kept awake with music, yelling, loud white noise or brief opportunities to stand. He then was subjected to eighty hours of nearly continuous interrogation until what was intended to be a 24-hour "recuperation." This recuperation was entirely occupied by a hospitalization for hypothermia that had resulted from deliberately abusive use of an air conditioner. . . . [After the] hospitalization . . . he was hooded, shackled, put on a litter and taken by ambulance to an interrogation room for twelve more days of interrogation, punc-

tuated by a few brief naps. He was then allowed to sleep for four hours before being interrogated for ten more days, except for naps of up to an hour. He was allowed 12 hours of sleep on January 1, but for the next eleven days, the exhausted and increasingly non-communicative prisoner was only allowed naps of one to four hours as he was interrogated.[23]

While Leso apparently registered no objections to al Qahtani's treatment, the FBI did. One FBI agent reported:

> In September or October of 2002 FBI agents observed that a canine was used in an aggressive manner to intimidate Detainee _____ after he had been subjected to intense isolation for over three months. During that time period, _____ was totally isolated (with the exception of occasional interrogations) in a cell that was always flooded with light. By late November, the detainee was evidencing behavior consistent with extreme psychological trauma (talking to non-existent people, reporting hearing voices, crouching in the corner of the cell covered with a sheet for hours on end).[24]

Al Qahtani's "interrogation" continued for at least six more weeks after the FBI reported he was in this state. The procedure was described by a top Pentagon official in late 2008 as meeting the legal definition of torture.[25] As of this writing in early 2010, three and a half years after the interrogation log of al Qahtani was published and after multiple ethics complaints were filed, Leso remains a member in good standing of the APA.

American Psychological Association

One might expect claims that psychologists were central actors in the administration's well-known program of torture and detainee abuse would have mobilized the APA to investigate, adopt measures to stop involvement, and punish perpetrators within the profession. Unfortunately, APA leadership took a different path. They decided to use the opportunity to curry favor with the military/intelligence establishment and the Bush administration. They encouraged, indeed asserted without evidence,[26] the necessity of having psychologists aid the interrogations.

Until the waning days of the Bush administration, in fall 2008, APA leaders uttered not one word of concern about the role of psychologists in abusing detainees, or in teaching others to abuse. Like the Bush administration, they condemned torture in resolution after resolution and insisted that psychologists would never participate in torture.[27] But when the PENS task force was created to formulate the association's ethics policy on interrogation, they appointed a majority of members from the military-intelligence establishment, including four with direct involvement in chains of command implicated in abuses.[28] Among those appointed was Banks, Army SERE Chief Psychologist, whose office trained Guantánamo interrogation staff, including Leso. Banks also wrote the instructions for the BSCTs,[29] which formed the basis for part of the task force report.

The APA also appointed Col. Larry James as chief of the BSCTs at Guantánamo from January to May 2003. In a recent memoir, entitled *Fixing Hell*, James tells a story of how he single-handedly stopped abuse at Guantánamo.[30] He claims that virtually all abuse ceased soon after his arrival in January 2003, and that any remaining abuse was the result of rogue staff acting contrary to standard operating procedures (SOPs). Unfortunately for James, the Camp Delta SOPs that were instituted in April 2003, during James's tenure, were leaked in November 2007 and paint a very different picture.[31] Consistent with the early BSCT emphasis on psychological abuse, these SOPs mandate that all new detainees were to be subjected to four weeks of isolation and other procedures designed "to enhance and exploit the disorientation and disorganization felt by a newly arrived detainee in the interrogation process . . . that concentrates on isolating the detainee and fostering dependence . . . on his interrogator."[32]

Adolescent Mohammed Jawad was subjected to this mandatory isolation upon his arrival in Guantánamo in February 2003, while James was fixing the hell there.[33] James told the PENS task force: "[T]he fact of the matter is that since Jan 2003, where ever we have had psychologists no abuses have been reported."[34] Here, James negates hundreds of press articles, official reports, and detainee accounts of widespread abuse occurring at Guantánamo long after psychologists became a regular presence at interrogations.[35] In order to maintain his claim, James denounces the press, the Defense Department Inspector General, the Red Cross, and his critics in his book and claims that he poked his head everywhere at Guantánamo, especially in the middle of the night, in order to ferret out hidden abuse. However, a quite different James appears in his February 2008 response to questions regarding new revelations about an ultra-secret Guantánamo camp, Camp VII:

> I learned a long, long time ago, if I'm going to be successful in the intel community, I'm meticulously—in a very, very dedicated way—going to stay in my lane . . . So if I don't have a specific need to know about something, I don't want to know about it. I don't ask about it.[36]

The APA also appointed Scott Shumate, former Chief Operational Psychologist, for the CIA's Counterterrorism Center, the branch in charge of the CIA's secret prisons where Zubaydah was tortured.[37] In her article, Eban actually places Shumate at the torture of Zubaydah.[38] Though allegedly distressed by the torture he witnessed there, Shumate remained at the Center for another year. Further, when he left government service, Shumate used his contact with the CIA detainees—"[h]e has been with several of the key apprehended terrorists"—as a bragging point for his private consulting.[39]

Another member of the PENS task force was Capt. Bryce Lefever, a former SERE psychologist who participated in interrogations in Afghanistan. Lefever, while speaking to a *Christian Science Monitor* reporter in August 2007 about U.S. citizen Jose Padilla's years of isolation, compared U.S. interrogation methods to the condemned Soviet techniques on which they are based:

> There's something to be said for sending the message that the gloves are coming off. You don't take a knife to a gunfight. . . . Their abuse was a systematic practice to conceal the truth. . . . If Padilla was abused, then it was for a righteous purpose—to reveal the truth.[40]

More recently, Lefever expressed similar views when he defended SERE psychologists who helped design the CIA's "enhanced interrogations" program during a *National Public Radio* (NPR) interview.[41] These opinions should not have been a surprise to those involved in the investigations, as Lefever expressed related sentiments on the PENS task force listserv, with no discernable objection from other members.[42]

The PENS meeting also included several observers with connections high in the military/intelligence establishment, such as the first psychologist at the National Security Agency, the former Assistant Director of Social, Behavioral, and Economic Policy for the Bush White House, and the organizer of a joint APA-FBI invitation-only conference called *Countering Terrorism: Integration of Practice and Theory.* CIA torture consultant Mitchell participated in that conference, as well as an APA-CIA invitation-only conference called *The Science of Deception*, which included both torture psychologists Mitchell and Jessen. Also present and key in certain decisions was a top APA official whose wife, a military psychologist, played an important role in revising the instructions for BSCTs under investigation by the task force.[43]

Not surprisingly, given its composition, the task force condemned torture, but ignored all evidence that torture was being practiced by the U.S. government or aided by psychologists. More centrally, they concluded:

> [I]t is consistent with the APA Ethics Code for psychologists to serve in consultative roles to interrogation and information-gathering processes for national security-related purposes. Acknowledging that engaging in such consultative and advisory roles entails a delicate balance of ethical considerations, the Task Force stated that psychologists are in a unique position to assist in ensuring that these processes are safe and ethical for all participants.[44]

The PENS task force was the paradigmatic example of how the APA dealt with the issue of psychologist involvement in abusive interrogations: ignore the issue of systematic government-sanctioned abuses, ignore or deny psychologist involvement, and assert the critical importance of having psychologists as protectors. In summary, the APA leadership uses eight distinct styles of response to deflect criticism about the roles of psychologists in interrogations and the role of the APA in promoting and protecting psychologist involvement.[45] These styles, all characterized by denial of social reality,[46] can be described in the approximate chronological order in which they were rolled out:

1. *Identification with the Aggressor,* in which APA leaders moved quickly after 9/11 to seek funding (for the psychology profession, not the organization) from and influence with the administration and the military/intelligence establishment. They staged joint conferences with the CIA and other security agencies on interrogations and related topics and engaged in extensive lobbying of intelligence officials.

2. *Rigging the Process*, in which an ethics task force (PENS) was created and secretly dominated by a majority of psychologists from the military/intelligence community to endorse an apparently already adopted "policy of engagement" in military and CIA interrogations.

3. *Denial*, in which APA leaders cast doubt upon reports that psychologists were aiding abusive interrogations, or minimized this involvement as the actions of a few "bad apples," rather than as part of a systematic government program. As former APA President Gerald Koocher stated in a 2006 "President's Column" piece in the *APA Monitor*: "A number of opportunistic commentators masquerading as scholars have continued to report on alleged abuses by mental health professionals."[47]

4. *Naming Names*, in which the issue turned into one of possible individual perpetrators and critics were challenged to name individual psychologists involved in torture. They were urged to provide definitive evidence of their involvement in specific abuses; failure to provide this evidence was used to discredit critics of APA policies.

5. *We Are Here to Help: "Safe and Ethical,"* in which APA leaders repeated, as if a mantra,[48] "psychologists have a critical role to play in keeping interrogations safe, legal, ethical, and effective,"[49] ignoring the massive amounts of evidence that psychologists were not keeping interrogations "safe, legal, and ethical," but actually participating in abuse and providing legal cover for torture.

6. *We Are No Different Than Others*, in which the positions of the American Medical Association and the American Psychiatric Association were distorted to make them virtually indistinguishable from the APA position, despite clear differences.[50]

7. *Parsing Pain*, in which the APA passed anti-torture resolutions with loopholes that were interpreted to allow continued participation by psychologists in many forms of psychological torture.[51]

8. *Repressive Tolerance and Endless "Dialog,"* in which the APA encouraged endless discussion in order to promote its position that participating in a program of abusive interrogations was a "complex issue," one on which "reasonable people" can differ, excuses that were then used to justify inaction.

Revelations, including release of the International Committee of the Red Cross report on the CIA's detention program,[52] the OLC memos, the SASC report on interrogations, and statements to NPR by a member of the PENS "ethics" task force defending SERE-based interrogations, have led the APA to adopt a new response—the *"We are Shocked!"* response. They act as if they just discovered that, perhaps, a few psychologists did indeed aid the torture regime and suddenly realized that some members might (unjustly) blame them for years of collusion and inaction. After years of revelations and APA denials, the best the APA Board could say on June 18, 2009, was:

> Information has emerged in the public record confirming that, as committed as some psychologists were to ensuring that interrogations were conducted in a safe and ethical manner, other psychologists were not. Although there are countless psychologists in the military and intelligence community who acted ethically and responsibly during the post-9/11 era, it is now clear that some psychologists did not abide by their ethical obligations to never engage in torture or other forms of cruel, inhuman, or degrading treatment. The involvement of psychologists, no matter how small the number, in the torture of detainees is reprehensible and casts a shadow over our entire profession. APA expresses its profound regret that any psychologist has been involved in the abuse of detainees.[53]

The Board also now recognizes that not all members feel satisfied with its (lack of) response to this crisis in the profession and in our society:

> We recognize that the issue of psychologist involvement in national security-related investigations has been an extremely difficult and divisive one for our association. We also understand that some of our members continue to be disappointed and others angered by the association's actions in this regard. Although APA has had a long-standing policy against psychologist involvement in torture, many members wanted the association to take a strong stand against any involvement of psychologists in national security interrogations during the Bush administration.[54]

The Board made no attempt to come to terms with the organization's years of denial and inaction.

Psychologists Fight Back: Civil Society in Action

The APA's policies promoting participation in detainee interrogations have not set well with several members. The leadership, however, are masters of denial, distraction, and delay, confusing and wearing down the opposition.

Nevertheless, many members have refused to be silent. Some have worked within the APA structures, shepherding resolutions through committees and engaging in closed-door negotiations. Others are outsiders, challenging the APA largely from an external vantage point. All, however, are working to convince, and, more importantly, to empower those psychologists disgusted by actions of some of their colleagues and the manipulations of the APA. In particular, the Internet has helped spread the message that the APA is abetting abuse.

As is true of virtually all social movements, activist psychologists were moved to act by a variety of issues, though three major overlapping concerns became prominent:[55]

- the historical record of psychologist participation in the U.S. government policy of detainee abuse and the disturbing absence of fundamental human rights in many of the U.S. detention centers during the war on terror;[56]
- the existence of special circumstances in the military's rigid hierarchy, the premium placed upon obedience, the severe consequences for failure to comply, the *need to know* philosophy that limits transparency, the primacy placed on loyalty above other values, and, in the detention facilities in particular,[57] extreme mandatory secrecy, the difficulty of obtaining independent feedback, the paucity of uninvolved colleagues for informal or formal ethical consultation, the extreme pressures to "get information" in a situation where many detainees have no information to give, which turns the traditional concept of the autonomous moral agent inappropriate for ethical policy-making on its head and creates what Lifton called "atrocity producing situations";[58]
- and the unique characteristics of psychology as a profession pledged to help and to "do no harm," the fundamental ethical principle of all health professionals.[59]

A range of aims arose out of these concerns. Throughout much of the Bush years, dissident members wanted, above all, a ban on psychologist interrogation support at sites like Guantánamo and the CIA's "black sites," where international law and the U.S. Constitution were being violated. Others wished to ban all direct psychologist participation in interrogations of individuals (as opposed to possible roles in general training or screening of interrogators), making the psychology position consistent with that of the American Medical Association regarding physicians;[60] also known as the *bright line* position.[61]

Yet another major aim that evolved gradually was revision of a 2002 APA ethics code section, which provided an exception when ethical standards conflict with other laws or orders.[62] Activists also sought investigation and accountability through the APA ethics process and state licensing boards for psychologists who have been identified as having possible involvement in abusive interrogations.[63] A final, and broader, goal was investigation and exposure of the extremely close ties between the APA leadership and the military intelligence establishment in general, and the apparent collusion of the APA in U.S. torture and detention abuse.[64]

In 2006, APA Council member Neil Altman proposed a moratorium on psychologist involvement in Bush-era detention sites that violated international law. The Board used parliamentary maneuvers to undermine this effort prior to the August 2007 Council of Representatives meeting. Instead, they substituted a generic anti-torture statement that banned psychologist participation in the use of certain abusive techniques while retaining loopholes that led some to wonder if it was deliberately designed to allow continued participation in U.S. torture.[65] After an intense struggle, these loopholes were finally closed at the APA's February 2008 Council meeting.[66]

Also in 2006, APA members started a movement of withholding dues pending association policy change. While never a serious economic threat, the organized group of several hundred psychologists proved a major moral challenge to APA leadership.

The broader movement was a decentralized alliance of ad hoc and more formal organizations, including the withhold dues movement, and existing organizations such as Psychoanalysts for Social Responsibility and Psychologists for Social Responsibility. A few APA divisions and several members of APA's Council of Representatives worked to change the policies, often in an incremental fashion, from within the association's official structure, while often maintaining some distance from the more outspoken members of the broader movement. Physicians for Human Rights provided substantial advice and support to this movement while simultaneously pressing the APA to change.

After the inadequate 2007 anti-torture resolution was passed, several prominent psychologists resigned their APA membership, including a former division President,[67] the founding Director of the association's Practice Directorate,[68] and the former Chair of the Ethics Committee.[69] In his resignation letter, the former chair described recent developments in the association:

> These changes [in APA policies in recent years] take APA so far away from its ethical foundation, historic traditions, and basic values, and from my own personal and professional view of our responsibilities, that I cannot support them with my membership.[70]

After the failure of the moratorium effort in Council, activists sought a new approach that went straight to the membership and did not rely upon support from the APA's committees and legislative body. They discovered a previously unused rule that allowed a member-initiated referendum to be put to a vote of the entire membership. The withhold dues movement drafted a proposal stating that APA members may not work in U.S. detention centers that are outside of or in violation of international law or the U.S. Constitution, "unless they are working directly for the persons being detained or for an independent third party working to protect human rights."[71] The referendum passed by 59 percent of voting members in September 2008.[72] Following its passage, however, struggles over the referendum's interpretation began and the APA delayed acceptance of the policy change until February 2009, after the Bush administration had left office. APA leaders also insisted that the referendum was unenforceable because it was not part of the ethics code, and avoided making any concrete statement as to the applicability of the referendum to any specific detention facility, including Guantánamo and Bagram. Referendum proponents are currently trying, without much success, to remedy both of these lapses.

At the time of this writing, the APA appears on the verge of taking an additional step toward reaffirming its Bush-era policies. In 2002, it added ethics standard 1.02 to the APA ethics code, which stated for the first time that, in the case of a conflict between the ethics code and "law, regulations, or other governing legal authority . . . psychologists may adhere to the requirements of the law, regulations, or other governing legal authority."[73] With echoes of the universally reviled Nuremberg—"I was just following orders"—Defense of Nazi doctors and others tried for war crimes after World War II, this standard has been deeply disturbing to many.[74] As early as 2005, the APA Council directed the Ethics Committee to evaluate and recommend an alternative to this standard; some discussions were held, but year after year, no action was taken.

At its August 2008 meeting, the Council again directed the Ethics Committee to make a recommendation at the August 2009 Council meeting. During the year, there was an open comment period in which over 80 psychologists participated via the APA website. Interestingly, a number of military psychologists strongly objected to changing this standard. Among them were PENS task force members Banks and James, as well as Debra Dunivin, a former BSCT psychologist at Guantánamo and wife of a former top APA official, Russ Newman, who played a major behind-the-scenes role in guiding the PENS task force.[75]

One month before the August 2009 Council meeting, the Ethics Committee made its recommendation. After four years of deliberations, it recommended no change in this standard. This recommendation met a blizzard of criticism. The Council united behind yet another proposal directing the very same Ethics Committee that had just expressed no urgency for change to develop a new plan for change. As this book goes to press, in January 2010, psychologists are yet again waiting to see if, this time, the APA will finally renounce the Nuremberg Defense.[76]

As the battle within psychology has played itself out over the last several years, a number of journalists and human rights advocates have become concerned with APA policies and begun to suspect that the issue runs deeper than merely bad policies.[77] They have rediscovered the open secret that professional psychology has long had deep connections with the military intelligence establishment, dating at least from World War II and the Cold War.[78] After 9/11, the APA leadership saw a major opportunity to prove the value of psychology to the defense and anti-terrorist efforts.

The connections between the APA and the military intelligence establishment must be further investigated as part of a necessary process to ensure transparency and accountability and to redeem the psychological profession and the APA. After the PENS listserv materials were publicly posted online in May 2009,[79] several psychological and human rights organizations called for investigations of possible collusion between the APA and the military intelligence establishment.[80] In response to the woefully inadequate June 18, 2009, letter from the APA Board cited above, a number of human rights organizations joined psychologists in co-signing a response to this letter.[81] These organizations recommended five actions for the APA to take in response to the crisis posed by psychologist participation in detainee abuse and torture:

1. Fully implement the 2008 referendum as an enforceable section of the APA Code of Ethics. This entails a public announcement that APA policy and ethical standards oppose the service of psychologists in detention facilities at Guantánamo Bay Detention Camp, Bagram Air Base, CIA secret prisons, or in the rendition program.

2. Annul the June 2005 PENS Report due to the severe and multiple conflicts of interest involved in its production.

3. Bring in an *independent* body of investigative attorneys to pursue accountability for psychologists who participated in or otherwise contributed to torture or cruel, inhuman, or degrading treatment. APA should also: (a) clarify the status of open ethics cases and (b) remove the statute of limitations for violations involving torture or cruel, inhuman, or degrading treatment, so as to allow time for information on classified activities to become public.

4. Develop a clear and rapid timetable to remove Sections 1.02 and 1.03 [the "Nuremberg defense" of following orders] from the APA Code of Ethics. [We note that the APA Ethics Committee has stated that they will not accept a defense of following orders to complaints regarding torture; this statement is a welcome improvement but is clearly inadequate as it is not necessarily binding on future committees nor does it cover abuses falling under the category of cruel, inhuman, or degrading treatment.] Revoke the equally problematic Section 8.05 of the Code, which dispenses with informed consent "where otherwise permitted by law or federal or institutional regulations," and Section 8.07, which sets an unacceptably high threshold of "severe emotional distress" for not using deception in the ethics of research design.

5. Retain an independent investigatory organization to study organizational behavior at APA. Due to potential conflicts of interest, independent human rights groups should be enlisted to select this investigatory entity. The study should address, among other things, possible collusion in the PENS process and the 2003 APA-CIA-Rand conference on the Science of Deception, attended by the CIA's apparent designers of their torture program [James Mitchell and Bruce Jessen] during which "enhanced interrogation" techniques were discussed. The study should explore how the APA governance system permits the accumulation of power in the hands of a very small number of individuals who are unresponsive to the general membership. It should also propose measures to return the APA to democratic principles, scientific integrity, and beneficence, including restructuring for greater transparency and the assimilation of diverse viewpoints.[82]

As this chapter is concluded, the story of psychologists and U.S. torture has not come to an end. It remains to be seen if the APA will take any of these five actions and how the APA membership, the broader psychological community, and the general public will respond, should the APA fail to act. The struggle is ongoing, just as the broader struggle to end torture and abuse by psychologists and other health professionals continues. These types of struggles are never definitively won. Human rights and human decency require an ongoing battle of civil society against state-sponsored abuses.

NOTES

1. For a detailed list of the notorious Justice Department documents, see George Washington University, "The Interrogation Documents: Debating U.S. Policy and Methods," *The National Security Archive*, http://www.gwu.edu/~nsarchiv/NSAEBB/NSAEBB127/ (last visited Sept. 2, 2009).

2. Jay S. Bybee, memorandum for John Rizzo regarding "Interrogation of al Qaeda Operative," Aug. 1, 2002, p. 17, http://luxmedia.vo.llnwd.net/o10/clients/aclu/olc_08012002_bybee.pdf (last visited Sept. 2, 2009).

3. Ibid.

4. For links to these documents, drafted by Assistant Attorney Generals Jay S. Bybee and Steven G. Bradbury, see American Civil Liberties Union, "The Bush Admin's Secret OLC Memos," *Accountability for Torture*, http://www.aclu. org/accountability/olc.html (last visited Sept. 2, 2009).

5. Steven G. Bradbury, memorandum to John Rizzo regarding, "Application of 18 USC §§ 2340-2340A," May 10, 2005, p. 4.

6. Ibid., at 5.

7. Physicians for Human Rights, *Break Them Down: Systematic Use of Psychological Torture by U.S. Forces* (2005); Physicians for Human Rights, *Broken Laws, Broken Lives: Medical Evidence of Torture By US Personnel and Its Impact* (2008); Physicians for Human Rights and Human Rights First, *Leave No Marks: Enhanced Interrogation Techniques and the Risk of Criminality* (2007).

8. See Michael Otterman, *American Torture: From the Cold War to Abu Ghraib and Beyond* (Australia: Griffin Press, 2007).

9. Anthony P. Doran, Gary Hoyt, and Charles A. Morgan III, "Survival, Evasion, Resistance, and Escape (SERE): Preparing Military Members for the Demands of Captivity," in *Military Psychology: Clinical and Operational Applications*, ed. Carrie H. Kennedy and Eric A. Zillmer, 241–61 (New York: Guilford Press, 2006).

10. See Katherine Eban, "The War on Terror: Rorschach and Awe," *Vanity Fair*, July 17, 2007, http://www.vanityfair.com/politics/features/2007/07/torture200707 (last visited Sept. 2, 2009).

11. See Jane Mayer, "The Black Sites: A Rare Look Inside the C.I.A.'s Secret Interrogation Program," *The New Yorker*, Aug. 13, 2007, http://www.newyorker. com/reporting/2007/08/13/070813fa_fact_mayer (last visited Sept. 2, 2009).

12. See Mark Benjamin, "The CIA's Torture Teachers," *Salon.com*, June 21, 2007, http://www.salon.com/news/feature/2007/06/21/cia_sere/ (last visited Sept. 2, 2009).

13. Eban, "Rorschach and Awe," *Vanity Fair*.

14. See Jane Mayer, *The Dark Side: The Inside Story of How the War on Terror Turned into a War on American Ideals* (New York: Doubleday, 2008); see also Scott Horton, "Six Questions for Jane Mayer, Author of *The Dark Side*," *Harper's Magazine*, July 14, 2008, http://www.harpers.org/archive/2008/07/hbc-90003234 (last visited Sept. 2, 2009).

15. See Stephen Soldz, "Former APA President Martin Seligman Denies Involvement in Developing CIA Tactics," *Psyche, Science, and Society*, July 14, 2008, http://psychoanalystsopposewar.org/blog/2008/07/14/former-apa-president-martin-seligman-denies-involvement-in-developing-cia-tactics/ (last visited Sept. 2, 2009); see also Andrew Sullivan, "Mayer on Seligman," *The Atlantic*, July 17, 2008 (last visited Sept. 2, 2009).

16. See Stephen Soldz et al., "Torture after Dark: Torture and the Strategic Helplessness of the American Psychological Association," *CounterPunch*, July 22, 2008, http://www.counterpunch.org/soldz07232008.html (last visited Sept. 2, 2009).

17. See Intl. Committee of the Red Cross (hereafter ICRC), *Report on the Treatment of Fourteen "High Value Detainees" in CIA Custody*, Feb. 2007, http://www.nybooks.com/icrc-report.pdf (last visited Sept. 2, 2009); see also Bradbury, memorandum regarding "Application of 18 USC §§ 2340–2340A."

18. See Jan Crawford Greenburg, Howard L. Rosenberg, and Adriane de Vogue, "Sources: Top Bush Advisors Approved 'Enhanced Interrogation," *ABC News*, Apr. 9, 2008, http://abcnews.go.com/TheLaw/LawPolitics/story?id=4583256&page=1 (last visited Sept. 2, 2009); Jan Crawford Greenburg, Howard L. Rosenberg, and Adriane de Vogue, "Bush Aware of Advisers' Interrogation Talks," *ABC News*, Apr. 11, 2008, http://abcnews.go.com/TheLaw/LawPolitics/story?id=4635175&page=1 (last visited Sept. 2, 2009).

19. U.S. Senate, Committee on Armed Services, *Inquiry into the Treatment of Detainees in US Custody* (hereafter *Levin Report*), Nov. 20, 2008, http://armed-services.senate.gov/Publications/Detainee%20Report%20Final_April%2022%20 2009.pdf (last visited Aug. 21, 2009).

20. Ibid., at xix.

21. See U.S. Dept. of Defense, *Review of DoD-Directed Investigations*; U.S. Senate, *Levin Report*; Sheri Fink, "Tortured Profession: Psychologists Warned of Abusive Interrogations, Then Helped Craft Them," *ProPublica*, May 5, 2009, http://www.propublica.org/article/tortured-profession-psychologists-warned-of-abusive-interrogations-505 (last visited Sept. 2, 2009).

22. Secret ORCON [Authoring agency classified by Originator Control], *Interrogation Log: Detainee 063*, Nov. 23, 2002, http://www.time.com/time/2006/log/log.pdf (last visited Sept. 2, 2009).

23. Steven H. Miles, "Medical Ethics and the Interrogation of Guantánamo 063," in *American Journal of Bioethics* 7, no. 4 (2007): 2, http://www1.umn.edu/humanrts/OathBetrayed/Guantanamo%20063.pdf (last visited Sept. 2, 2009).

24. T. J. Harrington, letter to Donald J. Ryder regarding "Suspected Mistreatment of Detainees," July 14, 2004, p. 2, http://www1.umn.edu/humanrts/OathBetrayed/FBI%204622-4624.pdf(last visited Sept. 2, 2009).

25. See Bob Woodward, "Detainee Tortured, Says U.S. Official," *Washington Post*, Jan. 14, 2009, p. A01, http://www.washingtonpost.com/wpdyn/content/article/2009/01/13/AR2009011303372.html (last visited Sept. 2, 2009).

26. See Kenneth S. Pope and Thomas G. Gutheil, "The American Psychological Association and Detainee Interrogations: Unanswered Questions," *Psychiatric Times* 25, no. 8 (2008).

27. See American Psychological Association (APA), *2006 Resolution Against Torture and Other Cruel, Inhuman, or Degrading Treatment or Punishment*, Aug. 9, 2006, http://www.apa.org/governance/resolutions/notortureres.html (last visited Sept. 2, 2009); APA, *Reaffirmation of the APA Position Against Torture and Other Cruel, Inhuman, or Degrading Treatment or Punishment and Its Application to Individuals Defined in the United States Code as "Enemy Combatants,"* Aug. 19, 2007, http://www.apa.org/governance/resolutions/councilres0807.html (last visited Sept. 2, 2009); APA, *Amendment to the Reaffirmation of the APA Position Against Torture and Other Cruel, Inhuman, or Degrading Treatment or Punishment and Its Application to Individuals Defined in the United States Code as "Enemy Combatants,"* Feb. 22, 2008, http://www.apa.org/governance/resolutions/amendo22208.html (last visited Sept. 2, 2009); Stephen Soldz and Brad Olson, "A Reaction to the APA Vote on Sealing Up Key Loopholes in the 2007 Resolution on Interrogations," *Psyche, Science, and Society*, Mar. 2, 2008, http://psychoanalystsopposewar.org/blog/2008/03/02/a-reaction-to-the-apa-vote-on-sealing-up-key-loopholes-in-the-2007-resolution-on-interrogations/ (last visited Sept. 2, 2009).

28. See Coalition for an Ethical Psychology, *Analysis of the American Psychological Association's Frequently Asked Questions Regarding APA's Policies and Positions on the Use of Torture or Cruel, Inhuman or Degrading Treatment During Interrogations*, Jan. 2008, http://psychoanalystsopposewar.org/blog/wp-content/uploads/2008/01/apa_faq_coalition_comments_v12c.pdf (last visited Sept. 2, 2009); Society for the Study of Peace Conflict and Violence, Peace Psychology Division 48, *American Psychological Association Presidential Task Force on Psychological Ethics and National Security: 2003 Members' Biographical Statements*, http://www.webster.edu/peacepsychology/tfpens.html (last visited Sept. 2, 2009); Mark Benjamin, "Psychological Warfare," *Salon.com*, July 26, 2006, http://www.salon.com/news/feature/2006/07/26/interrogation/ (last visited Sept. 2, 2009).

29. Morgan Banks, *Providing psychological support for interrogations, chapter 1: Purpose of psychological support to interrogation and detainee operations. Unofficial records of the APA Task Force on PENS, June 25–28, 2005*; Banks, *Providing psychological support for interrogations, chapter 2: The ethics of psychological support to interrogation. Unofficial Records of the APA Task Force on PENS, June 25–28, 2005.*

30. See Larry C. James and Gregory A. Freeman, *Fixing Hell: An Army Psychologist Confronts Abu Ghraib* (New York: Grand Central Publishing, 2008).

31. See William Glaberson, "Red Cross Barred from Guantánamo," *New York Times*, Nov. 16, 2007, http://www.nytimes.com/2007/11/16/washington/16gitmo.html (last visited Sept. 3, 2009).

32. Joint Task Force-Guantánamo, *Camp Delta Standard Operating Procedures (SOP)*, Mar. 1, 2004, 4.3, http://humanrights.ucdavis.edu/projects/the-guantanamo-testimonials-project/testimonies/testimonies-of-standard-operating-procedures/camp_delta_sop_2004.pdf.

33. See Amnesty Intl., *From Ill-Treatment to Unfair Trial. The Case of Mohammed Jawad, Child 'Enemy Combatant*,' AMR 51/09/2008, Aug. 13, 2008, http://www.amnesty.org/en/library/info/AMR51/091/2008/en (last visited Sept. 4, 2009).

34. See Psychological Ethics and National Security Task Force (hereafter PENS Task Force), "Email Messages From the Listserv of the American Psychological Association's Presidential Task Force on Psychological Ethics and National Security: April 22, 2005–June 26, 2006," *ProPublica*, p. 47, http://documents.propublica.org/docs/e-mails-from-the-american-psychological-association-s-task-force-on-ethics-and-national-security/original.pdf (last visited Sept. 4, 2009).

35. See Neil A. Lewis, "Red Cross Finds Detainee Abuse in Guantánamo," *New York Times*, Nov. 30, 2004, http://www.nytimes.com/2004/11/30/politics/30gitmo.html (last visited Sept. 3, 2004); Neil A. Lewis, "Fresh Details Emerge on Harsh Methods at Guantánamo," *New York Times*, Jan. 1, 2005, http://www.nytimes.com/2005/01/01/national/01gitmo.html (last visited Sept. 3, 2004); Neil A. Lewis, "Interrogators Cite Doctors' Aid at Guantánamo Prison Camp," *New York Times*, June 24, 2005, http://www.nytimes.com/2005/06/24/politics/24gitmo.html(last visited Sept. 3, 2004); Jane Mayer, "The Experiment," *The New Yorker*, July 11, 2005, http://www.newyorker.com/archive/2005/07/11/050711fa_fact4 (last visited Sept. 3, 2004). See also U.S. Dept. of Defense, *Review of DoD-Directed Investigations*; U.S. Dept. of Justice, *A Review of the FBI's Involvement in and Observations of Detainee Interrogations in Guantánamo Bay, Afghanistan, and Iraq*, May 2008, http://www.usdoj.gov/oig/special/s0805/final.pdf (last visited Sept. 3, 2004); U.S. Senate, *Levin Report*.

36. See Andrew O. Selsky, "AP Confirms Secret Camp Inside Guantánamo," *truthout.org*, Feb. 6, 2008, http://www.truthout. org/article/ap-confirms-secret-camp-inside-guantanamo (last visited Sept. 3, 2004).

37. See Society for the Study of Peace Conflict and Violence: Peace Psychology Division 48, "American Psychological Association Presidential Task Force on Psychological Ethics and National Security: 2003 Members' Biographical Statements," http://www.webster.edu/peacepsychology/tfpens.html (last visited Feb. 5, 2010).

38. See Eban, "Rorschach and Awe," *Vanity Fair*.

39. See Stephen Soldz, "Member of APA PENS Task Force Brags of Being with Tortured Prisoners," *Psyche, Science, and Society*, Apr. 27, 2007, http://psychoanalystsopposewar.org/blog/2007/04/27/member-of-apa-pens-task-force-brags-of-being-with-tortured-prioners/ (last visited Sept. 3, 2004).

40. See Warren Richey, "US Gov't Broke Padilla Through Intense Isolation, Say Experts," *Christian Science Monitor*, Aug. 14, 2007, p. 4, http://www.csmonitor.com/2007/0814/p11s01-usju.html?page=4 (last visited Sept. 4, 2004).

41. See Alix Spiegel, "Military psychologist says harsh tactics justified," *National Public Radio*, May 4, 2009, http://www.npr.org/templates/story/story.php?storyId=103787285 (last visited Sept. 4, 2004).

42. PENS Task Force, "Email Messages from the Listserv."

43. See Jean Maria Arrigo, "APA Interrogation Task Force Member Dr. Jean Maria Arrigo Exposes Group's Ties to Military," *Democracy Now!* Aug. 20, 2007, http://i1.democracynow.org/2007/8/20/apa_interrogation_task_force_member_dr (last visited Sept. 4, 2009); Coalition for an Ethical Psychology, *Analysis of the APA's FAQ's*; PENS Task Force, "Email Messages from the Listserv."

44. PENS Task Force, *Report on Psychological Ethics and National Security*, June 2005, p. 2, http://www.apa.org/releases/PENSTaskForceReportFinal.pdf (last visited Sept. 4, 2009).

45. See Stephen Soldz, "Closing Eyes to Atrocities: U.S. Psychologists, Detainee Interrogations, and Response of the American Psychological Association," in *Interrogations, Forced Feedings, and the Role of Health Professionals: New Perspectives on International Human Rights, Humanitarian Law, and Ethics*, ed. Ryan Goodman and Mindy Jane Roseman (Cambridge, MA: Harvard Law School, 2009).

46. See Stanley Cohen, *States of Denial: Knowing About Atrocities and Suffering* (Malden, MA: Blackwell, 2001).

47. See Gerald P. Koocher, "Speaking Against Torture," *Monitor on Psychology* 37, no. 2 (2006): 5, http://www.apa.org/monitor/feb06/pc.html (last visited Sept. 4, 2009).

48. See APA, *Frequently Asked Questions Regarding APA's Policies and Positions on the Use of Torture or Cruel, Inhuman or Degrading Treatment During Interrogations*, Oct. 2006, http://www.apa.org/releases/faqinterrogation.html (last visited Sept. 4, 2009).

49. See Olivia Moorehead-Slaughter, "Ethics and National Security," *Monitor on Psychology* 37, no. 4 (2006): 20, http://www.apa.org/monitor/apr06/security.html (last visited Sept. 4, 2009).

50. See Stephen Behnke, "Ethics and Interrogations: Comparing and Contrasting the American Psychological, American Medical and American Psychiatric Association Positions," *Monitor on Psychology* 37, no. 7 (2006): 66–67, http://www.apa.org/releases/PENSfinal_061606.pdf (last visited Sept. 4, 2009); Stephen Soldz, "Protecting the Torturers: Bad Faith and Distortions From the American Psychological Association," *CounterPunch*, Sept. 6, 2006, http://www.coun-

terpunch.org/soldz09062006.html (last visited Sept. 4, 2009); Stephen Soldz, "American Medical Association Emphasizes Interrogation Policy Differences with APA," *OpEdNews*, Aug. 28, 2006, http://www.opednews.com/articles/opedne_stephen__060828_american_medical_ass.htm (last visited Sept. 4, 2009).

51. See APA, *Reaffirmation of the APA Position Against Torture*; Mark Benjamin, "Will Psychologists Still Abet Torture?" *Salon.com*, Aug. 21, 2007, http://www.salon.com/news/feature/2007/08/21/psychologists/ (last visited Sept. 4, 2009); Coalition for an Ethical Psychology, *Analysis of the APA's FAQ's*; Soldz, "Protecting the Torturers"; Stephen Soldz, "What the US Reservations to UN Convention on Torture Really Means?" *Psyche, Science, and Society*, Sept. 13, 2006, http://psychoanalystsopposewar.org/blog/2006/09/13/what-the-us-reservations-to-un-convention-on-torture-really-means/ (last visited Sept. 4, 2009).

52. ICRC, *Report on "High Value Detainees."*

53. See Stephen Soldz, "APA Board makes major statement on torture," *Psyche, Science, and Society*, June 18, 2009, http://psychoanalystsopposewar.org/blog/2009/06/18/apa-board-makes-major-statement-on-torture/ (last visited Sept. 4, 2009).

54. Ibid.

55. See Stephen Soldz and Brad Olson, "Psychologists, Detainee Interrogations, and Torture: Varying Perspectives on Nonparticipation," in *The Trauma of Psychological Torture*, ed. Almerindo E. Ojeda, 70–91 (Westport, CT: Praeger, 2008).

56. See Bernice Lott, "APA and the Participation of Psychologists in Situations in which Human Rights Are Violated: Comment on 'Psychologists and the Use of Torture in Interrogations,'" *Analyses of Social Issues and Pub. Policy* 7, no. 1 (2007): 35–43; Neil Altman, *Resolution for a Moratorium on Psychologist Participation in Interrogations at US Detention Centers Holding Foreign Detainees, So-called 'Enemy Combatants': Summary and Overview*, 2006, http://www.apa.org/ethics/pdfs/2006moratoriumresolutionsummaryandoverview.pdf (last visited Sept. 4, 2009).

57. See Mark Costanzo, Ellen Gerrity, and M. Brinton Lykes, "The Use of Torture and Other Cruel, Inhumane, or Degrading Treatment as Interrogation Devices," *The Society for the Psychological Study of Social Issues*, June 21, 2006, http://www.spssi.org/index.cfm?fuseaction=Page.viewPage&pageId=1061&parentID=47 (last visited Sept. 4, 2009); Philip G. Zimbardo, "Thoughts on Psychologists, Ethics, and the Use of Torture in Interrogations: Don't Ignore Varying Roles and Complexities," *Analyses of Social Issues and Pub. Policy* 7, no. 1 (2007): 1–9, http://www.asap-spssi.org/pdf/0701Zimbardo.pdf (last visited Sept. 4, 2009).

58. Robert Jay Lifton, "Doctors and Torture," *New England Journal of Medicine* 351, no. 5 (2004): 415–16, http://content.nejm.org/cgi/content/full/351/5/415h (last visited Sept. 4, 2009).

59. See APA, "General Principle A," in *Ethical Principles of Psychologists and Code of Conduct*, June 1, 2003, http://www.apa.org/ethics/code2002.html#intro (last visited Sept. 4, 2009); Steven H. Miles, *Oath betrayed: America's Torture Doctors* (Berkeley: Univ. of California Press, 2009).

60. See American Medical Association (hereafter AMA), "Opinion 2.068: Physician Participation in Interrogation," *Code of Medical Ethics*, Nov. 2006, http://www.ama-assn.org/ama/pub/physician-resources/medical-ethics/code-medical-ethics/opinion2068.shtml (last visited Sept. 4, 2009); AMA, *Report of the Council on Ethical and Judicial Affairs: Physician Participation in Interrogation*, Res. 1, I-05, CEJA Report 10-A-06, 2006, http://www.ama-assn.org/ama1/pub/upload/mm/code-medical-ethics/2068a.pdf (last visited Sept. 4, 2009).

61. See Brad Olson and Stephen Soldz, "Positive Illusions and the Necessity of a Bright Line Forbidding Psychologist Involvement in Detainee Interrogations," *Analyses of Social Issues and Pub. Policy* 7, no. 1 (2007): 1–10; Leonard S. Rubenstein, "Complicity and the Illusion of Beneficence," in *Interrogations, Forced Feedings, and the Role of Health Professionals*, ed. Goodman and Roseman.

62. See Kenneth S. Pope and Thomas G. Gutheil, "Psychologists Abandon the Nuremberg Ethic: Concerns for Detainee Interrogations," *Intl. Journal of Law and Psychiatry* 32, no. 4 (2009): 161–66.

63. See Trudy Bond, "If Not Now, When?" *CounterPunch*, May 19, 2008, http://www.counterpunch.org/bond05192008.html (last visited Sept. 4, 2009).

64. See Coalition for an Ethical Psychology, *Analysis of the APA's FAQ's*; Frank Summers, "Making Sense of the APA: A History of the Relationship between Psychology and the Military," *Psychoanalytic Dialogues* 18, no. 5 (2008): 614–27.

65. See Stephen Soldz, "APA, Torture, and the CIA," *Psyche, Science, and Society*, Aug. 22, 2007, http://psychoanalystsopposewar.org/blog/2007/08/22/apa-torture-and-the-cia/ (last visited Sept. 8, 2009); Benjamin, "Will Psychologists Still Abet Torture?"; APA, "Reaffirmation of the APA Position Against Torture;" Editorial, "Human Wrongs: Psychologists Have No Place Assisting Interrogations at Places Such as Guantánamo Bay," *Houston Chronicle*, Aug. 23, 2007, B8, http://www.chron.com/CDA/archives/archive.mpl?id=2007_4410052 (last visited Sept. 8, 2009).

66. APA, *Amendment to the Reaffirmation of APA Position on Torture*; Soldz and Olson, "Reaction to the APA Vote," *Psyche, Science, and Society*.

67. See Stephen Soldz, "Noted Psychologist Beth Shinn Resigns from American Psychological Association," *Psyche, Science, and Society*, Oct. 7, 2007, http://psychoanalystsopposewar.org/blog/2007/10/07/noted-psychologist-beth-shinn-resigns-from-american-psychological-association/ (last visited Sept. 8, 2009).

68. See Bryant Welch, "Torture, Political Manipulation and the American Psychological Association," *CounterPunch*, July 28, 2008, http://www.counterpunch.org/welch07282008.html (last visited Sept. 8, 2009).

69. See Kenneth S. Pope, "Why I Resigned from the American Psychological Association," letter to Alan Kasdin, Feb. 6, 2008, http://kspope.com/apa/index.php (last visited Sept. 8, 2009).

70. Ibid.

71. See APA, *2008 APA Petition Resolution Ballot*, Aug. 1, 2008, http://www.apa.org/governance/resolutions/worksettingscon.html (last visited Sept. 8, 2009).

72. See Stephen Soldz and Brad Olson, "Psychologists Reject the Dark Side: APA Members Reject Participation in Bush Detention Centers," *Psyche, Science, and Society*, Sept. 22, 2008, http://psychoanalystsopposewar.org/blog/2008/09/22/psychologists-reject-the-dark-side/ (last visited Sept. 8, 2009).

73. See APA, "Ethical Standard 1.02," in *Ethical Principles of Psychologists and Code of Conduct*.

74. See Pope and Gutheil, "Psychologists Abandon Nuremberg Ethic," *Intl. Journal of Law and Psychiatry*.

75. See Arrigo, "Arrigo Exposes Group's Ties to Military," *Democracy Now!*

76. See APA Ethics Committee, *No Defense to Torture Under the APA Ethics Code*, June 2009, http://www.apa.org/ethics/standard-102/Ethics-Committee-Council-recommendation-0609.pdf (last visited Sept. 8, 2009).

77. See Arthur Levine, "Collective Unconscionable: How Psychologists, the Most Liberal of Professionals, Abetted Bush's Torture Policy," *Washington Monthly* 39, no. 1 (2007): 5; Amy Goodman, "A Torture Debate Among Healers," *Democracy Now!* Apr. 10, 2008, http://www.democracynow.org/blog/2008/4/10/amy_goodmans_new_column_a_torture_debate_among_healers (last visited Sept. 8, 2009); Amy Goodman and David Goodman, *Standing Up to the Madness: Ordinary Heroes in Extraordinary Time* (New York: Hyperion, 2008); David Goodman, "The Enablers: The Psychology Industry's Long and Shameful History with Torture," *Mother Jones*, Mar. 1, 2008, http://www.motherjones.com/politics/2008/03/enablers (last visited Sept. 8, 2009); Editorial, "Psychologists and Torture," *Boston Globe*, Aug. 20, 2008, http://www.boston.com/bostonglobe/editorial_opinion/editorials/articles/2008/08/30/psychologists_and_torture/ (last visited Sept. 8, 2009).

78. See James H. Capshew, *Psychologists on the March: Science, Practice, and Professional Identity in America, 1929–1969* (Cambridge, UK: Cambridge Univ. Press, 1999); Frank Summers, "Making Sense of the APA: a History of the Relationship Between Psychology and the Military," *Psychoanalytic Psychology* 25, no. 2 (2008): 280–94.

79. See PENS Task Force, "Email Messages from the Listserv."

80. See Stephen Soldz, "Psychologists for an Ethical APA Calls for APA Investigation and Resignations," *Psyche, Science, and Society,* May 2, 2009; Psychologists for Social Responsibility, *PsySR Statement Urges Independent Torture Commission to Examine Role of Psychologists and APA in Prisoner Abuse,* Apr. 23, 2009, http://www.psysr.org/about/pubs_resources/PsySR_Statement_on_Torture_Commission.pdf (last visited Sept. 8, 2009); Physicians for Human Rights, *PHR Calls for Investigation of American Psychological Association's Ties to Pentagon, PHR Library,* May 5, 2009, http://physiciansforhumanrights.org/library/news-2009-05-05.html (last visited Sept. 8, 2009); Coalition for an Ethical Psychology, "Time for an Independent Investigation of the Ties Between the APA and the Defense Establishment," *CounterPunch,* May 6, 2009, http://www.counterpunch.org/cep05062009.html (last visited Sept. 8, 2009).

81. Coalition for an Ethical Psychology et al., *Open Letter in Response to the APA Board,* June 29, 2009, http://psychoanalystsopposewar.org/blog/2009/06/29/open-letter-in-response-to-the-american-psychological-association-board/ (last visited Sept. 8, 2009).

82. Ibid. (emphasis added).

9

From Guantánamo to Berlin

Protecting Human Rights after 9/11

MICHAEL RATNER

The title of this chapter includes Berlin because it is one of the places where we at the Center for Constitutional Rights (CCR) have tried to hold former Secretary of Defense Donald Rumsfeld responsible for the horrors of Guantánamo Bay Detention Camp in Cuba (Guantánamo), as well as the worldwide U.S. torture program.

In June 2009, Spain moved forward with a serious case against the lawyers involved in the U.S. torture program and, perhaps against other high-ranking U.S. officials.[1] In the United States, the question of prosecuting the conspirators is front page news.[2] Meanwhile, the world justice system is closing in as well. It may take a few years, but the perpetrators will more than likely be held accountable for their actions some day.

Sadly, President Obama is doing all he can to thwart the possibility of a criminal investigation in the United States.[3] Obama has resisted even a commission of inquiry, much less appointment of a special prosecutor, saying we need to look forward and avoid a retrospective on the faults of the prior administration.[4]

Yet, prosecutions are intuitively forward-looking. We cannot ensure a future without torture unless we send a message to those who would torture again: torture and you will be prosecuted. Instead, the message sent is one of impunity. Obama may well retain the legal regime that underlies Guantánamo, which is, in essence, a preventive detention scheme. Rather than charge and try detainees in a court, prisoners are often held without arraignment. If Obama retains a similar scheme as the Bush era (e.g., with a bit more due process), an unmitigated human rights disaster will result.

Preventive detention is a line that should never be crossed. A central aspect of human liberty that has taken centuries to win is that no person shall be imprisoned unless he or she is charged and tried. Rewrapping Guantánamo in another location will haunt this country and the world for generations.

This chapter briefly tells the story of how CCR initiated the first Guantánamo cases challenging indefinite, incommunicado detention and how those cases became instrumental in exposing the Bush administration's torture program. One equation must be kept in mind: indefinite, incommunicado detention equals torture. This is not to say that the detention always constitutes torture, though it can. The primary purpose of secret detention, whether at Guantánamo or elsewhere, is to have a place of darkness—no lawyers, no relatives, and no press—where torture can be inflicted with impunity.

Guantánamo

CCR and I began our first cases and, in fact, the first Guantánamo cases, in February 2002. We were the first and for a long time the only human rights organization willing to handle them, asserting that one could not assume all the detainees were terrorists, and that they deserved the right to a court hearing to help determine whether or not we actually have the proper detainees.

CCR also challenged the popular refrain that since the terrorists did not give us any rights when they attacked the World Trade Center, we had no obligation to give them any rights. This assumes the detainees are the actual guys responsible for the attacks on the World Trade Center. However, even those who might be guilty must be treated humanely and lawfully. If we mistreat people, we will be mistreated ourselves. The manner in which we treat one group of people is the way we will be treated by others.

In fact, we have an obligation to uphold fundamental human rights, no matter what really happens in the world. We have a moral, legal, political, and pragmatic reason for treating people according to law and morality.

There is also the more personal question: Why are we at CCR defending those at Guantánamo and at other secret sites around the world? The classic, easy answer of every defense lawyer applies here. Our job is to defend people and that is what we do. That is the way our American system works: defend people and the truth will come out.

But for me, there was actually a deeper reason at the time. Because the rights that were being taken away by the Bush administration were so fundamental, particularly the right of *habeas corpus* and the right to be free from torture, I was terrified to believe that our democracy was coming to an end. After all, the right of *habeas corpus* dates clear back to the *Magna Carta* of 1215 and is the hallmark of any democracy.[5]

I looked at what was happening to our clients. I saw them a bit like canaries in a coal mine because what was happening to them really tells us about what will happen in this country and around the world going forward. If you can take away those rights and simply grab someone by the scruff of the neck and throw them into some offshore penal colony because they are non-citizen Muslims, those deprivations of rights will be employed against all. These are profound, hard-fought-for fundamental rights.

Now, the question is, "Why Berlin?" We have tried for a long time, since the first revelations in 2004, to achieve accountability for torture, climbing the chain of command to Bush, Cheney, Rumsfeld, and others, and we have failed utterly. We failed in Congress. We have basically failed at prosecuting torture conspirators in U.S. courts. Therefore, we attempted to use a concept called "universal jurisdiction" to hold them accountable in Berlin.[6]

Some crimes are considered international crimes, torture being one of those,[7] and Germany, as it turns out, partly because of its past, has the best single law for prosecuting people for serious violations of international human rights.[8] So, we filed the case in Germany, where U.S. soldiers who actually were involved in the torture were still stationed.

In addition, Germany possesses the history from which international human rights law emerged—Nuremburg and the aftermath of the Second World War.[9] "From Guantánamo to Berlin" contains the idea that we must have accountability someday for the tragedy of Guantánamo and the infamous torture program.

The most important event in the unraveling of our democratic rights post-9/11 occurred on November 13, 2001, when President Bush issued what he called "Military Order No. 1."[10] The implications of that order and the underlying grab for executive power were utterly and completely shocking. The breadth of these "commander-in-chief powers," or executive powers, or war powers, or whatever you call them, still haunt us today. As of June 2009, President Obama has not repudiated this order or its detention authority.

Military Order No. 1 had two very important aspects. First, it enabled the president to pick up any non-citizen anywhere in the world and throw him in prison anywhere in the world, essentially rendering him disappeared (though the terminology differed, the effect was basically the same).[11] Those so imprisoned would never have any right to access a court or legal representation and could be held incommunicado for as long as the president desired.

Basically, this was indefinite detention without a hearing, performed solely at the behest of the president. The abolition of the writ of *habeas corpus* refers to the right to go to court and ask the government, "Why are you holding me in prison?" That is not to say the government cannot hold people (although they must be properly charged and tried once detained), but the government must justify any and all detentions in a court of law.

The second part of the Order said that if the Bush administration decided to try someone, they could utilize "Military Commissions" (or possibly kangaroo courts), which were special courts specifically designed for trying enemy combatants.[12] (The Obama administration suspended the use of military commissions for four months, but on May 21, 2009, they were allowed to resume.)[13]

There was some debate at CCR about whether we should get involved. We did not really know who we would end up representing.[14] Were these going to be the people actually involved in the conspiracy to attack the World Trade Center? Certainly, we would not feel comfortable defending *them*.

Yet the idea that the president could just take human beings, throw them in prison forever, and deny them any access to a court was frightening. This is the power of a police state and not a democracy. So we decided to take the first of the Guantánamo cases: an Australian man named David Hicks, who was finally released from Guantánamo more than five years later.[15]

Once we decided to get involved in the Guantánamo cases, we knew we needed help from other lawyers. There were only a handful of us at CCR, and we had some serious trouble getting others to assist, likely because 9/11 had just occurred four months earlier. In fact, we could not get a single human rights organization to take a case; we could not get most other lawyers, even progressives, to help out.

The lawyers and human rights groups we talked to were afraid of two things: first, there was no way to win these cases because of extremely adverse legal precedents coming out of World War II and before; and second, they were afraid of the national outrage that would surely be directed against them.

In addition to David Hicks, we also represented the Tipton men, three Englishmen referred to by their hometown. We did not select these individuals directly, nor did we know any of the inmates personally. In fact, there were hundreds of detainees who needed representation. The foreign embassies of our clients had notified their families abroad, who in turn contacted us.

We went into court with a very straightforward proposition—that *habeas corpus* meant every single person detained has the right to go into court and say to the government: "Tell me why you are detaining me and give me the legal justification." As one might anticipate, the initial arguments before the courts were completely empty and the lower level judges looked at us like we were talking to a wall. Indeed, they thought we were completely out of our minds. After losing the first case in the lowest court, and again in the appellate court, we finally went to the Supreme Court in 2004, in *Rasul v. Bush*.[16]

In June 2004, we won *Rasul v. Bush* in the Supreme Court, 6 to 3, on the grounds that people detained in Guantánamo—and arguably people detained anywhere in the world by the United States—could go to court and file a writ of *habeas corpus* and force the government to answer the question, "What is the legal basis for my detention?" In turn, the government would have to demonstrate a legally viable justification. This seems reasonable in any nation that calls itself a civilized society.

Technically, the Supreme Court decided in our favor on the basis that *habeas corpus* is required not by the U.S. Constitution, but by federal statute. The Court avoided the constitutional question, which it would ultimately need to decide in 2008 in *Boumediene v. Bush*.[17] After our victory in *Rasul*, we started receiving letters the content of which were along the lines of "I feel better about America," and, "You've saved us." However, despite our success, we still had not had one federal court hearing for any of our clients by 2008, four years later.

Immediately after the *Rasul* victory began one of the great pages of legal history in the United States. First, we obtained the names of many, many more Guantánamo detainees. Our staff tracked down their families in Muslim countries around the world and identified almost all 400–500 detainees at Guantánamo in 2004. Then the law firms started stepping forward to take on cases *pro bono*. Today, almost every major law firm in the country represents detainees. We now coordinate a group of roughly 600 lawyers from across the country, most of whom have three or four clients each.

These men and women travel to Guantánamo at their own expense, visit clients, and represent them in court. It has been a magnificent chapter in American legal history, as lawyers are leading a righteous social movement to close the Guantánamo prison. Importantly, allowing lawyers to visit clients makes torture much more difficult. Although we did not get a *habeas corpus* hearing until our third victory in court, we were able to obtain lawyer visits to Guantánamo in the interim.

The next obstacle to achieving *habeas corpus* rights for the detainees arose in late 2005 when the Bush administration essentially told Congress, "Well, we don't like this idea that lawyers are going down to Guantánamo, doing all this litigation and asserting *habeas corpus* rights, so why don't you strip *habeas corpus* out of the federal statutes?" After all, the Supreme Court had not said *habeas corpus* was a constitutional right at this point, only a statutory right.

What resulted was the Bush administration's passage of *The Detainee Treatment Act* in 2005.[18] Although the Act eliminated the right of *habeas corpus*, we pressured the Democrats into including enough ambiguous language to avoid retroactive application to detainees. Again, the issue went to the Supreme Court, another year and a half after our victory in 2004. Our clients, meanwhile, had been in Guantánamo four or five years without any kind of hearing in court and without any disclosed basis for detention.

Eventually, in 2006, in the *Hamdan* case,[19] the Supreme Court said, Congress, you did not do it right. If you are going to strip *habeas corpus*, you cannot do it this way. And the Court again restored the right of *habeas corpus* to us. Once more we started to prepare for our cases, until the Bush administration went back to Congress and had the *Military Commission Act* passed in the fall of 2006.[20]

This time, Congress did what they had not done in the *Detainee Treatment Act*: they stripped *habeas corpus* retroactively and prospectively from everyone at Guantánamo, eliminating the right to *habeas corpus* for all detainees. They went even further to say that no non-citizen anywhere in the world who has been classified as an enemy combatant by the president has a right to *habeas corpus*."[21] This exceeded the bounds of Guantánamo, as the president could now arrest even a permanent resident in the United States, take him to Guantánamo or a "black site" like Bagram Air Force Base in Afghanistan, never disclose his kidnapping, and deny him any right to *habeas corpus*.

This was not just about Guantánamo anymore; this affected a much wider spectrum of non-citizens, even people in the United States. Before *Boumediene* there was no longer a statutory right to *habeas corpus*; it had been stripped. The only question left to be answered in *Boumediene* was whether the U.S. Constitution gives detainees a right to *habeas corpus*. That is, does it give that right to a non-citizen in Guantánamo, in particular, "outside the United States," or at least outside the 50 states?

The Constitution does not include much about *habeas corpus*, only that "[t]he privilege of the writ of *habeas corpus* shall not be suspended, unless when in cases of rebellion or invasion the public safety may require it."[22] So, the question is one of interpretation. Who does this cover and to what geographical location does it apply?

We lost the case 2–1 in the Court of Appeals on the issue of whether there is a constitutional right to *habeas corpus* for the detainees at Guantánamo. If the Supreme Court ultimately had decided against us, that would have been the end. The prisoners at Guantánamo, the people in Bagram, the detainees in secret sites and elsewhere, could remain there forever without any judicial review. Luckily, that frightening scenario did not occur. We won the case in the Supreme Court with a razor thin victory, 5–4.

The Court held that the U.S. Constitution guarantees prisoners at Guantánamo, and hopefully elsewhere, a right to *habeas corpus*. Remarkably, the right of *habeas corpus* hung by one justice in the Supreme Court. Finally, because of this victory, almost eight years after the first detentions, *habeas corpus* hearings began. By July 2009, some 30 or so detainees had *habeas corpus* hearings in federal court; almost all were found not to be "enemy combatants."[23]

Where are we at the time of this writing—summer 2009—with regard to Guantánamo? There are 225 detainees remaining. The situation remains desperate. Though lawyers are visiting continuously, there have still been four deaths, labeled suicides by the military.[24] And torture continues in the form of the response to hunger strikes.[25]

What the Bush administration did and what the Obama administration continues to do is force-feed strikers, a brutal process designed to torture the individual into ending the strike. At Guantánamo, within days, if not hours of a hunger strike, authorities strap the striker into a chair, head and all. They force a very thick feeding tube down through their noses and into their stomach without any anesthetic. This method usually breaks a hunger strike quickly because it is extremely painful and actually violates the prohibition against torture.[26]

It is our hope that, by the time you are reading this, torture and detention at Guantánamo will be a thing of the past. However, even if the physical prison is shuttered, the Obama administration apparently will continue detaining prisoners without charges and trial, albeit in other locations. As for Guantánamo itself, over 500 detainees have been released, almost all prior to the Obama administration.[27] We have secured their release, at least in part, because of protests by foreign citizens and foreign governments, which proved quite effective for the Europeans.[28]

More importantly, many of these detainees have been released because even the government acknowledges that the majority of these people should not have been there in the first place. Even today, there are 85 detainees who the United States admits are not guilty of anything.[29] There are presumably many more and, as the court hearings continue, increasing numbers of detainees will be found not to be "enemy combatants."

Who are or were the people at Guantánamo? Are they really the people I thought they were when we began this representation, the worst of the worst? Are they really people who are going to chew through hydraulic cords and bring down airplanes? In fact, they usually turn out not to be. The so-called worst people, the so-called high-value detainees, were not taken to Guantánamo; they were put in secret detention facilities. We do not know where they are or how many of those detainees exist, though the government publicly transferred 14 from secret sites to Guantánamo in fall 2006.[30]

It was my hope that the Guantánamo prison would have been closed on January 22, 2010, as Obama promised. But congressional funding was not forthcoming and the prison remains open as this book goes to press. Moreover, the policies underlying that off-shore prison may sadly become part of the permanent legal landscape of the U.S. legal system, in particular the practices of preventive detention and military commissions. Other prison sites, such as Bagram, will continue to operate in the dark, denying detainees any access to lawyers or courts and perhaps replicating some of what we now know as Guantánamo.[31]

And the practice of torture—applied liberally at Guantánamo, will inevitably continue at other detention sites. When the first detainees were sent to Guantánamo, I did not actually suspect they were being tortured. I thought it was an indefinite detention and interrogation camp, but not a torture center. Now I know better. As early as 2004, clients told me about being shackled and locked to a large metal bolt in the center of the floor. The temperature was lowered and raised to extremely uncomfortable levels.

The men were stripped, hooded, sometimes put in isolation, and deprived of sleep for extended periods. I heard stories about women sexually harassing detainees and interrogators frightening them with vicious, un-muzzled military dogs. These torture methods, now known as the "Rumsfeld techniques," were apparently standard operating procedures at Guantánamo.[32]

Documents emerged exposing Rumsfeld's set of approved torture techniques for Guantánamo, including exploitation of phobias, such as exposure to dogs, as Arabs have a special aversion to dogs. Realistically, however, anyone—whether they are Arab or not—would be afraid of growling dogs thrust into their faces or genitals. Another technique was to remove religious items and comfort items, including the *Koran*. Others included stripping, hooding, sleep deprivation, stress positions, and standing for long periods. In giving his approval of these methods, Rumsfeld added these words, "I stand for 8–10 hours a day. Why is standing limited to 4 hours?"[33] Thus, the torture was approved and authorized from the highest level of our government.

Often, people ask whether torture works. However, there are moral, legal, and ethical reasons why torture should never be used, without exception. As to whether it works, based on the anecdotal evidence from CCR clients, it does not. Those enduring torture will say anything to end the torture and it will be exactly what the torturers want to hear. In fact, even the FBI believes that there are much better interrogation techniques to obtain vital information and apparently refused to participate in torture practices at Guantánamo.[34]

What, then, is the future of the torture program? While President Obama has more or less outlawed torture (though some exceptions exist in the Army Field Manual permitting cruel treatment) that is not sufficient to permanently eliminate torture.[35] There must be accountability by means of criminal prosecutions, especially of the higher-ups who authorized the program. This includes, among others, former President George W. Bush, former Vice President Dick Cheney, former CIA Director George Tenet, former Secretary of Defense Donald Rumsfeld and the administration's lawyers who enabled the torture program.

Until this occurs, a future president can, with the stroke of a pen, put the United States back in the torture business. If we can run a torture program and by inaction give impunity to its perpetrators, every other country in the world can do so as well. The United States has torn what was once the all-enveloping fabric of human rights law. It cannot be sewn back together without accountability of key conspirators.

NOTES

1. See Craig Whitlock, "Spain's Judges Cross Borders in Rights Cases," *Washington Post*, May 24, 2009, http://www.washingtonpost.com/wp-dyn/content/article/2009/05/23/AR2009052301795.html (last visited July 22, 2009).

2. Ibid.

3. See David M. Herszenhorn and Carol Hulse, "Senate Leaders Oppose Interrogation Inquiry Panel," *New York Times*, Apr. 23, 2009, http://thecaucus.blogs.nytimes.com/2009/04/23/senate-leaders-opposes-interrogation-inquiry-panel/?hp (last visited July 22, 2009).

4. Bobby Ghosh and Michael Scherer, "Obama: Still Opposed to Truth Commission," *TIME*, May 21, 2009, http://www.time.com/time/nation/article/0,8599,1900035,00.html (last visited July 22, 2009).

5. *Magna Carta*, signed by King John, Runnymede, U.K., June 15, 1215.

6. See International Court of Human Rights, "Universal Jurisdiction" (1999), http://www.ichrp.org/en/projects/201 (last visited July 22, 2009).

7. See, for example, *Convention Against Torture and Other Cruel, Inhuman, or Degrading Treatment or Punishment*, G.A. res. 39/46 [annex, 39 U.N. GAOR Supp. (No. 51) at 197, U.N. Doc. A/39/51 (1984)], *entered into force* June 26, 1987.

8. See A. Hays Butler, "The Growing Support for Universal Jurisdiction," in *Universal Jurisdiction: National Courts and the Prosecution of Serious Crimes under International Law*, ed. Stephen Macedo, 73, nn. 39–41 (Philadelphia: Univ. of Pennsylvania Press, 2006).

9. See Steven J. Ratner and Jason S. Abrams, *Accountability for Human Rights Atrocities in International Law* (Oxford: Oxford Univ. Press, 2001), 187–90.

10. George W. Bush, Military Order, "Detention, Treatment, and Trial of Non-Citizens in the War against Terrorism," *Federal Register* 66, no. 222 (Nov. 2001).

11. Ibid. at sec. 1(f), sec. 2(a), 3(a), 4(c), 7(b).

12. Ibid.

13. Barack Obama, "Protecting Our Security and Our Values" (speech, National Archives Museum, Washington, DC, May 21, 2009).

14. See Katherine Q. Seelye, "Threats and Responses: the Detainees; Some Guántanamo Prisoners Will be Freed, Rumsfeld Says," *New York Times*, Oct. 23, 2002, http://www.nytimes.com/2002/10/23/world/threats-responses-detainees-some-Guantánamo-prisoners-will-be-freed-rumsfeld.html (last visited July 24, 2000).

15. Phil Mercer, "Guántanamo Bay Detainee Back Home in Australia," *Voice of America*, May 20, 2007, http://www.voanews.com/english/archive/2007-05/2007-05-20-voa13. cfm?CFID=259379931&CFTOKEN=67784988&jsessionid=88302ce81d22d7b4aaa3152847445bd58576 (last visited July 22, 2009).

16. *Rasul v. Bush*, 542 U.S. 466 (2004).

17. *Boumediene v. Bush*, 128 S.Ct. 1923 (2008).

18. *Detainee Treatment Act of 2005*, Public Law 109-148, Title X, 109th Cong., 1st sess. (Dec. 30, 2005).

19. *Hamdan v. Rumsfeld*, 548 U.S. 557 (2006).

20. *Military Commissions Act of 2006*, Public Law 109-366, 109th Cong., 2nd sess. (Oct. 17, 2006).

21. Ibid.

22. *U.S. Constitution*, art. 1, § 9.

23. See, e.g., *el Gharani v. Bush*, 593 F.Supp.2d 144 (D.D.C. 2009); *Boumediene v. Bush*, 579 F.Supp.2d 191 (granting five detainees' *habeas* petitions); Amnesty International, *U.S.A. Judge Orders Guantánamo Detainee Released After Seven and a Half Years in Detention* (June 24, 2009), http://www.amnestyusa.org/document.php?id=ENGAMR510802009 (last visited July 23, 2009).

24. "Guantánamo 'suicide' inmate named," BBC News, June 1, 2007, http://news.bbc.co.uk/2/hi/americas/6710505.stm (last visited July 23, 2009).

25. See Tim Golden, "Tough U.S. Steps in Hunger Strike at Camp in Cuba," *New York Times*, Feb. 9, 2006, http://www.nytimes.com/2006/02/09/politics/09gitmo.html (last visited July 23, 2009); "Doctors Attack U.S. Over Guantánamo," *BBC News*, March 10, 2006, http://news.bbc.co.uk/2/hi/americas/4790742.stm (last visited July 23, 2009); World Medical Association (WMA), *Declaration on Hunger Strikers* (Malta: 1991), http://www.wma.net/e/policy/h31.htm (last visited July 23, 2009).

26. See "Doctors Attack U.S. Over Guantánamo," *BBC News;* Golden, "Tough U.S. Steps in Hunger Strikes."

27. Barack Obama, Executive Order, "Review and Disposition of Individuals Detained at the Guantánamo Naval Base and Closure of Detention Facilities," *Federal Register* 74, no. 16 (Jan. 2009).

28. "Guantánamo Clouds E.U.-U.S. Meeting," *BBC News*, June 21, 2006, http://news.bbc.co.uk/2/hi/europe/5099732.stm (last visited July 27, 2009).

29. U.S. Department of Defense, *Detainee Transfer Announced*, News Release 201-07, Dec. 17, 2006, http://www.defenselink.mil/releases/release.aspx?releaseid=10301 (last visited July 23, 2009).

30. Sheryl Gay Stolberg, "President Moves 14 Held in Secret to Guantánamo," *New York Times*, Sept. 7, 2006, http://www.nytimes.com/2006/09/07/us/07detain.html (last visited July 23, 2009).

31. "Obama to Appeal Detainee Ruling," *New York Times*, Apr. 10, 2009, http://www.nytimes.com/2009/04/11/world/asia/11bagram.html (last visited July 27, 2009).

32. Margulies, *Guantánamo and the Abuse*, 63–65, 107; Rose, "How We Survived," *The Observer*.

33. U.S. Department of Defense, action memo regarding use of interrogation techniques, Dec. 2, 2002, http://www.gwu.edu/~nsarchiv/NSAEBB/NSAEBB127/02.12.02.pdf (last visited July 23, 2009).

34. Eric Lichtblau and Scott Shane, "Report Details Dissent on Guantánamo Tactics," *New York Times*, May 21, 2008, http://www.nytimes.com/2008/05/21/washington/21detain.html?partner=rssuserland&emc=rss&pagewanted=all (last visited July 24, 2009).

35. Barack Obama, address to the Joint Session of Congress (speech, U.S. Congress, Washington, DC, February 24, 2009), http://www.whitehouse.gov/the_press_office/remarks-of-president-barack-obama-address-to-joint-session-of-congress/ (last visited July 24, 2009); also see U.S. Department of the Army, *Field Manual 22-2.3: Human Intelligence Collector Operations*, Sept. 2006, Appendix M, http://www.army.mil/institution/armypublicaffairs/pdf/fm2-22-3.pdf (last visited July 24, 2009).

10

Mass Torture in America

Notes from the Supermax Prisons

LANCE TAPLEY

Exterminate all the brutes!
Joseph Conrad, *Heart of Darkness* [1]

The American prison system has become a monster. Our incarceration rate is *nearly four times* what it was in 1980, more than five times the world average and the highest in the world. We have 4.5 percent of the world's population and almost 25 percent of its prisoners—over 2.3 million human beings—behind bars, two-thirds of them black or Hispanic, and millions more on probation or parole. Annually, their detention costs close to $30,000 per prisoner. Despite the expense, two-thirds of ex-convicts return to prison within three years. And no matter how many prisons we build, they become overcrowded.[2]

One could conclude from these facts that Americans have become a harsher people over the past 30 years. Other well-known facts could be cited to support this argument: the resurrection and persistence of capital punishment, the callous treatment of immigrant detainees, and the military and CIA torture at Abu Ghraib and Guantánamo. But less well known is our very harshest domestic product: Tens of thousands of prisoners, many of them mentally ill, are kept in a network of extraordinarily cruel super-maximum-security, solitary-confinement prisons or units within prisons called supermaxes. Constructed beginning in the mid-1980s, supermax facilities exist in almost every state and in the federal prison system; many are separate prisons. They constitute a network of mass torture unique in the world and in history. This network has close parallels to the notorious American torture overseas, but it is much more vast, and it is torture of our own citizens.

The Torture of Michael James

"They beat the shit out of you," said Michael James, hunched near the smeared Plexiglas separating us in a concrete-walled cubicle off the visitors' room of the Maine State Prison in Warren. He was talking about the cell "extractions" he had endured at the hands of supermax guards. "They push you, knee you, poke you," he said, his voice ardent but faint through the speaker. "They slam your head against the wall and drop you on the floor while you're cuffed." James lifted his manacled hands to a scar on his chin. "They split it wide open. They're yelling 'Stop resisting! Stop resisting!' when you're not even moving." He'd been sprayed with Mace countless times, he said, and had spent long periods strapped into a restraint chair.

When you lay eyes on Michael James, you first notice the scars on his shaved head, including a deep, horizontal gash. He got that by scraping his head on the cell door slot, which guards use to pass in food trays. "They were messing with me," he explained, referring to guards who taunted him. "I couldn't stand it no more." He added: "I've knocked myself out by running full force into the wall."

James, who is in his twenties, has been beaten all his life, first by family members: "I was punched, kicked, slapped, bitten, thrown against the wall." He began seeing mental-health workers when he was four and taking psychiatric medication when he was seven. He only made it through the second grade in public school, spending most of his early youth in homes for disturbed children. He said he was bipolar, and before and after he was in prison he also accumulated diagnoses of antisocial-personality, attention-deficit-hyperactivity, post-traumatic-stress, and oppositional-defiance disorders.

James got in trouble with the law as a juvenile, but his real problems began after a doctor took him off his medications when he was 18. On the street, he got into "selling drugs, robbing people, fighting, burglaries." Soon he was handed a 12-year sentence. Of the four years James had been in prison when I met him, he had spent all but five months in solitary confinement. The isolation is "mental torture, even for people who are able to control themselves," he said.

In addition to solitary confinement and physical brutality, the Maine Department of Corrections has tortured James in another way that recalls American treatment of Islamist detainees. It could be called legal torture. In 2007, James went on trial for 10 felony assaults on guards—kicking, punching, throwing his feces at them. His court-appointed lawyer, Joseph Steinberger, tried what was apparently a novel defense and convinced a jury in Rockland, the nearest big town to the prison, to find James "not criminally responsible" by reason of insanity. Steinberger thought the verdict was a landmark because it called into question the state's practice of keeping men like James in solitary confinement. After the verdict, as the law required, the judge committed James to a state mental hospital.

But state officials saw the verdict as another kind of landmark. Never before in Maine had a prisoner been committed to the mental hospital after being tried for assault on guards. Apparently worried that inmates might attack guards as a ticket to the hospital, the Department of Corrections refused to send James there, arguing that he first had to serve out the remaining 10 years of his sentence.

University of Maine law professor Orlando Delogu said at the time he thought state officials were taking a page out of President George W. Bush's legal books, which Delogu described as, "We only enforce the law that appeals to us." He saw a parallel between the state's position in the James case and the Bush administration's denial of standard U.S. legal rights to prisoners at Guantánamo.

After a year of appeals, the judge finally succeeded in getting James into the hospital, though he conceded to the state that James's time there would not count against his sentence, which he'll have to serve after he's cured, however long that takes.

At one point, Steinberger wrote about his client to Maine's Democratic governor, John Baldacci, begging him to intervene and send James to the hospital:

> He continually slits open his arms and legs with chips of paint and concrete, smears himself and his cell with feces, strangles himself to unconsciousness with his clothing. . . . He also bites, hits, kicks, spits at, and throws urine and feces on his guards.[3]

The governor declined Steinberger's request.

Abuse Is Standard Practice

In the extractions that Mike James suffers up to five times a day, five hollering guards wearing helmets and body armor charge into a cell. The point man smashes a big shield into the prisoner, knocking him down. The others spray Mace into his face, push him onto the bed, and twist his arms behind his back to handcuff him, connecting the cuffs by a chain to leg irons. Then they haul him into the corridor, cut off all his clothes, and carry him screaming through the cell block while they continue to Mace him. They put him in an observation room, and bind him to a special chair. He remains there for hours, naked and cold, yelling and mumbling.[4]

A scene like this might have played out at Abu Ghraib, where American soldiers tormented captured Iraqis. But as described to me by prisoners and guards, and as vividly revealed in an official video of an extraction that was leaked to me (the prison ironically records each extraction to prove the inmate was not mistreated), the guards' behavior is the standard reaction to disobedience in the Maine prison system's Special Management Unit, colloquially known as the supermax. This separate 100-cell building lies within the 925-inmate, all-male prison, hidden in the woods in the incongruously pretty coastal village of Warren, just off touristy Route 1. The prisoner's disobedience might be a refusal to put his hands through the food slot to be handcuffed before being taken to the showers. In supermaxes around the country, such extractions occur routinely.

Underlying the extractions and the other routines in the supermax is the concept of total control. The accepted definition of a supermax is a "control unit" subjecting inmates to prolonged solitary confinement (often for months, sometimes for years); tight restrictions on movement outside the cell (usually, an inmate is in handcuffs and ankle shackles, with a guard on either side); little or no counseling or education; and zero-tolerance to disobedience. Supermaxes were built to house, theoretically, "the worst of the worst," the most violent or disruptive prisoners. But inmates may be taken from the prison's general population and put in a supermax for a variety of reasons besides violence, including possession of contraband like marijuana or tobacco; an accusation by one inmate against another such as of gang membership; disobedience of a guard's order; and even the benign motivation of protection from other inmates. But by many accounts mental illness is the most common denominator; mentally ill people have a hard time following prison rules.

In Maine's supermax, which is typical, an inmate spends 23 hours a day alone in a tiny cell. Five days a week in good weather he gets an hour alone in a small cage outdoors (some prisoners are permitted outside in small groups). Radios and television are forbidden. Feces, urine, and blood may coat cell and corridor walls, floors, and ceilings—splattered there by insane or enraged men. Guards often deprive the prisoner of sleep, as does the usual pandemonium; like ghosts, some inmates howl in agony. Cell lights are constantly on. Minimal, cold food is shoved through the unsanitary slot in the door. The prisoner receives limited medical, mental-health, and dental care—he's not allowed a toothbrush, for example, but has a ribbed, plastic nub that fits over a finger. He gets a shower a few times a week and the opportunity for an occasional telephone call and "no contact" access to a visitor. What a prisoner has to do to get out of the supermax is usually not revealed to him. Variations in this treatment exist: In some states, TVs or radios are allowed.

Can supermax treatment legitimately be called torture? The United States is a party to the Convention Against Torture and Other Cruel, Inhuman or Degrading Treatment or Punishment (CAT). Under that treaty, torture is official treatment that causes "severe pain or suffering, whether physical or mental" when it's inflicted as punishment or for coercion. CAT specifies that torture "does not include pain or suffering arising only from, inherent in or incidental to lawful sanctions."[5] The suffering that occurs in a supermax prison, however, does not arise from lawful sanctions. It is a consequence of an administrative decision, not a court's, and the inmate has little ability to lawfully challenge his or her placement or supermax conditons because of the severe restrictions placed on inmate lawsuits by the 1996 Prison Litigation Reform Act.[6]

Severe pain and suffering as punishment are plainly the norm in a supermax. Even when mental suffering alone is considered—ignoring, for example, the supermax cell extractions—the prolonged solitary confinement of American prisoners has increasingly been described by UN agencies or human rights organizations as cruel, inhuman, degrading, or torture.[7]

The Worst Form of Torture

The official beatings known as extractions are dramatic, but isolation is without question the worst form of torture inflicted on supermax inmates. It frequently maims and sometimes kills them—both the many who are mentally ill when they enter the supermax and those who develop mental illness while there. In 2007 psychiatrist Stuart Grassian, a leading researcher on the effects of solitary confinement, told *Time*, "We're taking criminals who are already unstable and driving them crazy."[8] Grassian believes supermaxes produce a "specific syndrome" characterized by "agitation, self-destructive behavior, and overt psychotic disorganization." He also notes memory lapses and other cognitive difficulties, "primitive aggressive fantasies," paranoia, loss of control over impulses, and, especially, hallucinations of all sorts.[9]

Grassian's is the consensus view. "Research on effects of solitary confinement has produced a massive body of data documenting serious adverse health effects," writes Peter Scharff Smith, a Danish researcher who has conducted the most comprehensive survey of the medical literature pertaining to prisoners in solitary.[10] "All human beings experience isolation as torture," writes Harvard Medical School professor Atul Gawande in a 2009 *New Yorker* article summarizing solitary confinement research. Besides hallucinations, Gawande lists such effects as compulsive pacing, screaming, depression, lethargy, despair, rage, and even catatonia.[11] The effects may start within a few days, involve as many as three-quarters of supermax inmates, and often become permanent. Another expert on solitary confinement, psychiatrist Terry Kupers, writes that "being held in isolated confinement for longer than three months causes lasting emotional damage if not full-blown psychosis and functional disability."[12]

As Mike James's behavior illustrates, particularly predictable symptoms of supermax isolation are self-mutilation (in prison, known as "cutting up") and throwing feces, urine, and blood at guards. Suicide attempts are another. An early, intriguing psychological study of solitary confinement, published in 1976, examined men held in the small segregation unit of the Maine State Prison, which was then in Thomaston. The study found, "Almost every prisoner sent to solitary has attempted to commit or has contemplated suicide."[13]

Also predictable is the reaction of prison officials to these symptoms. A 2009 investigation of the Tamms supermax in Illinois by the *Belleville News-Democrat* depicted Faygie Fields, a schizophrenic imprisoned for killing a man in a drug deal. He regularly cut his arms and throat with glass and metal, swallowed glass, and smeared his feces all over his cell.

> Prison officials charged him $5.30 for tearing up a state-owned sheet to make a noose to kill himself. . . .
>
> If he hadn't been charged with crimes in prison, Fields could have been paroled in 2004 after serving 20 years of a 40-year sentence. But Fields must serve all the extra time for throwing food, urine and committing other offenses against guards. That amounts to 34 years, or 54 years total, that he must serve before becoming eligible for parole in 2038, at age 79.[14]

Perversely, "prisoners who can't handle profound isolation are the ones who are forced to remain in it," Gawande observes.

The Scope of the Torture

How many human beings in this country are kept in these conditions? Daniel Mears, a criminologist at Florida State who has done the most complete study of this question, reports that in 2004, supermaxes in 44 states held about 25,000 people. The federal system currently has about 11,000 prisoners in solitary, according to the Bureau of Prisons.[15] Mears's number includes exact counts and, when the prison systems didn't supply the data or it was unreliable (often the case), educated guesses. Mears told me his number was very conservative. Other research pegs the supermax total as high as 100,000; these studies sometimes include more broadly defined control units that, for example, lock people in cells 23 hours a day with another prisoner (some inmates think this is worse than solitary).[16]

This American system of extrajudicial punishment has no equivalent. There are supermax-type prisons or units within prisons in other countries, but they are few and small. In 2004 Corey Weinstein, a San Francisco physician, toured prisons in the United Kingdom on behalf of the American Public Health Association. In one he was shown "eight of the forty men out of the 75,000 [in England and Wales] considered too dangerous or disruptive to be in any other facility." But seven of the eight "were out of their cells at exercise or at a computer or with a counselor or teacher. . . . With embarrassment the host took us to the one cell holding the single individual who had to be continuously locked down."[17]

Supermax systems don't exist abroad not just because the American attitude toward prisoners is exceptional, but also due to the expense. Since supermax buildings are so high-tech and close management of single-celled prisoners is so labor-intensive, supermaxes "typically are two to three times more costly to build and operate than other types of prisons," Mears writes.[18] No other nation has been willing to spend that kind of money. Indeed, the gigantic American supermax system is probably unique in the history of imprisonment. In the gulags and concentration camps of the Soviet Union, Nazi Germany, and other totalitarian nations, prisoners were rarely kept in solitary confinement.

But there are parallels with some institutions abroad. Comparing the Tamms supermax in Illinois with the two most notorious locations of U.S. military torture of terrorist suspects, at Guantánamo Bay in Cuba and in Iraq, Stephen Eisenman, author of the book *The Abu Ghraib Effect*, told the *Belleville News-Democrat*, "The pattern of suicide, cutting, depression, and hallucination at Gitmo and Abu Ghraib is repeated at Tamms."[19] At Guantánamo, according to the Center for Constitutional Rights, 70 percent of the prisoners have been kept in solitary confinement.[20]

Prisoners who follow the news invariably see an irony in the substantial negative reaction of some Americans to the mistreatment of several hundred foreign terrorist suspects while, to little public outcry, tens of thousands of American citizens are held in equal or worse conditions in the United States. They also find it ironic that the Obama administration plans to shut down the detention center at Guantánamo and ship its prisoners to a supermax in the United States.

The Torture of Deane Brown—Part 1

In my first interviews of Maine supermax prisoners, I found Deane Brown to be the most articulate. He was highly intelligent, and I asked him to organize interviews with other inmates. He was also compassionate—more interested in alleviating the suffering of the mentally ill prisoners in the supermax than in his own difficulties. In his forties, a big man with long, dark hair, a Fu Manchu beard, and lively eyes, he had been sentenced to 59 years for a string of burglaries in the mid-1990s. He joked about being given a longer sentence than the man who had murdered his brother.

Brown had been put in the supermax for possession of a razor blade, screwdriver, soldering iron, and wire—all of which he claimed he used for fixing other inmates' televisions and electronic devices. He was known as a mechanical and electronics wizard, but officials viewed him as an escape risk, he said, though "there was no charge against me for trying to escape," and he had no history of trying. Under a U.S. Supreme Court decision, [21] which he cited, supermax prisoners are entitled to due process in connection with their placement in such a restrictive setting, but like most jailhouse lawyers Brown saw the prison grievance system as a farce.

Since being sent to the supermax, Brown had become concerned about his teeth, which were visibly loose and coated with gray plaque. Though he wasn't violent or suicidal, like other inmates in solitary he wasn't allowed a toothbrush or floss. He said the device that fits over a fingertip, which he showed me, didn't work to keep his teeth clean. He felt his health was also threatened by the supermax's lack of hygiene. The food cart was "dragged through feces," and "the ceiling was plastered with feces."

"It's supposed to be an administrative program for correcting behavior, but it's creating animals," he said. "I saw a guy eat his own feces." When I winced, Brown apologized: "I know it's distressing."

The Torture of Joseph Reeves

"I had my arm broken while handcuffed behind my back while face down on the floor and Maced so I couldn't see," recounted Joseph Reeves, a narrow-faced man in his twenties with a wispy goatee and tattooed, pale skin. Guards broke his arm during this extraction, he said: "They said I wouldn't open my hands, but I was handcuffed and I blacked out. My hands were clenched." When he came back from the hospital, the prison staff, suspecting contraband in the cast, cut it off, and so the arm didn't heal properly, he added.

Reeves also was upset with what he called sexual intimidation in the form of frequent strip searches and "butt searches"—exposing one's anus to guards to prevent the hiding of contraband. This is part of the universal supermax routine, even when the prisoner may have had no physical contact with another human being for a long period.

Reeves was serving a five-year term for robbery and gun possession. Much of it had been spent in the supermax. After my interview, he sent me pages from an Amnesty International publication on how supermax isolation, degradation, threats, and "monopolization of perception" constitute torture.

The Torture of Deane Brown—Part 2

After my first interviews with Reeves, Brown, James, and other super-max inmates were published in the *Portland Phoenix* in November 2005, accompanied by the video of a cell extraction posted on the *Boston Phoenix*'s website, a controversy ensued.[22] The Maine Civil Liberties Union and organizations representing the mentally ill began pressing the governor and the legislature's Criminal Justice Committee to reform the supermax. Governor Baldacci was compelled to state that Corrections would fix any problem. The Corrections commissioner, Martin Magnusson, declared that he would embark on reforms. Magnusson, a heavy-set man in his early sixties who once had been the prison's warden, never disputed my published accounts of supermax practices. In admitting the need for reform, he implicitly confirmed them.

Soon, the number of cell extractions dropped radically. Magnusson reported in 2008 that they had dropped from 133 in 2005 to only two in 2007, which seemed to prove they hadn't been necessary.[23] He asked federal experts to advise on how the supermax could be run differently. Deane Brown was released back into the general population.

But Brown was now on a mission to reform the prison. He fed me inside information such as a guard supervisor's highly critical memo on prison management. (Brown was well-liked by the guards, who shared their complaints with him.) He also aired the prison's dirty laundry in calls to a local radio station. In late 2006, prison authorities finally did what they often do with troublemakers—they "shipped him out," trading him for a Maryland prisoner. Brown wound up in the Baltimore supermax, 500 miles from family, friends, and news media in Maine. In Maryland, where he has been shifted from prison to prison, he has almost died from staff negligence in dealing with his diabetes, has been beaten by inmates, and has become despondent.

Around the time Brown was sent out of state, Corrections barred me from the prison. Journalism organizations protested vigorously on my behalf, but a year passed before I got back in for interviews. In my renewed interviews and in mail from supermax inmates, I learned that not much had changed despite Magnusson's promises, aside from the decline in cell extractions. Unless solitary confinement was abandoned, not much could really change.

The Taunting of Ryan Rideout

Indeed, the Maine supermax horrors continued apace. For example, late on the night of October 5, 2006, a severely mentally ill young man, Ryan Rideout, hanged himself from the sprinkler in his cell. Seeing him prepare to do this, the nearby inmates had frantically pressed their cells' panic buttons. But guards had turned off the alarm system, and this was "the direct cause" of Rideout's death, according to a wrongful-death lawsuit filed in federal court by his mother.[24]

The suit also claims that when a guard making his rounds found Rideout hanging, he first taunted him instead of immediately sounding an alarm. This same guard had allegedly taunted Rideout earlier, telling him he "didn't have the balls" to kill himself. The suit also claims that before Rideout was cut down and futilely given medical aid, guards took time to put him in handcuffs and ankle shackles. It contends, too, that the prison's mental-health staff had taken away his needed psychiatric medications.

Prison officials have mostly denied the accusations, but prisoners who watched and heard events unfold from nearby cells wrote or spoke to me, independently confirming most of the allegations in detail. Moreover, the claims of officials were called into question after a daily newspaper quoted the prison warden as saying Rideout was not considered a suicide risk. In fact, he was the most notorious suicide risk in the state. He had made headlines three times within three weeks in 2004, when he had threatened to jump from the top of a four-story building in downtown Bangor. His threats closed off traffic each time, until police talked him down.

After Rideout was imprisoned for burglary, he made his first suicide attempt in March 2006. The suit alleges that guards responded by extracting him from his cell using Mace and dragging him naked through the cell block to put him in a restraint chair for hours. After a second suicide attempt, the prison charged him with criminal mischief for breaking the sprinkler he had used to try to hang himself. He was fined $130. Rideout finally succeeded on his third try.

"The idea that you would prevent suicides by being concerned about the mental health of prisoners is not something they consider," attorney Joe Steinberger told me angrily, referring to prison officials. To them, "suicidal behavior is punishable behavior."

After a prison investigation, the guard who allegedly taunted Rideout was fired.

The Supermax Boom

Maine's supermax opened in 1992 several miles from the old Thomaston prison, a high-walled landmark built in 1824. The new Warren prison was built around the supermax, opening in 2002. Literally and metaphorically, the supermax's solitary confinement is at the core of the stark, low, high-tech prison with its radiating "pods" for prisoners.

Atul Gawande asks:

> If prolonged isolation is—as research and experience have confirmed for decades—so objectively horrifying, so intrinsically cruel, how did we end up with a prison system that may subject more of our own citizens to it than any other country in history has?[25]

This is an essential question, but answering it is not easy. No thorough account exists to explain exactly why supermaxes were rapidly constructed across the country over the past 25 years—and, especially, in the 1990s. Researchers agree, however, that the supermax boom was connected to America's prisoner population explosion. As this sudden increase threw some prisons into turmoil, with larger numbers of violent inmates and more gang activity, supermaxes became the perceived way to quiet the tumult by segregating the most troublesome prisoners and deterring others from creating trouble.

But a veteran federal official, George Keiser, Chief of the National Institute of Corrections Community Corrections Division, which is part of the Department of Justice, told me supermaxes were "a fad," and scholars agree they were built without knowledge they would be effective. They were also a response to another frustration: "For a time, there was a thought that nothing worked" to rehabilitate prisoners, Keiser said. "Corrections" was abandoned. Wardens concluded that their task was to suppress violence, especially against guards.[26] But tax money poured into supermax construction also because they were "the animal of public-policy makers," Keiser said. The beast was fed by tough-on-crime politicians who capitalized on fears incited by increasing news-media sensationalism in covering crime.

Behind the supermax craze loom the forces driving the shocking growth of the country's entire penal system. For academic researchers, the competing but likely complementary explanations include the longer mandatory sentences resulting from the media-induced "moral panics";

the lobbying of the bureaucratic, union, and corporate prison-industrial complex; the deinstitutionalization of mental patients, throwing them onto the streets without enough community care and, eventually for many, into the jails and prisons; and the War on Drugs, whose casualties include roughly 20 percent of America's prisoners.[27]

Deeper in the background, according to Ruth Wilson Gilmore, a University of Southern California geographer and author of *Golden Gulag*, there was a corporate-globalizing American economy in which "a certain kind of labor market collapsed"—the American manufacturing economy. A number of people who might have had a future in that labor market turned to stealing or drug-dealing to make a living. The political reaction to a large, unemployed, "modestly educated," alienated, and disproportionately African American and Hispanic segment of the working class was an "iron-fisted" attitude that turned to "saturation policing" as well as saturation imprisonment.[28]

The clenching of the iron fist began about the time Ronald Reagan was inaugurated president, in 1981, when the country veered sharply to the political right and began to deal severely with threats to order and privilege. In 1983, turmoil in the federal penitentiary in Marion, Illinois, led to a permanent lockdown and the first supermax.

Supermax Prisons Don't Work

Norman Kehling—a small, balding, middle-aged man—is serving 40 years in the Maine State Prison for an arson in which, he told me, no one was hurt. He was in the supermax for trafficking in heroin. I asked him about the mentally ill men there. "One guy cut his testicle out of his sack," he said. "They shouldn't be here." He added: "This place breeds hate. What they're doing obviously isn't working."

In meeting the objective that wardens cite for supermaxes of decreasing violence against guards and inmates in the prison's general population, there's "no empirical evidence to support the notion that supermax prisons are effective," according to a 2008 comprehensive study published in *The Prison Journal*.[29] As for the goal of deterrence—act out and you'll be thrown in the hole—a similar study concluded, "deterrence as a correctional policy does not work."[30] And no one claims that within the supermax extreme behavior is stopped by extreme punishment; it becomes worse.

When enraged supermax inmates go back into the prison general population or the outside world, as the overwhelming majority do, the supermax dramas play out on larger stages. Because of the growth of supermaxes, psychiatrist Kupers writes, "We are seeing a new population of prisoners who, on account of lengthy stints in isolation units, are not well prepared to return to a social milieu."[31] In the worst cases, supermax graduates—sometimes released from solitary confinement directly onto the street—"may be time bombs waiting to explode," writes criminologist Hans Toch.[32]

The bombs are already going off. In July 2007 Michael Woodbury, then 31, walked into a New Hampshire store and in a botched robbery shot and killed three men. Not long before, he had completed a five-year stint for robbery and theft at the Maine State Prison, part of it in the supermax. One day, when Woodbury was being taken to court, he told reporters, "I reached out and told them I need medication. I reached out and told them I shouldn't be out in society. I told numerous cops, numerous guards." While in prison, he said, he had given a four-page "manifesto" to a prison therapist saying he "was going to crack like this." His father said his son was mentally ill and didn't get proper treatment in prison.[33] Woodbury pleaded guilty and received life imprisonment.

Dumping Grounds for the Mentally Ill

Although there is considerable scientific acceptance of the fact that supermax isolation can make prisoners mentally ill, there's even broader acceptance that supermaxes make mentally ill inmates worse. Grassian, the psychiatric expert, writes: "Solitary confinement often results in severe exacerbation of a previously existing mental condition."[34]

In a 2002 report, the Maine chapter of the National Alliance for the Mentally Ill discussed the state supermax's "vicious cycle of infractions, isolation, increased psychiatric symptoms, additional infractions, and additional time in isolation."[35] The group's director told a newspaper that supermax practices "might have crossed into the realm of torture."[36]

On all sides of the supermax issue there is no dispute that U.S. prisons have become dumping grounds for the mentally ill. "That's true of every [correctional] system," the deputy Maine Corrections commissioner, Denise Lord, told me. Forty percent of Maine's prison inmates are on psychiatric medicine, she said. A Maine Civil Liberties Union survey in 2003 of inmates throughout the state's prison system found close to that percentage of prisoners describing themselves as mentally ill.[37] Nationally, a 2006 U.S. Department of Justice study concluded that more than half of prison and jail inmates reported mental-health problems.[38] In a *New York Times* op-ed in 2007, law and criminology professor Bernard Harcourt succinctly described the cause: "Over the past 40 years, the United States dismantled a colossal mental health complex and rebuilt—bed by bed—an enormous prison."[39] Danish researcher Smith reports that studies show the mentally ill in prison are disproportionately found in control units.[40]

Toward Rehabilitation: Away from Cruelty

Justice Department expert George Keiser told me the supermax idea was "not one of our brightest lights." The path away from it, he said, is "the new direction in corrections . . . evidence-based policy and practice." "Evidence-based" is a buzz phrase. In the corrections context it means something proven to work in reducing the chance an ex-convict will return to crime and prison—known as recidivism—as well as in reducing prison violence and disorder. The scientific evidence, Keiser said, points away from punishment and toward treatment, toward changing behavior instead of warehousing prisoners.

In other words, the movement is forward to the past: toward corrections, once (and still the nominal) goal of prisons. Even political conservatives will be pleased with this new direction, Keiser said: "We will save money. We will have fewer new crimes. We will have fewer victims." A smarter approach to changing behavior can immediately be put to work in supermaxes, he suggested. In the case of an inmate who is acting up, instead of "exerting force" on him—as in a cell extraction—a correctional officer might tell the inmate that he'll call his mother: "You might not think it would work, but sometimes it works."

The sharp drop in extractions within the Maine supermax proves that smarter and less cruel approaches to prisoner behavior could be implemented virtually overnight by changing guard behavior. Taking inmates out of insanity- and rage-producing solitary confinement, of course, would be the most effective reform. But for supermaxes to be shut down or greatly shrunk—for the torture to be stopped—legislatures would have to provide resources for mentally ill prisoners to be properly treated rather than locked away, and they and other difficult inmates would need to be offered rehabilitation programs to occupy their time, reverse tendencies toward crime, and give them hope for the future.

There is better social-science evidence today than there was 30 years ago that prisoner rehabilitation can take place. Proven practices include drug treatment, cognitive-behavior group therapy, general education, and vocational education.[41] But for public money to be available for these programs, the still-growing number of convicts pouring into the prisons would have to slow down. This trend has continually eaten up corrections budgets. The supermax problem cannot be untangled from the larger dilemma of the entire penal system.

The cost of the prison system has begun to concern even the toughest-on-crime legislator. Because of economic concerns, the rate of growth in the number of people imprisoned in the United States has recently begun to slow.[42] One would think that the economic argument against supermaxes would have political traction, since supermaxes are so expensive. Still, lawmakers are hesitant to spend money on the care and rehabilitation of prisoners, even if there are cost savings in the long run. Politicians could be accused of coddling criminals. And especially in a bad economy funds for state services are a low priority. In the case of supermaxes it might be difficult for legislatures to abandon such a relatively new, massive investment. Even among criminologists who recognize that supermaxes are expensive failures, the consensus appears to be that "supermax prisons are here to stay."[43]

Forcing the Issue Legally

But state legislatures and corrections departments could be forced to act. One way is through the courts—convincing judges that supermax practices violate the Eighth Amendment's prohibition against cruel and unusual punishment. There is mixed legal precedent here. In 1890, the Supreme Court sharply criticized solitary confinement, and in 1940 the court referred to it as a form of torture.[44] But in recent decades the high court and other courts have refused to characterize solitary confinement per se as unconstitutional. The Supreme Court's basic position on prison litigation is that great deference should be shown to prison officials.[45]

There is an emerging consensus in the courts that mentally ill people, at least, should not suffer supermax conditions. A key case is the 1995 federal appeals court ruling in *Madrid v. Gomez* that forbade, as unconstitutionally cruel, keeping mentally ill inmates in the Security Housing Unit of the Pelican Bay State Prison in California.[46] The American Civil Liberties Union and other groups have successfully sued several states over supermax conditions, focusing on the treatment of the mentally ill. In a Wisconsin case in 2002, for example, the state agreed not to put seriously mentally ill prisoners in solitary confinement.[47] But 15 years after *Madrid*, any nationwide consensus about keeping the mentally ill out of supermaxes is honored much more in the breach than in the observance.

Federal civil rights law allows the Justice Department to pursue state and local correctional officials for prisoner abuse through civil proceedings, and occasionally it does.[48] A recent development in Maine's ongoing prison saga occurred after the April 2009 murder of a 64-year-old, wheelchair-bound sex offender. He died in the supermax, where he had been put after a beating by inmates several days before. When accusations were made that guards and medical staff had allowed him to die by ignoring his wounds, human rights groups asked the Justice Department's Civil Rights Division to launch an investigation of the prison, which its Special Litigation Section agreed to consider (as I write this, no decision has been made). If President Obama's Justice Department turns out to be truly progressive, it could have a big effect on supermax confinement.

International law is sometimes cited as a way to end supermax torture. The United States ratified the Convention Against Torture, thereby making it American law, but the Senate considerably qualified our country's obligations under the treaty.[49] Although the Senate agreed that mental torture includes "procedures" that disrupt "profoundly the senses or the personality," the list of qualifications have so restricted the treaty's use that "the placement of even mentally ill prisoners in prolonged solitary confinement would not constitute torture even if the mental pain caused thereby drove the prisoner to commit suicide," writes legal scholar Jules Lobel.[50]

Moreover, the Senate limited the treaty's enforcement by making it "non-self-executing," which means it requires an enabling U.S. law before it could be used by victims in U.S. prisons. There is a federal law passed in 1995 outlawing torture, but, ironically, it only applies to American citizens outside the United States or foreigners "present" in the United States.[51] Not even the events of Abu Ghraib and Guantánamo resulted in prosecutions under this statute. Even when the Convention Against Torture is not enforced, however, organizations such as the National Lawyers Guild support citing it to heighten public consciousness on prisoner-treatment issues—and public shame.[52]

Forcing the Issue through Grass-Roots Activism

Another alternative is citizen pressure to force state legislators to abolish supermaxes or eliminate prolonged solitary confinement. In Illinois, a grass-roots group has been fighting for years to "end psychological torture" at the Tamms supermax, though so far it has succeeded only in extracting promises from a new corrections commissioner to improve conditions.[53] In 2008, a pioneer in opposing supermax torture, the American Friends Service Committee, began a national STOPMAX Campaign with the goal of abolishing supermaxes, but the organization has not been able to raise the money to mount an aggressive effort.[54] A prison-reform coalition in Maine has been working for several years toward the eventual goal of abolition. In early 2010, it began lobbying the legislature to pass a bill to limit solitary confinement to 45 days and forbid seriously mentally ill inmates from being kept in the supermax.[55] Also in early 2010, the National Religious Campaign Against Torture, which has been active in opposing American torture at Guantánamo, began a campaign to end supermax torture.[56]

The public, however, is still largely hostile or indifferent to the fate of convicted criminals. A national soul-searching may be needed before that attitude changes. But there is a possible forum for this discussion on the horizon. Democratic Senator Jim Webb of Virginia has introduced a bill in Congress, the National Criminal Justice Commission Act, to create a blue-ribbon commission "to look at every aspect of our criminal justice system with an eye toward reshaping the process from top to bottom."[57] Prison activists view the bill with some hope.

Socially Acceptable Hatred

Bo Lozoff, a man who calls himself the prisoner's "spiritual friend" and who visits hundreds of institutions a year giving inspirational talks to inmates, told me, "Prisoners are the new niggers, gooks, kikes."[58] That is, criminals are the present-day, socially acceptable objects of vicious hatred.

In the summer of 2007, I covered a talk by Lozoff—who is sixtyish, salty, and sarcastic—when he spoke at the Unitarian Universalist Church in the erstwhile fishing town of Belfast, Maine, now a retirement haven. The audience was a group of 70 liberal folk, most on the well-to-do side. Sitting cross-legged on a blue mat, Lozoff spoke about the need to relieve the suffering of prisoners. When he asked for questions, I was surprised by the number of people who were not receptive to his plea and more interested in how his spiritual advice could help them. As a thunderstorm rumbled around us, a couple of people spoke about self-esteem: Don't we have to be psychologically strong before we can help others?

"That's spiritual Reaganomics," Lozoff replied. "The trickle-down theory. When I get my shit completely together, then I can trickle it down to others." The ghost of Ronald Reagan must not have appreciated that remark. With a peal of thunder, lightning struck nearby, and the lights went out.

In the darkness, I thought about how criminologists had found no evidence for the utility of supermaxes but rather evidence that they make prisons and the larger society more dangerous. Yet these experts doubt this archipelago of agony will be abolished—because of the huge investment, but also because supermaxes serve something else besides rational utility. "The object of torture is torture," George Orwell wrote in 1984.[59] Like much other criminal violence, the torturing of prisoners in supermaxes is not rational but expressive, to use a social-science term. It is punitive rage and revenge, and those are what the torture provokes in turn from supermax inmates, as it destroys them mentally. As author Gary Wills wrote about the American prison system before the first supermax was established, it engages in "the psychic incineration of our fellow citizens."[60]

In an earlier interview with me, Lozoff had connected hatred toward prisoners and its horrifying outcome in the supermax to a profound unhappiness permeating America. This unhappiness results from what he called our "narcissistic" or selfish, consumerist society. Selfishness is unhappy, I reflected, because in that condition we are alone, and alienated people strike out at—or ignore—others. Even in this nice church group, the self-orientation quotient was quite high.

But when the lights came on and the meeting ended, I saw a middle-aged woman with glistening eyes. I asked her what she had taken away from Lozoff's talk. "We're all prisoners, and we're all free," she said. She told me she was going to work to help prison inmates.

NOTES

1. See Joseph Conrad, *Heart of Darkness: Complete, Authoritative Text with Biographical and Historical Contexts, Critical History, and Essays from Five Contemporary Critical Perspectives,* 2nd edition, ed. Ross C. Murfin (Boston: Bedford/St. Martin's, 1996), 66.

2. See U.S. Dept. of Justice (DOJ), *Key Facts at a Glance: Incarceration Rate, 1980–2007,* http://www.ojp.usdoj. gov/bjs/glance/tables/incrttab.htm (last visited Sept. 16, 2009); DOJ, Prison Statistics: Summary Findings, http://www. ojp.gov/bjs/prisons.htm (last visited Sept. 16, 2009); DOJ, *Prison Inmates at Midyear 2008—Statistical Tables,* http://www.ojp.usdoj.gov/bjs/abstract/pimo8st. htm (last visited Sept. 16, 2009); International Centre for Prison Studies (ICPS), *Prison Brief—Highest to Lowest Rates,* http://www.kcl.ac.uk/depsta/law/research/ icps/worldbrief/ (last visited Sept. 16, 2009); ICPS, *Prison Brief for the United States of America,* http://www.kcl.ac.uk/depsta/law/research/icps/worldbrief/ wpb_country.php?country=190 (last visited Sept. 16, 2009); ICPS, *World Prison Population List,* 8th ed.; Pew Center on the States, *One in 31: The Long Reach of American Corrections,* 2009, http://www.pewcenteronthestates.org/uploaded-Files/PSPP_1in31_report_FINAL_WEB_3-26-09.pdf (last visited Sept. 16, 2009); DOJ, *Recidivism of Prisoners Released in 1994,* NCJ 193247, June 2002, http:// www.ojp.usdoj.gov/bjs/pub/pdf/rpr94.pdf (last visited Sept. 16, 2009); Ryan G. Fischer, "Are California's Recidivism Rates Really the Highest in the Nation? It Depends on What Measure of Recidivism You Use," *The Bulletin* 1, no. 1 (2005), http://ucicorrections.seweb.uci.edu/pdf/bulletin_2005_vol-1_is-1.pdf (last visited Sept. 16, 2009); David Crary, "Budget Woes Prompt States to Rethink Prison Policy," *San Francisco Chronicle,* Jan. 10, 2009, http://www.sfgate.com/ cgi-bin/article.cgi?file=/n/a/2009/01/10/national/a093301S65.DTL (last visited Sept. 16, 2009).

3. Joseph Steinberger, e-mail to Governor John E. Baldacci, July 4, 2006.

4. The Maine Department of Corrections claims the prison stopped stripping inmates naked in cell extractions in 2005.

5. United Nations (UN), *Convention Against Torture and Other Cruel, Inhuman or Degrading Treatment or Punishment,* Dec. 10, 1984, UN Treaty Series, vol. 1465, 85.

6. P.L. 104–34, 110 Stat. 1321 (2006); 42 U.S.C. § 1997e (1994 ed. & Supp. II).

7. See Manfred Nowak, "Interim Report of the UN Special Rapporteur on Torture and Other Cruel, Inhuman or Degrading Treatment or Punishment," UN General Assembly, 29 July 2008, A/63/175.

8. Jeffrey Kluger, "Are Prisons Driving Prisoners Mad?" *Time*, Jan. 26, 2007, http://www.time.com/time/magazine/article/0,9171,1582304,00.html (last visited Sept. 16, 2009).

9. Stuart Grassian, "Psychiatric Effects of Solitary Confinement," emailed statement from author, version of "a declaration submitted in September 1993 in *Madrid v. Gomez*, 889F.Supp.1146."

10. Peter Scharff Smith, "The Effects of Solitary Confinement on Prison Inmates: A Brief History and Review of the Literature," in *Crime and Justice 34*, ed. Michael Tonry (Chicago: Univ. of Chicago Press, 2006), 475.

11. Atul Gawande, "Hellhole," *The New Yorker*, Mar. 30, 2009, http://www.newyorker.com/reporting/2009/03/30/090330fa_fact_gawande (last visited Sept. 16, 2009).

12. Terry A. Kupers, "What to Do with the Survivors: Coping with the Long-term Effects of Isolated Confinement," *Criminal Justice and Behavior* 35, no. 8 (2008): 1006.

13. Thomas Benjamin and Kenneth Lux, "Constitutional and Psychological Implications of the Use of Solitary Confinement: Experience at the Maine State Prison," *Capital University Law Review* 5 (1976): 66.

14. George Pawlaczyk and Beth Hundsdorfer, "Ex-Warden: Ill. Supermax 'Very, Very Hard Time,'" *Marion Daily Republican*, Aug. 6, 2009, http://www.mariondaily.com/news/x1331798434/Ex-warden-Ill-supermax-very-very-hard-time (last visited Sept. 16, 2009).

15. See Daniel P. Mears, "Evaluating the Effectiveness of Supermax Prisons" (Washington, DC: Urban Institute, 2006), ii, http://www.urban.org/Uploaded-PDF/411326_supermax_prisons.pdf (last visited Sept. 16, 2009). For the number of federal supermax prisoners, see Stephanie Chen, "'Terrible Tommy' spends 27 years in solitary confinement," CNN, Feb. 2, 2010, at www.cnn.com/2010/CRIME/02/25/colorado.supermax.silverstein.solitary/index.html?hpt=Sbin (last visited Mar. 16, 2010).

16. See Maoist Internationalist Ministry of Prisons, Nationwide Survey of Control Units, http://abolishcontrolunits.org/research (last visited Sept. 16, 2009).

17. Corey Weinstein, "Perpetrators and Enablers of Torture in the US," unpublished paper, emailed by author Sept. 17, 2009.

18. Daniel P. Mears, "An Assessment of Supermax Prisons Using an Evaluation Research Framework," *The Prison Journal* 88, no. 1 (2008): 46.

19. See George Pawlaczyk and Beth Hundsdorfer, "Expert: Tamms Inmates Show Signs of Torture," *Belleville News-Democrat*, Aug. 5, 2009, http://www.bnd.com/news/local/story/870776.html (last visited Sept. 16, 2009).

20. Center for Constitutional Rights, "Solitary Confinement at Guantanamo Bay," http://ccrjustice.org/learn-more/faqs/solitary-confinement-guantanamo-bay (last visited Jan. 17, 2010).

21. See *Wilkinson v. Austin*, 125 S. Ct. 2384 (2005).

22. See Lance Tapley, "Torture in Maine's Prison," *Portland Phoenix*, Nov. 11, 2005, http://www.portlandphoenix.com/features/top/ts_multi/documents/05081722.asp. (last visited Jan. 17, 2010). Includes link to video.

23. See Lance Tapley, "Imprisoned Facts," *Portland Phoenix*, http://thephoenix.com/boston/news/62324-imprisoned-facts/ (last visited Jan. 17, 2010).

24. *Choate v. Merrill*, 2009 WL 1469015 (D-ME).

25. Gawande, "Hellhole."

26. Jesenia M. Pizarro and Raymund E. Narag, "Supermax Prisons: What We Know, What We Do Not Know, and Where We Are Going," *The Prison Journal* 88, no. 1 (2008): 24–25.

27. See DOJ, *Drugs and Crime Facts, Drug Law Violations: Correctional Populations and Facilities*, http://www.ojp.gov/bjs/dcf/correct.htm#jail (last visited Sept. 16, 2009).

28. See Ruth Wilson Gilmore, *Golden Gulag: Prisons, Surplus, Crisis, and Opposition in Globalizing California* (Berkeley: Univ. of California Press, 2007). See also Lance Tapley, "Prison Madness Explained," *Boston Phoenix*, Mar. 28, 2007, http://thephoenix.com/Boston/News/36449-Prison-madness-explained/?rel=inf (last visited Sept. 17, 2009).

29. Pizarro and Narag, "Supermax Prisons," 29.

30. Jesenia Pizarro and Vanja M. K. Stenius, "Supermax Prisons: Their Rise, Current Practices, and Effect on Inmates," *The Prison Journal* 84, no. 2 (2004): 259.

31. Kupers, "Survivors," 1011.

32. Hans Toch, "The Future of Supermax Confinement," *The Prison Journal* 81, no. 3 (2001): 381.

33. David Sharp, "Suspect Admits to N.H. Triple-Slaying," *Boston Globe*, July 6, 2007, http://www.boston.com/news/local/articles/2007/07/06/suspect_admits_to_nh_triple_slaying/ (last visited Sept. 16, 2009).

34. Grassian, "Psychiatric Effects."

35. See Citizen's Committee on Mental Illness, Substance Abuse, and Criminal Justice and Nami Maine, Report on the Current Status of Services for Persons with Mental Illness in Maine's Jails and Prisons, Sept. 2002, p. 3, http://www.prisonpolicy.org/scans/maine/maine_mental_illness_2002.pdf (last visited Sept. 16, 2009).

36. See Emmet Meara, "Lawmaker Seeks Review of Supermax Policies," *Bangor Daily News*, Mar. 24, 2001, B-1.

37. See Maine Civil Liberties Union (MCLU), *The Health Status of Maine's Prison Population: Results of a Survey of Inmates Incarcerated by the Maine Department of Corrections* (Portland, ME: MCLU, 2003), 14.

38. See Doris J. James and Lauren E. Glaze, *Mental Health Problems of Prison and Jail Inmates*, NCJ 213600, Sept. 2006, http://www.ojp.usdoj.gov/bjs/pub/pdf/mhppji.pdf (last visited Sept. 16, 2009).

39. Bernard E. Harcourt, "The Mentally Ill, Behind Bars," *New York Times*, Jan. 15, 2007, http://www.nytimes.com/2007/01/15/opinion/15harcourt.html (last visited Sept. 16, 2009).

40. Smith, "Effects of Solitary Confinement," 455.

41. See Steve Aos, Marna Miller, and Elizabeth Drake, "Evidence-Based Public Policy Options to Reduce Future Prison Construction, Criminal Justice Costs, and Crime Rates," Washington State Institute for Public Policy, October 2006, http://www.wsipp.wa.gov/pub.asp?docid=06-10-1201 (last visited Jan. 17, 2010).

42. See DOJ, *Prisoners in 2008*, http://bjs.ojp.usdoj.gov/index.cfm?ty=pbdetail&iid=1763 (last visited Jan. 17, 2010).

43. See Pizarro and Narag, "Supermax Prisons," 36.

44. See *In re Medley*, 134 U.S. 160 (1890); *Chambers v. Florida*, 309 U.S. 227, 237 (1940).

45. See *Turner v. Safley*, 482 U.S. 78, 78-79 (1987).

46. *Madrid v. Gomez*, 889 F. Supp. 1146 (N.D. Cal. 1995).

47. See American Civil Liberties Union (ACLU), "District Court Approves ACLU Settlement, Orders Improvements at Wisconsin's 'Supermax,'" Mar. 8, 2002, http://www.aclu.org/prison/conditions/14640prs20020308.html (last visited Sept. 16, 2009); Judgment of June 24, 2002, Jones'El v. Berge, 2002 WL 32362655 (W.D.Wis.); http://www.aclu.org/FilesPDFs/order%20and%20settlement%20agreement.pdf (last visited Sept. 16, 2009).

48. For the principal authority, see The Civil Rights of Institutional Persons Act, 42 U.S.C. § 1997 (1980).

49. See Implementation of the Convention Against Torture, 8 C.F.R. § 208.18; also, S. Treaty Doc. 100-20.

50. Jules Lobel, "Prolonged Solitary Confinement and the Constitution," *Univ. of Penn. Journal of Constitutional Law* 11, no. 1 (2008): 138, http://papers.ssrn.com/sol3/papers.cfm? abstract_id=1428922 (last visited Sept. 16, 2009).

51. See 18 U.S.C. §§ 2340 and 2340A. Only one prosecution, in fact, has taken place, of Charles "Chuckie" Taylor, Jr., the U.S.-citizen son of the Liberian dictator Charles Taylor. In 2008, he was convicted in Florida for torture that took place in Liberia.

52. See, e.g., National Lawyers Guild, http://www.nlg.org (last visited Sept. 16, 2009); The Meiklejohn Civil Liberties Institute, http://www.mcli.org (last visited Sept. 16, 2009).

53. See Pawlaczyk and Hundsdorfer, "Expert: Tamms Inmates Show Signs of Torture."

54. See American Friends Service Committee, "STOPMAX," http://www.afsc.org/stopmax/ (last visited Sept. 16, 2009).

55. See Maine Coalition to End the Abuse of Solitary Confinement, http://www.maineprisonjustice.org/ (last visited Jan. 17, 2010).

56. See National Religious Coalition Against Torture, http://www.nrcat.org/ (last visited Jan. 17, 2010).

57. See National Criminal Justice Commission Act, http://thomas.loc.gov/cgi-bin/query/D?c111:1:./temp/~c111vbCg5X:: (last visited Jan. 18, 2010).

58. See Bo Lozoff, *We're All Doing Time: A Guide for Getting Free* (Durham, NC: Human Kindness Foundation, 1985).

59. See George Orwell, *Nineteen Eighty-Four* (New York: Harcourt, Brace, & World, 1949), 267.

60. Gary Wills, "The Human Sewer," *New York Review of Books* 22, no. 5 (1975).

PART III

Accountability for Torture

11

The Law of Torture and
Accountability of Lawyers
Who Sanction It

JEANNE MIRER

This chapter[1] provides a comprehensive background to the legal issues underpinning the call by the National Lawyers Guild (NLG) to prosecute and dismiss from their jobs such persons as then Deputy Assistant Attorney General John Choon Yoo,[2] then Assistant Attorney General Jay Bybee,[3] and others who caused to be drafted or participated in the drafting of memoranda that authorized acts of torture and other cruel, inhuman, or degrading treatment.[4] The memoranda were written at the request of high-ranking U.S. officials in order to insulate them from the risk of future prosecution for subjecting detainees in U.S. custody to torture. This chapter also explains the legal reasons why all who authorized the use of torture by giving legal advice to justify it are subject to prosecution under international and U.S. domestic law.

Torture is prohibited in the United States by the Constitution, laws, executive statements, judicial decisions, and treaties. In fact, the United States has repeatedly criticized countries that use torture. The prohibition against torture is absolute, applies to all persons in U.S. custody during times of peace and war, and constitutes a *jus cogens* norm.[5] However, the legal memoranda drafted by government lawyers purposely or recklessly misconstrued and/or ignored *jus cogens*, customary and international law, and various U.S. treaty obligations, and in so doing facilitated the torture of many detainees in U.S. custody.

The Prohibition against Torture Is a Jus Cogens Norm

Jus cogens norms are accepted and recognized by the international community as a whole and no deviation from them is permitted. Countries also have universal jurisdiction over violations of these basic principles, enabling them to prosecute offenders extraterritorially. In international criminal law, crimes designated as violations of *jus cogens* norms include the duty to prosecute or extradite, the non-applicability of statutes of limitations, the non-applicability of any immunities, up to and including heads of state, and the non-applicability of the defense of "obedience to superior orders."[6]

Other *jus cogens* norms include slavery, genocide, and wars of aggression, all of which are, like norms of customary international law, legally binding. No affirmative executive act may undercut the force of these prohibitions, nor may a legislature pass legislation legalizing such acts or immunizing those responsible from prosecution. *Jus cogens* norms differ from norms which have attained the status of customary international law by dint of their universal and non-derogable (deviation never allowed) character. Also, they are peremptory, that is, they trump any other inconsistent international or national law.

The right to be free from torture and other cruel, inhuman, or degrading treatment was recognized in Article 5 of the *Universal Declaration of Human Rights*.[7] It is contained in Article 7 of the *International Covenant on Civil and Political Rights*,[8] and Article 5(2) of the *American Convention on Human Rights*.[9] Torture is outlawed under the *Rome Statute* which created the International Criminal Court (ICC).[10] The U.S. Army's *Field Manual 34-52* makes clear that techniques of interrogation are to be established under the rules laid out by The Hague and Geneva Conventions. The manual is unambiguous in prohibiting the use of torture and any other coercion in interrogation of prisoners.[11]

Article 17 of the 1949 *Third Geneva Convention* prohibits physical or mental torture and any other coercive action against prisoners of war, and Article 130 classifies a violation of Article 17 as a "grave breach" of the *Geneva Conventions*.[12] The *Fourth Geneva Convention* prohibits an occupying power from torturing protected persons (Article 32) or engaging in any other "measures of brutality" (Article 283).[13] Common Article 3 (that is, Article 3 in each of the conventions) prohibits torture as well as inhuman, humiliating, and degrading treatment of those who are taking no active part in hostilities, or any persons in detention who may be members of armed forces who have laid down their arms, or those who are *hors de combat*.[14]

The 1984 *Convention against Torture and Other Cruel, Inhuman or Degrading Treatment or Punishment* (*Torture Convention* or *CAT*) codified the prohibitions against torture into specific rules. It prohibits "torture and other acts of cruel, inhuman, or degrading treatment or punishment."[15] Also, the *CAT* criminalizes acts that result in torture and limits impunity by denying all possible refuge to torturers. The *Torture Convention* is also categorical: "No exceptional circumstances whatsoever, whether a state of war, or a threat of war, internal political instability or any other public emergency, may be invoked as a justification for torture."[16]

Because this prohibition has achieved universal recognition and attained *jus cogens* status, it is part of the highest and most compelling law across the globe. Thus, the conduct of Yoo and the others who sought to provide legal cover for torture and cruel treatment must be examined accordingly.

The Convention against Torture, the Torture Statute, and the War Crimes Act

Several developments have led to the prohibition of torture attaining *jus cogens* status. First, the UN General Assembly adopted the *CAT* in 1984 to strengthen existing prohibitions against torture and other cruel, inhuman, or degrading treatment.[17] In addition, the United States ratified the *International Covenant on Civil and Political Rights* (ICCPR)[18] in 1992 and the *Torture Convention* in 1994.[19] Finally, the British House of Lords decided to extradite Augusto Pinochet for prosecution in 1999 based on his promoting and condoning acts of torture while in power, which was based in part on the existence of the *Torture Convention*.[20]

Article 1 of the *CAT* defines torture as:

1. Any act by which severe pain or suffering, whether physical or mental, is intentionally inflicted on a person for such purposes as obtaining from him or a third person information or a confession, punishing him for an act he or a third person has committed or is suspected of having committed, or intimidating or coercing him or a third person, or for any reason based on discrimination of any kind, when such pain or suffering is inflicted

by or at the instigation of or with the consent or acquiescence of a public official or other person acting in an official capacity. It does not include pain or suffering arising only from, inherent in or incidental to lawful sanctions.

Article 2 requires that "[e]ach State Party shall take effective legislative, administrative, judicial or other measures to prevent acts of torture in any territory under its jurisdiction." It also provides, "An order from a superior officer or a public authority may not be invoked as a justification of torture."

In ratifying the *CAT*, the United States included various "reservations," "understandings," and "declarations" (RUD's), despite the fact that international law does not permit RUD's that violate the object and purpose of the treaty.[21] Through Article VI, Section 2 of the United States Constitution (Supremacy Clause), upon ratification, the convention becomes "the Supreme Law of the Land." Pursuant to the language of the treaty, Congress statutorily criminalized torture and any conspiracy to commit such acts.

The opinions sought by Bush officials from Yoo and the other lawyers address actions taken by U.S. officials outside the United States, in the various "black sites" as well as U.S. bases in Afghanistan and Guantánamo. At that time, the administration argued that these locations were outside the United States and beyond the reach of any U.S. court.[22] However, unlike the *CAT*, which is site-specific, the U.S. statute applies to actions that take place extraterritorially.[23] Thus, the jurisdictional argument is moot.

The United States Prohibits Torture and Other Cruel, Inhuman, or Degrading Treatment

Over 25 years ago, the U.S. Court of Appeals for the Second Circuit in *Filartiga v. Peña-Irala* declared that the prohibition against torture is universal, obligatory, specific, and definable.[24] Consistent with the principle attaining *jus cogens* status, since *Filartiga*, every other U.S. circuit court that has considered the issue has held that torture violates well-established customary international law.[25]

In 2004, Congress declared that "the Constitution, laws, and treaties of the United States and the applicable guidance and regulations of the United States government prohibit the torture or cruel, inhuman, or degrading treatment of foreign prisoners held in custody of the United States," here or abroad.

Further, Congress affirmed that "no detainee shall be subject to torture or cruel, inhuman, or degrading treatment or punishment that is prohibited by the Constitution, laws, or treaties of the United States." Finally, Congress reiterated, "the policy of the United States is to . . . investigate and prosecute, as appropriate, all alleged instances of unlawful treatment of detainees in a manner consistent with the international obligations, laws, or policies of the United States."[26]

Bush's Order and the Torture Memos

Houston Law Center Professor Jordan Paust noted:

A common plan to violate customary and treaty-based international law concerning the treatment and interrogation of so-called terrorist and enemy combatant detainees and their supporters captured during the U.S. war in Afghanistan emerged within the Bush administration in 2002.[27]

On February 7, 2002, President Bush announced that Geneva's Common Article 3 did not apply to alleged Taliban and al-Qaeda members. Bush declared, however, "As a matter of policy, the United States Armed Forces shall continue to treat detainees humanely and, *to the extent appropriate and consistent with military necessity*, in a manner consistent with the principles of Geneva."[28]

In the summer of 2002, the Pentagon sought advice on whether the army was bound by its field manual in interrogating prisoners at Guantánamo. An advisory memo written by Col. Diane Beaver, a U.S. Army lawyer, attempted to circumvent the manual's constraints on interrogation.[29] Before issuing her opinion, Beaver was visited by lawyers from Washington, DC, including David Addington, William Haynes, and others who made it clear that those at the top of the administration sought permission to deviate from the strictures of the field manual.[30]

Beaver's advisory opinion concluded that international obligations are irrelevant and that because the detainees were not prisoners of war, the *Geneva Conventions* did not apply. Before Beaver issued her opinion, however, the Department of Justice (DOJ) was providing advice on whether interrogation techniques, which were assumed to be legal under U.S. law, could violate the *CAT*[31] and expose the United States to prosecution at the ICC.[32]

There are many lawyers in the DOJ's Office of Legal Counsel who are cognizant of the legal duties of the United States under ratified treaties. The Bush administration, however, turned to political appointees, Deputy Assistant Attorney General John Yoo and Assistant Attorney General Jay Bybee, for these opinions.[33]

On January 9, 2002, Yoo submitted a memorandum opinion titled "Application of Treaties and Laws to al Qaeda and Taliban Detainees." Co-authored with Special Counsel Robert J. Delahunty, the memo purported to address "the effect of international treaties and federal laws on the treatment of individuals detained by the U.S. Armed Forces during the conflict in Afghanistan."

This memo argued that the president was not bound by international laws in the war on terror. Instead, it concluded that "any customary international law of armed conflict in no way binds, as a legal matter, the President or the U.S. Armed Forces concerning the detention or trial of members of al-Qaeda and the Taliban." The memo found it proper to deny international legal protections to detainees and exempt those who do so from liability.[34]

Yoo also authored a memorandum opinion dated August 1, 2002, titled "Standards of Conduct for Interrogation under 18 U.S.C. ss. 2340–2340A." This opinion was addressed to Alberto Gonzales from Jay Bybee, but was reportedly drafted by Yoo. In this memo, Yoo/Bybee redefined torture to include only acts inflicting physical pain equivalent in intensity to the pain accompanying serious physical injury, such as organ failure, impairment of bodily function, or even death, a much narrower definition than provided by the *CAT* and the U.S. torture statute.[35]

In 2007, a March 14, 2003, Yoo memorandum entitled, "Military Interrogation of Alien Unlawful Combatants Held outside the United States," became public. This 81-page memo again reiterates that the president is not bound by federal laws. "Such criminal statutes, if they were misconstrued to apply to the interrogation of enemy combatants, would conflict with the Constitution's grant of the Commander in Chief power solely to the President." Yoo unequivocally states that the president is not bound by laws that prohibit torture, assault, maiming, stalking, and war crimes.[36]

This memo failed to acknowledge that the prohibition of torture is a *jus cogens* norm, and wrongly declares that the president is free to override customary international law at his discretion. In *The Paquete Habana*, however, more than 100 years ago, the Supreme Court held that customary international law is part of the law of the United States, which must be ascertained and applied by the judiciary.[37] In 1984, Justice O'Connor wrote for the court, "power, delegated by Congress to the Executive Branch, and a relevant congressional-Executive arrangement must not be exercised in a manner inconsistent with . . . international law."[38]

Finally, the memo suggests that those who engaged in torture during interrogations may claim legal defenses of military necessity and self-defense, notwithstanding the *jus cogens* status of the norm, the absolute prohibition of the *CAT*, and the elimination of a military necessity defense in the *Geneva Conventions*.[39]

The August 2002 Yoo Torture Memo Is Withdrawn

Many scholars have opined on the legal deficiencies of the several torture memos drafted by Yoo and others.[40] Referring back to the discussion of *jus cogens*, there is no legal basis for presidential immunity. No one has the power to re-write the *CAT*'s definition of torture and allow aggressive interrogation techniques that violate the treaty. The *war* on terror does not exempt the executive branch from the legal restraints on warfare conduct, as codified by *Geneva Conventions*.[41]

After the exposure of the atrocities at Abu Ghraib and the disclosure of the August 1, 2002, memo, the DOJ withdrew the Yoo memos on June 1, 2004. A new opinion was written by Daniel Levin, acting Assistant Attorney General Office of Legal Counsel, dated December 30, 2004. This memo specifically rejects Yoo's definition of torture, stating: "Under the language adopted by Congress in sections 2340–2340A, to constitute 'torture,' the conduct in question must have been 'specifically intended to inflict severe physical or mental pain or suffering."[42]

With respect to "specific intent," the Levin memo cites Wayne R. LaFave, who writes in his treatise on criminal law:

With crimes which require that the defendant intentionally cause a specific result, what is meant by an "intention" to cause that result?

Although the theorists have not always been in agreement . . . , the traditional view is that a person who acts . . . intends a result of his act . . . under two quite different circumstances: (1) when he consciously desires that result, whatever the likelihood of that result happening from his conduct; and (2) when he knows that that result is practically certain to follow from his conduct, whatever his desire may be as to that result.[43]

The 2005 Bradbury Memos to the CIA Echo the Yoo/Bybee Justifications of Torture

In 2009, three memos written by attorney Steven G. Bradbury to CIA General Counsel John Rizzo in 2005, regarding individual techniques and combined techniques of interrogation, as well as U.S. obligations under *CAT*, were released to the public.[44] These memos describe in excruciatingly cold and clinical detail the use of torture, euphemistically called, "enhanced interrogation techniques."[45] Each technique, including the use of waterboarding, was found by Bradbury not to constitute torture.

Thus, the changes from the Yoo to the Levin memo appear to be changes only in words, not substance.[46] That is, even with the changed definition of torture, every "enhanced interrogation technique" allowed by the Yoo memo was allowed under the Bradbury memos and found to be permissible under both the torture statute and Article 16 of the *CAT*.

One such technique is "shackling," where the detainee's feet are shackled to the floor and his hands are cuffed and chained to the ceiling. Often the detainee is wearing nothing but a diaper and deprived of sleep for up to 180 hours. Many of Bradbury's justifications for these techniques contain bizarre analogies. For example, he relies on the fact that people in the United States use weight loss products containing less than 1,000 calories a day to justify the use of a complete liquid diet of "Ensure Plus" for detainees. Bradbury also concludes that the use of waterboarding is permissible, even though he recognizes that it poses a "threat of imminent death."[47]

It is difficult to imagine how a lawyer could have determined the listed techniques did not violate the *CAT*. All appear not only to sanction but to encourage the intentional infliction of severe physical and/or mental pain or suffering to obtain a "confession," or to intimidate, coerce, or discriminate against him.[48]

Hamdan v. Rumsfeld

On June 29, 2006, the U.S. Supreme Court ruled in *Hamdan v. Rums-feld* that Guantánamo detainees were entitled to the protections provided under Geneva's Common Article 3. The Court invoked the legal precedents sidestepped by John Yoo and others. Joining the majority, Justice Kennedy pointedly observed that violations of Common Article 3 are considered 'war crimes.'

Specifically, *Hamdan* addressed the procedural due process rights of Guantánamo detainees and found that military commissions used for trying them did not pass muster under Common Article 3. Moreover, the court found that the Geneva Conventions protected detainees against torture, and cruel, inhuman, or other degrading treatment.[49]

Four months later, President Bush signed the *Military Commissions Act*,[50] which was enacted ostensibly to correct procedural defects referred to in *Hamdan*, and create a new legal defense for misconduct arising from the "detention and interrogation of aliens" between September 11, 2001, and December 30, 2005.[51]

*Lawyers Complicit in Promoting or Facilitating Torture,
Cruel, Inhuman, or Degrading Treatment Cannot Claim
Shield against Culpability Based on Being Lawyers*

The Yoo/Bybee memos were either prospective—for the purpose of advising the executive of the limits (or lack thereof) of its authority, or retrospective—for the purpose of justifying already approved actions. Although they purport to be the former, it now appears they were written after the Bush administration began using torture. Regardless, there are only two conclusions one can draw from the memos.

First, the purpose of the memos was not to give the president a full understanding of the legal issues, but to provide legal cover for a premeditated illegal policy. Second, the drafters did not present all possible conclusions and consequences, and thus failed to meet the requisite professional standard of care, constituting legal malpractice. No one, and certainly not the NLG, has accused Yoo of being completely incompetent.

Yoo, Bybee, Bradbury and others advised that detainees held at black sites, prisons in Afghanistan, and Guantánamo were only entitled to protection from certain severe forms of torture, comparable to organ failure and/or death. In effect, these memos provided the "green light" for interrogators to engage in other illegal techniques. Therefore, these attorneys knew, or should have known, that as a direct result of their counsel, detainees would be tortured.

> [The "torture memos" written by the DOJ lawyers, along with] presidential and other authorizations, directives, and findings substantially facilitated the effectuation of the common, unifying plan to use coercive interrogation and that use of authorized coercive interrogation tactics were either known or substantially foreseeable consequences.[52]

John Yoo even admitted, "[the coercive interrogation] policies were part of a common, unifying approach to the war on terrorism.[53]

The NLG has taken a position consistent with Professor Sands' conclusion in his chapter in this volume, "Terrorists and Torturers," that giving political cover makes a lawyer complicit in the decision to torture.[54] Thus, there can be no two opinions on whether those involved in the decision to torture should be held accountable. Yoo and other lawyers who were involved in the drafting of opinions justifying the use of torture are just as responsible as those who authorized and carried out the orders. All must be held equally accountable.

Some have criticized the NLG for targeting lawyers who were "merely fulfilling their duty by giving advice." However, the NLG is not only targeting the lawyers, as the organization has continually called for prosecution of all who are responsible for these crimes and not just the lower-ranking enlisted people. These men and women, though culpable, should not simply serve as scapegoats for the entire administration. The lawyers cannot be shielded by their obligation to fulfill professional responsibilities, nor does the attorney-client privilege extend to maintaining confidentiality in this matter.

Following World War II, Josef Altstoetter and 15 other German lawyers were prosecuted before a U.S. military tribunal. Many were convicted of international crimes based on legal advice they had provided. The tribunal found that, despite the fact that many were following "legal" orders, the lawyers and judges of Nazi Germany bore a particular responsibility for the regime's crimes. In fact, many were convicted of war crimes and crimes against humanity for advising Hitler on how to "legally" disappear political suspects.[55]

However, that case alone should not expose Yoo and his cohorts to liability for the legal advice provided. Their memos were not written for the purpose of advocacy. If they were defending the president in an impeachment case, or before the ICC, they would be free to argue, however vainly, their novel positions. But they cannot divorce themselves from the consequences of rendering defective legal advice and should not receive immunity or impunity.

Those Who Approved or Authorized Torture Cannot Avoid Prosecution

The legal principles and reasoned arguments discussed above can lead to one conclusion and one conclusion only: If the U.S. Attorney General properly followed the law, he would have to appoint a special independent prosecutor to investigate and prosecute anyone who assisted in designing, approving, or implementing a program of torture and cruel, inhuman, and degrading treatment.

In the current political climate, however, such prosecutions are not imminent. When the Bradbury memos were released, President Obama stated that no one in the CIA who took action in reliance on the improper legal advice would be prosecuted. Despite having read the as yet unreleased CIA Inspector General's report, Attorney General Eric Holder is only considering appointment of a special prosecutor to investigate interrogators and pursue criminal liability against those whose actions went beyond the techniques described by Bradbury and exceeded legal bounds.[56]

The mantra Obama uses to avoid holding anyone else accountable is the need to look forward, not backwards. Some claim that to prosecute all those involved would be too divisive, or an unwise use of resources in light of the economic crisis. Potential proponents of accountability, such as House Speaker Nancy Pelosi, have been threatened by supporters of Bush's interrogation program. They claim that she would be part of any investigation because she was briefed about the use of these techniques and approved them.[57]

Notwithstanding the desire of elected officials to avoid accountability, the law requires prosecution. There has been a growing movement and drum beat among progressive forces to make sure that those responsible for these heinous and illegal acts are brought to account.[58] Congressman John Conyers introduced a bill that would create a 9/11 type commission to investigate crimes of the Bush administration, including torture and other activities, such as illegal wiretapping and extraordinary rendition.[59] This bill continues to gain sponsors and the NLG is actively supporting it.

In 2008, Jose Padilla, who, after being designated as an enemy combatant, spent almost three years in solitary confinement at a brig in North Carolina, sued John Yoo for mental and emotional damages resulting from the detention. Yoo was named as a major architect of the policies that deprived Padilla of his constitutional rights. So far, this case has survived a motion to dismiss. The court squarely confronted the political tension between actions designed to protect national security during a "war on terror" and the constitutional rights of citizens, and came down on the side of ensuring that constitutional rights are protected even during times of combat. The court stated, "We must preserve our commitment at home to the principles for which we fight abroad."[60]

It may take time before all of the individuals responsible for the unspeakable acts visited upon those taken into U.S. custody after 9/11 are brought to justice. But, to ensure that it never happens again, it is essential to hold those who perpetrated these acts accountable for their illegal conduct. Impunity should not be an option.

NOTES

1. This chapter was originally drafted in 2007 when, upon release of the first Yoo/Bybee memos, the National Lawyers Guild (NLG) declared that these individuals and all of those who ordered the torture of detainees should be held accountable for their actions. As an organization of lawyers, law students, legal workers, and jailhouse lawyers, the NLG was particularly concerned that lawyers in the Office of Legal Counsel and the Attorney General were used to try to provide legal justifications for the use of torture or other cruel, inhuman, or degrading treatment. Initially, this writing was issued as an NLG White Paper on this same topic. The law as originally stated remains substantially the same, but it has been updated to include recent developments. See NLG, *White Paper on the Law of Torture and Holding Accountable Those Who Are Complicit in Approving Torture of Persons in U.S. Custody*, http://nlg.org/news/statements/NLGWhitePaper_Yoo.doc (last visited July 29, 2009).

2. John Choon Yoo is currently a Professor of Law at University of California, Berkeley.

3. Jay Scott Bybee is currently a federal judge on the United States Court of Appeals for the Ninth Circuit.

4. The *Convention Against Torture*, as well as other treaties to which the United States is a party, prohibits torture and other cruel, inhuman, or degrading treatment or punishment. The term "torture" will be generally used in this chapter, but cruel, inhuman and degrading treatment are also prohibited. United Nations (UN), *Convention Against Torture and the Other Cruel, Inhuman or Degrading Treatment or Punishment* (hereafter *Convention Against Torture*), Dec. 10, 1984, S. Treaty Doc. No. 100-20 (1988), 1465 U.N.T.S. 85 G.A. Res. 39/46, U.N. GAOR, 39th Sess. Supp. No. 51, at 197, U.N. Doc. A/39/51 (1984), reprinted in 23 I.L.M. 1027 (1984).

5. See, e.g., *Siderman de Blake v. Republic of Argentina*, 965 F.2d 699, 714 (9th Cir. 1992); *Regina v. Bow Street Metro. Stipendiary Magistrate Ex Parte Pinochet Ugarte (No. 3)*, [2000] 1 AC 147, 198; *see also* Restatement (Third) of Foreign Relations Law of the United States § 702, note 5.

6. UN, *Vienna Convention on the Law of Treaties* (hereafter *Vienna Convention*), May 23, 1969, art. 53, 64 8 I.L.M. 679, 698–99 (1969); also see Karen Parker, *"Jus Cogens*: Compelling the Law of Human Rights," 12 *Hastings Intl & Comp. L. Rev.* 411 (1989).

7. UN, *Universal Declaration of Human Rights*, art. 5, G.A. res. 217A (III), U.N. Doc A/810 (1948).

8. UN, *International Covenant on Civil and Political Rights* (hereafter *ICCPR)*, art. 7, Dec. 16, 1966, 999 U.N.T.S. 171 (ratified by the United States on June 8, 1992).

9. Organization of American States, *American Convention on Human Rights*, art. 5(2), Nov. 22, 1969, O.A.S.T.S. No. 36, 1144 U.N.T.S. 123.

10. International Criminal Court (ICC), *Rome Statute*, July 12, 1998, A/CONF.183/9.

11. U.S. Department of Army, *Field Manual 34–52: Intelligence Interrogation*, May 8, 1987, http://www.fas.org/irp/doddir/army/fm34-52.pdf (last visited July 29, 2009).

12. *Convention Relative to the Treatment of Prisoners of War* (*Geneva Convention III*), art. 17, 130, Aug. 12, 1949.

13. *Convention Relative to the Protection of Civilian Persons in Time of War* (*Geneva Convention IV*), art. 32, 283, Aug. 12, 1949.

14. *Geneva Conventions of 1949*, art. 3, Aug. 12, 1949.

15. UN, *Convention Against Torture*.

16. Ibid. at art. 2(2).

17. See J. Herman Burgers and Hans Daniels, *The United Nations Convention Against Torture: A Handbook on the Convention Against Torture and Other Cruel, Inhuman or Degrading Treatment or Punishment* (Dordrecht, Netherlands: Martinus Nijhoff Publishers, 1988).

18. 138 Cong. Rec. 7967, 8070 (1992)

19. 136 Cong. Rec. 36007, 36198 (1990); although the Senate approved ratification in 1990, the United States did not deposit its documentation with the UN
until implementing legislation was passed in 1994.

20. *Regina v. Bartle*, 2 W.L.R. 827 (H.L.) March 24, 1999.

21. See UN, *Vienna Convention*, art. 19. "Understandings" differ from "reservations." An understanding cannot change an international legal obligation
under the convention. Under international law, where there is conflict between
international obligation and domestic law, international law will govern. It is
clear that the *Convention Against Torture* would not tolerate national legislation
that would give less protection. See Jordan J. Paust, *Beyond the Law: The Bush
Administration's Unlawful Responses in the "War" on Terror* (New York: Cambridge Univ. Press, 2007), 33–34, 189–91, 59n, 63n.

22. Military personnel or any other person who commits or has committed
torture would be covered by the *War Crimes Act*, and may be punished up to life
in prison or if death occurs, may be executed. 18 U.S.C. §2441(a). A "war crime"
includes any conduct:

> (1) defined as a grave breach in any of the international conventions signed
> at Geneva 12 August 1949, or any protocol to such convention to which the
> United States is a party;
> (2) prohibited by Article 23, 25, 27, or 28 of the Annex to the Hague Convention
> IV, Respecting the Laws and Customs of War on Land, signed 18 October 1907;
> (3) which constitutes a violation of common Article 3 when committed in
> the context of and in association with an armed conflict not of an interna-
> tional character. . . (18 U.S.C §2441(b)).

23. 18 U.S.C. §§2340–2340A. §2340 provides that:

> (1) "torture" means an act committed by a person acting under color of law
> specifically intended to inflict severe physical or mental pain or suffering
> (other than pain or suffering incidental to lawful sanctions) upon another
> person within his custody or physical control;

§2340A provides in part:

> (a) Offense.- Whoever outside the United States commits or attempts to
> commit torture shall be fined under this title or imprisoned not more than
> 20 years, or both, and if death results to any person from conduct prohib-
> ited by this subsection, shall be punished by death or imprisoned for any
> term of years or for life. . . .
> (c) Conspiracy.- A person who conspires to commit an offense under this
> section shall be subject to the same penalties (other than the penalty
> of death) as the penalties prescribed for the offense, the commission of
> which was the object of the conspiracy.

24. *Filartiga v. Pena-Irala,* 630 F.2d 876 (2nd Cir. 1980).

25. *Abebe-Jira v. Negewo,* 72 F.3d 844, 847 (11th Cir. 1996). See also, e.g., *Kadic v. Karadzic,* 70 F.3d 232, 243 (2d Cir. 1995) (noting than torture is prohibited by "universally accepted norms of international law") (quoting *Filartiga*); *Hilao v. Marcos,* 103 F.3d 789 (9th Cir. 1996)*: In re Estate of Ferdinand Marcos, Human Rights Litigation,* 25 F.3d 1467, 1475 (9th Cir. 1994); *Siderman de Blake v. Republic of Argentina,* 965 F.2d 699, 717 (9th Cir. 1992); *Mehinovic v. Vuckovic,* 198 F. Supp.2d 1322 (N.D. Ga.2002); *Doe v. Islamic Salvation Front,* 993 F. Supp. 3, 8 (D.D.C. 1998); *Doe v. Unocal,* 963 F. Supp. 880, 890 (C.D. Cal. 1997); *Xuncax v. Gramajo,* 886 F. Supp. 162 (D. Mass. 1995); *Paul v. Avril,* 901 F. Supp. 330 (S.D. Fla. 1994) (imposing civil liability for acts of torture).

26. U.S. Congress, *Sense of Congress and Policy Concerning Persons Detained by the United States,* Pub. L. No. 108-375, 118 Stat. 1811, §1091(a)(1)(6), (a)(8),(b) (2) (Oct. 28, 2004).

27. See Jordan Paust, "Criminal Responsibility of Bush Administration Officials with Respect to Unlawful Interrogation Tactics and the Facilitating Conduct of Lawyers," in this book; "Executive Plans and Authorizations to Violate International Law Concerning Treatment and Interrogation of Detainees." Paust, *Beyond the Law,* 1.

28. George W. Bush, memorandum to White House officials regarding "Humane Treatment of Taliban and al Qaeda Detainees," February 7, 2002, http://www.pegc.us/archive/White_House/bush_memo_20020207_ed.pdf (last visited July 29, 2009) [emphasis added].

29. Col. Beaver relied on Bush's executive order of February 7, 2002, that the detainees at Guantánamo were not prisoners of war and therefore allegedly not covered under the *Geneva Conventions.*

30. The book *Torture Team* demonstrates that the decision to seek to use these methods came from the very top and that significant pressure was placed on Beaver to write an opinion that provided justification for what Addington and others wanted to do. See Philippe Sands, *Torture Team: Rumsfeld's Memo and the Betrayal of American Values* (New York: Palgrave MacMillan, 2008).

31. See ibid.

32. Although the United States has not ratified the Rome Statute, violations of the statute in countries which have ratified it could subject persons within the territory to prosecution. See International Criminal Court, *Rome Statute,* A/CONF.183/9, July 12, 1998.

33. From the chronology provided by Philippe Sands in his *Vanity Fair* article entitled "The Green Light," it is known that the lawyers for the president, vice president, and secretary of defense, to wit: Addington, Haynes, Gonzales, Yoo,

and Bybee, met in Guantánamo to discuss the use of various interrogation techniques which were being proposed to be used on various detainees. It is also now known from news reports (most notably ABC News) that meetings were held at the White House in which the specific interrogation/torture techniques to be applied to various detainees were discussed and approved. See Philippe Sands, "The Green Light," *Vanity Fair*, May 2008, http://www.vanityfair.com/politics/features/2008/05/Guantánamo200805 (last visited July 28, 2009).

34. John Yoo and Robert Delahunty, memorandum for William J. Haynes II regarding "Application of Treaties and Laws to al Qaeda and Taliban Detainees," January 9, 2002, http://www.gwu.edu/~nsarchiv/NSAEBB/NSAEBB127/02.01.09.pdf (last visited July 29, 2009).

35. Jay Bybee, memorandum to Alberto R. Gonzales regarding "Standards of Conduct for Interrogation under 18 U.S.C. §§ 2340–2340A," Aug. 1, 2002, http://www.washingtonpost.com/wp-srv/nation/documents/dojinterrogation-memo20020801.pdf (last visited July 29, 2009).

36. John C. Yoo, memorandum to William J. Haynes II regarding "Military Interrogation of Alien Unlawful Combatants Held Outside the United States," March 14, 2003, http://www.aclu.org/pdfs/safefree/yoo_army_torture_memo.pdf (last visited July 29, 2009).

37. *The Paquete Habana*, 175 U.S. 677 (1900).

38. *TransWorld Airlines v. Franklin Mint Corp.*, 466 U.S. 243, 261 (1984). Every relevant federal case has recognized that the president is bound by the laws of war. See, e.g., Paust, *Beyond the Law*, 20–22 and cases cited.

39. Yoo, memorandum regarding "Military Interrogation."

40. See, e.g., Philippe Sands, *Lawless World: America and the Making and Breaking of Global Rules—from FDR's Atlantic Charter to George W. Bush's Illegal War* (New York: Penguin Group, 2006); Marjorie Cohn, *Cowboy Republic: Six Ways the Bush Gang Has Defied the Law* (Sausalito, CA: PoliPointPress, 2007), 34–37; Paust, *Beyond the Law*, 9–11, 29–30, 146, 148–49.

41. See UN, *International Convention for the Suppression of Terrorist Bombings*, A/52/653, Nov. 25, 1997. Indeed, this convention treats "terrorists" as criminals, whose punishments are subject to criminal law of the country at issue.

42. Daniel Levin, memorandum opinion for the Deputy Attorney General regarding "Legal Standards Applicable Under 18 U.S.C. §§ 2340–2340A," Dec. 30, 2004, http://www.usdoj.gov/olc/18usc23402340a2.htm (last visited July 29, 2009).

43. Wayne R. LaFave, *Substantive Criminal Law* (St. Paul, MN: West Group, 1986), § 5.2(a), 341.

44. See Stephen G. Bradbury, memorandum to CIA Senior Counsel John Rizzo regarding "Application of U.S.C. §§ 2340–2340A to Certain Techniques That May Be Used in the Interrogation of a High Value al Qaeda Detainee" (hereafter *Individual Techniques Memo*), May 10, 2005; Stephen G. Bradbury, memorandum to CIA Senior Counsel John Rizzo regarding "Application of 18 U.S.C. §§ 2340–2340A to the Combined Use of Certain Techniques in the Interrogation of High Value al Qaeda Detainees" (hereafter *Combined Techniques Memo*), May 10, 2005; Stephen G. Bradbury, memorandum to CIA Senior Counsel John Rizzo regarding "Application of United States Obligations Under Article 16 of the Convention Against Torture to Certain Techniques that May Be Used in the Interrogation of High Value al Qaeda Detainees" (hereafter *CAT Memo*), May 30, 2005.

45. The memos define three categories of techniques: "baseline, corrective and coercive." The baseline techniques were imposed upon the detainee's arrival to the interrogation facility for the purpose of "demonstrat[ing] to the [detainee] that he has no control over basic human needs, and helping to make him 'perceive and value his personal welfare, comfort, and immediate needs more than the information he is protecting" (internal quotations omitted). Bradbury, *Combined Techniques Memo*, 5. Three techniques are used to bring the detainee to this state, sleep deprivation, nudity, and dietary manipulation. The primary method of sleep deprivation is called "shackling." Bradbury, *Individual Techniques Memo*, 11–13.

46. Yoo, memorandum regarding "Military Interrogation." Also released in 2009 was another memo dated August 1, 2002 signed and authored by Yoo which provided the rationale for excluding detainees from protections against torture and articulating the same definition of torture as his other August 1, 2002 memo to Alberto Gozales. See John C. Yoo, memorandum to Alberto R. Gonzales regarding interrogation methods that do not violate prohibitions against torture, Aug. 1, 2002, http://news.findlaw.com/wp/docs/doj/bybee80102ltr.html (last visited July 29, 2009).

47. When NLG President Marjorie Cohn testified before the House Judiciary Committee's Subcommittee on the Constitution, Civil Rights, and Civil Liberties about Bush's interrogation policies, Congressman Trent Franks (R-AZ) stated that former CIA Director Michael Hayden had confirmed that the Bush administration only waterboarded Khalid Sheikh Mohammed, Abu Zubaydah, and Abd al-Rahim al-Nashirit for one minute each. (See House Judiciary Subcommittee, "Testimony of Marjorie Cohn Before the Subcommittee on the Constitution, Civil Rights, and Civil Liberties," May 6, 2008). One of the newly released torture memos reveals that Mohammed was waterboarded 183 times and Zubaydah was

waterboarded 83 times. See Scott Shane, "Waterboarding Used 266 Times on Two Suspects," *New York Times*, April 19, 2009, http://www.nytimes.com/2009/04/20/world/20detain.html (last visited July 28, 2009). One of Stephen Bradbury's 2005 memos asserted that "enhanced techniques" on Zubaydah led to the identification of Mohammed and an alleged bomb plot by Jose Padilla. See Marjorie Cohn, "Torture Used to Link Saddam with 9/11," *Huffington Post*, April 27, 2009, http://www.huffingtonpost.com/marjorie-cohn/torture-used-to-link-sadd_b_190848.html (last visited July 28, 2009). But FBI special agent Ali Soufan, who interrogated Zubaydah, wrote in the *New York Times* that Zubaydah gave up that information under traditional interrogation methods, before the harsh techniques were used. Ali Soufan, "My Tortured Decision," *New York Times*, April 22, 2009, http://www.nytimes.com/2009/04/23/opinion/23soufan.html?_r=1 (last visited July 28, 2009). It later appeared that these techniques were being used on these subjects to try to get them to admit a connection between Iraq and 9/11. See Cohn, "Torture Used to Link Saddam."

48. See UN, *Convention Against Torture*, art. 1.

49. *Hamdan v. Rumsfeld*, 584 U.S. 557, 126 S. Ct. 2749 (2006).

50. *Military Commissions Act of 2006*, Public Law 109-366, 109th Cong., 2nd sess. (Oct. 17, 2006).

51. Attempts to immunize those complicit in torture from civil or criminal liability are not permitted in the context of the violation of a *jus cogens* norm; hence, the language in the *Military Commissions Act* creating this legal defense is not a blanket grant of immunity. See, e.g., Jordan J. Paust et al., *International Criminal Law: Cases and Materials,* 3rd ed. (Durham, NC: Carolina Academic Press, 2007), 51–78, 100–114. Furthermore, there can be no immunity, including Head of State immunity, or statute of limitations for violation of a *jus cogens* norm. In addition, universal jurisdiction will apply to those accused of violating *jus cogens* norms, enabling extraterritorial prosecution. See UN, *Vienna Convention*, art. 53, 64; Parker, *"Jus Cogens:* Compelling the Law of Human Rights."

52. See Jordan J. Paust, "International Crimes within the White House," 10 *N.Y. City L. Rev.* 339, 345 (2007).

53. John Yoo, Remarks on National Public Radio, Dec. 15, 2005. See also John Yoo, *War by Other Means: An Insider's Account of the War on Terror* (New York: Atlantic Monthly, 2006), 190–91.

54. See Philippe Sands, "Terrorists and Torturers," in this book.

55. See *United States of America v. Alstoetter et al.* ("The Justice Case"), 3 T.W.C. 1 (1948), 6 L.R.T.W.C. 1 (1948), 14 Ann. Dig. 278 (1948); *The Nuremburg Trials: The Justice Trial,* http://www.law.umkc.edu/faculty/projects/ftrials/nuremberg/Alstoetter.htm#Commentary (last visited July 29, 2009).

56. See David Ignatius, "Kicking the CIA (Again)," *Washington Post*, July 15, 2009, http://www.washingtonpost.com/wp-dyn/content/article/2009/07/15/AR2009071502393.html (last visited July 29, 2009). Given the potential that lower level interrogators will point to authority from higher ups, it may be impossible to contain the targets of prosecution to these persons and this might prevent Attorney General Holder from acting.

57. See Debra J. Saunders, "What Did Pelosi Know and When Did She Know It?" *San Francisco Chronicle*, April 30, 2009, http://www.sfgate.com/cgibin/article.cgi?f=/c/a/2009/04/30/EDM117AH31.DTL (last visited July 29, 2009). While Speaker Pelosi denies she was told that enhanced interrogation techniques were in use, even if she did know, calling for prosecutions or a truth commission years after she learned of these techniques would make her a hypocrite, not a likely candidate for criminal prosecution as a violator of the *jus cogens* norm. In order to convict someone of a crime, several elements must be established. Under the Model Penal Code, for example, these elements include the requirement of: (1) a voluntary act (otherwise known as *actus reus*); (2) a culpable mental state (otherwise known as *mens rea*); and (3) causation. See American Law Institute (ALI), *Model Penal Code* §§ 1.13, 2.01–2.03 (Washington, DC: ALI, 1962). Although one could perhaps argue that if Pelosi had knowledge of the torture program, and failed to protest it, this would satisfy the *mens rea* requirement, there is still no evidence of a voluntary act or causation.

58. See NLG, "NLG Votes for Impeachment of President Bush and Vice President Cheney," Nov. 6, 2007, http://www.nlg.org/news/index.php?entry=entry071106-092734 (last visited July 29, 2009); NLG, "NLG Calls on Boalt Hall to Dismiss Law Professor John Yoo, Whose Torture Memos Led to Commission of War Crimes," April 9, 2008, http://www.nlg.org/news/index.php?entry=entry080409-083133 (last visited July 29, 2008); ACLU, "ACLU Asks Justice Department to Appoint Independent Prosecutor to Investigate Torture," March 18, 2009, http://www.aclu.org/safefree/torture/39060prs20090318.html (last visited July 29, 2009); David Swanson, "200 Orgs Ask for Special Prosecutor for Cheney and Bush," May 12, 2009, http://www.opednews.com/articles/200-Orgs-Ask-for-Special-P-by-David-Swanson-090512-194.html (last visited July 29, 2009); Human Rights Watch, "Letter to Holder Supporting Criminal Prosecution for Counterterrorism Abuses," July 20, 2009, http://www.hrw.org/en/news/2009/07/20/letter-holder-supporting-criminal-prosecution-counterterrorism-abuses (last visited July 29, 2009).

59. U.S. Congress, *To Establish a National Commission on Presidential War Powers and Civil Liberties*, HR 104, 111th Cong., 1st sess., Jan. 6, 2009.

60. *Padilla v. Yoo*, F.Supp.2d, 2009 WL 1651273 (N.D.Cal., 2009). The decision was written by Judge Jeffrey White, a 2002 George W. Bush appointee.

12

Terrorists and Torturers

PHILIPPE SANDS

International law? I better call my lawyer. . . . I don't know
what you're talking about by international law.
George W. Bush, December 11, 2003

What do you do, as an international lawyer, when your client asks you to advise on the international rules prohibiting torture? Do you start with the rules, ask yourself how an international court—or your allies—might address the issues, and reach a balanced conclusion? Or do you focus on narrower issues of the relevance, applicability, and enforceability of the international rules in the national context, and reach a conclusion that you know—if you ask yourself the question—no international court would accept? Let me put it another way. Do you advise or do you provide legal cover?

When the now notorious Abu Ghraib photographs and testimonies entered the public domain, we did not know that lawyers in the U.S. Department of Justice and elsewhere in the administration had provided detailed legal advice to the U.S. government on the international torture rules. But during the weeks that followed, a rich source of leaked legal memos and opinions shed light on the logic which provided context in which Abu Ghraib could happen. The documents argued, in short, that the international rules were inapplicable, irrelevant, or unenforceable. They suggested that interrogation practices could be defined without reference to the constraints placed on the United States by its international obligations. So long as the practice was consistent with U.S. law, it would be fine. The advice ignored the plain language of the 1984 Convention against Torture and other treaties and rules which bound the United States. The advice ignored the definition of torture in international law, and the prohibition against torture under any circumstances. Even more outrageously, it proposed defenses, immunities, and impunity. In an effort to limit the damage, the White House declassified and released a great deal of material, although by no means all the advice. But it turned out that the White House material had not been reviewed very carefully. Some of it was even worse than the earlier leaked material. Parts of the advice were then disavowed.

The photographs were monstrous, and so were the legal opinions. How did it come to this, at the beginning of the twenty-first century, after more than 50 years of human rights and humanitarian law? How could the government of a country so strongly committed to the rules set its lawyers on such a task? And how could it be that the lawyers would get it so badly wrong?

The "war on terrorism" has led many lawyers astray. This phony "war" has been used to eviscerate well-established and sensible rules of international law, which the United States has in the past supported, relied upon, and often created. In the minds of the politically appointed legal advisers, the argument runs something like this: (1) the United States faces an unparalleled threat, presenting a clear and present danger; (2) all necessary means may be used to obtain information from captives, who are to be treated as combatants rather than ordinary criminals; and (3) international law is inapplicable and/or unenforceable and/or irrelevant, and in any case, the rules of international law must be interpreted to allow a threatened state to do everything necessary to protect itself. I should make it clear that this is not the kind of legal analysis that would be applied by the vast majority of legal advisers in the U.S. State Department or the U.S. Army's Judge Advocate General's Corps, or by legal advisers to the British government or any other government in the world. The advice I would have expected to see would run something like this. There are two sets of international rules governing torture and interrogation practices: a first set prohibits torture; a second set provides that torture cannot be used against terrorists, whether they are combatants or criminals. The governing principle must be: do unto others as you would have them do unto you.

Torture and other cruel and inhuman treatment have been internationally outlawed since the end of the Second World War. The 1948 Universal Declaration of Human Rights stated, "No one shall be subjected to torture or to cruel, inhuman or degrading treatment or punishment."[1] It allows for no exceptions. Similar language can be found in the International Covenant on Civil and Political Rights (Article 7)[2] and the American Convention on Human Rights (Article 5(2)).[3] Both are binding on the United States. The 1949 Geneva Convention III[4] prohibits physical or mental torture and any other form of coercion against a prisoner of war (Article 17). It designates such acts as "grave breaches" of the Convention (Article 130). Geneva Convention IV[5] prohibits an occupying power from torturing any protected person (Article 32), as well as other "measures of brutality" (Article 283). And the 1977 Geneva Protocol I[6]—the relevant provision of which reflects customary law—prohibits "torture of all kinds" and any other outrages on personal dignity, against any person under any circumstances. Even the threat of such acts is banned (Article 75(2)). These are the standards to which all detainees are entitled as of right.

The 1984 Convention against Torture takes these general obligations and codifies them into more specific rules. It prohibits torture and "other acts of cruel, inhuman or degrading treatment or punishment."[7] It criminalizes torture and seeks to end impunity for any torturer by denying him all possible refuge. The House of Lords ruled that Augusto Pinochet's claim to immunity could not withstand the 1984 Convention. The Convention defines torture broadly: "any act by which severe pain or suffering, whether physical or mental, is intentionally inflicted on a person." It encompasses acts which have been authorized—or acquiesced in—by a public official, and it includes acts carried out to obtain from the victim or from a third person information or a confession (Article I). The Convention is categorical that there will be no circumstances—even a "war against terrorism"—in which torture is permitted:

> No exceptional circumstances whatsoever, whether a state of war or a threat of war, internal political instability or any other public emergency, may be invoked as a justification for torture.[8]

Similarly, the Statute of the International Criminal Court treats torture and other inhumane acts as war crimes and crimes against humanity.[9] These are parts of the Rome Statute that the United States has not objected to.

This is one area in which the rules of international law are clear. It does not matter whether a person is a criminal, or a warrior combatant, or a lawful combatant or an unlawful combatant, or an al-Qaeda militant, or a private American contractor. He may not be tortured. He may not be subjected to other cruel, inhuman, or degrading treatment. If he is, then the perpetrator of such acts must be punished under the criminal law. And any person who threatens torture, or who is complicit or participates in torture, is also to be treated as a criminal. Complicity can include a commanding officer or a political official. It can include a prime minister or a president.

This absolute prohibition is related to the second set of rules, addressing the status of the terrorists: are they to be treated as criminals or combatants? The answer will depend on the particular individual. If he was a member of the Taliban's regular armed forces, or of Saddam Hussein's Republican Guard, then he is a combatant, and must be treated as such. Once caught, he is entitled to protection under international humanitarian law, including the Geneva Conventions and Protocols. Even if it is suspected that he has information which may assist in the "war on terrorism," there are strict constraints on his interrogation. He cannot be tortured or treated inhumanely under any circumstances.

What if he is a suspected member of al-Qaeda who is thought to have planned a suicide attack? Or an insurgent in Iraq after the March 2003 conflict, who is suspected of laying roadside bombs targeting the Coalition Provisional Authority? Is he a combatant or a criminal? International law generally treats such people as criminals, not warriors. Britain adopted that approach in respect of the IRA, whose claims to be treated as combatants were always rejected, largely on the grounds that applying the laws of war would add legitimacy to their efforts. The 1997 International Convention for the Suppression of Terrorist Bombings[10] followed that reasoning, and made it a criminal offense to bomb a public place or a state or government facility with the aim of causing death or destruction. The United States, Britain, and more than 120 other states supported that approach. States which are parties to the 1997 Convention agreed to subject any person who is thought to have engaged in terrorist activities to criminal process, by prosecuting them or extraditing them to a country that will prosecute them. The United States became a party in June 2002, after 9/11.

Nowhere does the 1997 Convention say that theses criminals are exempt from the ordinary protections of the law or that you can torture them or treat them inhumanely. Quite the contrary. The Convention explicitly guarantees "fair treatment" to any person who is taken into custody under its provisions. That includes the rights and guarantees under "applicable provisions of international law, including the international law of human rights."[11]

Taken together, the rules prohibiting torture and criminalizing terrorism allow no exceptions. The rationale is simple: torture is morally wrong. According to the U.S. Army's *Field Manual*,[12] it is a poor technique that leads to unreliable results. In 1999, the Israeli Supreme Court handed down a landmark ruling that prohibited the Israeli Security Services from using physical abuse on suspected terrorists during interrogation. "This is the destiny of democracy," wrote Chief Justice Barak, "as not all means are acceptable to it, and not all practices employed by its enemies are open before it."[13] His words have a strong resonance today:

Although a democracy must often fight with one hand tied behind its back, it nonetheless has the upper hand. Preserving the Rule of Law and recognition of an individual's liberty constitutes an important component in its understanding of security. At the end of the day, they strengthen its spirit and its strength and allow it to overcome its difficulties.[14]

The Supreme Court said that it was not deciding whether the so-called necessity defense could be available. This might be invoked in the "ticking time-bomb argument" (where an arrested suspect is thought to hold information concerning the location of a bomb which has been set and will explode imminently).[15] Such a case would have to be decided on its own merits, as and when it arose. What the state could not do, ruled the Israeli Supreme Court, was to invoke a necessity argument to justify directives and authorizations which would use "liberty-infringing physical means" during the interrogation of those suspected of terrorist activities. The Court noted the absolute prohibition on torture and cruel, inhuman, and degrading treatment in international law: there were no exceptions and "there is no room for balancing."[16]

The events of 9/11 reopened a door of the kind which the Israeli Supreme Court wanted to close. Very shortly after the attacks, the Bush administration set in motion the procedures which led from the interrogation centers at Kandahar, Bagram, and Guantánamo to the torture of detainees at Abu Ghraib and elsewhere. According to media reports, former President Bush signed a secret order giving new powers to the CIA and authorizing it to set up a series of detention facilities outside the

United States, and to question those held in them with "unprecedented harshness."[17] Guantánamo was established as a place to gather information beyond the constraints of international law and U.S. law. The U.S. Supreme Court's ruling in *Rasul v. Bush*[18] in June 2004 initiated the unraveling of that effort. What the Supreme Court has not yet addressed, but which U.S. federal courts may yet have to consider, is whether the interrogation regime at Guantánamo was consistent with U.S. domestic law and America's international obligations. The Guantánamo model of interrogation techniques seems to have been applied in Afghanistan, and to have been exported to Iraq, including to Abu Ghraib, where the Geneva Conventions are recognized as being applicable.

We know nothing about the covert CIA regime. As to Guantánamo, the full story is yet to be told, including how far up the hierarchy the decision-making went. But much is known. The first detainees arrived on January 11, 2002. They were subjected to interrogations in accordance with the principles set out in the U.S. Army's *Field Manual 34-52*, which was published in 1987. *FM 34-52*, as it is known, sets out "the basic principles of interrogation doctrine and establishes procedures and techniques applicable to Army intelligence interrogations."[19] It makes clear that the principles and techniques of interrogation are to be used within the constraints established by The Hague[20] and Geneva Conventions. *FM 34-52* is unambiguous in its prohibition of the use of force, or threats of force. It says:

> The use of force, mental torture, threats, insults, or exposure to unpleasant and inhumane treatment of any kind is prohibited by law and is neither authorized nor condoned by the U.S. Government. Experience indicates that the use of force is not necessary to gain the cooperation of sources for interrogation. Therefore, the use of force is a poor technique, as it yields unreliable results, may damage subsequent collection efforts, and can induce the source to say whatever he thinks the interrogator wants to hear. However, the use of force is not to be confused with psychological ploys, verbal trickery, of other non-violent and non-coercive ruses used by the interrogator in questioning hesitant or uncooperative sources. . . . Additionally, the inability to carry out a threat of violence or force renders an interrogator ineffective should the source challenge the threat. Consequently, from both legal and moral viewpoints, the restrictions established by international law, agreements, and customs render threats of force, violence, and deprivation useless as interrogation techniques.[21]

According to the Pentagon, by the summer of 2002, it had become clear that *FM 34-52* was not producing the desired results. The Pentagon wanted to use "additional interrogation techniques" on Guantánamo detainees who were alleged to have close connections to the al-Qaeda leadership and planning figures, including "financiers, bodyguards, recruiters and operators."[22] This included individuals who were "assessed to possess significant information on al-Qaeda plans," and who demonstrated resistance to the relatively light interrogations set out in *FM 34-52*.[23]

Lt. Col. Diane Beaver, a U.S. Army lawyer, was asked to advise on the legal position. More aggressive interrogation techniques than the ones referred to in *FM 34-52*, she wrote, "may be required in order to obtain information from detainees that are resisting interrogation efforts and are suspected of having significant information essential to national security."[24] Her memorandum of October 11, 2002, described the problem: the detainees were developing more sophisticated interrogation resistance strategies, because they could communicate amongst themselves and debrief each other. This problem was compounded by the fact that there was no established policy for interrogation limits and operations at Guantánamo and "many interrogators have felt in the past that they could not do anything that could be considered 'controversial.'"[25] According to her memorandum, America's international obligations are irrelevant and interrogation techniques—including forceful means and restraints on torture—are governed exclusively by U.S. law.

Her analysis provides a useful insight on how to get around international law. Bush's Executive Order of February 7, 2002, determined that the detainees were not prisoners of war. It followed, therefore, that "the Geneva Conventions limitations that ordinarily would govern captured enemy personnel interrogations are not binding on U.S. personnel conducting detainee interrogations at [Guantánamo]."[26] In fact, Beaver went even further: "no international body of law directly applies."[27] She was not saying that there are no international rules; rather, the international rules are either not applicable or not enforceable. To reach this extraordinary conclusion, she reviewed various international conventions which establish binding norms for the United States—including the 1984 Convention against Torture, the International Covenant on Civil and Political Rights, and the American Convention on Human Rights—and then explained why not one of them creates any obligations which could actually be applied so as to constrain interrogators. This was either because the United States had entered reservations which gave primacy to U.S.

federal law, or because the treaty was not "self-executing" (meaning that although it might bind the United States under international law, it did not create rights for individuals which they could enforce in the national courts). It is striking that no mention is made of customary international law, reflected in particular in Article 75 of the 1977 Geneva Protocol I. *FM 34-52*'s reference to the "restrictions established by international law, agreements, and customs" is simply bypassed. The logic of the argument is grotesque. It means that international law is irrelevant. Can you imagine how the United States would react if another country tortured an American and defended it by saying, "Oh, terribly sorry, but the international treaty we signed up to which prohibits torture isn't enforceable in our domestic law so we don't have to apply it"? That is Beaver's logic.

In the meantime, over at the U.S. Department of Justice, her civilian colleagues had not been idle. On August 1, 2002, a few months before Beaver produced her advice, Alberto Gonzales, Counsel to President Bush, received two memoranda. Apparently these were not related to Guantánamo, but to interrogations carried out elsewhere, including those conducted by the CIA.

One memorandum was from John Yoo, a Deputy Assistant Attorney General.[28] He had been asked whether interrogation methods used on captured al-Qaeda operatives, which were lawful under a U.S. statute, could nonetheless lead to prosecution at the International Criminal Court (ICC), or violate the 1984 Convention against Torture. The question seems to have arisen to address the possibility that an interrogation carried out on the territory of a country which had joined the ICC might fall foul of the ICC rules. Yoo is known in academic circles as a skeptic about international law, and his opinion is replete with basic errors of law. Since the United States is not a party to the Rome Statute, he wrote, the United States "cannot be bound by the provisions of the ICC treaty nor can U.S. nationals be subject to ICC prosecution."[29] The first point is right, but the second is wrong. Individuals, not states, are defendants before the Court. If a CIA operative commits torture, rising to the level of a war crime or a crime against humanity, on the territory of a state which is a party to the Statute, then he can be prosecuted at the ICC. The Rome Statute is totally clear on that point. A first-year law student could work that out.

As regards the Convention against Torture, Yoo concluded that American participation was premised on the view that the definition of torture in the Convention was "in the exact terms" of the relevant U.S. federal statute. This is significant, because the Convention sets a lower threshold for acts to be defined as torture. On Yoo's analysis, then, if an act was not to be defined as torture under U.S. law, then it could not be torture under the Convention. The argument is hopeless. It is one of the most basic rules of international law that in the event of a conflict between an international rule and a domestic rule, the international rule will prevail. Once the rule is overridden—as Yoo proposes—there is no international law left. If that were the case, then why bother negotiating a treaty on torture? Each state would be free to substitute its own definitions for those of the Convention. But more seriously, Yoo has misunderstood what the United States did in ratifying the Convention. It did not enter a "reservation" redefining torture and setting the bar at a higher level; it entered an "understanding." This is an entirely different thing. Whilst a reservation can change the international legal obligation, an "understanding" cannot. Yoo writes that Germany commented on the United States' reservations, but, "do not oppose any U.S. reservation outright." In fact, Germany said the understandings "did not touch upon the obligations of the United States of America as State Party to the Convention."[30] So it is the definition in the Convention—the international definition—which prevails. No amount of willful misreading by a politically appointed Justice Department legal adviser can change that.

The second memorandum received by Gonzales was a longer one from Jay Bybee, an Assistant Attorney General and, presumably, Yoo's boss.[31] It addressed the standards of conduct required by the 1984 Convention against Torture, as implemented by U.S. federal law. Administration officials have confirmed that the Bybee memo "helped provide an after-the-fact legal basis for harsh procedures used by the CIA on high-level leaders of al-Qaeda."[32] *Newsweek* magazine has reported that the August 1, 2002, memo was prompted by CIA questions about what to do with those captives alleged to be top-ranking al-Qaeda terrorists, such as Ibn al-Shaykh al-Libi and Abu Zubaydah, who had turned uncooperative.[33] Relying on the same starting point as Beaver and Yoo—we are supreme and our law trumps everything—Bybee dispenses with all established canons of treaty interpretation and concludes that torture covers only the most extreme acts, limited to severe pain which is difficult for the victim to endure. "Where the pain is physical," he writes, "it must be of an intensity akin to that which accompanies serious physical injury such as death or organ failure." Anything less, he implies, will not be torture and will be permissible. And where the pain is mental, then it "requires suffering not just at the moment of infliction but it also requires lasting psychological harm, such as seen in mental disorders like post-traumatic stress disorder."[34] This is the most shocking legal opinion I have ever come across. Such "legal" analysis, by a lawyer who is now a federal judge, bears no relation to the definition which the United States and 120 other countries signed up to in the Convention against Torture.

And it gets worse. According to Bybee, the U.S. Congress can no more interfere with the president's conduct of the interrogation of enemy combatants than it can dictate strategic or tactical decisions on the battlefield. So the president is freed from all legal constraints. Laws that would prevent the president from gaining the intelligence he believes necessary to prevent attacks upon the United States would be unconstitutional.[35] The U.S. Assistant Attorney General concludes that under the current circumstances, certain criminal law defenses of necessity and self-defense could justify interrogation methods needed to prevent a direct and imminent threat to the United States and its citizens. This overrides the Convention against Torture's absolute prohibition on torture in all circumstances. But that prohibition is not applicable in U.S. law, advises Bybee, because it has not been included in the relevant federal statute. The U.S. Congress must therefore have intended to permit the "necessity of wartime defense" for torture.[36] Finally, he concludes that self-defense could allow a government defendant to argue that using torture in an interrogation could be justified, "on the basis of protecting the nation from attack."[37]

The assessment of international law is plain wrong. I can't comment on the position under U.S. law but I am happy to defer to Harold Koh, former dean of the Yale Law School and an acknowledged expert in U.S. constitutional and international law: the memos are "blatantly wrong. It's just erroneous legal analysis. The notion that the president has the constitutional power to permit torture is like saying he has the constitutional power to commit genocide."[38] The analyses of Beaver, Bybee, and Yoo are deeply flawed, and scary. Anyone who has even the most rudimentary understanding of international law will see that. Yet these are the memoranda the White House was willing to put in the public domain.

The "global war on terrorism" was therefore used to justify the need for "additional interrogation techniques"—at Guantánamo, in Afghanistan and in Iraq, and secretly elsewhere under CIA control. Against the backdrop of this legal advice, the U.S. Army's Lt. Col. Jerald Phifer requested approval for a new "interrogation plan" at Guantánamo.[39] The additional techniques—going beyond *FM 34-52*—were divided into three categories. Category I included two techniques: yelling and deception. Category

II required additional permission and included the use of stress positions (such as standing) for up to four hours, the use of falsified documents, isolation for up to 30 days, deprivation of light and auditory stimuli, hooding during questioning and transportation, 28-hour interrogations, removal of comfort items (including religious items), removal of clothing, forced grooming (shaving of facial hair, etc.), and using detainee-specific phobias (such as fear of dogs) to induce stress. Category III was to be used only for "exceptionally resistant detainees," who would normally number no more than 3 percent of the total (that would be 20 people at Guantánamo). This category required approval by the Commanding General, with appropriate legal review and information sent to the Commander of the U.S. Southern Command (USSOUTHCOM). It covered the "use of scenarios designed to convince the detainee that death or severely painful consequences are imminent for him and/or his family," exposure to cold weather or water, use of a wet towel and dripping water to induce the misperception of suffocation, and use of mild non-injurious physical contact such as grabbing, poking in the chest with the finger, and light pushing. All of these are inconsistent with international law, as are most of the Category II techniques. Nevertheless, Phifer's memorandum implied that even more might be available: it added that any of the Category III techniques "that require more than light grabbing, poking or pushing will be administered only by individuals specifically trained in their safe application."[40]

In another memorandum of the same day—October 11, 2002—Major General Michael E. Dunleavy concluded that these techniques did not violate U.S. or international law.[41] He relied on Beaver's legal analysis, which had determined that no international laws were actually applicable. Beaver gave the green light to all three techniques, although not without reservation. The use of a wet towel to induce suffocation should be used with caution, she wrote, because, "foreign courts have already advised about the potential mental harm this may cause." Pushing and poking "technically" constituted assault. And the U.S. Torture Statute specifically mentioned death threats as an example of "inflicting mental pain and suffering." Nevertheless, she concluded that the proposed methods of interrogation should be approved, subject to proper training and prior legal and medical review before their application.[42]

Others were cautious about Category III. General James T. Hill wrote to the Chairman of the U.S. Joint Chiefs of Staff, asking that lawyers from the Department of Defense and the Department of Justice review Category III. He was unclear whether all techniques in Category III were legal under U.S. law, he wrote, and was "particularly troubled by the use of implied or expressed threats of death of the detainee or his family."[43] But he wanted as many options as possible at his disposal.

If any legal reviews were carried out, they have not been made publicly available. However, it appears that there were no legal objections to techniques that plainly violate the 1984 Convention against Torture and the requirements of the Geneva Conventions, including Protocol I. It would be interesting to know what the lawyers at the U.S. State Department would have made of all this. Perhaps they never got a chance to have their say. On December 2, 2002, Donald Rumsfeld personally approved Categories I and II. He also approved the grabbing, poking, and pushing technique in Category III.[44] As to the other Category III techniques, he concluded that while these could be legally available, a blanket approval was not warranted "at this time." "I stand for 8–10 hours a day," Rumsfeld added in a handwritten comment. "Why is standing limited to 4 hours?"[45]

The approval remained in force only six weeks, and was rescinded by Rumsfeld on January 15, 2003. When this fact was made public in June 2004, it stated that Rumsfeld had "learned that some officials had concern about the implementation of these techniques."[46] No further explanation was provided. But more was needed, beyond *FM 34-52*. So Rumsfeld directed the Pentagon's General Counsel to establish a Working Group on the interrogation of detainees held by the U.S. armed forces. The Group was headed by Mary Walker, the U.S. Air Force's General Counsel. It included top civilian and uniformed lawyers from each military branch, and consulted with the Justice Department, the Joint Chiefs of Staff, the Defense Intelligence Agency and other intelligence agencies.[47] Again it seems the State Department was excluded.

The Working Group reported on April 4, 2003. It recommended 35 interrogation techniques to be used on unlawful combatants outside the United States, subject to certain limitations. The legal analyses put forward by Yoo and Bybee were broadly accepted, with the effect that international law could be taken as imposing no constraints above and beyond U.S. law. A military lawyer who assisted in preparing the report said that political appointees heading the Working Group wanted to assign to the president virtually unlimited authority on matters of torture.[48] Military lawyers were uncomfortable with that approach, and focused on reining in the more extreme interrogation methods, rather than challenging the president's constitutional powers.[49] The report accepted the principle that unlawful acts might not give rise to criminal liability, in view of the necessity and self-defense arguments. And it concluded that the prohibition against torture "must be construed as inapplicable to interrogations undertaken pursuant to [the President's] Commander-in-Chief Authority."[50] This sweeping conclusion brushed aside 50 years of international laws.

On April 16, 2003, Donald Rumsfeld approved the use of only 24 of these techniques, for the purpose of interrogating unlawful combatants at Guantánamo. Seven techniques went beyond what *FM 34-52* allowed. Four of the techniques could only be used with Rumsfeld's approval because, it was said, other countries might consider them to be inconsistent with the Geneva Conventions. They were the use of incentives to cooperate, "pride and ego down" (referring to the exploitation of a prisoner's loyalty, intelligence, or perceived weakness), good-cop-bad-cop interrogation, and isolation.

Rumsfeld did not approve 11 of the 35 techniques recommended by the Working Group, at least in this document. They included mild physical contact, threats to transfer to a third country, use of prolonged interrogations, forced grooming, prolonged standing, sleep deprivation, physical training, and slapping. They also included one technique which appeared in the Abu Ghraib photographs, namely increasing anxiety by use of aversions ("simple presence of a dog without directly threatening action") and they included removal of clothing and hooding, two techniques which U.S. Senators found especially troubling when they questioned Rumsfeld's Deputy, Paul Wolfowitz, on May 13, 2004:

SENATOR REED: Mr. Secretary, do you think crouching naked for 45 minutes is humane?

MR. WOLFOWITZ: Not naked, absolutely not.

SENATOR REED: So if he is dressed up that is fine? . . . Sensory deprivation—which would be a bag over your head for 72 hours—do you think that is humane?

MR. WOLFOWITZ: Let me come back to what you said, the work of this government . . .

SENATOR REED: No, no. Answer the question, Mr. Secretary. Is that humane?

MR. WOLFOWITZ: I don't know whether it means a bag over your head for 72 hours, Senator. I don't know.

SENATOR REED: Mr. Secretary, you're dissembling, non-respon-
sive. Anybody would say putting a bag over someone's head for 72
hours, which is . . .

MR. WOLFOWITZ: It strikes me as not humane, Senator.

SENATOR REED: Thank you very much Mr. Secretary.[51]

The materials released by the White House raised a great number of
questions. Were these the only techniques approved? Were other techniques approved for use by the CIA or other agencies? How are the
approved techniques to be squared with the accounts given by released
Guantánamo detainees? The accounts by the British detainees, if accurate,
describe practices that go beyond Rumsfeld's revised standards. Tarek
Dergoul has reported being poked, kicked, punched, shaved, exposed to
intense heat and cold, deprived of sleep, and being kept chained in painful
positions. He claims he was threatened with return to an Arab country
where he was told he would be subjected to full-blown torture.[52] These
are some of the 11 techniques recommended by the Pentagon's Working
Group Report in April 2003, but not approved by Rumsfeld. This inevitably raises a question: did interrogators exceed their orders, or was a parallel system of interrogations established which permitted application of
the eleven techniques?

That question needs to be answered because similar techniques—and
others which were even worse—appear to have been used in Afghanistan
and Iraq. The situation in Iraq should have been very different, since the
United States accepted that the Geneva Conventions were applicable. But
it is plain that the Conventions were not respected in relation to all the
detainees. In January 2004, Joseph Darby, a low-ranking American soldier, spilled the beans. An internal inquiry was carried out, but Congress
was not informed. Why, asked Senator Robert Byrd, was the report on
abuse "left to languish on the shelf at the Pentagon unread by the top leadership until the media revealed it to the world?"[53] In the spring of 2004,
media photographs and reports described graphic abuse and torture at
Abu Ghraib prison, Saddam Hussein's former punishment center, turned
into a U.S. POW camp. They had been taken from the summer of 2003
onward. The most notorious included a picture of a hooded detainee
standing on a box with what appeared to be electrode wires attached to his
fingers and genitals. Another showed First Class Lynndie England holding a leash tied to the neck of a naked man on the floor. Others depicted a
terrified detainee cowering naked before dogs, a hooded detainee appar-

ently handcuffed in an awkward position on top of two boxes in a prison hallway, a soldier kneeling on naked detainees, a hooded detainee collapsed over a railing to which he was handcuffed, and two soldiers posing over the body of Manadel al-Jamadi, a detainee who had allegedly been beaten to death by the CIA or civilian interrogators in the prison's showers. Would the United States accept the treatment of its nationals in this way, under any circumstances?

Also in the spring of 2004, a Red Cross report condemning the treatment of Iraqi prisoners was leaked. It described violations of the Geneva Conventions which had been documented or observed while the International Committee of the Red Cross (ICRC) had been visiting Iraqi prisoners of war, civilian internees and other persons protected by the Geneva Conventions, between March and November 2003. The leaked extracts described brutality causing death or serious injury, physical or psychological coercion during interrogation, prolonged solitary confinement in cells devoid of daylight, and excessive and disproportionate use of force. The ICRC report described the ill treatment as "systematic . . . with regard to persons arrested in connection with suspected security offenses or deemed to have an 'intelligence' value."[54] In some cases, wrote the ICRC, the treatment was "tantamount to torture."

The rules governing interrogations in Iraq have been less easy to identify. Until August 2003, the rules set out in *FM 34-52* applied. At the end of August, Maj. Gen. Geoffrey Miller, who was head of detention operations at Guantánamo, visited Iraq. According to Lt. Gen. Keith Alexander, a Deputy Chief of Staff for U.S. Intelligence, Miller's mission was "to help get the most we could out of human intelligence operations in Iraq as a whole."[55] He visited Abu Ghraib. By September 9, Miller had completed a review and recommended a new interrogation policy that "borrowed heavily" from the approved Guantánamo procedures.[56] On September 14, Lt. Gen. Ricardo Sanchez, the ground commander in Iraq, authorized rules which allowed the harsh procedures *not* permitted at Guantánamo, including sleep deprivation and stress (crouching) positions for up to an hour. Military lawyers objected, and a month later—on October 12—Sanchez restricted the policy. The new procedures were claimed to be consistent with the Geneva Conventions. Nevertheless, as the *New York Times* described, troubling practices were tolerated, including forced nudity, slapping, handcuffing, hooding, and intimidation with dogs. The picture that emerges from the documents, interviews, and congressional testimony "points to a broader pattern of misconduct and knowledge about it stretching up the chain of command."[57] It was only in May 2004, after the press got hold of the details of the procedures, that coercive practices were reported to have been ended. Whether that included any CIA interrogations which may have been taking place is not known.

As the media obtained the material, the Bush administration came under increased pressure to explain its commitment to international rules, and the Geneva Conventions in particular. Bush's General Counsel, Alberto Gonzales (who became Attorney General in the second George W. Bush administration), made it clear that the administration had never authorized torture, but he left open the possibility that agencies other than the Department of Defense might have engaged in interrogation by reference to different rules. During his press conference on June 22, 2004, he was asked whether interrogation went beyond the 24 methods approved for Guantánamo, either through a "special access program" or through another government agency. "We're not going to comment on anything beyond what is accepted [by the] Department of Defense," he responded, adding that there was a directive throughout the entire government that every agency was to follow the law and could not engage in torture.[58] But whose definition of the law? And torture defined by whom? By Beaver or Bybee? By the Working Group? When he was asked whether the CIA was subject to the 24 categories of interrogation techniques, he responded: "I'm not going to get into questions related to the CIA." When pushed, he responded: "I'm not going to get into discussions about the CIA, except to repeat what I just said, and that is that the techniques that they used that have been approved—they've been approved and vetted by the Department of Justice—are lawful and do not constitute torture."[59] This fell far short of the denial that the 35 techniques recommended by the Working Group Report—which adopted the Department of Justice's approach—might actually be in use by some other agency, including the CIA.

Gonzales did disavow some of the earlier memoranda that had been drafted, including Bybee's memo of August 1, 2002. "Unnecessary, over-broad discussions in some of these memos that address abstract legal theories, or discussions subject to misinterpretation, but not relied upon by decision-makers," he said, "are under review." To the best of his knowledge, he added, the memos did not make it into the hands of soldiers in the field or to the president. They did "not reflect the policies that the administration ultimately adopted."[60] But that disavowal did not extend to the memoranda's findings on international law, which were incorporated more or less unchanged into the April 2003 Working Group Report, which remained in effect.

Over time, a great deal more information will emerge. But even at this stage, it seems pretty clear that the legal minds which created Bush's doctrine of pre-emption in the use of force and established the procedures at the Guantánamo detention camp led directly to an environment in which the monstrous images from Abu Ghraib could be created. Disdain for global rules underpins the whole enterprise. The international rules on torture, the treatment of prisoners of war, and human rights norms do not apply, or they add nothing to U.S. law, or they are not enforceable. These three techniques for avoiding international legal obligations can be added to the 17 or 24 or 35 techniques of interrogation. In this way, the rules put in place by the United States after the horrors of the Second World War are side-stepped, and the "war on terror" is brought into disrepute.

What I find most remarkable is that such a scheme could have been put in place for the treatment of foreigners, of non-Americans, where respect for the international rules was bound to be raised. It is clear that many American military lawyers and legal advisers in the U.S. State Department were horrified by what was happening. Some took active steps to stop the new rules and practices from being adopted. When their efforts failed, they alerted others with leaks to the press, for which we must be thankful. Temporarily, however, it was the Yoo's and the Bybee's and the Gonzales's of the administration that prevailed. They seem never to have asked themselves, as David Scheffer queried, "Would we tolerate such treatment of U.S. prisoners? If the answer is no, then the subject is closed."[61] Nor, it seems, did they detain themselves for very long in deliberating whether their duty, as lawyers, was to ensure respect for the international rules or, rather, to provide legal cover for their political masters.

NOTES

Reprinted from *Lawless World* by Philippe Sands, copyright (c) 2005, 2006 by Philippe Sands. Used by permission of Viking Penguin, a division of Penguin Group (USA) Inc.

1. Universal Declaration of Human Rights, art. 5, G.A. res. 217A (III), U.N. Doc A/810 (1948).

2. International Covenant on Civil and Political Rights (hereafter ICCPR), art. 7, Dec. 16, 1966, 999 *U.N.T.S.* 171 (ratified by the United States on June 8, 1992).

3. American Convention on Human Rights, art. 5(2), Nov. 22, 1969, *O.A.S.T.S.* No. 36, 1144 *U.N.T.S.* 123.

4. Convention Relative to the Treatment of Prisoners of War (Geneva Convention III), art. 17, 130, Aug. 12, 1949.

5. Convention Relative to the Protection of Civilian Persons in Time of War (Geneva Convention IV), art. 32, 283, Aug. 12, 1949.

6. Protocol I Additional to the Geneva Conventions, art. 75(2), June 8, 1977.

7. Convention Against Torture and Other Cruel, Inhuman or Degrading Treatment or Punishment, art. 16, Dec. 10, 1984, 1465 *U.N.T.S.* 85.

8. Ibid. at art. 2(2).

9. Rome Statute, July 12, 1998, A/CONF.183/9.

10. International Convention for the Suppression of Terrorist Bombings, Nov. 25, 1997, A/52/653.

11. Ibid. at art. 14.

12. U.S. Dept. of Army, *Field Manual 34-52: Intelligence Interrogation*, ch. 1, May 8, 1987, http://www.fas.org/irp/doddir/army/fm34-52.pdf (last visited July 29, 2009).

13. Supreme Court of Israel, *Decision on GSS Practices*, ¶39, Sept. 6, 1999, reproduced in *International Legal Materials*, vol. 38 (1999), 1471.

14. Ibid.

15. Ibid. at ¶14; see also John Lango, "Fundamental Human Rights and the Coercive Interrogation of Terrorists in an Extreme Emergency," in this volume.

16. Supreme Court of Israel, *GSS Practices*, at ¶23, 38.

17. See, for example, John Barry, Michael Hirsh, and Michael Isikoff, "The Roots of Torture," *Newsweek*, May 24, 2004, http://www.newsweek.com/id/105387/page/1 (last visited Sept. 28, 2009). See also George W. Bush, memorandum regarding "Humane Treatment of al Qaeda and Taliban Detainees," Feb. 7, 2002, http://www. washingtonpost.com/wp-srv/nation/documents/020702bush.pdf (last visited Sept. 28, 2009).

18. *Rasul v. Bush*, 542 U.S. 466 (2004).

19. U.S. Army, *Field Manual*, Preface.

20. Located in a western metropolitan region of the Netherlands, the Hague is home to over 150 international organizations, including the International Court of Justice (ICJ) and the International Criminal Court (ICC), which are involved in the development and interpretation of international legal norms and the punishment of offenders.

21. U.S. Army, *Field Manual*, ch. 1.

22. U.S. Dept. of Defense, "DoD Provides Details on Interrogation Process," News Release no. 596-04, June 22, 2004, http://www.defenselink.mil/releases/release.aspx?releaseid=7487 (last visited Sept. 28, 2009).

23. Ibid.

24. Diane Beaver, memorandum to Commander of Joint Task Force 170 regarding "Proposed Counter-Resistance Strategies," Oct. 11, 2002, JTF 170-SJA, p. 1.

25. Ibid.

26. Ibid.

27. Ibid.

28. John C. Yoo, memorandum to Alberto R. Gonzales regarding interrogation methods that do not violate prohibitions against torture, Aug. 1, 2002, http://news.findlaw.com/wp/docs/doj/bybee80102ltr.html (last visited Sept. 28, 2009). This and other memoranda are reprinted in R. Greenberg and J. Dratel, *The Torture Papers: The Road to Abu Ghraib* (New York: Cambridge Univ. Press, 2005).

29. Ibid.

30. Ibid.

31. Jay S. Bybee, memorandum to Alberto R. Gonzales regarding "Standards of Conduct for Interrogation under 18 U.S.C. §§ 2340–2340A," Aug. 1, 2002, http://www.washingtonpost.com/wpsrv/nation/documents/dojinterrogation-memo20020801.pdf (last visited July 29, 2009).

32. David Johnston and James Risen, "U.S. Memos Provide Basis for CIA Coercion," *New York Times*, June 28, 2004, p. 6.

33. See Michael Hirsh, John Barry, and Daniel Klaidman, "A Tortured Debate," *Newsweek*, June 21, 2004, http://www.newsweek.com/id/54093 (last visited Sept. 28, 2009).

34. Bybee, memo to Gonzales regarding "Standards of Conduct for Interrogation," p. 46.

35. Ibid.

36. Ibid. at p. 41.

37. Ibid. at p. 45.

38. Harold Koh is quoted in Edward Alden, "Dismay at Attempt to Find Legal Justification for Torture," *Financial Times*, June 10, 2004, p. 7.

39. Jerald Phifer, memorandum regarding "Approval for Counter-Resistance Strategies," JTF 170-J2, Oct. 11, 2002.

40. Ibid.

41. See Michael E. Dunleavy, memorandum regarding "Counter-Resistance Strategy," Oct. 11, 2002.

42. See Beaver, memo on "Proposed Strategies," at pp. 6–7.

43. James T. Hill, memorandum regarding "Counter-Resistance Techniques," Oct. 25, 2002, http://news.findlaw.com/hdocs/docs/dod/hill102502mem.html (last visited Sept. 28, 2009).

44. See William J. Haynes, memorandum to Donald Rumsfeld regarding "Counter-Resistance Techniques," Nov. 27, 2002, http://www.washingtonpost.com/wp-srv/nation/documents/dodmemos.pdf (last visited Oct. 9, 2009).

45. See Donald Rumsfeld, approved memorandum regarding "Counter-Resistance Techniques," Dec. 2, 2002, http://www.gwu.edu/~nsarchiv/NSAEBB/NSAEBB127/02.12.02.pdf (last visited Sept. 28, 2009).

46. See Jim Garamone, "White House, DoD Discuss Interrogation Process," *Dept. of Defense News*, June 23, 2004, http://www.defenselink.mil/news/newsarticle. aspx?id=26221 (last visited Sept. 28, 2009).

47. See Jess Bravin, "Security or Legal Factors Could Trump Restrictions, Memo to Rumsfeld Argued," *Wall Street Journal*, June 7, 2004, p. A1.

48. Ibid.

49. Ibid.

50. U.S. Dept. of Defense, "Working Group Report on Detainee Interrogations in the Global War on Terrorism," Mar. 6, 2003, p. 21.

51. U.S. Senate Armed Services Committee, Hearing on Contingency Reserve Fund Request for FY05, 108th Cong., 2nd sess., *Federal News Service*, May 13, 2004.

52. See David Rose, "They Tied Me Up Like a Beast and Began Kicking Me," *The Observer*, May 16, 2004, http://www.guardian.co.uk/world/2004/may/16/terrorism.guantanamo (last visited Dec. 19, 2009).

53. See Guy Dinmore and James Harding, "Rumsfeld Stays Vague on What and When," *Financial Times*, May 8, 2004, p. 3.

54. See Editorial, "Violations Were 'Tantamount to Torture," *Guardian*, May 8, 2004, http://www.guardian.co.uk/world/2004/may/08/iraq (last visited Sept. 28, 2009).

55. Alberto Gonzales, Press Briefing, White House, Washington DC, June 22, 2004, http://georgewbush-whitehouse.archives.gov/news/releases/2004/06/20040622-14.html (last visited Sept. 28, 2009).

56. See Douglas Jehl, "U.S. Rules on Prisoners Seen as a Back and Forth of Mixed Messages to GI's," *New York Times*, June 22, 2004, p. A7, http://www.nytimes.com/2004/06/22/politics/22ABUS.html (last visited Sept. 28, 2009).

57. Ibid.

58. Gonzales, Press Briefing, June 22, 2004.

59. Ibid.

60. Ibid.

61. See Alden, "Dismay at Attempt to Find Legal Justification for Torture," p. A7.

13

Criminal Responsibility of Bush Administration Officials with Respect to Unlawful Interrogation Tactics and the Facilitating Conduct of Lawyers

JORDAN J. PAUST

Between December 2001 and January 2002, Vice President Cheney and highest level Bush administration officials crafted a common plan to violate customary and treaty-based international law concerning the treatment and interrogation of so-called terrorist and enemy combatant detainees and their supporters captured during the U.S. war in Afghanistan.[1] A major part of the plan was to deny protections under the customary laws of war and treaties that require humane treatment of all persons who are detained during an armed conflict, regardless of their status and regardless of any claimed necessity. President Bush personally approved secret detention of persons for harsh interrogation on September 17, 2001, and he approved the denial of treaty-based protections on February 17, 2002. Also in early 2002, a still secret presidential finding reportedly signed by Bush, Condoleezza Rice, and John Ashcroft approved use of the criminal interrogation tactic known as waterboarding. White House Counsel Alberto Gonzales had facilitated the denial of law of war protections for detainees in January 2002. In April 2002, he played a more direct role when he personally approved use of several unlawful interrogation tactics on a top al-Qaeda operative months before the infamous August 2002 cover memos written by then Department of Justice lawyers Jay Bybee and John Yoo. These memos were designed to facilitate use of coercive interrogation as part of what John Yoo has admitted was a "common, unifying" plan devised by an "inner circle" of the Bush administration.

The common plan and authorizations have criminal implications, since denials of protections under the laws of war are violations of the laws of war, and every violation of the laws of war is a war crime.[2] Numerous other war crimes and other treaty violations occurred during what became a program of serial and cascading criminality devised and approved or facilitated by the inner circle of highest level officials and facilitated by several compliant lawyers in the Department of Justice, the White House, and the CIA. This chapter outlines general types of criminal responsibility that pertain as well as some of the harsher coercive forms of interrogation authorized, approved, and abetted during the Bush program. It then discusses the main facilitating memoranda written by lawyers from the Office of Legal Counsel in the Department of Justice. Finally, I address whether the so-called Bybee memos can provide a golden shield for others within the Executive branch.

Types of Criminal Responsibility for Ill-Treatment

At least four general types of criminal responsibility exist under international law with respect to torture and other outlawed treatment. First, it is obvious that direct perpetrators of violations of the Geneva Conventions, other laws of war, the Convention Against Torture, and crimes against humanity (such as secret detention or the forced disappearance of persons) have direct liability. Leaders who issue authorizations, directives, findings, and orders to commit acts that constitute international crimes, such as former President Bush, Alberto Gonzales, and former Secretary of Defense Rumsfeld, may also be prosecuted as direct perpetrators of crimes.[3]

Second, any person who aids and abets torture has liability as a complicitor or aider and abettor before the fact, during the fact, or after the fact.[4] Liability exists whether or not the person knows that his or her conduct is criminal or, for example, that the conduct of the direct perpetrator of torture is criminal or even constitutes torture as such.[5] Under customary international law, a complicitor or aider and abettor need only be aware that his or her conduct (which can include inaction) would or does assist a direct perpetrator or facilitates conduct that is criminal.[6] In any case, ignorance of the law is no excuse. Clearly, several memo writers and others during the Bush administration abetted the "common, unifying" plan to use "coercive interrogation," and their memos and conduct substantially facilitated its effectuation.[7] Therefore, prosecution or extradition of several former members of the Bush administration for criminal complicity would be on firm ground.

Third, individuals can also be prosecuted for participation in a "joint criminal enterprise,"[8] which the International Criminal Tribunal for Former Yugoslavia has recognized can exist in at least two relevant forms: (1) where all the accused "voluntarily participate in one aspect of a common plan" and "intend the criminal result [whether or not they knew it was a crime], even if not physically perpetrating the crime"[9]; and (2) where "(i) the crime charged is the natural and foreseeable consequence of the execution of that enterprise, and (ii) the accused was aware that such a crime was a possible consequence of the execution of that enterprise, and, with that awareness participated in that enterprise."[10]

Fourth, civilian or military leaders with *de facto* or *de jure* authority, such as former President Bush and former Secretary of Defense Rumsfeld, can also be liable for dereliction of duty with respect to acts of torture and cruel, inhuman, or degrading treatment engaged in by subordinates when (1) the leader knew or should have known that subordinates were about to commit, were committing, or had committed international crimes; (2) the leader had an opportunity to act; and (3) the leader failed to take reasonable corrective action, such as ordering a halt to criminal activity or initiating a process for prosecution of all subordinates reasonably accused of criminal conduct.[11]

Unlawful Tactics Used during the Bush Administration

Among specific interrogation tactics authorized by President Bush and/ or Secretary Rumsfeld, Secretary Rice, Attorney General Ashcroft, White House Counsel and later Attorney General Gonzales, and several others within the Bush administration and used on detained persons that manifestly and unavoidably constitute torture are waterboarding or a related inducement of suffocation,[12] use of dogs to create intense fear,[13] threatening to kill the detainee or family members,[14] and the cold cell or a related inducement of hypothermia.[15] Although the intentional use of sexual violence and rape as tactics are recognizably torture,[16] some forms of sexual humiliation that were authorized and used might not have constituted severe pain or suffering within the international legal definition of torture. Nonetheless, they can be manifestly inhumane or degrading and, therefore, equally unlawful.

Many of these illegal tactics, including waterboarding and the "cold cell," were addressed and expressly and/or tacitly approved during several meetings of the National Security Council's Principals Committee in the White House during 2002 and 2003 that were attended by Dick Cheney, his lawyer David Addington, Condoleezza Rice, Donald Rumsfeld, George Tenet, John Ashcroft, and others who facilitated their approval and use, including John Yoo.[17] With respect to the configurative contributions of his team, President Bush was quoted as stating, "Yes, I'm aware our national security team met on this issue. And I approved."[18]

Some of the Facilitating Memos

During President Bush's admitted "program" of "tough" interrogation and secret detention or forced disappearance[19] and as part of the well-documented "common, unifying" plan to deny Geneva law protections and to use and attempt to justify serial and cascading criminality in the form of "coercive interrogation,"[20] the administration used shifting definitions of "torture" as if the manifest illegality of its approved interrogation tactics could be defined away.

The First 2001 Bybee Memo

The so-called Bybee torture memo,[21] completed in August 2002 by John Yoo and Jay Bybee, set forth what had become the Bush administration's preferred but patently improper standard regarding "torture." According to the Bybee memo, "torture" should involve far more than the widely known treaty-based and customary international legal test of "severe" physical or mental pain or suffering (the same test set forth in 18 U.S.C. § 2340(1)), and the definition of "severe" "must rise to the level of death, organ failure, or the permanent impairment of a significant bodily function."[22] The memo was written *after* several of the White House meetings during which an inner circle (and John Yoo) had discussed and approved or facilitated use of specific interrogation tactics[23] and was created expressly with respect to "the conduct of interrogations outside the United States" and "possible defenses that [allegedly] would negate any claim that certain interrogation methods violate" a particular federal statute.[24] It was also written several months *after* Alberto Gonzales had "signed off" several times on the use of a number of harsh interrogation tactics at the request of CIA personnel.[25] Since the memo writers had refused to use the widely known test with respect to torture, the Bybee memo was facially devoid of legal propriety and blatantly facilitated use of criminal interrogation tactics. The servile memo had also made the patently erroneous claim that, as a matter of law, "necessity and self-defense could justify interrogation methods needed to elicit information."[26]

Criticism of the memo grew so widespread in the United States and abroad that it was eventually withdrawn and replaced by a 2004 memo that at the time of this writing is still classified. However, John Yoo prepared a second Bybee memo in August 2002 that addressed specific interrogation tactics.[27]

The Second Bybee Memo

The second August 1, 2002 Bybee memo[28] was declassified and released on April 16, 2009. It provides further evidence of serial criminality that was authorized by an inner circle of Bush advisers and knowingly facilitated by memo writers in the Department of Justice. The second Bybee memo was apparently a "cover" memo to memorialize "previous oral advice" in July 2002 regarding use of "ten [SERE] techniques" for interrogation and to assuage evident concern that persons who authorize, facilitate, or use them might be prosecuted under the U.S. torture statute.

The advice was manifestly erroneous with respect to use of at least two interrogation tactics—waterboarding and the "box." The Bybee memo admitted and necessarily warned that waterboarding "produces the perception of 'suffocation and incipient panic'" and "constitutes a threat of imminent death."[29] Furthermore, persons undergoing SERE training are aware of "precautions," the memo noted,[30] but waterboarded detainees in CIA control would not be aware of "precautions" while admittedly experiencing "incipient panic" and the "threat of imminent death."

Additionally, the Bybee memo admitted and necessarily warned that placing a human being in a "small confinement box" "without light" for "two hours" can cause pain and mental harm,[31] but argued that it would not cause "substantial" physical pain, "substantial" interference with the individual's cognitive abilities, or "fundamentally" alter his personality.[32]

Along with the "box," there was to be an "introduction of an insect" that foreseeably can cause "trepidation" (i.e., dread or even terror) in a person who was admittedly expected "to have a fear of insects."[33]

The memo was clearly designed to facilitate use of waterboarding and use of the "box" and a fear-enhancing insect during interrogation and expressly noted their unavoidable and probable effects. As such, the second Bybee memo is another smoking gun. It documents knowledge of the factual quality of international crime and provides clear evidence of criminal responsibility, not merely with respect to those who authorized and used these techniques, but also with respect to those who were aware of the fact that their memo would facilitate the proposed use of such forms of ill-treatment and what would be their actual and probable effects. As noted at the beginning of the chapter, criminal complicity can occur when a memo writer is aware that his or her conduct can or will facilitate conduct of a direct perpetrator. The person who aids and abets need not know that the conduct of the direct perpetrator is criminal or whether it does in fact constitute "torture" or some other widely known criminally proscribed conduct such as cruel or inhumane treatment. It suffices that an accused was aware of the relevant factual circumstances and "need not have known that . . . [conduct of a direct perpetrator would amount] to an 'inhumane act' either in the legal or moral sense."[34]

The advice in the second Bybee memo was also facially erroneous because (1) physical pain that is "severe" within the definition of torture (addressing "severe physical or mental pain or suffering")[35] manifestly need not occur over "a protracted period of time"; (2) physical "suffering" that is "severe" manifestly need not occur over "a protracted period of time"; and (3) mental harm that is "severe" within the definition of torture need not "disrupt profoundly" or "fundamentally" change a person's personality.[36] Advice that is manifestly in error can provide no cover.

Moreover, the advice was shoddy and unprofessional. First, the advice was memorialized in connection with a request from CIA to use waterboarding, the "box," and a fear-enhancing insect, and other tactics for interrogation of a detainee held outside the United States. The CIA "asked . . . whether certain proposed conduct would violate" the torture statute.[37] It must have been clear to a professional, however, that the torture statute would not pose the only legal obstacle to use of the tactics the CIA had in mind and that far more than torture is criminally proscribed. For example, torture, cruel, and inhumane treatment are proscribed under two sets of federal statutes that allow prosecution of relevant customary and treaty-based laws of war,[38] but there was no attention to such legislation or to any laws of war in the second Bybee memo. Torture, cruel, and inhumane treatment are also proscribed under the Convention Against Torture,[39] and foreign states and international tribunals can prosecute such conduct, but there was no attention to any international agreement, customary international law in any relevant form, or the clear possibility of prosecution in foreign and international fora. There was merely a facially improper reading of one U.S. federal statute. Such advice, in view of clearly relevant law criminally proscribing cruel and inhumane treatment as well as torture and the CIA's request to use certain tactics abroad where foreign jurisdiction pertains, was at best shoddy and seriously unprofessional. Its apparently unquestioned receipt by John Rizzo at CIA is equally troubling and clearly left CIA personnel in harm's way.

Second, instead of using computer-assisted research to identify whether waterboarding, the water cure, or related forms of induced suffocation are "torture" (much less cruel or inhumane treatment), the Bybee memo states that it was "drawing upon" a few cases decided under the Torture Victim Protection Act. Several easily discoverable federal and state court cases make clear that waterboarding is a form of "torture."[40] U.S. Country Reports on Human Rights Practices of various countries published by the U.S. Department of State and available online prior to the second Bybee memo and for years thereafter also make clear that waterboarding is known by the Executive to be a form of "torture."[41] Additionally, federal cases addressing cruel treatment in violation of the Eighth Amendment clearly demonstrate that use of waterboarding would also constitute cruel treatment.[42] Discoverable cases and Executive Country Reports on Human Rights Practices also demonstrate that a "threat of imminent death" constitutes torture.[43]

Since the second Bybee memo only addressed possible cover with respect to one federal statute that addresses torture, clearly it was in no way a shield with respect to possible criminal liability under two forms of legislation allowing prosecution of war crimes, which include not merely torture but also cruel or inhumane treatment. Since relevant federal and state court cases and Executive Country Reports were easily discoverable by a lawyer (and the Bybee memo was a lawyer-to-lawyer memo), I assume that the memo can in no way provide cover for a lawyer in the

Bush administration. Additionally, the Bybee memo clearly was in no way a potential shield with respect to violations of various treaty-based and customary international laws prosecutable in foreign courts that can exercise universal jurisdiction[44] over international crime or in the International Criminal Court.[45]

The March 2003 Yoo Memo

A March 14, 2003 memo written by John Yoo for William Haynes[46] (after several of the White House meetings of the Principals Committee) had, in the new head of OLC Jack Goldsmith's words, "contained abstract and overbroad legal advice, but the actual techniques approved by the [defense] department were specific."[47] In December 2003, Goldsmith finally decided to withdraw the March 2003 Yoo memo, but he told Ashcroft and Haynes that he allowed DOD "to continue to employ the twenty-four techniques."[48]

The March 2004 Goldsmith Memo

In March 2004, a draft memo penned and "circulated" by Jack Goldsmith fit perfectly within the common, unifying plan to deny Geneva protections and engage in secret detention and coercive interrogation by claiming that persons in Iraq can be transferred "to another country to facilitate interrogation"[49] despite the clear, absolute, and criminal prohibition of the transfer of any non-prisoner of war out of occupied territory under the Geneva Civilian Convention and customary international law.[50] To "facilitate interrogation," the Goldsmith memo also made the patently erroneous claim that a detainee who was not lawfully in Iraq could be denied protections under Geneva law.[51]

Goldsmith's book and that of Jane Mayer paint an interesting picture of Goldsmith's involvement in the Bush program. They both note that he had flown to GTMO with Addington, Philbin, Rizzo, and others, where they were briefed and "witnessed an ongoing interrogation," and he thought that "the United States could not . . . be bound by any customary laws of war to confer legal protections" to detainees at GTMO. Thus, Goldsmith must have known by 2004 what transfer to "facilitate interrogation" meant under the Bush program in terms of likely tactics to be used, and he must have been aware of the fact that his memo would facilitate secret detention and coercive interrogation. He admits that while at OLC in DOJ in October 2003, before writing his 2004 memo, he had "been beset by doubts" about the Bush program and prior memos, but did not protest against the use of any unlawful tactics or resign. While under Haynes at DOD, Goldsmith admits that "[a]s a . . . critic of many aspects of the international human rights movement . . . [he] was the perfect person for the assignment" to oppose use of human rights law and the law of war.[52]

The 2005 Bradbury Memos

BRADBURY I

In May 2005, long after International Committee of the Red Cross and widespread public condemnation of various tactics as illegal, a memo penned by Steven G. Bradbury in OLC at DOJ[53] and approved by then Attorney General Alberto Gonzales provided what has been reported as "an expansive endorsement of the harshest interrogation techniques ever used by the Central Intelligence Agency," including waterboarding and use of "frigid temperatures."[54] The memo addressed specific CIA interrogation tactics and concluded that each was lawful under the federal torture statute despite the obvious fact that the statute is incompatible with U.S. obligations under the Convention Against Torture.[55] Like the second Bybee memo, the Bradbury memo argued erroneously that "[w]hat guidance there is comes from decisions that apply . . . the Torture Victims [sic] Protection Act,"[56] thereby ignoring a rich set of U.S. federal and state court opinions addressing specific tactics such as waterboarding, threats to kill, and the cold cell as "torture," as well as several relevant U.S. Executive Country Reports on Human Rights Practices. With respect to waterboarding, the Bradbury memo noted that it "has been used by the CIA on three high-level al Qaeda detainees, two of whom were subjected to the technique numerous times," and admitted that it "induces a sensation of drowning . . . based on a deeply rooted physiological response" and "usually does cause fear and panic."[57] Media have reported that the IG's report also warned that some of the CIA tactics were criminal, something not mentioned in Bradbury's memo.

The Bradbury memo also addressed use of the "cold cell," termed "water dousing," and addressed use of water at 41, 50, and 59 degrees Fahrenheit and noted the danger of hypothermia.[58] With respect to "nudity," the memo noted that it "is used to cause psychological discomfort . . . particularly . . . for cultural or other reasons," can involve "full-time closed-circuit video monitoring" that the detainee is aware of, and can be used to "exploit the detainee's fear of being seen naked," especially "by females."[59] Nudity admittedly can cause humiliation but, Bradbury argued, nudity "cannot be said to cause 'suffering.'"[60]

With Bybee-esque result-oriented reasoning, the Bradbury memo argued that "severe physical pain" must be "extreme in intensity and difficult to endure"[61] and that "severe physical suffering" must be "both extreme in intensity and significantly protracted in duration or persistent over time" and must persist "for a significant period of time."[62] In other words, contrary to common sense, it was argued that one could not have "severe physical suffering" for a short time. Armed with this restrictive definitional orientation, the memo concluded that waterboarding that can occur during two "sessions" within 24 hours that can each last two hours would not cause "severe physical suffering"[63] and, because the torture statute added a word ("prolonged") that simply does not exist as a limitation in the CAT's definition of torture (or in any other international legal instrument), the memo concluded that waterboarding does not cause "prolonged" mental suffering.[64]

BRADBURY II

The second Bradbury memo addressed combined use of certain techniques. Although the second memo was more cautionary and noted that the effects of combined use of tactics in a given instance are "difficult to assess"[65] and "difficult to calculate,"[66] that the combined effect with waterboarding "is particularly difficult to judge,"[67] and that "inferences" and "assumptions" have to be made,[68] the conclusion was offered that combined uses would still be lawful, especially given the definitional orientations used in the first memo. Interestingly, the second memo recognized that some methods are "coercive" (e.g., walling, water dousing, stress positions, and "confinement in the 'small box'")[69] and "'place the detainee in more physical and psychological stress,'"[70] but, given the restrictive definitional orientations, supposedly they would not constitute torture. Sleep deprivation "might cause physical distress in some cases" and "lower . . . tolerance for pain,"[71] the memo noted, but would not meet the memo's restrictive definitional criteria for physical "suffering"[72] nor, the memo opined, would waterboarding used in combination with other tactics.[73]

BRADBURY III

The third Bradbury memo was supposed to address what seems to have been partly admitted in the first two memos, that some CIA tactics can involve cruel, inhuman, or degrading treatment. But the third Bradbury memo directly addressed only the international legal prohibitions of such treatment under the CAT (and not customary international law reflected in the CAT that is universally applicable,[74] the Geneva Conventions, the ICCPR, and so forth) and began with a misread of the phrase in Article 16 of the CAT that requires a party to the CAT to prevent such treatment "in any territory under its jurisdiction."[75] The third Bradbury memo argued that such territory only includes territory "over which the United States exercises" *de jure* or *de facto* authority "as the government,"[76] did not include territory where the CIA was conducting interrogations and, therefore, Article 16 of the CAT allegedly did not apply. However, the generally shared interpretation that is also recognized by the Committee Against Torture is that the "provisions of the Convention . . . apply to, and are fully enjoyed, by all persons under the effective control of its authorities, of whichever type, wherever located in the world . . . [including] in all places of detention under its *de facto* effective control."[77]

The second error was Bradbury's assumption that a unilateral U.S. reservation concerning a putative limitation of the reach of Article 16's prohibitions to merely conduct that was already proscribed under the U.S. Constitution reflected U.S. obligations under the treaty,[78] but this is not correct and the reservation is void *ab initio* as a matter of law.[79] Compounding this error, Bradbury turned to certain U.S. cases regarding a "shocks the conscience" test with respect to the Fifth Amendment of the U.S. Constitution in an attempt to create a supposed limit to treaty-based protection if ill-treatment is not arbitrary or is justified,[80] despite the Convention's clear absolute prohibition of cruel, inhuman, or degrading treatment and the warning in Article 2(2) that "[n]o exceptional circumstances whatsoever, whether a state of war or a threat of war . . . or any other public emergency, may be invoked as a justification of torture."[81] Of course, it is also well-understood that outside the CAT the same prohibition of cruel, inhuman, and degrading treatment is absolute and there is no necessity exception in any relevant treaty or customary international law.[82] Such international law is also a necessary background for interpretation of the CAT.[83]

Armed with his two major misconceptions about the treaty's reach, Bradbury concluded that no violation of Article 16 could occur, despite his recognition, for example, that waterboarding is "coercive," "traumatic," and "induces fear and panic"[84] and that "[u]se of interrogation practices like those we consider here in ordinary criminal investigations might well 'shock the conscience.'"[85]

Incredibly, the third Bradbury memo paid some attention to U.S. Executive Country Reports on Human Rights Practices, noted that the reports list some tactics as "'[p]sychological torture'" if they involve food and sleep deprivation, noted that "'methods of torture'" included "'stripping and blindfolding victims . . . and dousing victims with cold water,'" noted one report's listing of "'having cold water thrown on' detainees as either torture or 'ill-treatment,'" but dismissed "[t]he State Department's inclusion of nudity, water dousing, sleep deprivation, and food deprivation among the conduct it condemns" (while Bradbury also conveniently ignored Country Reports addressing waterboarding and other inducement of suffocation) as providing merely "some indication of an executive foreign relations tradition," as opposed, he argued, to a constitutional standard attentive to "'traditional executive behavior, . . . contemporary practice, and . . . the standards of blame generally applied to them.'"[86] "A United States foreign relations tradition of condemning torture," Bradbury argued unconvincingly, "says little about the propriety of the CIA's interrogation practices."[87] In an outrageously inept slam at the State Department's consistent conclusions over a number of years regarding the nature of certain tactics as violations of human rights law, Bradbury opined that such legal conclusions were merely "a matter of diplomacy" and "diplomatic relations" and, allegedly therefore, "not reliable evidences of United States executive practices."[88] On May 31, 2005, under pressure from Cheney, Attorney General Gonzales attended a National Security Council's Principals Committee and, armed with the Bradbury memos, obtained approval of the full list of tactics.[89]

In July 2006, soon after the Supreme Court had ruled that detainees are entitled at a minimum to the rights reflected in common Article 3 of the Geneva Conventions,[90] President Bush signed a new executive order re-authorizing unlawful interrogation tactics such as waterboarding and the "cold cell" while furthering his program of coercive interrogation and secret detention.[91] In September 2006, President Bush admitted that a CIA program had been implemented using secret detention and "tough" forms of treatment, and he stated that the program would continue.[92]

Lame Excuses

The Bybee Memo as Golden Shield

Some news media have referred to the Bybee torture memo as "the Golden Shield," as if it can shield those who planned, authorized, ordered, abetted, or perpetrated torture, cruel, inhumane, or degrading treatment from criminal prosecution.[93] However, the shield is made of fool's gold and is full of holes. For example, orders or authorizations to engage in interrogation tactics that will manifestly produce what the community will judge to be torture, cruel, inhumane, or degrading treatment are orders or authorizations to engage in conduct that is manifestly illegal. The ploy "I did not know that waterboarding was unlawful or torture" will not work, since waterboarding is manifestly unlawful and is a form of torture;[94] and if it is not torture, it is cruel, and if it is not cruel, it is inhumane and, therefore, it is necessarily unlawful under common Article 3 of the Geneva Conventions, Articles 1 and 16 of the CAT, Article 7 of the ICCPR, customary international law reflected in the above, and other relevant international law. Importantly, no memo stated that waterboarding is not cruel or inhumane under international law. Furthermore, the Bybee memos were written after specific tactics had been used and, therefore, were inoperative as any putative "shield" regarding such conduct. The mere fact that a particular tactic was approved in an Executive memo is not a defense.

Additionally, President Bush and several high-level officials were warned or on notice of legal improprieties regarding denial of Geneva protections, secret detention, and use of coercive tactics.[95] Some of the International Committee of the Red Cross warnings of widespread, intentional unlawful treatment and a "system of abuse" had even become public, which usually occurs after warnings to government officials and quiet diplomacy have failed.[96] Criminal conduct was also widely reported for several years by various media and NGO's, such as Amnesty International, Human Rights Watch, Human Rights First, the American Bar Association, the ACLU, and the Center for Constitutional Rights. Moreover, for many years before and during the Bush administration, the Executive's own Country Reports on Human Rights Practices had listed several relevant tactics as torture.[97] In 2006, in the face of known illegalities of the Bush administration, a rare resolution of the American Society of International Law, created because of the tireless efforts of Professor Ben Davis, reaffirmed what every professional international lawyer had known, that "[t]orture and cruel, inhuman, or degrading treatment of any person . . . are prohibited by international law from which no derogations are permitted."[98] The U.S. Congress had made this point earlier in October 2004.[99]

Secretary Rice Merely Conveyed the Authorization to Waterboard[100]

A report of the Senate Select Committee on Intelligence declassified in April 2009 states that "[o]n July 17, 2002, according to CIA records, the Director of Central Intelligence (DCI) [Tenet] met with the National Security Adviser [Rice], who advised that the CIA could proceed with its proposed interrogation of Abu Zubaydah. This advice . . . was subject to a determination of legality by OLC."[101] The report adds that on July 26 (a week before the infamous second Bybee memo that provides its own evidence of complicity),[102] "OLC orally advised the CIA that the Attorney General [Ashcroft] had concluded . . . that use of waterboarding was lawful."[103] As noted above, however, Alberto Gonzales had already signed off on use of various harsh tactics on several occasions prior to the July 17 meeting.[104] ABC News also reported in 2005 that "current and former CIA officers [stated that] there was a presidential finding, signed in 2002, by President Bush, Condoleezza Rice and then-Attorney General John Ashcroft approving" waterboarding.[105] Instead of taking the fall for Bush's nefarious behavior, Rice declared at Stanford University in April 2009: "I didn't authorize anything. I conveyed the authorization of the administration to the agency, that they had a policy authorization, subject to the Justice Department's clearance."[106]

Whether or not she advised that the CIA could proceed with waterboarding or conveyed the authorization of the president to proceed with waterboarding, and whether or not she signed the 2002 presidential finding, Rice has admitted that she intended to engage in conduct that would knowingly facilitate the use of waterboarding if OLC would also approve. As such, she is reasonably accused of aiding and abetting waterboarding, whether or not she actually approved its use on another person on July 17, 2002, earlier in 2002,[107] or later in 2002 and 2003 during several meetings addressing waterboarding and other unlawful tactics.

As noted above, criminal complicity can occur when a person is aware that his or her conduct can or will assist or facilitate conduct of a direct perpetrator. The person who aids and abets need not know that the conduct of the direct perpetrator is criminal or whether it does in fact constitute "torture" or some other widely known and unavoidably criminal conduct such as cruel or inhumane treatment. It suffices that an accused was aware of the relevant factual circumstances and even a direct perpetrator "need not have known that his or her act . . . amounted to an 'inhumane act' either in the legal or moral sense."[108] Furthermore, all acts of assistance, by words or acts and omissions, that lend encouragement or support will also suffice if the accused knows or is aware that such conduct can or will facilitate the use of what happens to be an illegal tactic.

In context, Rice's statement is unavoidably an admission of what the tribunals recognize as the "factual quality" of the crime—in this case, the factual quality of aiding and abetting waterboarding. She has admitted that she engaged in conduct (the conveyance of a policy authorization of President Bush to engage in waterboarding) that, at the time, she must clearly have known or been aware can or will facilitate use of waterboarding. It does not matter whether she knew the law, that waterboarding is criminally proscribed, or that waterboarding is torture or cruel and inhumane.

Perhaps what Rice had in mind while fingering Bush and pointing to his authorization of waterboarding was a defense of superior orders. She claimed: "If it was authorized by the President, it did not violate our obligations under the Convention."[109] Quite clearly, however, the president cannot lawfully authorize a violation of a treaty[110] and, in view of an express and unavoidable constitutional mandate under Article II, Section 3, the president must faithfully execute the laws.[111] Under international and U.S. domestic law, there would be no defense if her claim is merely that anything the president authorized is lawful. That defense did not work for Germans accused at Nuremberg[112] and it will not work here.

Superior orders? The test is whether the order or authorization approved conduct that is manifestly or clearly conduct that is unlawful,[113] such as torture or cruel or inhumane treatment. Is waterboarding manifestly torture or cruel or inhumane? That's the real issue and, since several federal and state court cases and U.S. Executive Country Reports on Human Rights Practices of other countries had already expressly recognized that waterboarding, the water cure, and other forms of induced suffocation are a method of "torture,"[114] it is obvious that waterboarding is manifestly and clearly unlawful, as well as cruel and inhumane. Indeed, what person would not recognize the inhumane effects of waterboarding that was not part of voluntary training that will end, but part of a planned process of coercive interrogation involving pain and an inducement of suffocation that, as the second Bybee memo expressly warned, creates "incipient panic" and a "threat of imminent death"?[115]

There is also possible criminal responsibility to explore with respect to Rice's conduct during several meetings of the National Security Council's Principals Committee in the White House from 2002 to 2003 and May 31, 2004, during which waterboarding and other unlawful tactics were addressed and expressly and/or tacitly approved or abetted.[116] The meetings raise issues not merely of accomplice liability, but also of liability of co-conspirators and what international criminal tribunals recognize as participation in a joint criminal enterprise. The meetings clearly were a major part of what is now the Bush legacy of serial and cascading criminality.

Vice President Cheney Thought It Necessary[117]

Former Vice President Dick Cheney made public statements about his role in assuring approval and use of manifestly unlawful interrogation tactics such as waterboarding during the eight-year Bush administration. According to Cheney, he has "[n]o regrets" that he was directly involved in the approval of severe interrogation methods, including waterboarding, and he has admitted that he was involved in helping to get the process cleared by President Bush. Although Bush delegated national security matters to Cheney in the early years and all such matters went through him, Cheney stated that "this was a presidential-level decision. And the decision went to the President. He signed off on it."[118]

On September 16, 2001, Cheney publicly declared that "[a] lot of what needs to be done . . . ["on the dark side"] will have to be done quietly, . . . using . . . methods that are available to our intelligence agencies . . . to use any means at our disposal, basically, to achieve our objective."[119] He added: "we'll have the kind of treatment of these individuals that we believe they deserve."[120] For the next two years, many of his preferences were effectuated by his top lawyer, David Addington. Moreover, it has been reported that Cheney attended meetings of the National Security Council's Principals Committee in the White House Situation Room during 2002 and 2003, at which specific tactics such as waterboarding and the "cold cell" were addressed and expressly and/or tacitly approved and abetted.[121] It has also been reported that during this time there was "live feed" or "real time" viewing of parts of actual interrogations, including that of al Qahtani at Guantánamo Bay, Cuba. Cheney also had his own office at CIA headquarters where he could review details.

According to the Center for Constitutional Rights (CCR), SERE tactics were being used against detainees at Guantánamo in September 2002 and during October 2002, military intelligence interrogators "used military dogs in an aggressive manner to intimidate" al Qahtani.[122] In November 2002, FBI Deputy Assistant Director Harrington reported that al Qahtani had exhibited symptoms of "extreme psychological trauma."[123] Around the third week in November, he was subjected to what was known as the "First Special Interrogation Plan," a plan to use tactics later detailed in an 84-page log describing their use during a six-week period. CCR reported that among several tactics used were: threats against his family, forced nudity and sexual humiliation, threats and attacks by dogs, beatings, and the cold cell or exposure to low temperatures for prolonged times.[124]

Each of these tactics is patently illegal under the laws of war, human rights law, and the Convention Against Torture, among other relevant international legal proscriptions and requirements. As I document elsewhere, death threats, use of dogs to create intense fear, beatings, the cold cell or a related inducement of hypothermia, and waterboarding are each manifest forms of "torture"[125] that are absolutely prohibited under all circumstances and regardless of the status of the victim. In fact, there are 29 U.S. judicial opinions and seven U.S. Executive Country Reports on Human Rights Practices, among other cases and materials, recognizing that waterboarding and related inducements of suffocation are "torture."[126] If they were not torture, they would also be absolutely prohibited as cruel, inhuman, or degrading treatment, along with the other tactics mentioned. Cheney's direct involvement is clear evidence of complicity in international crime, if not also participation in a criminal conspiracy. In fact, it has been reported that when Cheney found out that a CIA Inspector General's report warned that several such tactics were criminal, he became irate and ordered the Inspector General to his office.[127]

What is Cheney's excuse? He claims that there was a need to engage in the illegal tactics, but others have affirmed that there was no need to engage in illegal interrogation tactics and that, on the contrary, it was well known by professionals that reliable intelligence must be obtained by lawful means of interrogation. Furthermore, it is well understood that under every relevant treaty-based and customary international law there is no such thing as a necessity defense with respect to outlawed tactics that are torture or cruel, inhumane, or degrading treatment.[128] Such forms of ill-treatment are strictly prohibited in all circumstances. More generally, it is well established that the laws of war are to be strictly applied during war when our national security is seriously threatened by enemies who have killed and will kill our nationals in the future.

Some have argued that there is a common law necessity defense that might be available if conduct was actually necessary. One of the August 1, 2002 Bybee memos made this claim when citing *United States v. Bailey*.[129] The Bybee memo failed to note, however, that the Supreme Court's opinion expressly warned that "[i]f there was a reasonable, legal alternative to violating the law . . . the defense will fail" and the defendant must prove "that given the imminence of the threat, violation of . . . [a law] was his *only* reasonable alternative."[130] Whether or not a threat of a major attack continued each year for eight years and was always imminent, reasonable legal alternatives with respect to time-honored forms of interrogation designed to obtain reliable intelligence clearly were always available. In fact, the CIA Inspector General's report found there was no evidence that the illegal interrogation tactics prevented any credible threats,[131] and it is known that lawful forms have often worked faster and more reliably against high-level al-Qaeda detainees, sometimes within an hour or a little longer.[132] Thus, necessarily, a judge must rule that, as a matter of law, the alleged necessity defense is unavailable and that the fact that a few secreted files might indicate whether torture led to useful information in a given instance is legally irrelevant. Interestingly, a 2005 Bradbury memo affirmed that "[a] good motive, such as to protect national security, does not excuse conduct that is specifically intended to inflict severe physical or mental pain or suffering," that specific intent to engage in conduct "is distinguished from motive."[133]

Additionally, as a matter of law, the defense is not available if relevant law sets an absolute standard, such as the various treaty-based and customary international legal prohibitions of torture and cruel, inhumane, or degrading treatment in all circumstances. Furthermore, as a matter of law, both treaty-based and customary international law, as supreme federal law under the U.S. Constitution, will trump inconsistent common law whether or not there might be such a common law defense to ordinary crime when international law has not been violated.

Conclusion

It is likely that in the months and years ahead, more revelations regarding the serial and cascading criminality of the Bush administration will occur, but clearly there is enough information available concerning the "common, unifying" plan devised by an "inner circle" of the Bush administration (including former Vice President Cheney) to engage in "coercive" interrogation[134] that can form the basis for criminal indictments or extradition of a number of former members of the inner circle, including those who authorized, ordered, or abetted war crimes, crimes against humanity, crimes under the CAT, and crimes under various other forms of treaty-based and customary international law. Quite clearly, various memo writers and other lawyers are also reasonably accused of complicity with respect to such forms of international crime. As noted, a memo writer who is an aider and abetter need only be aware that his or her memo would or does assist or facilitate conduct that is criminal, such as use of waterboarding, dogs to create intense fear, or the cold cell. A complicitor need not know the law or that use of such tactics constitutes "torture." Indeed, if they were not torture, they would be criminally proscribed in any event as cruel or inhumane treatment. The facilitating conduct of some of the lawyers obviously went beyond the writing of desired memos.

There is an unavoidable customary and treaty-based duty of every state to take action to end impunity and to either initiate prosecution of or to extradite those who are reasonably accused of international crime. Within the United States, President Obama and Attorney General Holder share that responsibility.

The Bush-Cheney "dirty war" tactics and autocratic policies have not only created criminal and civil liability, but also served our enemies and degraded this country, its values, and its influence. As patriots of democratic freedom understand, they threaten our democracy and the rule of law. It is time to end impunity. It is time for a change.

NOTES

1. See Jordan J. Paust, *Beyond the Law: The Bush Administration's Unlawful Responses in the "War" on Terror* (New York: Cambridge Univ. Press, 2007), 1.

2. See, e.g., ibid. at 1, 133 n.2.

3. See, e.g., Jordan J. Paust et al., *International Criminal Law: Cases and Materials*, 3rd ed. (Durham, NC: Carolina Academic Press, 2006), 32, 35, 51–73. See also, infra notes 17–34. This and the next three paragraphs are borrowed from Jordan J. Paust, "Prosecuting the President and His Entourage," 14 *ILSA J. Int'l & Comp. L.* 539, 542–43 (2008).

4. See, e.g., Convention Against Torture and Other Cruel, Inhuman or Degrading Treatment or Punishment, art. 4(1), Dec. 10, 1984, 1465 U.N.T.S. 85 [hereinafter CAT]; Paust et al., *Int'l Criminal Law*, 35, 44–49; Paust, *Beyond the Law*, 18, 24, 30, 165, 167, 185, 193, 199, 277.

5. See, e.g., Rome Statute of the International Criminal Court, arts. 25(3)(c)–(d), 30, 32(2), 2187 U.N.T.S. 90, July 17, 1998, in force, July 1, 2002, [hereinafter Rome Statute of the ICC]. See also *The Prosecutor v. Dario Kordic, Mario Cerkez*, Case No. ICTY-95-14/2-A, Judgment, ₵ 311 (Dec. 17, 2004); Guenael Mettraux, "Crimes Against Humanity in the Jurisprudence of the International Criminal Tribunals for the Former Yugoslavia and for Rwanda," 43 *Harv. Int'l L.J.* 237, 297 n.323 (2002); Committee Against Torture, Gen. Comm. No. 2, Implementation of Article 2 by States Parties, ₵ 9, U.N. Doc. CAT/C/GC/2 (Jan. 24, 2008) [hereinafter CAT Comm. Gen. Comm.]; Jordan J. Paust, "Rice, Waterboarding and Accountability," *JURIST*, May 8, 2009, http://jurist.law.pitt.edu/forumy/2009/05/rice-waterboarding-and-accountability.php (last visited Jan. 13, 2010); Jordan J. Paust, "The Second Bybee Memo: A Smoking Gun," *JURIST*, April 22, 2009, http://jurist.law.pitt.edu/forumy/2009/04/second-bybee-memo-smoking-gun.php (last visited Jan. 13, 2010).

6. See, e.g., *The Prosecutor v. Tihomir Blaskic*, Case No. ICTY-95-14-T-A, Judgment, ₵ 50 (Jul. 29, 2004); *The Prosecutor v. Anto Furundzija*, Case No. ICTY-95-17/1-T, Judgment, ₵ 236–38, 245–46, 249 (Dec. 10, 1998); *The Prosecutor v. Jean Kambanda*, Case No. ICTR-97-23-S, Judgment and Sentence, ₵ 39 (Sept. 4, 1998); *Almog v. Arab Bank*, PLC, 471 F. Supp.2d 257, 286–87 (E.D.N.Y. 2007). At the International Military Tribunal for the Far East concerning the Trial of Koiso, an ex-Prime Minister, guilt was established where the accused knew that treatment of prisoners "left much to be desired" and he had asked for a full inquiry but did not resign from office or act more affirmatively to stop illegal treatment. *United States et al. v. Kuniaki Koiso et al.*, IMTFE, Judgment, 1177–78 (Nov. 1, 1948). Cf. Rome Statute of the ICC, art. 25(3)(c). The forms of criminal complicity recognized in Kambanda and Koiso seem to be particularly relevant to meetings of former Vice President Cheney and other high-level officials of the Bush administration in the White House during 2002 and 2003. See infra notes 17–34.

7. See, e.g., infra notes 17–34.

8. See, e.g., Paust et al., *Int'l Criminal Law*, 32, 37–38; Allison Marston Danner, "Joint Criminal Enterprise," *International Criminal Law: Enforcement* 3, no. 483 (2008).

9. See, e.g., *The Prosecutor v. Radoslav Brdjanin*, Case No. ICTY-99-36-T, Judgment, ₵ 264 (Sept. 1, 2004). Concerning the Bush administration's "common, unifying" plan to deny rights and protections under international law and to use unlawful interrogation tactics, see, e.g., Paust, *Beyond the Law*, 6–19, 25–30; infra notes 12–20.

10. *The Prosecutor v. Brdjanin*, ICTY-99-36-T, ₵ 265; *Prosecutor v. Blaskic*, ICTY-95-14-T-A, ₵ 50.

11. See, e.g., Paust et al., *Int'l Criminal Law*, 51–89. The President of the United States and the Secretary of Defense, among others, have *de jure* command authority. Further, this type of leader responsibility for dereliction of duty is part of customary international law that is part of the supreme law of the land in the United States. It has also been incorporated by reference in 10 U.S.C. § 818, which incorporates all violations of the laws of war as offenses against the laws of the United States. See Jordan J. Paust, "The Absolute Prohibition of Torture and Necessary and Appropriate Sanctions," 43 *Val. L. Rev.* 1535, 1569 n.106 (2009). Leader responsibility incorporated through such a statute (then, through the same language found in the 1916 Articles of War) was recognized by the Supreme Court in *In re Yamashita*, 327 U.S. 1, 15–16 (1946); see also, *The Prosecutor v. Zejnil Delalic et al.*, Case No. ICTY-96-21-T, Judgment, ¶ 338 (Nov. 16, 1998). It has also been used with respect to civil sanctions against leaders. See, e.g., *Kadic v. Karadzic*, 70 F.3d 232, 242 (2d Cir. 1995); *Xuncax v. Gramajo*, 886 F. Supp. 162, 171–72 (D. Mass. 1995); Jordan J. Paust, Jon M. Van Dyke, and Linda A. Malone, *International Law and Litigation* (St. Paul, MN: West Group, 2009), 25, 367–70, 373, 382, 385–88, 440, 449.

12. See, e.g., 29 U.S. federal and state court opinions and 7 U.S. Country Reports on Human Rights Practices in Paust, "Absolute Prohibition," n.69; *Saadi v. Italy*, Case No. 37201/06, Eur. Ct. H.R., ¶ 143 (Feb. 28, 2008); *Baldeón-Garcia v. Peru*, Case No. 147, Inter-Am. Ct. H.R. (ser. C), ¶ 123, 125 (Apr. 6, 2006); *Tibi v. Ecuador*, Case No. 114, Inter-Am. Ct. H.R. (ser. C), ¶ 148–49 (Sept. 7, 2004).

13. See, e.g., Paust, *Beyond the Law*, 12–16, 25–27, 43, 155, 159–62, 173–75, 256; Bob Woodward, "Detainee Tortured, Says U.S. Official," *Washington Post*, Jan. 14, 2009, A1; *Rasul v. Rumsfeld*, 414 F. Supp.2d 26, 27 (D.D.C. 2006); *Haitian Refugee Center v. Civiletti*, 503 F. Supp. 442, 493 (D.C. Fla. 1980); *Chitayev and Chitayev v. Russia*, Case No. 59334/00, Judgment, Eur. Ct. H.R., ¶ 159 (Jan. 18, 2007).

14. See, e.g., 7 U.S. federal and state court opinions and other citations in Paust, "Absolute Prohibition," n.71; Paust, *Beyond the Law*, 13, 16, 154 n.105, 158 n.122; U.S. Dep't of State, 1999 Country Reports on Human Rights Practices, Iraq.

15. See, e.g., 14 U.S. federal and state court opinions and other citations in Paust, "Absolute Prohibition," n.72; *Elci and Others v. Turkey*, Case No. 23145/93, Judgment, Eur. Ct. H.R., ¶ 646 (Nov. 13, 2003); U.S. Dep't of State, 1999 Country Reports on Human Rights Practices, Egypt; U.S. Dep't of State, 1999 Country Reports on Human Rights Practices, Turkey. A variation of the "cold cell" involves stripping a person naked, placing the person in a cold room, and dousing the person with water in order to produce hypothermia that can turn the body blue and produce violent shaking and even death.

16. See, e.g., *Farmer v. Brennan*, 511 U.S. 825, 852, 854 (1994) (Blackmun, J., concurring); *Doe I v. Unocal Corp.*, 395 F.3d 932, 945 (9th Cir. 2002); *Zubeda v. Ashcroft*, 333 F.3d 463, 472 (3d Cir. 2003); *Kadic v. Karadzic*, 70 F.3d at 242; In re Extradition of Suarez-Mason, 694 F. Supp. 676, 682 (N.D. Cal. 1988); *The Prosecutor v. Dragoljub Kunarac, Radomir Kovac, and Zoran Vukovic*, Case Nos. ICTY-96-23 and ICTY-96-23/1-A, Judgment, ¶ 137, 150–51, 153 (June 12, 2002); *The Prosecutor v. Alfred Musema*, Case No. ICTR-96-13-T, Judgment and Sentence, ¶ 222 (Jan. 27, 2000); Torture Victims Relief Act, 22 U.S.C. § 2152; and other citations in Paust, "Absolute Prohibition," n.74.

17. Jan Crawford Greenburg, Howard L. Rosenberg, and Ariane de Vogue, "Bush Aware of Advisers' Interrogation Talks," ABC News, Apr. 11, 2008, http://abcnews.go.com/print?id=4635175; and other citations in Paust, "Absolute Prohibition," n.76.

18. Ibid.

19. See, e.g., Paust, *Beyond the Law*, 29, 179–80 n.22. Concerning Bush admissions, authorizations, directives, and findings, see, e.g., ibid. at x, 7–8, 17, 26, 28–30, 32, 35, 145–47, 176, 179–80; House Committee on the Judiciary, Reining in the Imperial Presidency: Lessons and Recommendations Relating to the Presidency of George W. Bush, Jan. 13, 2009, p. 136 [hereinafter House Comm. Report], http://judiciary.house.gov/hearings/printers/110th/IPres090113.pdf.

20. See, e.g., Paust, *Beyond the Law*, 27–30, 32; Jane Mayer, *The Dark Side: The Inside Story of How the War on Terror Turned into a War on American Ideals* (New York: Doubleday, 2008), 150, 185, 198–99, 304, 307, 311–12; John Yoo, *War By Other Means: An Insider's Account of the War on Terror* (New York: Atlantic Monthly, 2006), ix, 30, 35, 39–40, 43, 171–72, 177–78, 190–92, 200, 202 (2006); House Comm. Report, 110–46; Ximena Marinero, "UN Torture Investigator Calls on Obama to Charge Bush for Guantánamo Abuses," *JURIST*, Jan. 21, 2009, http://jurist.law.pitt.edu/paperchase/2009/01/un-torture-investigator-calls-on-obama.php (last visited Jan. 13, 2010). John Yoo wrote that he had also flown with other lawyers to Guantánamo in early January 2002. Yoo, *War By Other Means*, 18, 38–39, 44. Those lawyers knew that persons transferred to Guantánamo were held in secret detention because their names were not released. Such constitutes a form of forced disappearance, a crime against humanity that during an armed conflict is also a war crime. See Paust, "Absolute Prohibition," n.21.

21. See Paust, *Beyond the Law*, 11, 150 n.89.

22. Ibid. at 151 n.90.

23. See Greenburg, Rosenberg, and de Vogue, "Bush Aware of Advisers' Talks," ABC News; U.S. Senate Armed Services Committee, Inquiry Into the

Treatment of Detainees in U.S. Custody, Dec. 20, 2008, xv–xvi [hereinafter Senate ASC Report], http://armedservices.senate.gov/Publications/EXEC%20 SUMMARY-CONCLUSIONS_For%20Release_12%20December%202008.pdf (last visited Jan 13, 2010).

24. See Paust, *Beyond the Law*, 150 n.89.

25. Ari Shapiro, "Did White House OK Earliest Detainee Abuse?" NPR, remarks, NPR, May 20, 2009, http://www.npr.org/templates/story/story.php?storyId=104350361 (last visited Jan. 15, 2010).

26. Ibid. at 11. Cf. Paust, "Absolute Prohibition," nn.1, 9, 11, 14, 67, and accompanying text.

27. See supra note 23; Jack Goldsmith, *The Terror Presidency: Law and Judgment Inside the Bush Administration* (New York: W.W. Norton, 2007), 150–51, 155. Concerning Goldsmith's subsequent role, see Paust, "Absolute Prohibition," nn.90–92.

28. Jay S. Bybee, Memorandum for John Rizzo, Acting General Counsel of the Central Intelligence Agency, Interrogation of al Qaeda Operative, Aug. 1, 2002, http://www.washingtonpost.com/wp-srv/nation/pdf/OfficeofLegalCounsel_Aug2Memo_041609.pdf (last visited Jan. 13, 2010). Rather incredibly, as of this writing, Rizzo is still with the CIA.

29. Ibid. at 4, 15.

30. Ibid. at 15.

31. Ibid. at 10, 13.

32. Ibid. at 13.

33. Ibid. at 3, 10, 13.

34. Paust, "Rice, Waterboarding and Accountability."

35. See, e.g., CAT, art. 1. The federal statute is incompatible with the CAT's definition because it limits severe mental suffering to "prolonged" mental harm caused merely by four types of conduct. 18 U.S.C. § 2340(2)(A)–(D). The Committee Against Torture under the auspices of the CAT has already found the U.S. legislation to be incompatible with Article 1 of the CAT. See, e.g., Paust, "Absolute Prohibition," 1570, n.107.

36. Cf. Bybee, Memorandum for John Rizzo, 11, 13–16.

37. Ibid. at 1, 18.

38. See, e.g., Paust, *Beyond the Law*, 145 n.47, 189 n.51.

39. CAT, art. 16. See also Paust, *Beyond the Law*, 2–5, 30–33.

40. See supra note 12.

41. Ibid.

42. Paust, "Absolute Prohibition," 1563, n.83.

43. See supra note 14.

44. Concerning universal jurisdiction, see, e.g., Paust et al., *Int'l Criminal Law*, 155–74; Paust, Van Dyke, and Malone, *Int'l Law and Litigation*, 559–74. Concerning the universal duty either to initiate prosecution or to extradite those who are reasonably accused and non-immunity, see, e.g., Paust, "Absolute Prohibition," 1537–43.

45. Regarding potential ICC jurisdiction over U.S. nationals, see, e.g., Paust, "Absolute Prohibition," 1571–72, n.111.

46. John C. Yoo, Memorandum for William J. Haynes II, General Counsel of the Department of Defense, Re: Military Interrogation of Alien Unlawful Combatants Held Outside the United States (Mar. 14, 2003), http://www.aclu.org/pdfs/safefree/yoo_army_torture_memo.pdf (last visited Jan. 13, 2010).

47. Goldsmith, *The Terror Presidency*, 151.

48. Ibid. at 153–55. Goldsmith was referring to Rumsfeld's 24 techniques. Ibid. at 153. Concerning these tactics, see Paust, *Beyond the Law*, 15, 158–59 n.122.

49. See Paust, "Absolute Prohibition," n.96; Paust, *Beyond the Law*, 18, 163 n.148; Goldsmith, *The Terror Presidency*, 99–100, 119, 136, 153; Mayer, *Dark Side*, 198–99, 261–63. Cf. Goldsmith, *The Terror Presidency*, 29 (stating that he did not know about the CIA's interrogation program before starting at DOJ in October 2003, but thereafter he did not oppose use of any tactic or secret detention), 40–41 (stating that the conclusion in his OLC opinion of October 2003 was personally communicated to Gonzales and Addington, that all Iraqis of any status in occupied Iraq have protections under the Geneva Civilian Convention), 59. On March 19, 2004, Goldsmith sent his memorandum to Taft, Haynes, Bellinger, and Muller (CIA General Counsel) and copied it to David Leitch. Concerning the September trip to GTMO, see also Senate ASC Report, xvi.

50. See Geneva Convention Relative to the Protection of Civilian Persons in Time of War, Aug. 12, 1949, arts. 49, 147, 75 U.N.T.S. 287; Paust, *Beyond the Law*, 18, 30, 163–64 nn. 147–52; Rome Statute of the ICC, art. 8(2)(a)(vii), (b)(viii); Protocol Additional to the Geneva Conventions of 12 August 1949, and Relating to the Protection of Victims of International Armed Conflicts, June 8, 1977, art. 85(4)(a), 1125 U.N.T.S. 3. The rights, duties, and prohibitions reflected in the 1949 Geneva Conventions are customary international law. See, e.g., Paust, *Beyond the Law*, 8, 134 n.8. It is widely known that any violation of the laws of war is a war crime. Ibid. at 133 n.2.

51. See Paust, *Beyond the Law*, 18, 163–64 nn. 149–52. There are no gaps in protection from torture or cruel, inhuman, or degrading treatment and denial of rights to minimum due process because of the status of a detainee. See, e.g., ibid. at 1–4, 8, 42, 70, 138 n.20, 183–88, 190 n.59, 215 n.27, 267 n.15, 294 n.171;

Hamdan v. Rumsfeld, 548 U.S. 557, 629–31, 631 n.63 (2006). In particular, rights, duties, and prohibitions reflected in common Article 3 of the Geneva Conventions are customary international law applicable in all armed conflicts. Paust, *Beyond the Law*, 2–3, 136–38 nn. 17, 19; *Hamdan v. Rumsfeld*, 557 U.S. at 631 n.63.

52. See Paust, "Absolute Prohibition," n.96.

53. Steven G. Bradbury, Memorandum for John A. Rizzo, Senior Deputy General Counsel, Central Intelligence Agency, Re: Application of 18 U.S.C. §§ 2340–2340A to Certain Techniques That May Be Used in the Interrogation of a High Value al Qaeda Detainee (May 10, 2005) [hereinafter Bradbury I], http://luxmedia.vo.llnwd.net/o10/clients/aclu/olc_05102005_bradbury46pg.pdf (last visited Jan. 18, 2010).

54. Scott Shane, David Johnston, and James Risen, "Secret U.S. Endorsement of Severe Interrogations," *New York Times*, Oct. 4, 2007, http://www.nytimes.com/2007/10/04/washington/04interrogate.html?pagewanted=all (last visited Jan. 13, 2010). See also Senate ASC Report, xvi; House Comm. Report, 134.

55. See supra note 35. Cf. Bradbury I, 3, 18.

56. Bradbury I, 3, n.4.

57. Ibid. at 13, 41–42. Cf. quoted language from the second Bybee memo in Bybee, Memorandum for John Rizzo, 4, 15.

58. Bradbury I, 9–10, 34.

59. Ibid. at 7–8.

60. Ibid. at 32.

61. Ibid. at 22.

62. Ibid. at 23. See also Steven G. Bradbury, Memorandum for John A. Rizzo, Senior Deputy General Counsel, Central Intelligence Agency, Re: Application of 18 U.S.C. §§ 2340–2340A to the Combined Use of Certain Techniques in the Interrogation of High Value al Qaeda Detainees, May 10, 2005, p. 16 [hereinafter Bradbury II], http://luxmedia.vo.llnwd.net/o10/clients/aclu/olc_05102005_bradbury_20pg.pdf (last visited Jan. 18, 2010). It has been reported that Daniel Levin "drafted much of Mr. Bradbury's lengthy May 2005 opinion authorizing the 13 methods." Scott Shane and David Johnston, "Lawyers Agreed on the Legality of Brutal Tactic," *New York Times*, June 6, 2009, http://www.nytimes.com/2009/06/07/us/politics/07lawyers.html (last visited Jan. 15, 2010).

63. Bradbury II, 42.

64. Ibid. at 43.

65. Ibid. at 3.

66. Ibid. at 15.

67. Ibid. at 17.

68. Ibid. at 9, 17.

69. Ibid. at 5–6.

70. Ibid. at 5–6, quoting a Background Paper on CIA's Combined Use of Interrogation Techniques from Rizzo's office and "transmitted Dec. 30, 2004." See ibid. at 3.

71. Ibid. at 14, 16.

72. Ibid. at 16.

73. Ibid. at 16–17.

74. See, e.g., Paust, *Beyond the Law*, 4–5, 143 n.41, 144 n.43, 190 n.59.

75. CAT, art. 16.

76. Steven G. Bradbury, Memorandum for John A. Rizzo, Senior Deputy General Counsel, Central Intelligence Agency, Re: Application of United States Obligations Under Article 16 of the Convention Against Torture to Certain Techniques that May Be Used in the Interrogation of High Value al Qaeda Detainees, May 30, 2005, pp. 1–2 [hereinafter Bradbury III], http://i.cdn.turner.com/cnn/2009/images/05/22/bradbury.pdf (last visited Jan. 18, 2010). See also CAT, art. 16.

77. Committee Against Torture, Consideration of Reports Submitted by States Parties Under Article 19 of the Convention, ¶ 15, 24, U.N. Doc. CAT/C/USA/CO/2 (May 2006). See also, e.g., Paust, *Beyond the Law*, 173 n.1, 187 n.43, 188 n.45, 199–200 n.145.

78. See Bradbury III, 2.

79. See, e.g., Paust, *Beyond the Law*, 5, 32–33, 97, 143–44, 157, 189–90. The putative reservation was actually phrased merely as a unilateral understanding as to what the U.S. "considers" itself to be bound by. See ibid. at 143 n.43.

80. See Bradbury III, 2–3, 28, 30, 37.

81. CAT, art. 2(2).

82. See, e.g., CAT Comm. Gen. Comm., ¶ 1.

83. See, e.g., Vienna Convention on the Law of Treaties, art. 31(3)(c), 1155 U.N.T.S. 331 (May 23, 1969).

84. Bradbury III, 14–15. Cf. Bybee, Memorandum for John Rizzo, 4, 15; Bradbury I, 13, 41–42.

85. Bradbury III, 32.

86. See ibid. at 32, 36.

87. Ibid. at 37.

88. See ibid. at 36 n.30.

89. James Comey wrote that he "explained to . . . [A.G. Gonzales] that some of this stuff is simply awful." James Comey, email to Chuck Rosenberg, May 31, 2005, http://documents.nytimes.com/justice-department-communication-on-interrogation-opinions#p=7 (last visited Jan. 15, 2010).

90. See *Hamdan v. Rumsfeld*, 548 U.S. at 633, n.63.

91. See Scott Shane, David Johnston, and James Risen, "Secret U.S. Endorsement of Severe Interrogations," *New York Times*, Oct. 4, 2007, http://www.nytimes.com/2007/10/04/washington/04interrogate.html?pagewanted=all (last visited Jan. 15, 2010), adding that Bradbury had "reviewed and approved" the 2006 executive order. Bush re-authorized unlawful tactics after their general outlawry the year before in the Detainee Treatment Act. See Department of Defense Appropriations Act, title X Public Law 109–48, 119 Stat. 2680, Dec. 30, 2005, § 1003(a).

92. See, e.g., Paust, *Beyond the Law*, 29.

93. See, e.g., Greenburg, Rosenberg, and de Vogue, "Bush Aware of Advisers' Talks," ABC News.

94. See supra note 12.

95. See, e.g., Paust, *Beyond the Law*, 5–8, 14–17, 19, 50–51, 162–63 nn.143–45, 173 n.1, 176 nn.11–12, 188 n.45; Senate ASC Report, xviii-xxi; Jane Mayer, "The Memo," *The New Yorker*, Feb. 27, 2006; Shane, Johnston, and Risen, "Secret U.S. Endorsement," *New York Times*; Paust, "Absolute Prohibition," nn.22, 73. A 2002 memo to Haynes warned against use of SERE tactics and affirmed that waterboarding is "torture." See Peter Finn and Joby Warrick, "In 2002, Military Agency Warned Against 'Torture,'" *Washington Post*, Apr. 25, 2009, http://www.washingtonpost.com/wp-dyn/content/article/2009/04/24/AR2009042403171.html (last visited Jan. 15, 2010).

96. See, e.g., Paust, *Beyond the Law*, 17, 19, 162 nn.143–44, 163 n.145, 268 n.15.

97. See supra notes 12, 14–15.

98. See American Society of International Law, Resolution Adopted, Mar. 30, 2006, http://www.asil.org/events/am06/resolutions.html (last visited Jan. 15, 2010).

99. See Paust, *Beyond the Law*, 177 n.13.

100. This subsection is revised from Paust, "Rice, Waterboarding and Accountability."

101. See U.S. Senate Select Committee on Intelligence, OLC Opinions on the CIA Detention and Interrogation Program, Apr. 22, 2009, 3–4 [hereinafter Senate SCI Report]; Paust, *Beyond the Law*, 28, 158 n.89.

102. See "Some of the Facilitating Memos," earlier in this chapter.

103. Senate SCI Report, 4.

104. See Shapiro, "Earliest Detainee Abuse," NPR.

105. See, e.g., Paust, *Beyond the Law*, 28, 179 n.19.

106. Condoleeza Rice, remarks, Apr. 27, 2009, http://www.youtube.com/watch?v=ijEED_iviTA&feature=related (last visited Jan. 15, 2010) http://www.stanforddaily.com/cgi-bin/?p=1030140.

107. See Senate SCI Report, 3. There was a mid-May 2002 Rice meeting with CIA General Counsel, Ashcroft, Gonzales, and others to discuss particular interrogation tactics, including waterboarding.

108. See supra note 5.

109. Rice, remarks, Apr. 27, 2009.

110. See, e.g., Jordan J. Paust, *International Law as Law of the United States* (St. Paul, MN: West Group, 2003), 169–73; Paust, Van Dyke, and Malone, *Int'l Law and Litigation*, 125, 136–38, 240–41, 319–27. More particularly, every relevant judicial opinion since the beginning of the United States has recognized that the president and all persons within the Executive branch are bound by the laws of war. See, e.g., Paust, *Beyond the Law*, 169–72 nn.181, 187, 190–95; Paust, Van Dyke, and Malone, *Int'l Law and Litigation*, 323–24.

111. U.S. Constitution, art. 2, sec. 3.

112. See *United States of America v. Wilhelm Von Leeb et al.*, 15 Intl.L.Reps. 3176 (1949).

113. See, e.g., ibid.; Paust et al., *Int'l Criminal Law*, 100–120.

114. See supra note 12.

115. See Bybee, *Memorandum for John Rizzo*, 4, 15.

116. See Greenburg, Rosenberg, and de Vogue, "Bush Aware of Advisers' Talks," ABC News. Regarding the meeting of May 31, 2005, where all Principles approved the full list of tactics addressed in the May 10 and 30, 2005 Bradbury memos to Rizzo; see Comey, email to Rosenberg, Apr. 27, 2005.

117. This subsection is revised from Jordan J. Paust, "The Complicity of Dick Cheney: No 'Necessity' Defense," *JURIST*, May 18, 2009, http://jurist.law.pitt. edu/forumy/2009/05/complicity-of-dick-cheney-no-necessity.php (last visited Jan. 15, 2010).

118. See Jim Acosta and Ed Hornick, "Cheney Ramps Up Attacks on Both Sides of the Aisle," CNN, http://www.cnn.com/2009/POLITICS/05/11/cheney. attacks/index.html (last visited Jan. 15, 2010).

119. See Paust, *Beyond the Law*, 12.

120. Dick Cheney, remarks to the U.S. Chamber of Commerce, Nov. 14, 2001, http://georgewbush-whitehouse.archives.gov/vicepresident/news-speeches/speeches/vp20011114-1.html (last visited Jan. 26, 2010).

121. See Greenburg, Rosenberg, and de Vogue, "Bush Aware of Advisers' Talks," ABC News.

122. See Center for Constitutional Rights, "al Qahtani v. Bush, al Qahtani v. Gates," http://ccrjustice.org/ourcases/current-cases/al-qahtani-v.-bush,-al-qahtani-v.-gates (last visited Jan. 15, 2010).

123. Ibid.

124. Ibid. Of course, Abu Zubaydah had already been subjected to torture by the CIA. See Shapiro, "Earliest Detainee Abuse," NPR; see "Some of the Facilitating Memos," earlier in this chapter.

125. See supra notes 12–15.

126. See supra note 12.

127. See, e.g., Mayer, *The Dark Side*, 288–89.

128. See, e.g., Paust, *Beyond the Law*, 2–5, 11.

129. *United States v. Bailey*, 444 U.S. 394 (1980).

130. Ibid. at 410–11 (emphasis added).

131. See, e.g., CIA Inspector General, Special Review: Counterterrorism Detention, and Interrogation Activities, no. 2003-7123-IG, May 7, 2004, ¶ 220–21, http://luxmedia.vo.llnwd. net/o1o/clients/aclu/IG_Report.pdf (last visited Jan. 26, 2010); Bradbury III, 9–10; Senator John D. Rockefeller, speaking to support the 2008 Intelligence Authorization Bill, Feb. 13, 2008, http://rockefeller.senate.gov/press/record.cfm?id=292883 (last visited Jan. 15, 2010); Mayer, *Dark Side*, 330–31.

132. See, e.g., U.S. Senate Committee on the Judiciary, Testimony of Ali Soufan, May 13, 2009, http://judiciary.senate.gov/hearings/testimony.cfm?id=3842&wit_id=7906 (last visited Jan. 15, 2010); Finn and Warrick, "Military Agency Warned Against 'Torture'"; Matthew Alexander and John Bruning, *How to Break a Terrorist: The U.S. Interrogators Who Used Brains, Not Brutality, to Take Down the Deadliest Man in Iraq* (New York: Free Press, 2008); Steven M. Kleinman, "The Promise of Interrogation v. the Problem of Torture," 43 *Valpo. L. Rev.* 1577 (2009).

133. Bradbury I, 28.

134. See, e.g., Paust, *Beyond the Law*, 5–19, 23–24, 26–30.

⁄⁄ 14 ⁄⁄

Torture, War, and Presidential Power

Thoughts on the Current Constitutional Crisis

THOMAS EHRLICH REIFER[1]

Why is there this inability to reckon with the moral and spiritual facts?

Bishop Bell[2]

A Liberal Culture of Torture[3]

The year 2009 initially brought sharp relief to torture abolitionists in the United States and around the world, as President Obama, in his first week in office, signed three executive orders: (1) closing Guantánamo in January, 2010; (2) creating a task force to examine policies toward prisoners caught up in the "war on terror"; and (3) mandating lawful interrogations in compliance with the Army *Field Manual* and international agreements.[4] All of these appeared to be major victories for the movement against torture and in favor of international humanitarian law and adherence to related international treaties.

Yet, virtually as fast as the orders were signed, the Obama administration began to backtrack radically on key areas affecting the question of torture and related war crimes. What appeared to be a clear difference between the candidates during the presidential campaign quickly morphed into an increasingly blurred similarity between Obama and what Professor David Luban calls the "liberal ideology of torture" that now pervades life in the United States and some of its allies.[5]

Even if Guantánamo were eventually to be shut down—a prospect made more difficult by Congress's stripping of project funding—the administration has made clear that prisoners caught up in the so-called war on terror will be subject to the same legal black hole as detainees at Guantánamo and a host of prison sites across the globe. In July 2009, the Obama administration announced that it reserved the right to imprison at least non-U.S. citizens for indefinite periods, *even if* they are acquitted by military commissions, the notorious tribunals established by the Bush administration and approved by Congress through the infamous Military Commissions Act.[6] This act, widely referred to as the Torture Act, is considered by many as one of the worst pieces of legislation ever enacted.

In the summer of 2009, the Obama administration declined requests from UN human rights investigators for private interviews with Guantánamo prisoners and for information on secret CIA prisons around the world.[7] Among the Kafkaesque ideas being considered by the administration is draft legislation that would change the Military Commissions Act and military law to allow prisoners facing the death penalty to plead guilty without a trial, facilitating executions while awaiting further revelations of torture.[8] Existing law requires that those tried in such cases be proven guilty, even in instances where the defendant wishes to plead guilty.

The Senate Armed Services Committee's "Levin Report," released in late April 2009, revealed that the Bush administration's program of torture was motivated in part by the desire to induce false confessions linking Iraq and al-Qaeda, as well as to uncover non-existent weapons of mass destruction (WMD) programs, in order to justify the invasion and occupation of Iraq.[9] Some of the charts used by U.S. military personnel and the CIA in this quest came from a 1957 Air Force study of Chinese Communist torture techniques, which were used to extract false confessions from tortured U.S. prisoners during the Korean War.[10]

Many hoped this shocking evidence would at last lead to criminal prosecution of high officials for war crimes and other high crimes and misdemeanors. Instead, the U.S. press basically ignored these revelations, which implicated what Luban calls the "torture lawyers of Washington" and other high officials directly in the Bush administration's illegal war of aggression in Iraq.[11] Such war constitutes the "supreme international crime" for which perpetrators were hanged at Nuremberg.[12]

Lies and related practices of secrecy and deception by the Bush administration in the run-up to the Iraq War were crucially aided by coerced confessions. Indeed, torture did work, at least to an extent, by helping extract some false statements that were then used to gain congressional approval of the U.S. invasion of Iraq.[13] Yet, despite congressional documentation, the Obama administration continues to shield the executive branch under a cloak of secrecy to prevent further revelations about the widespread use of torture. Instead of protecting national security, torture by U.S. forces arguably constitutes one of the greatest ongoing threats to U.S. and world security in recent memory.[14] Nevertheless, efforts to end U.S. practices of torture and the occupation of Iraq have not yet proved successful.

In February 2009, soon after the Obama administration took office, the *New York Times* ran a story about the incoming CIA director titled, "Panetta Open to Tougher Methods in Some C.I.A. Interrogation."[15] The administration had already implied that it would continue the practice of extraordinary rendition by failing to prohibit the practice in the January 2009 executive orders.[16] Then, in March 2009, President Obama's Justice Department came to the defense of the preeminent "torture lawyer," John Yoo,[17] arguing that former "enemy combatants" have no right to sue U.S. government officials responsible for their torture.[18]

When U.S. district judge Jeffrey White queried incredulously: "You're not saying that if high public officials commit clearly illegal acts, a citizen subject to those acts has no remedy in this court?" Justice Department attorney Mary Mason replied affirmatively, noting that unless Congress explicitly authorized such a lawsuit, former torture victims had no recourse to the courts.[19] Soon thereafter, Richard Haas, president of the Council on Foreign Relations, argued against prosecution of officials, stating, "Criminalizing legitimate policy differences will paralyze the conduct of foreign policy."[20]

At the time of this writing, it is clear that the new administration is not complying with the UN Convention Against Torture, the Geneva Conventions, or other obligations under international and domestic law, as reports from the *Washington Post* and other reputable news organizations indicate that torture continues at various U.S. prisons overseas.[21] This is not the time for complacency, but rather for what Dr. Martin Luther King, Jr., called the "fierce urgency of now."[22] We must look back to understand how torture, the cancer of democracy, metastasized in our body politic to critically and honestly examine what can be done to ensure, at a minimum, that such practices end immediately and never occur again.

The September 11 terrorist attacks and the resultant declaration of an endless "war on terror" provided the context for the rapid proliferation of U.S. torture practices. The invasion of Iraq, which led to insurgency, sectarian violence, and larger civil war under U.S. occupation, as well as the subsequent military action against Afghanistan, have also been instrumental in the proliferation of torture.

The "torture memos" also played a crucial role in stripping important human rights protections from U.S. detainees in the "war on terror" and providing President Bush with virtually untrammeled authority in foreign affairs. This is evidenced by the signing statements of President Bush that openly thwart the will of the elected representatives of the people.[23] On September 25, 2001, almost immediately after the 9/11 attacks, Yoo penned a memorandum opinion for Timothy Flanigan, Deputy Counsel to the President, entitled: "The President's Constitutional Authority to Conduct Military Operations Against Terrorists and Nations Supporting Them."[24] The memo argued that the president has seemingly unlimited power in the "war on terror" to make war upon any country or groups he deems necessary in response to September 11, 2001, or to prevent further attacks, without even consulting Congress, and to take all measures necessary to protect the country, even if such measures violate the law.[25]

Soon thereafter, on January 9, 2002, Yoo and Robert J. Delahunty drafted a legal opinion that exceeded even the Justice Department's argument that the United States did not have to comply with international law in dealing with prisoners in the "war on terror." The authors argued that international law as a whole did not apply to the United States, including customary international law dealing with armed conflict. This meant, effectively, that al-Qaeda and the Taliban were beyond the protections of the Geneva Conventions, a position President Bush adopted quickly thereafter. Other memos authored by Yoo and his colleagues maintained that Guantánamo detainees were beyond the reach of law, attempting to create a legal black hole where no law applied and torture could be practiced with impunity.[26]

As a result, the Bush administration enacted a host of new policies exercising this new power by arresting foreign nationals and U.S. citizens, holding many without charges or trial, at times secretly, and denying them the right to consult a lawyer. For the first time, U.S. terror suspects were being disappeared, a term heretofore typically associated with U.S.-sponsored military regimes in Latin America. Up to a hundred or more persons have died in custody, many from torture.[27] At one time, there were some 50,000 persons held at Guantánamo and dozens of sites in Iraq and Afghanistan, not to mention the network of CIA prisons in Eastern Europe and around the world.

In a series of internal and public memos, the Bush administration ignored well-founded international agreements, including the Geneva Conventions and the Convention Against Torture and Other Cruel, Inhuman or Degrading Treatment or Punishment, as well as the U.S. War Crimes Act, the U.S. Torture Act, and the U.S. Constitution.[28] Yet, as legal scholar Michael Ramsey states, "The combination of the Supremacy Clause and the Take Care Clause seems to amount to a specific constitutional prohibition on such unauthorized executive suspensions of treaties that are the supreme law of the land."[29] The war crimes and crimes against humanity committed at Guantánamo, Abu Ghraib, and elsewhere are in fact "crimes of obedience," as Herbert Kelman has argued.[30]

Checking and Balancing

Lt. Cdr. Charles Swift was a lawyer in the U.S. Navy Judge Advocate General Corps assigned to defend Guantánamo prisoner Salim Ahmed Hamdan. He and others successfully sued the president and the Secretary of Defense over the new military tribunals. Swift noted: "The whole purpose of setting up Guantánamo Bay is for torture. Why do this? Because you want to escape the rule of law."[31] In the historic 2006 decision, *Hamdan v. Rumsfeld*, the Supreme Court declared Bush's military tribunals illegal under U.S. and international law, including the Geneva Conventions and the Uniform Code of Military Justice.[32]

Yet soon thereafter, under pressure from the Bush administration, the then Republican-controlled Congress ran a legislative end-game around the Supreme Court by passing the Military Commissions Act. It purported to strip *habeas corpus*, judicial review, and Geneva protections from those captured in the "war on terror," while allowing for confessions obtained via "coercion." Furthermore, the act retroactively immunized interrogators for any criminal acts and rejected the notion that the rape of a detainee would constitute torture.[33] The act narrowly redefined torture and cruel and unusual punishment by excluding serious pain or suffering that does not involve "significant loss or impairment of the function of a bodily member, organ, or mental faculty," or "extreme" physical pain, or, "a substantial risk of death."[34]

Ironically, in 2007, on the same day President Bush stated that George Washington "believed that the freedoms we secured in our Revolution were not meant for America alone,"[35] the U.S. Court of Appeals, in *Boumediene v. Bush*, upheld the Military Commissions Act in a 2 to 1 decision. Effectively, the court stripped federal judges of the ability to review the imprisonment of Guantánamo prisoners, despite two previous Supreme Court rulings that federal statutes allowed courts to consider *habeas corpus* petitions challenging their imprisonment.[36]

Subsequently, on June 12, 2008, in a 5-4 vote, the U.S. Supreme Court reversed the Court of Appeals,[37] holding that prisoners could in fact petition the federal courts for redress via *habeas corpus*. The high court thus struck down the heart of the two legislative acts that sought to deny this constitutional right, the Detainee Treatment Act of 2005 and the Military Commissions Act of 2006.[38]

Unfortunately, as noted above, military commissions are being revived under President Obama, with the proviso that even acquittals will not stop the administration from detaining prisoners indefinitely.[39] Those who are complicit in the torture policy are not limited to the executive branch. A series of stories originally appearing in the *Washington Post* revealed that several members of Congress, including some Republicans and Democratic House Speaker Nancy Pelosi, Rep. Jane Harman, who later became the head of the House Intelligence Committee, and Sen. Jay Rockefeller, who acceded to head of the Senate Intelligence Committee (all Democrats), were briefed on the CIA torture program as early as 2002:

> For more than an hour, the bipartisan group . . . was given a virtual tour of the CIA's overseas detention sites and the harsh techniques . . . [including] waterboarding, a practice that years later would be condemned as torture by Democrats and some Republicans on Capital Hill. . . .
>
> But on that day, no objections were raised. Instead, at least two lawmakers in the room asked the CIA to push harder, two U.S. officials said. "The briefer was specifically asked if the methods were tough enough," said a U.S. official who witnessed the exchange.[40]

According to Porter Goss, Chair of the House Intelligence Committee from 1997 to 2004 and CIA Director from 2004 to 2006, "the reaction in the room was not just approval but encouragement."[41]

These revelations constituted the first confirmation of earlier statements by the Bush administration that congressional leaders had in fact been briefed on such programs, though controversy rages about the extent of their knowledge and approval. In this regard, Nazi high official Albert Speer's belated acknowledgment of officials' moral imperative to overcome willful ignorance of crimes against peace and crimes against humanity seems especially pertinent. Indeed, U.S. officials, elected representatives, and even the U.S. public must consider allocating responsibility for potential war crimes.[42] As Noam Chomsky asserted long ago, there is a need for the "denazification" of U.S. society.[43]

What makes this story more extraordinary is that even when the Abu Ghraib torture scandal was revealed publicly in the spring of 2004, these elected representatives and government officials said nothing publicly, though timely revelations could have led to the truly independent investigations necessary to reveal those responsible for these crimes of obedience.

The first order of business for the progressive movement, Congress, and the Obama administration is to end the wars in Iraq and Afghanistan (which provide the context for torture operations) and end Guantánamo-type imprisonment. Other important initiatives include repealing the Military Commissions Act/Torture Act, restoring *habeas corpus* for U.S. prisoners everywhere, and ending the abominable practice of torture forever.[44]

In order to ensure that such practices are permanently brought to an end, we must reclaim our constitutional system of government with three co-equal branches. A step forward in this regard would be to appoint a Special Prosecutor with subpoena power to investigate and prosecute officials and their lawyers for willful violations of the U.S. Constitution and international law. In so doing, we could become a beacon of light and a source of hope, carrying through on a promissory note to torture survivors everywhere, that we shall stand with you and beside you, to change the world, to make it safe once again for you and your children. This will require hard work and arduous effort, and the willingness to be honest about who we are, who we want to be, and what we have become. Let us begin.

NOTES

1. For Sister Dianna. Thanks to Noam Chomsky, Marjorie Cohn, Tom Dobrzeniecki, Daniel Ellsberg, David Luban, Christina Shaheen, and Jordan Paust for assistance. I of course take full responsibility for the content herein. A longer version of this chapter is available online at the Transnational Insti-

tute, where the author is an Associate Fellow; see http://www.tni.org/article/
tom-reifer-o. See also "Lawyers, Torture, and Aggressive War," in Ramsey Clark,
Thomas Ehrlich Reifer, and Haifa Zangana, *The Torturer in the Mirror* (New York:
Seven Stories Press, 2010.)

2. See Andrew Chandler, "The Church of England and the Obliteration
Bombing of Germany in the Second World War," *English Historical Review* 108,
no. 429 (1993): 939.

3. This phrase is inspired by the important work of David Luban (see foot-
notes 5 and 32).

4. See Barack Obama, Executive Orders, Jan. 22, 2009, http://www.white-
house.gov/briefing_room/executive_orders/ (last visited Aug. 23, 2009).

5. See David Luban, "Liberalism, Torture, and the Ticking Time Bomb," in
The Torture Debate in America, ed. Karen J. Greenberg (New York: Cambridge
Univ. Press, 2007), 36.

6. U.S. Congress, *Military Commissions Act of 2006*, Pub. L. no. 109-366, 120
Stat. 2600 (Oct. 17, 2006). For details of the campaign to repeal the act, see, e.g.,
http://www.actagainsttorture.org/repeal-mca.html (last visited Aug. 21, 2009).

7. See Colum Lynch, "U.S. Rebuffs U.N. Requests for Guantánamo Visits,
Data on CIA Prisons," *Washington Post*, July 23, 2009 (last visited Aug. 23, 2009).

8. See William Glaberson, "U.S. May Permit 9/11 Guilty Pleas in Capital
Cases," *New York Times*, June 5, 2009, http://www.nytimes.com/2009/06/06/us/
politics/06gitmo.html (last visited Aug. 30, 2009).

9. See U.S. Senate, Armed Services Committee, *Inquiry Into the Treatment of
Detainees in U.S. Custody* ("Levin Report"), Nov. 20, 2008, http://levin.senate.gov/
newsroom/supporting/2008/Detainees.121108.pdf (last visited Dec. 21, 2009).

10. See Scott Shane, "China Inspired Interrogations at Guantánamo," *New
York Times*, July 2, 2008, A01, 14.

11. See Luban, "Liberalism," in *The Torture Debate*, 52

12. See Marjorie Cohn, *Cowboy Republic: Six Ways the Bush Gang Has Defied
the Law* (Sausalito, CA: PoliPointPress, 2007), 9–28. For links to several articles
about the historical tribunal, see "The Nuremburg Trial," *Times Online*, http://
www.timesonline.co.uk/tol/system/topicRoot/The_Nuremberg_Trials_/ (last
visited Aug. 23, 2009).

13. See Michael Isikoff and David Corn, *Hubris* (New York: Crown Books,
2007).

14. See, for example, Laura K. Donohue, *The Costs of Counterterrorism: Power,
Politics, and Liberty* (New York: Cambridge Univ. Press, 2008). See also Noam
Chomsky, "The Torture Memos," May 24, 2009, http://www.chomsky.info/arti-
cles/20090521.htm (last visited Aug. 21, 2009).

15. Mark Mazzetti, "Panetta Open to Tougher Methods in Some C.I.A. Interrogation," *New York Times*, Feb. 5, 2009, http://www.nytimes.com/2009/02/06/us/politics/06cia.html (last visited Aug. 21, 2009).

16. See Barack Obama, *Executive Order: Ensuring Lawful Interrogations*, Jan. 22, 2009, http://www.whitehouse.gov/the_press_office/EnsuringLawfulInterrogations/ (last visited Aug. 21, 2009).

17. See Bob Egelko, "Obama Lawyers Argue to Drop Yoo Torture Suit," *San Francisco Chronicle*, Mar. 7, 2009 (last visited Aug. 21, 2009).

18. The term "enemy combatant" is a phrase that has no legal standing in international law. Like the prisons at Guantánamo, it was invented by the Bush administration for the sole purpose of evading the law. In this sense it is exactly that type of "categorical inequality" that sociologist Charles Tilly referred to in his book *Durable Inequality*. See Charles Tilly, *Durable Inequality* (Los Angeles: Univ. of California Press, 1998). See also Peter Jan Honigsberg, *Our Nation Unhinged* (Los Angeles: Univ. of California Press, 2009), 15–22.

19. Bob Egelko, "U.S. Lawyers Defend Bush Torture Memo Writer," *San Francisco Chronicle*, Mar. 7, 2009, A7.

20. Richard N. Haas, "The Interrogation Memos and the Law," *Wall Street Journal*, May 1, 2009, A17.

21. See, e.g., Joshua Partlow and Julie Tate, "2 Afghans Allege Abuse at U.S. Site," *Washington Post*, Nov. 28, 2009, http://www.washingtonpost.com/wp-dyn/content/article/2009/11/27/AR2009112703438_pf.html (last visited Dec. 18, 2009).

22. Martin Luther King, Jr., "I Have a Dream" (speech, Lincoln Memorial, Washington, DC, Aug. 28, 1963), http://www.usconstitution.net/dream.html (last visited Aug. 23, 2009).

23. See Charlie Savage, *Takeover: The Return of the Imperial Presidency and the Subversion of American Democracy* (New York: Back Bay Books, 2008). See also Tom Reifer, "September 11th, Terrorism and the Globalization of Human Rights," *Transnational Institute News*, Sept. 2008 http://www.tni.org/detail_page.phtml?act_id=18652 (last visited Aug. 23, 2009).

24. John C. Yoo, "The President's Constitutional Authority to Conduct Military Operations Against Terrorists and Nations Supporting Them," memorandum to the Deputy Counsel to the President, Sept. 25, 2001, http://www.usdoj.gov/olc/warpowers925.htm (last visited Aug. 23, 2009).

25. Reprinted in Karen J. Greenberg and Joshua L. Dratel, eds., *The Torture Papers: The Road to Abu Ghraib* (New York: Cambridge Univ. Press, 2005), 3–24. See also Glenn Greenwald, *How Would a Patriot Act? Defending American Values from a President Run Amok* (San Francisco: Working Assets, 2006).

26. A 2006 analysis by Seton Hall University Law School found that only 5% of Guantánamo's prisoners had been captured by the United States. The remainder were captured by the Northern Alliance, Afghan warlords, and Pakistani intelligence, who many times sold them for bounty. A mere 8% were "even alleged to be al-Qaeda fighters," some 55%, or 280 persons, were not alleged to have engaged in hostile activities against the United States, with the remaining 45 percent accused of acts such as fleeing U.S. forces. Mark Denbeaux, *Report on Guantánamo Detainees: A Profile of 517 Detainees through Analysis of Department of Defense Data*, Feb. 6, 2006, http://law.shu.edu/publications/GuantánamoReports/Guantánamo_report_final_2_08_06.pdf (last visited Aug. 23, 2009).

An additional key point here, as Piero Gleijeses notes, is that, "with or without its gulag, [Guantánamo] is a monument to U.S. arrogance." Piero Gleijeses, "Cuba or the Base," *London Review of Books*, Mar. 26, 2009, http://www.lrb.co.uk/v31/n06/gleio1_.html. On the history of U.S. relations with Cuba, see Lars Schoultz, *That Infernal Little Cuban Republic* (Chapel Hill: Univ. of North Carolina Press, 2009).

27. See Glen Greenwald, "The Suppressed Fact: Deaths by U.S. Torture," *Salon.com*, June 30, 2009, http://www.salon.com/opinion/greenwald/2009/06/30/accountability/ (last visited Aug. 23, 2009).

28. For an analysis demonstrating that the U.S. president is legally bound by the Geneva Conventions, see Derek Jinks and David Sloss, "Is the President Bound by the Geneva Conventions?" 90 *Cornell Law Review* 97 (2004).

29. Michael D. Ramsey, "Torturing Executive Power," 93 *Georgetown Law Journal* 1213 (2005), 1234, 1240, 1252. See also Michael D. Ramsey, *The Constitution's Text in Foreign Affairs* (Cambridge, MA: Harvard Univ. Press, 2007).

30. Herbert C. Kelman, "The Policy Context of Torture: A Social-Psychological Analysis," *Intl. Review of the Red Cross* 87, no. 857 (2005):123–34, http://www.icrc.org/Web/eng/siteeng0.nsf/html/review-857-p123 (last visited Aug. 23, 2009). See also the path-breaking work of Herbert C. Kelman and V. Lee Hamilton, *Crimes of Obedience: Towards a Social Psychology of Authority and Responsibility* (New Haven: Yale Univ. Press, 1989).

31. See Marie Brenner, "Taking on Guantánamo," *Vanity Fair*, Mar. 2007, 328–41, http://www.vanityfair.com/politics/features/2007/03/Guantánamo200703?printable=true&currentPage=all. (last visited Aug. 23, 2009). See also Jonathan Mahler, *The Challenge* (New York: Farrar, Straus & Giroux, 2009).

32. *Hamdan v. Rumsfeld*, 548 U.S. 557 (2006). In this case, the Supreme Court rejected President Bush's decision to strip Geneva protections from al-Qaeda and the Taliban, holding that Geneva's common article 3 applies in the "war on terror," even to al-Qaeda, and "forbids torture." See David Luban, *Legal Ethics*

and Human Dignity (New York: Cambridge Univ. Press, 2007), 204–5. See also Neal Kumar Katyal, "The Supreme Court, 2005 Term, Comment: *Hamdan v. Rumsfeld*: The Legal Academy Goes to Practice," 120 *Harvard Law Review* 65 (2006).

33. On the Military Commmissions Act, see Howard Ball, "Bush Trumps the Supreme Court: The 2006 Military Commissions Act," in *Bush, the Detainees, and the Constitution: The Battle Over Presidential Power in the War on Terror* (Lawrence: Univ. Press of Kansas, 2007) 175–86. See also Jordan Paust, *Beyond the Law* (New York: Cambridge Univ. Press, 2007), 120–27.

34. U.S. Congress, *Military Commissions Act* of 2006.

35. See Sheryl Gay Stolberg, "Defending Nation's Latest War, Bush Recalls Its First," *New York Times*, Feb. 20, 2007, http://www.nytimes.com/2007/02/20/washington/20bush.html (last visited Aug. 23, 2009).

36. *Boumediene v. Bush*, 476 F.3d 981 (D.C. Cir. 2007).

37. *Boumediene v. Bush*, 553, U.S. 723 (2008).

38. See Karen J. Greenberg and Joshua L. Dratel, eds., *The Enemy Combatant Papers: American Justice, the Courts, and the War on Terror* (New York: Cambridge Univ. Press, 2008), 997–1008. See also Karen Greenberg, *The Least Worst Place: Guantánamo's First 100 Days* (New York: Oxford Univ. Press, 2009).

39. See Jess Bravin, "Detainees, Even If Acquitted, Might Not Go Free," *Wall Street Journal*, July 8, 2009, http://online.wsj.com/article/SB124699680303307309.html (last visited Aug. 23, 2009).

40. Jody Warrick and Dan Eggen, "Hill Briefed on Waterboarding in 2002," *Washington Post*, Dec. 9, 2007, A01, http://www.washingtonpost.com/wp-dyn/content/article/2007/12/08/AR2007120801664.html (last visited Aug. 23, 2009).

41. Ibid. Jane Harman and Nancy Pelosi have stated that they registered objections or at least raised questions about the waterboarding, with Harman asking in a letter if the president had approved such techniques. Pelosi has further alleged being misled by the CIA, stating that she was not told that these techniques were then being used, only that they were in the armory of possible techniques. According to a top aide, though, Pelosi learned that torture techniques such as waterboarding were being used as early as 2003. See Paul Kane, "Top Pelosi Aide Learned of Waterboarding in 2003," *Washington Post*, May 9, 2009, http://www.washingtonpost.com/wp-dyn/content/article/2009/05/08/AR2009050803967.html (last visited Aug. 23, 2009).

42. On Speer's relevance for U.S. officials, see Dan Ellsberg, "The Responsibility of Officials in a Criminal War," in *Papers on the War* (New York: Random House, 1972). See also Gitta Sereny, *Albert Speer: His Battle with Truth* (New York: Vintage, 1995).

43. See Noam Chomsky, *American Powers and the New Mandarins* (New York: New Press, 1969), 16–17.

44. See the brilliant and fundamental work of Judith Lewis Herman, *Trauma and Recovery: The Aftermath of Violence—From Domestic Abuse to Political Terror* (New York: Basic Books, 1997); "Symposium: War, Terrorism, and Torture: Limits on Presidential Power in the 21st Century," *Indiana Law Journal* 81, no. 4 (2006). See also Pat Barker, *Regeneration* (New York: Penguin, 1993), about the life and treatment of the decorated British officer Seigfried Sassoon, a war hero turned anti-war activist in World War I.

About the Contributors

MARJORIE COHN is a professor at Thomas Jefferson School of Law and past president of the National Lawyers Guild. Her books include *Cowboy Republic: Six Ways the Bush Gang Has Defied the Law* and *Rules of Disengagement: The Politics and Honor of Military Dissent*. The 2008 recipient of the Peace Scholar of the Year Award, she has testified before Congress about Bush administration torture policy. See www.marjoriecohn.com.

RICHARD FALK is Albert G. Milbank Professor Emeritus of International Law at Princeton University and Visiting Distinguished Professor in Global and International Studies at the University of California, Santa Barbara. His most recent books are *The Costs of War: International Law, the UN, and World Order after Iraq* and *Achieving Human Rights*.

MARC D. FALKOFF, an assistant professor at Northern Illinois University College of Law, represents 17 Yemeni prisoners at Guantánamo Bay. He is the compiler and editor of *Poems from Guantánamo: The Detainees Speak*, a best-selling anthology of prisoner poetry.

TERRY LYNN KARL, Ph.D., the Gildred Professor of Political Science and Latin American Studies at Stanford University, publishes about the politics of oil and transitions to democracy. She was the expert witness in five human rights trials, including the murder trial of Salvadoran military officers for the killing of six Jesuit priests in 1989.

JOHN W. LANGO, Ph.D., is a professor of philosophy at Hunter College of the City University of New York. The author of *Whitehead's Ontology*, he specializes in metaphysics and ethics.

JANE MAYER, an award-winning staff writer for *The New Yorker*, writes about politics and the war on terror. She is the author of the best-selling book, *The Dark Side: The Inside Story of How the War on Terror Turned into a War on American Ideals.*

ALFRED W. MCCOY is the J.R.W. Smail Professor of History at the University of Wisconsin–Madison. He is the author of *A Question of Torture: CIA Interrogation, From the Cold War to the War on Terror.*

JEANNE MIRER, an attorney practicing in New York, is president of the International Association of Democratic Lawyers. She founded the International Commission for Labor Rights and she represents Vietnamese victims of Agent Orange.

SISTER DIANNA ORTIZ joined the Ursuline Sisters of Mount Saint and traveled to Guatemala to teach Mayan children. Abducted and tortured there, she later founded the Torture Abolition and Survivors Support Coalition International. Her autobiography is *The Blindfold's Eyes: My Journey from Torture to Truth.*

JORDAN J. PAUST is the Mike and Teresa Baker Law Center Professor of International Law at the Law Center of the University of Houston. The author of *Beyond the Law: The Bush Administration's Unlawful Responses in the "War" on Terror*, he has published over 165 articles, book chapters, papers, and essays.

BILL QUIGLEY is the legal director of the Center for Constitutional Rights and a law professor at Loyola University New Orleans. He is the author of *Ending Poverty As We Know It: Guaranteeing a Right to a Job at a Living Wage* and *Storms Still Raging: Katrina, New Orleans and Social Justice.*

MICHAEL RATNER, president of the Center for Constitutional Rights, represented Guantánamo detainees in the United States Supreme Court in *Rasul v. Bush* (2004) and *Boumediene v. Bush* (2008). He is the author of *The Trial of Donald Rumsfeld: A Prosecution by Book.*

THOMAS EHRLICH REIFER is an assistant professor of sociology and an affiliated faculty in Ethnic Studies at the University of San Diego. He specializes in the study of large-scale, long-term social change and world-systems analysis, including terrorism, human rights, and U.S. militarism.

PHILIPPE SANDS QC is a barrister and a law professor in England. His cases include *ex parte Augusto Pinochet* (House of Lords, counsel for Human Rights Watch). He is the author of *Torture Team: Rumsfeld's Memo and the Betrayal of American Values* and *Lawless World: America and the Making and Breaking of Global Rules*.

STEPHEN SOLDZ, Ph.D., is a professor and director of the Center for Research, Evaluation, and Program Development at the Boston Graduate School of Psychoanalysis. He is president of Psychologists for Social Responsibility and a leader in the movement to remove psychologists from involvement in U.S. torture and abusive interrogations.

LANCE TAPLEY, a freelance investigative journalist, is a political writer for the *Portland Phoenix* in Maine. His series on torture in Maine's Supermax prison won a national first-place award from the Association of Alternative Newsweeklies.

Index

CPSIA information can be obtained
at www.ICGtesting.com
Printed in the USA
JSHW020153211221
21401JS00008B/277